CW00709123

Ayresome Park Memories

Evening Gazette

Ayresome Park Memories

Eric Paylor and John Wilson

First published in Great Britain by
The Breedon Books Publishing Company Limited
Unit 3, The Parker Centre, Mansfield Road, Derby, DE21 4SZ
1995, updated edition 2004.

Dedication

Since the original Ayresome Park Memories book was first published in 1995, some of the most famous 'Boro legends who contributed their reminiscences have sadly passed away. We dedicate this updated edition to their memory and thank them for the pleasure they gave countless generations of supporters over the years. We respectfully remember: Ralph Birkett, Ronnie Dicks, Micky Fenton, George Hardwick, Willie Maddren, Wilf Mannion, Harold Shepherdson, Geoff Walker and Ray Yeoman.

ISBN 1 85983 434 5

Printed and bound by Butler & Tanner Ltd, Frome, Somerset.

Contents

Introduction and Acknowledgements

IT'S HARD to believe, but 2005 marks the 10th anniversary of Middlesbrough FC's historic move from Ayresome Park to the Riverside Stadium. At the time of the departure traditionalists questioned its wisdom, but there can be no doubt that the new state-of-the-art facility, fully equipped for the 21st century, has enabled 'Boro to compete at the highest level of the modern game.

However, over the past decade, life has never been dull for the club's supporters: Middlesbrough's first major trophy was finally secured in 2004, the manager changed from Robson to McClaren, a diminutive Brazilian called Juninho arrived, left and returned. A protracted three-point spat with the FA led to relegation, swiftly followed by promotion back to the top flight. Major cup final appearances, which were once the strict province of other, more fashionable clubs, became a regular occurrence, and 'Boro established themselves in the Premiership with commendable average crowds of over 30,000. In other words, the usual rollercoaster ride.

In order to mark the 10th anniversary of Ayresome Park's closure, we felt it would be appropriate to update the first edition of the book to include some of the many supporters' memories we received following the initial publication. And also to take the opportunity to finally complete the Ayresome Park story by describing what happened to the site of the famous and much-loved old ground.

However, the fundamental objectives of the original book remain unchanged. Firstly, to chronicle the history of Ayresome Park. Secondly, to highlight all the major matches which took place at the stadium over the years. Thirdly, to record for posterity the players' and supporters' reminiscences of a sporting venue which, for 92 years, was an important, integral and indelible part of life on Teesside.

Hopefully, the mix of original and new material will rekindle readers' favourite memories and ensure that while Ayresome Park has faded even further into the mists of time it is never completely forgotten.

Acknowledgements

NATURALLY this book could not have been completed without the co-operation of many people.

Primarily, we must thank the *Middlesbrough Evening Gazette* and its editor in 1995, Ranald Allan, for granting us access to the newspaper archives and photographic library. We are also grateful to the newspaper's editor in 2004, Steve Dyson, for continuing with that arrangement.

Our appreciation is extended to Keith Lamb, the Chief Executive of Middlesbrough Football Club, for granting us permission to peruse the club's minutes. Without this invaluable facility, the history of Ayresome Park would have been incomplete.

We also convey our gratitude to the countless number of ex-'Boro players, supporters and celebrities who generously gave up their time to record their evocative memories and reminiscences.

Finally, the text is supplemented with many photographs from the *Evening Gazette* and various private collections. Therefore we would like to acknowledge the assistance received from the following organisations and individuals: Janet Barker of the Cleveland Archive, George Baxter, Harry Bell, Don Birkett, George Camsell, Larry Bruce of Middlesbrough Reference Library, Jackie Carr, Edward Cole, Edna Dennis, Jack Hatfield, John and Rosemarie Hickton, Olivia Iceton, Dave Jamieson, Margaret Larkin, Doug Moody, *The Northern Echo*, Joe Scott, Olga Thompson and Rolando Ugolini.

Foreword

by John Hendrie

I ENJOYED every single minute of my six years at Middlesbrough Football Club. It was one of the happiest times of my whole playing career. In fact the club has continued to be very good to me ever since I left in 1996. So my affection is as strong as ever.

It's great that my work with 'Boro TV Extra also gives me the opportunity to keep in touch with my many friends on Teesside. I've always had a superb rapport with the fans and they make me very welcome.

I always felt that 'Boro fans were special. That's why I was delighted for them when 'Boro finally won their first trophy by beating Bolton Wanderers in the Carling Cup Final.

It was the first step towards realising the dream of chairman Steve Gibson, who wants to make 'Boro one of the best and most respected clubs in the country. The Gibson passion was first kindled at Ayresome Park and is burning more brightly than ever at the Riverside Stadium.

Naturally most of my career with 'Boro was spent playing at Ayresome Park. When you look back now, the old stands and the less-than-adequate facilities off the pitch seem to belong to a different era. They are part of another time, of course. But for me, and no doubt for many of those fans who still cheer on the lads at the Riverside, the memories of Ayresome Park will never be forgotten.

I played in some great games there, scored some memorable goals, and was very fortunate to earn the distinction of being the last player to score a league goal at the old stadium. I'll certainly never forget that goal against Luton Town on a hot afternoon in front of a capacity crowd. After all, the photograph of the last goal at Ayresome Park has pride of place on my kitchen wall, the hub of the Hendrie household. You can't take away memories like that. They are priceless.

That's why I'm honoured to be asked to write the foreword to the second edition of *Ayresome Park Memories*. I've known Eric Paylor and John Wilson for many years and I know they feel as passionate about the 'Boro as I do.

Like me, many of their own football memories are forever entwined in the old stadium. That's why they were encouraged to write *Ayresome Park Memories* in the first place. And here we are, looking ahead to a second edition. The first edition was a complete sell-out and I'm sure that this updated version will be just as eagerly snapped up by the fans.

Looking back, I can still recall the day I arrived at Middlesbrough, and it was amazing how every season at Ayresome Park seemed to be a rollercoaster. Even so, it seems incredible that so many years have passed since I scored those goals in that final league game. But that's part of the beauty of football. It has so many ups and downs at the time, but it leaves you with nothing but happy memories. Many of those memories are encapsulated in this book, which is a fitting testament to the old stadium and some of the great moments from a now bygone era. I'm sure that 'Boro fans old and young will enjoy reading this book and remember the history of a great football club.

The earliest known view of Ayresome Park. The main stand looks hardly any different in 1903 to how it was in 1995.

The Story of a Stadium 1903-1986

THE summer of 1903 was an exciting time for the people of Teesside, because their brand new state of the art football stadium at Ayresome was due to be unveiled.

Officials of the Middlesbrough Football and Athletic Club Limited had worked wonders to have the stadium, suitably named Ayresome Park, almost completed in time for the start of the 1903-04 season.

It had been a desperate battle against time and the club was very much in the hands of local contractors and construction workers. The 'Boro directors originally planned to move from their headquarters at Linthorpe Road in another 12 months, but the alarm bells started ringing when they failed to negotiate the renewal of their lease on the Linthorpe Road Ground.

The loss of the lease left 'Boro with no alternative. There was no suitable stadium in Middlesbrough which was capable of housing First Division football, even on a temporary basis.

So 'Boro's officials rushed through their plans to construct the new stadium and also to move the old grandstand at Linthorpe Road to Ayresome Park for use as a second stand.

Negotiations to buy the land at Ayresome had started some years earlier. In fact work had begun to drain the site as early as January 1901, when the original inhabitants – a group of gypsies – were moved off. The land was relatively flat and was ideal for a new sports stadium. However, it was low lying and much of it was under water during spells of wet weather. So the drainage work was crucial towards creating a suitable playing area.

The news that the Linthorpe Road lease would definitely not be renewed was relayed to the 'Boro directors on 29 December 1902. It left very little time for decision making. There would be few problems laying out the pitch, but the grandstand presented a problem.

'Boro were determined to erect an impressive grandstand which would be as modern as any found elsewhere in the Football League. Immediately they issued advertisements inviting tenders for the stand, which they envisaged would be 75 yards long and seat around 2,000 spectators. The cost was not to exceed £1,750. The important thing as far as the directors were concerned was to commission a grandstand which matched the club's status. 'Boro were a First Division side and needed a stadium which would be a credit to the town and an awe-inspiring spectacle for all their visitors.

With this in mind, 'Boro approached Glasgow architect Archibald Leitch to design the new stadium. Leitch was primarily a mechanical engineer, based in Glasgow, who had worked closely with councils and public bodies in his native Scotland.

In the early 1900s, Leitch branched out into football and introduced revolutionary ideas which were immediately picked up by the leading Scottish clubs. He did work at Ibrox and Parkhead, before masterminding the construction of Hampden Park in 1903.

At this stage Leitch was largely unknown in England. But when news of his ideas and his achievements spread to the North of England, they were brought to the attention of the 'Boro board. The directors were impressed by his work, though to be fair there were few engineers specialising in football stadiums at that time.

'Boro pinned their faith in the Scot and were not to be disappointed. Naturally it was a gamble because Leitch had not previously worked in England, but his work at Ayresome Park was to prove a stepping stone towards supervising the construction of dozens of stadiums south of the border, including Roker Park at Sunderland.

Leitch wasted no time in coming up with the design, the integral part of which was a two-tier grandstand, running virtually the whole length of the north side of Ayresome Park. The grandstand was innovative in that it had a barrel roof, with a small semi-circular gable, topped by an ornate wrought-iron flourish.

In the event, Leitch's stand was much longer than the 'Boro directors had envisaged, so they were delighted with the plans. The total length of the stand was to be 274ft 6in. The front of the roof was supported by ten posts, standing 30ft 6in apart.

Entry to the stand was to be gained by four pay boxes at the rear of the construction and at the foot of the staircases at each end of the stand. There would also be two transfer pay boxes from the terrace to the Main Stand.

One of the most impressive features was the array of facilities provided for the use of club officials underneath the stand. On the right-hand side were offices, including directors' and secretary's rooms and a telegraph office. On the left was a gymnasium, with a billiard room behind it. In the middle were smart dressing-rooms, bathrooms for both teams, a referee's room and toilets for general use.

It was the magnificent new grandstand that 'Boro were looking for and they were happy to give Leitch the go-ahead. Another bonus was the cost of the construction. – £1,521, well within the budget allowed by the board. Even so, the erection of the grandstand was only a small part of the work needed to complete the whole stadium. 'Boro had to pay for thousands of tons of earth to be transported by horse-drawn wagons to the site to provide embankments for the terracing at the east and west ends of the ground. The two ends were known initially as the Linthorpe Road End and Workhouse End respectively.

Leitch's initial plan was for three sides of the stadium to be open ends. But the directors were determined to erect a second stand on the south side.

So the former Main Stand at the Linthorpe Road Ground was dismantled into sections and carried to Ayresome Park, where it was re-erected as the official South Stand.

Even so, it was a rather ramshackle affair, being just over half the length of the new grandstand. But it helped to provide extra seats and more cover from the elements for the supporters, in addition to completing the overall effect of the new-look stadium.

Once the stands were in place and the huge mounds of earth piled up at each end, 'Boro then set about having the stadium enclosed by a wooden fence. The total cost of the work, from start to finish, was £11,957. Naturally the directors did not have the cash to hand and much of the cost was financed by loans.

The work continued at great pace during the summer but while Ayresome Park was capable of receiving its first paying spectators at the beginning of September, it was still far from completed. In fact workmen were labouring furiously to complete the installation of the seating in the grandstand.

As a result, most of the grandstand had to be closed off to the public when Ayresome Park hosted its very first match on a bright Tuesday evening on 1 September 1903.

'Boro unveiled their new stadium to the public with a prestigious pre-season friendly against Glasgow Celtic. The Scottish club were going through a transitional stage, having failed to win their championship in the previous five seasons.

However, the Scots were still a very good side and were formidable opponents. The match also provided a rare opportunity for the Teesside football fans to see a team in action from north of the border.

At the same time, the match against Celtic was not the official opening of Ayresome Park. It was merely designed to get the 'Boro players in the mood for the new First Division season. In the event the friendly game attracted a healthy crowd of around 7,000, though it was less than the club had been drawing for League fixtures at Linthorpe Road.

The match was a useful pipe-opener for 'Boro, coming only four days before the start of the new season. 'Boro had made their bow in the First Division only 12 months earlier and finished a respectable 13th out of the 18 clubs. There was a great deal of hope for improvement in the new season, especially in a new stadium.

'Boro's ground staff had worked hard to get the pitch in good condition for the big kick-off. The grass had been sown shortly after the drainage work was completed and provided as good a playing surface as could be found in the Football League.

'Boro approached their task in determined fashion and were unfortunate not to take the lead when skipper Joe Cassidy hit the crossbar with an overhead kick. Celtic goalkeeper Adams was also called on to make several fine saves to keep the Scots in the game at the interval.

In the second half 'Boro's spirited efforts paid dividends when they scored what proved to be the winning goal. It came from the penalty spot after 'Boro centre-forward Sandy Brown was tripped by Celtic defender McLeod inside the area. Willie White, a new signing from Dundee, made no mistake with the spot kick.

It was a good start to Ayresome Park's career, though it didn't help 'Boro to make a winning start to their First Division programme. They were away to Sheffield Wednesday in their opening game and lost 4-1. Andy Brown netted their consolation goal.

Unfortunately it was the shape of things to come for 'Boro, because they failed to win a single away game all season in the First Division.

The defeat failed to dampen the enthusiasm of 'Boro's excited fans, who were eagerly anticipating the official opening of Ayresome Park in the first home League fixture against local rivals Sunderland on Saturday, 12 September.

The fixtures could hardly have been kinder to 'Boro, because the derby clash with Sunderland was a big game whatever the occasion. And, as an opening match at the new Ayresome Park, it could not have been planned any better.

The stadium was to be officially opened by James Clifton Robinson, who was the managing director of the Electric Tram Company. Quite why Mr Robinson was invited is not clear, though he was clearly an important public figure and was apparently a noted and witty speaker.

Mr Robinson was to officially open the main gate at Ayresome Park with a gold key, which was specially made for the occasion. The key was put on official display during the week leading up to the match at the home of Councillor T.Gibson Poole in Linthorpe Road. Hundreds of fans went to inspect it.

The day of the big game arrived with a distinct threat of rain hanging over Ayresome Park. However, it failed to dampen the enthusiasm of the fans, even bearing in mind that the vast majority of them would be standing out in the open throughout the proceedings.

There were few latecomers and a mammoth crowd, estimated at around 30,000, packed into Ayresome Park long before the official ceremony was due to begin. Both stands were packed, except for a tiny part of the grandstand, which was still not officially open because the work of installing the seats was not yet complete. Naturally the vast majority of the fans were standing on the two embankments.

Clifton Robinson duly performed the official opening of the gates, after receiving the gold key from 'Boro chairman R.W.Williams. Mr Robinson then addressed the packed throng and he went on to make a humorous and well-received speech.

Secretary-manager John Robson also made a speech and said that the new stadium had been his ambition of the last ten years He added that he would not be satisfied until 'Boro had won the English Cup. Little did Mr Robson know that if he

John Robson, who was secretary-manager of the 'Boro when the club moved to Ayresome Park. It's one of those unusual coincidences that the first and last managers at Ayresome Park were both called Robson.

R.W. Williams, the 'Boro chairman when the club moved to Ayresome Park. He was one of 11 directors suspended in 1906 for illegal payments to players.

lived to be 150, he would still be waiting to realise the full extent of his ambition.

Following the completion of the speeches, the excitement increased to a crescendo as the crowd anticipated the start of the match. 'Boro's fortunes were reported in the *Evening Gazette* by Old Bird, who wrote: 'It was an enormous crowd, exceptionally so for a threatening afternoon. Every enclosure was filled with an eager throng and thin lines of smoke told of the consumption of much tobacco.'

The fans had paid 6d entry into Ayresome Park, plus an extra 9d if they wanted to transfer to the stands. The final receipts of around £1,000 were a club record.

The packed ground mainly consisted of men and boys and included Jim Windross and Fred Hardisty, who were members of 'Boro's first-ever football team.

The two teams took to the field to rapturous applause, with Joe Cassidy winning the toss for 'Boro and electing to defend the Linthorpe Road goal. The kick-off was taken by Sunderland centre-forward Hogg at 3.15pm, amid a great roar.

A first-half goal from Cassidy was enough to give 'Boro an interval lead, but Gemmell brought the small travelling band of Sunderland supporters into song when equalising after the restart. 'Boro regained the lead through Sandy Brown, but there was to be no fairy-tale ending as goals from Hogg and Robinson earned the Rokermen both points from a 3-2 victory.

The defeat failed to weaken the high excitement around the stadium and the celebrations continued long into the night.

The famous badge of Middlesbrough Football Club up until liquidation in 1986. The three ships pay tribute to the town's once thriving port, and it's fitting that 'Boro have built their new stadium in the town's former dockland.

When the Edwardians decided to celebrate something they did it properly. During the evening songs were rendered by Bobby Artherton, T.Edwards, J.Young and Councillor Alf Mattison. After all, there was no television for the supporters to go home to in those days.

At the end of the night, the company accompanied Clifton Robinson to Middlesbrough Railway Station and gave him a rousing send-off.

The whole day had been planned and executed to perfection and even the rain stayed away. The match was trouble free, as might have been expected at that time.

However, there was one unfortunate fatality among the fans, even though it happened well away from Ayresome Park. Thomas Sterling, 34, a Sunderland fan from Jarrow, collapsed and died on his way from the station to the stadium.

'Boro's fans had to wait another two weeks for the next match at Ayresome Park, which produced the first League win at the stadium and also the first in the First Division that season.

Small Heath, later to become Birmingham City, were the visitors and 'Boro won 3-1. It was a hot afternoon, yet the attendance dropped considerably from the opening game to a still more than respectable 18,000.

'Boro opened the scoring after 25 minutes through Cassidy, though Howard equalised for Small Heath two minutes later following a mix-up in the home defence. However, Cassidy scored again four minutes after the restart and 'Boro spent the rest of the match in control. Brown added the third goal in the 70th minute.

'Boro went on to win nine of their 17 home games in that inaugural season at Ayresome Park. Despite the lack of success on their travels, it was good enough to ensure that 'Boro climbed to tenth position in the First Division.

Attendances fell to around 12,000 by the end of the season, which was well below capacity. However, it was still a reasonable first season for the fledgling stadium, which had witnessed an exceptional crowd in the November when 25,000 watched 'Boro beat Sheffield United 4-1.

Ayresome Park also staged its first big FA Cup-tie in that first season. It came in the third round of the competition, which was also the quarter-final. 'Boro had cruised through to the last eight by recording victories at Millwall and Preston North End, which turned out to be their only away wins of the season.

'Boro were drawn away from home again in the third round but forced a creditable replay in a goalless draw against Manchester City at Hyde Road. Ayresome Park was absolutely heaving as 34,000 fans packed into the stadium for the Wednesday afternoon replay. However, it was to be the first of many FA Cup disappointments at the stadium.

Sandy Brown predictably scored for 'Boro, but City were the better team on the day and won 3-1. In the following 92 seasons at Ayresome Park, 'Boro were to get no nearer to winning the Cup.

Even so, the 'Boro directors had good reason to be satisfied with the events of Ayresome's first season. The club made a healthy profit of £3,314 and had consolidated its place in the First Division.

Despite the fine start, 'Boro found it difficult to maintain the momentum. The following season there was a dropping off in the level of interest by the supporters and 'Boro recorded a loss for the first time since turning professional.

They also went very close to losing their First Division status, which would have been a financial disaster if it had taken place, especially as 'Boro had only just started to pay off the loans which were arranged to finance the building of Ayresome Park.

'Boro avoided the drop to the Second Division and averted disaster, by doing something which shocked the football world. They paid the then unbelievable world record fee of £1,000 to bring experienced forward Alf Common to Ayresome Park

The 'Boro boys pictured at the start of their second season at Ayresome Park. Back row (left to right): J.Cassidy, J.Hogg, J.Frail, J.Blackett. Middle: J.Robson (manager), S.Aitken, A.Davidson, A.Jones, R.Page, C.Harper (trainer). Front row: E.Gettins, J.Bell, A.Brown, R.Atherton, J.Thackeray.

from Sunderland. 'Boro were immediately labelled as spendthrifts and were called unprofessional. People said it was better to go down with your head held high, rather than to buy your First Divisions status. Sunderland, who were laughing all the way to the bank, were also heavily criticised. They were regarded as moneygrabbers.

But the object of the exercise as far as the 'Boro directors were concerned was to stay in the First Division. The purchase of Common was an investment to avoid possible financial ruin and to that extent the money was well spent.

Common was not the greatest player. But he was a bustling attacker with an eye for goal. He scored four goals in his ten appearances for 'Boro before the end of the season, including the winner at Sheffield United on his debut and it was enough to avoid the dreaded drop.

Even so, many 'Boro fans were not too impressed with this method of buying survival and average gates actually fell to below the 10,000 mark after Common's arrival. In modern times you could expect to double your gates by paying a world record fee for a striker.

The same season that Common signed, 'Boro staged their first full international at Ayresome Park, when England drew 1-1 with Ireland. Tim Williamson, 'Boro's highly regarded 20-year-old goalkeeper, was called up to make his debut for England in the match and helped attract a huge crowd of around 24,000.

Unfortunately it wasn't a debut to remember for the North Ormesby-born 'keeper. Williamson suffered the embarrassing misfortune of dropping the ball behind his own goal-line to hand Ireland their goal on a plate. Naturally it was a disappointment for both player and fans, who paid gate receipts of more than £1,000.

The season ended on a bad note for 'Boro because they were reported to the Football Association by several shareholders for making irregular payments to players. The club's auditors confirmed that the payments had been made.

A Commission of Inquiry was set up by the FA, but dragged on and on. In fact it was a full six months before the 'Boro directors admitted that they had broken the rules. They admitted to the FA that £400 in bonuses had been paid to players over the previous two years. At the time players were permitted to receive no more than £208 a year.

The FA fined 'Boro £250 and suspended 11 of the 12 directors, including the chairman R.W.Williams and Alf Mattison, from 1 January 1906, until 1 May 1908. 'Boro's outside-right Teddy Gettins was fined £10 for making false statements.

There was very little sympathy for 'Boro throughout the game. They were not a popular club following the signing of Alf Common and were now firmly in place as the bad boys of football.

However, 'Boro did have problems to overcome, notably the problem of operating with a one-man board. It was left to civic dignatory Lieutenant Colonel T.Gibson Poole to come to the rescue and form a new board of directors.

It wasn't an easy task, especially as the club had only £20 in the bank and the players were owed back wages. However, Gibson Poole gathered a new board together and set about

Alf Common, whose signing caused a national outcry when 'Boro paid a world-record fee of £1,000 to buy him from Sunderland in 1905.

Everybody knows that 'Boro created a British record when paying £1,000 to sign Alf Common from neighbours Sunderland in February 1905. What isn't known is that 'Boro failed to sign Common from Sheffield United for £400 in March 1903. Their bid was rejected, Common moved to Sunderland for £520 four months later, and 'Boro eventually had to break the bank to get him.

trying to generate a new image for the club. It wasn't to turn out exactly how the fans might have expected.

In addition to a new chairman, 'Boro started the new season with a new manager. Former Sunderland manager Alex Mackie took over from John Robson, who had been absolved of all involvement in the payment of the illegal bonuses.

The new board of directors were not prepared just to sit back and rest on their laurels and they hit the headlines again when they made the shock signing of the legendary England international forward Steve Bloomer from Derby County in the spring of 1906.

Once more 'Boro bought big to stave off the threat of relegation. Bloomer was one of several new men drafted in and the signings proved to be extremely successful.

Another quality signing at the time was another England international, right-winger Billy Brawn, who was snapped up from Aston Villa. Again it was money well spent. Clearly nobody could accuse 'Boro of lack of ambition at that time.

However, the constant buying proved to be a drain on the club's limited finances. The new directors were forced to dip into their own pockets on several occasions to pay the bills. In fact Lt-Col T.Gibson Poole had even paid the £250 fine imposed on the previous board by the FA from his own bank account.

As a result, 'Boro started to cook the books a little bit. It wasn't surprising that 'Boro's reputation was suspect and the FA, acting on information, set up another Commission of Inquiry to examine 'Boro's books. This was held in Manchester at the end of the 1905-06 season.

Lt-Col Poole and manager Mackie were called to the Commission to give evidence. The Commission discovered that there was general malpractice in the books and that 'Boro had improperly paid a bonus of £10 to Steve Bloomer for re-signing for the new season.

The outcome was a £50 fine for the club and it was made absolutely clear to Lt-Col Poole that future book entries should be made properly and that all transactions should be fully disclosed. In fact two members of the FA management committee were instructed to visit Ayresome Park regularly to make spot checks.

The Commission held on to the club's books so that they could make further investigations and reported, in the November, that they were unable to account for the total gate money at Ayresome Park and that expenses were suspect. Lt-Col Poole, it was alleged, had often taken custody of the gate takings and he was ordered to pay back almost £500 to the club.

The Colonel escaped without further punishment, though Mackie, who had already announced his retirement, was suspended in any case. Steve Bloomer was suspended for 14 days and missed two matches.

Despite all this public humiliation, things were starting to look up for the 'Boro fans. The club started the 1906-07 season with a formidable forward line of Brawn, Bloomer, Common, Fred Wilcox and James Thackeray. They were a match for any defence.

Even so, it took new player-manager Andy Aitken some time to get the team into gear. They made a disappointing start to the season, but then recovered and finished mid-table.

The following year, Aitken patched up the defence and their record was the best in the First Division. As a result 'Boro went on to finish sixth. It was Ayresome Park's best season so far and turned out to be one of the best ever.

At the same time, 'Boro could not free themselves of their financial problems, though they had stopped resorting to underhand methods of solving them.

In 1908-09 'Boro made a loss of £1,674 which set the alarm bells ringing loudly. The directors were forced to introduce a series of severe cuts, and Aitken was unable to enter the transfer market. There were few problems with the team, however, because 'Boro finished ninth in the First Division.

The following season was the start of a new era at Ayresome Park when one George Washington Elliott made his first-team debut for 'Boro. Sunderland-born Elliott was to go on and play a major part in 'Boro's early history, scoring 213 goals in 365 appearances. He also played three games for England and was a great favourite on the terraces.

When Elliott first came into the team as a promising 20-year-old inside-forward, Bloomer and Common were still permanent fixtures in the line-up. However, both soon moved on to new pastures. Bloomer returned to Derby and Common joined Arsenal after being awarded a free transfer by the FA because 'Boro could not afford to pay him a £250 benefit.

The financial noose was tightening all the time and with the club's receipts down by £1,000, a crisis meeting was held in the Victoria Hall in the summer of 1910. Gibson Poole, who by that time was the mayor of Middlesbrough and the whole board threatened to resign unless shareholders and season-ticket holders advanced £500 to pay the summer wage bill.

The money was forthcoming, though Gibson Poole must have argued the situation very well because 'Boro had made a profit of £356 on the season, comparing very favourably to the disastrous loss of the previous season.

'Boro made a fine start to the 1910-11 season, but once again all the success on the pitch was wasted by the unsavoury events off it. This time Lt-Col Poole and manager Andy Walker, who had been in charge for only six months, were charged with bribery by the FA. Just when 'Boro were on the verge of losing their bad boy image, they were back to square one.

The bribery charge stemmed from the derby match against Sunderland at Ayresome Park on 3 December 1910. It came about largely for political reasons and was generally regarded as

One of the earliest surviving action shots from Ayresome Park. 'Boro are pictured playing Liverpool on 21 November 1908. A goal from Steve Bloomer was enough to give 'Boro victory.

A 'Boro team group from 1908. Back row (left to right): T.Heslop, J.C.Brown (assistant secretary), A.Campbell, A.E.Forbes (director), A.A.Hassell, F.France (director), D.Gordon, T.R.Bell. Second row: Jack Ingleby (trainer), T.Burdon (director), J.A.Groves, A.Aitken (manager), J.Watson, J.H.Gunter (director), J.McKenzie, C.G.Hunt, F.Pentland, J.R.Smiles (vice-chairman). Seated: F.Wilcox, J.H.Hall, J.L.Jones, S.Aitken (captain), Col T.G.Poole (chairman), S.Bloomer, T.Wilson, D.Cail, E.Verrill. Front row: J.Haxby, H.Kent, A.Oribin, J.Miller, J.Thackeray, W.Barker, T.Dixon, S.McClure.

This group of capped 'Boro players from 1910 includes Steve Bloomer, back row left, John L.Jones, back second right, Jimmy Watson, front left, Alf Common, front centre, and Donald McLeod, front right.

Paul Frith, one of 'Boro's best known early trainers, and the immediate predecessor to the great Charlie Cole.

a political rather than a football matter. It came about because 'Boro chairman Gibson Poole was the town's Conservative candidate in the forthcoming general elections. In fact voting was to take place the following Monday.

It was felt, quite rightly, if 'Boro were to win the derby match, then this would considerably help Lt-Col Poole's chances of being elected. The Liberals were favourites to win the seat, so Gibson Poole needed every bit of help he could get.

Clearly he could count on the help of the 'Boro players, who would be busting a gut to beat Sunderland in any case. Most of them had been campaigning on his behalf beforehand.

Unfortunately it all rather got out of hand. Andy Walker is said to have approached the Sunderland captain Charlie Thomson, before the game and offered him £10 plus £2 each for the other Sunderland players if 'Boro could win the match for the Colonel's sake.

These allegations, made by Thomson, were passed on to his trainer, Billy Williams. The trainer reported what he had been told to Fred Taylor, the Sunderland chairman and from then on it became a major incident. Taylor reported the matter to the FA.

Ironically, the alleged bribe was academic because 'Boro won the game by 1-0 with a goal from outside-left James Nichol. And the result made not the slightest difference to Gibson Poole, who was soundly beaten at the election.

However, the FA were forced a call another Commission of Inquiry. It was becoming a regular occurrence. This time the FA were ready to throw the book at 'Boro, especially as the club had only recently been fined £100 for making an illegal approach to an Airdrie player, which had led to a four-week suspension for Walker.

The Commission met on 16 January 1911 and were satisfied that a bribe had been made to Thomson. Their action was predictable. Gibson Poole and Walker received lifetime bans.

The Commission's report stated: 'Middlesbrough has in the past been guilty of a number of breaches of the rules and regulations of the FA, some of them of a very serious character. These offences have been committed while Col Poole has been chairman and the Commission are satisfied that the club have been largely under his domination.'

'Boro had to pay the expenses of the inquiry, the result of which sent shock waves running through the town. There was strong criticism of Gibson Poole, who had been a leading civic figure in Middlesbrough for many years. There was also plenty of sympathy for Andy Walker, who, it was felt, was the scapegoat. A petition calling for Walker's reinstatement was signed by 12,500 people, but it was ignored by the FA.

At the same time, the Commission made it absolutely clear to the remaining members of the 'Boro board that this was the very last chance for the club. They had broken the rules on too many occasions in the past. If there was a similar reoccurrence, it was highly likely that the club would be thrown out of the Football League.

'Boro were the bad apple of English soccer and clearly needed a new image. It came, almost immediately, with the arrival of a new chairman, Phil Bach, who went on to become one of the most respected figures in the game. Bach also appointed a new manager, Tom McIntosh, who was to lead the team up until the start of World War One.

One of the chairman's first tasks was to try to generate some good news. Even the local Press had contained too many damning headlines about the club. So, in the summer of 1911, Mr Bach announced a new look for Ayresome Park. Railway sleepers were to be laid in front of the Main Stand to accommodate a standing terraced area. The total cost was £2,500, which represented quite an outlay for the cash-strapped club. More positive headlines followed as a result of the 'Boro's achievements on the pitch. In November 1911, 'Boro forced their way to the top of the First Division. It was a great moment for the North-East as a whole, because Newcastle United were second and Sunderland in third place. However, 'Boro could not maintain their level of performance and had to be satisfied with seventh position at the end of the season.

There was more good news from the directors on 2 May 1912, when it was announced that Ayresome Park had finally been purchased. 'Boro had paid off their loans and were now owners of the stadium.

The year was a notable one in another sense, for a certain Charlie Cole joined the Ayresome Park staff as assistant trainer. Cole, who was a carpenter by trade, was a top local athlete and athletics' coach, so his experience was invaluable in helping to keep 'Boro's professionals in trim – especially as most training in those days involved running around the pitch. Cole became assistant to regular trainer Paul Frith.

On the playing side, the legendary Carr brothers from South Bank were all now at Ayresome Park. The first brother to break through was inside-forward Jackie, quickly followed by George in the same position and then centre-half William, who was known as Puddin'. In future years a fourth brother Henry, or Pep, was to represent the club.

The best of them all was Jackie, who went on to become one of 'Boro's all-time greats. He became a regular first-team player at the age of 21 in 1913 and played his last game for the club at the age of 38, winning two England caps along the way.

While Jackie was starting to make an impact, it was the attacking combination of George Elliott and inside-forward Walter Tinsley which was leading the way. The duo developed

One of 'Boro's all time great sides in 1911-12 which finished seventh in the First Division. Back row (left to right): J.G.Pallister (director), T.Bell (gateman), B.Davies, J.Pickering. Second row: J.Nichol, Dr Brownlee, H.Chapelhow, S.Cail, T.H.McIntosh (secretary-manager), J.Fell, W.James, J.J.Walton, Lucas. Third row: C.W.Beckwith (director), H.Cook, A.Layton, W.Barker, A.Jackson, E.Verrill, J.Crozier, E.Eyre, W.Duguid, J.M.Colbeck. Fourth row: W.Metcalfe (director), D.McLeod, J.French (director), R.G.Williamson, captain, P.Bach (chairman), J.Weir, E.Turner (director). Front row: P.Frith (trainer), G.W.Elliott, J.Carr, G.Burton, H.Leonard, F.B.Pentland, W.Carr, J.Stirling, C.Cole (assistant trainer).

Goalkeeper Tim Williamson was with 'Boro for so long that he received two benefits. The first was a benefit game, against Chelsea at Ayresome Park on 19 April 1913, when 'Boro lost 3-0. The second was a benefit payment of £1,000 awarded at the end of his 21-year career with the club. Tim also received a silver tea and coffee service from chairman Phil Bach at a special board meeting in the Grand Hotel on 17 May 1923.

This useful 'Boro side in 1921 featured the three Carr brothers from South Bank. Back row (left to right): W.Birrell, J.Carr, J.Mordue. Second row: P.Donaghy, R.Pender, W.Fox, R.G.Williamson, W.Carr, G.Carr, C.Cole (trainer). Third row: J.Marshall, A.Wilson, S.Davidson, G.W.Elliott, T.Ellerington. Front row: T.Urwin, W.Murray.

a terrific understanding and were largely responsible for 'Boro achieving their highest-ever League placing in 1913-14.

Elliott rammed in 31 goals, including home hat-tricks against Sunderland, Blackburn Rovers and Sheffield Wednesday. Tinsley, signed from Sunderland in the December, scored 19 goals in only 23 appearances, including hat-tricks at home to Aston Villa and Liverpool.

As a result, 'Boro recovered well from a poor start to finish third. It was a season they have never bettered, or even matched. 'Boro finished eight points behind the runaway champions Blackburn, who had been crushed 3-0 at Ayresome Park in the January thanks to Elliott's hat-trick.

'Boro had also completed a double over runners-up Aston Villa during the season, beating the Midlanders 5-2 at Ayresome Park with the help of Tinsley's hat-trick.

Despite these successes, 'Boro in general were going through a difficult period and had to settle for an average attendance of just under 15,000 despite enjoying their best season ever.

'Boro were unable to build on their success and fell away to 12th position the following season. Then came the intervention of World War One, during which 'Boro relinquished control of the stadium. Ayresome Park was requisitioned by the Army for use as a training centre for the troops.

Football was first played on Ayresome Park again early in 1919, when Tim Williamson, Jackie Carr and George Elliott were all regulars in Northern Victory League games.

The Football League restarted the following season, with the 'Boro team having a similar look. However, the club was still mourning the sad loss of Andy Jackson, 'Boro's highly talented young centre-half, who was tragically killed during the war.

'Boro twice finished eighth in the First Division shortly after the war and had a good side. Jackie Carr and Elliott won England honours in the early 1920s and Jack Marshall, Andy Wilson and Andy Davison all played for Scotland. Wilson was arguably the top centre-forward in Britain at the time despite having to wear a glove over a paralysed hand as a result of a war injury.

The board also found the cash after the war to make

This side of the late 1920s contained 'Boro's famous attack of Pease, Birrell, Camsell, Carr and Williams. Back row (left to right): Frank Twine, Johnny McKay, Jimmy Mathieson, John Smith, Joe Peacock, Charlie Cole (trainer), Bob Ferguson. Front row: Billy Pease, Joe Miller, George Camsell, Billy Birrell, Jackie Carr, Owen Williams.

Manager Herbert Bamlett was sacked at a special meeting of the Middlesbrough board on 31 December 1926. It was rather surprising because 'Boro had won five of their previous six games, drawing the other and scoring 29 goals in the process. They were also pushing for promotion. New manager Peter McWilliam did take 'Boro into the First Division at the end of that season. Unfortunately, the Football League refused to sanction Bamlett receiving a Second Division championship medal.

improvements to the stadium. Fourteen tiers of concrete steps were erected in part of the Linthorpe Road End, which previously was an earthen bank.

There was a notable addition to the staff in 1922, when Charlie Flintoff joined the groundstaff. Charlie arrived at the club at the same time as the pitch was relaid. He was eventually to progress to chief groundsman and was respected throughout the game for his playing surfaces until his retirement in 1954, aged 71.

Unfortunately 'Boro's form began to wane in season 1923-24 and suddenly the club was in grave danger of losing its First Division status for the first time since Ayresome Park was opened.

Tim Williamson had retired at the end of the previous season after playing 602 League and Cup games in his 22-year career. Wilson was also transferred to Chelsea early in the season, which proved to be a bad piece of business. Marshall, too, had moved on, to Welsh side Llanelli.

'Boro started badly by losing six of their first eight games but had recovered by Christmas. However, they won only once in the second half of the season – beating Blackburn by 2-0 at Ayresome Park – and finished bottom.

Attendances began to dip sharply the following season as 'Boro struggled to adapt to the Second Division. 'Boro had gambled on bringing in Herbert Bamlett as manager in place of Jimmy Howe in the previous season, but Bamlett had been unable to avoid relegation. However, he began to put a new side together and results improved every season, culminating in 'Boro romping away with the Second Division title in season 1926-27.

It was a remarkable season, which restored Teesside's football pride and the fans responded by returning in their thousands. The average crowds zoomed to almost 22,000, including a new Ayresome Park record capacity of 43,754 for a Christmas holiday game at home to Manchester City. Most of the fans were delighted with the attacking skills and flair of Bamlett's new side, especially centre-forward George Camsell. The 25-year-old powerhouse smashed the Football League goalscoring record with a remarkable 59 goals in only 37 appearances.

Camsell, who had been signed from Durham City in 1925, was a relative unknown when he stepped into the 'Boro first team because of an injury to regular centre-forward Jimmy McClelland.

George was drafted in after 'Boro had failed to win any of their first four games. He scored seven goals in the next six games as 'Boro won the lot. There was no looking back, with Camsell's positive style of play and quick bursts through the middle causing havoc for Second Division defences.

'Boro's forward line of Billy Pease, Billy Birrell, Camsell, Jackie Carr and Owen Williams remains one of the best remembered in the club's history. But they had a lot of other quality players like goalkeeper Jimmy Mathieson and tough wing-half Don Ashman. While Camsell took most of the headlines, Pease also set a new club record number of goals for a winger when notching 25 – which earned him an England cap against Wales.

Unfortunately 'Boro found themselves back in Division Two after only 12 months, despite Camsell scoring 33 First Division goals. They hadn't done too badly, finishing with 37 points. But it was an exceptional season and was enough to leave them in bottom position.

'Boro's dismal form at Ayresome Park contributed largely to them dropping down, because they won only two games at home in the second half of the season.

It was a huge blow to end up back in the Second Division again. But 'Boro were fighters and their second stay in the second flight lasted only one season.

'Boro were the best side and won the championship by two points from Grimsby Town. Camsell again top-scored with 33 goals, while Pease made another cracking contribution with 28.

This time 'Boro were determined to return to the First Division to stay. Peter McWilliam who had replaced Herbert Bamlett shortly before 'Boro won their first promotion, was worldly wise and brought First Division stability.

'Boro celebrated their return to Division One by announcing major ground improvements to the West End. They had concrete terracing installed to replace the old railway sleepers and also erected crash barriers. The concreting cost £3,235 and the barriers £785.

A corrugated fence was installed at the Linthorpe Road End for £485.2s, while the home dressing-room floor was relaid with pitch pine. 'Boro paid £10 to have the canteen under the grandstand flagged, while the concrete steps from the players' entrance to the playing pitch were levelled at a cost of £16.

And to brighten up the stadium, 'Boro paid £40 to Kent and Brydon Limited to plant 400 shrubs and evergreens at the Linthorpe Road End.

Unfortunately the Ayresome pitch was not as luxurious as it was to become after World War Two. The pitch was reported to be infested with plantains and 12 boys were engaged during the summer to clear the weeds at a wage of £1 per week.

A rare aerial view of Ayresome Park in 1934, showing the old South Stand which had been transported from the Linthorpe Road ground in 1903.

Despite the refurbishment costs, plus the return to Division One, 'Boro decided to hold season tickets at £3.6s 6d.

'Boro's team was gradually changing. International defenders Joe Miller and Maurice Webster were the foundations of the side, while 'Boro had the skilful Bobby Bruce in midfield. Pease and Camsell were still knocking in the goals up front.

However, 'Boro needed a 3-1 home win against Bolton Wanderers on the final Saturday of the season to stay up in their first season back in Division One. Camsell scored twice in the game to take his tally to 31.

The highlight of the season came when 'Boro reached the fifth round of the FA Cup – a rare achievement – though they lost 2-0 to Arsenal at Ayresome Park in front of the season's biggest crowd of more than 42,000.

At the end of the season 'Boro lost one of its characters when Jackie Carr, now 38, moved on to Blackpool after giving great service at Ayresome Park. He had joined 'Boro in 1911.

'Boro went through some difficult financial times in the early 1930s. The Depression did not only hit businesses and families. It hit football clubs as well.

The result was that the directors could not spare the cash to enter the transfer market in a big way. However, there was a great need to continue to produce players of First Division quality so, at a crucial and far-reaching board meeting, the directors made the forward thinking decision to start producing and nurturing their own young talent.

The first move in this direction was to adopt both South Bank and South Bank East End's nursery clubs. It was an inspirational move. South Bank was a breeding ground for dozens of hungry, skilful footballers and in fact 'Boro had already signed a teenage striker called Mick Fenton from the East End club in 1932. There had been a danger of missing out on some of these promising youngsters, because clubs from all over the country were running the rule over the lads from the East End and St Peter's clubs. So 'Boro got in first and started the ball rolling with a £50 payment to South Bank and £15 to East End in 1934.

However, it was from St Peter's where 'Boro unearthed one of their greatest gems. 'Boro director Bob Rand watched the St Peter's against Thornaby Juniors match in March 1936 and ran the rule over a tiny inside-forward called Wilfred Mannion.

Rand reported: "Mannion (17½, 5ft 4in, 9st 11lb) is a clever little player, but very small. Wolves have been after the player but he will not sign for anyone until after the junior cup final."

Mannion was true to his word and in the September joined 'Boro as a professional for £3.10s a week. Eight months later, 'Boro plucked another jewel from South Bank, this time from East End. He was 17-year-old George Hardwick, who accepted terms of £4 winter and £3 summer wages, plus an extra £1 when he was in the first team. Both players were to go on to become great internationals.

'Boro had come through their financial problems and in 1936 the board announced the biggest overhaul of Ayresome Park since the ground was opened in 1903.

On 15 June 1936, Dorman Long & Co were awarded a contract to build a new South Stand. 'Boro desperately needed to replace the current stand, which was small and antiquated and was a relic of the former Linthorpe Road ground. In fact it still had a slate roof.

The new South Stand was to be an impressive structure, 250ft long and stretching virtually the full length of the south side of the stadium. It would accommodate 9,000 fans and have all the modern facilities. The seats were to have timber backs, while concrete steps were to be laid in front of the stand, instead of ashes and railway sleepers.

The estimated cost was £13,407 and included a down

Tom Griffiths, 'Boro's experienced Welsh international defender, poses for a photographer in 1934 with youngsters Bobby Stuart (left) and Micky Fenton (right).

In July 1930, Ayresome Park was opened up to thousands of Middlesbrough schoolchildren so that HRH The Prince of Wales could meet them on his visit to Teesside.

Players and officials enjoy a day out at Saltburn in 1934. The picture includes secretary Herbert Glasper, back row, second left, and manager Peter McWilliam, third row, left, both of whom were rarely photographed during their times with the 'Boro.

***Top:* Action from 'Boro's 4-1 home win against Aston Villa at Ayresome Park on 15 December 1934 *and below:* 'Boro prepare to leave Warwick Street for a coach trip to an away game, led by Ralph Birkett, wearing the trilby. Also includes a very young Harold Shepherdson, Billy Brown and Micky Fenton.**

payment of £3,407 to Dorman Long with the remainder to follow, with interest, in installments. Dormans wanted to erect a clock at the top of the front of the stand at a cost of £110, but the board decided against it.

However, the erection of a brand new south stand was only part of the refurbishment. 'Boro announced that Dorman Long were to put in foundations and cover the West End of the stadium. It was great news for the fans who regularly stood in the pouring rain. The cost of the waterproof was £2,714.

In addition, 'Boro also decided to recover the North Stand, this contract, for £726.8s 6d, was awarded to William Clark & Co. Clark also fitted a new staircase to the East End for £37.10s. Mundell & Co carried out work to repair urinals and the turnstile houses in the South Stand and also made minor alterations to the East End. They were paid £83.10s for the work.

When we aren't playing football at Ayresome Park, we can play golf! Bobby Baxter illustrates the finer points of the game to Paddy Nash, Wilf Mannion and George Hardwick.

Work started virtually immediately on the refurbishment and carried on through much of the 1936-37 season. However, not everybody was happy with the magnificent new South Stand. The occupiers of 82-88 Clive Road wrote to the club to say that the stand had considerably darkened their front rooms and asked what the board intended to do about it. The directors wrote back to say that no infringement of light had taken place, so they would be doing nothing.

The South Stand was officially opened on Saturday, 4 September 1937, in 'Boro's first home game of the season against Stoke City. 'Boro celebrated with a victory when goals from Billy Forrest and Micky Fenton produced a 2-1 win. A big luncheon was held beforehand in the Grand Hotel at 5s 6d a head. The opening ceremony was performed by Mr C.E.Sutcliffe, the president of the Football League.

'Boro continued to spend money on Ayresome Park right up until World War Two. In February 1938, work was completed on new staircases at the West and East Ends of the ground by Bainbridge & Co at a cost of £118.16s 9d.

That summer the whole stadium received a spruce-up, at a total cost of more than £600. It included painting the stands and the important job of concreting the billiard-room floor! Overall the stadium looked in great shape and once again 'Boro could boast of a ground as good as any other in the country.

They had also been putting together a team which was as good as any in the land. Highly-respected new manager Wilf Gillow started to assemble a team in the mid-1930s and continually improved it in the years leading up to the war.

In 1936, 'Boro reached the quarter-finals of the FA Cup for the first time since 1904. Their Wembley hopes were dashed by a sixth round 3-1 defeat at Grimsby Town.

Even so, there was justifiable belief by the supporters that honours were just around the corner. In 1937 goalkeeper Dave Cumming was signed from Arbroath, giving strength at the back to a squad which already included big stars like Billy Brown, Bobby Stuart, Bobby Baxter, Billy Forrest, Benny Yorston and Tommy Cochrane.

George Camsell was still going strong, but his 18 League goals in 1936-37 were eclipsed by those of Stockton-born Micky Fenton, who hit 22. All in all, 'Boro were on the verge of producing arguably the best side in their history. Cumming, Jack Milne and Baxter were all Scottish internationals, while Fenton was called up to play for England against Scotland in 1938. 'Boro were as good as anybody.

In 1937-38 'Boro finished fifth in the First Division and the following season were fourth. Everybody believed that they would do it the next year. But, in September 1939, the insanity of Adolf Hitler led to World War Two ending competitive football at Ayresome Park for seven seasons.

The majority of the 'Boro squad rushed to join the Armed Forces and many of them were lost to Teesside as they guested for other clubs during the war years. They played for whichever club was nearest to their barracks. George Hardwick, for example, played for Chelsea and won a wartime FA Cup Final winner's medal, while Micky Fenton played for Blackpool.

'Boro continued to play matches in the Football League North, which was essentially a friendly League and themselves were hosts to several notable guests like Matt Busby.

In July 1940, Ayresome Park became home to two air-raid shelters, which were erected by Middlesbrough Council on the club's land adjoining Ayresome Park Road at a rent of one shilling a year.

It was not until 1945, when the war was coming to an end, that 'Boro gradually moved towards becoming a fully functional club again. The 1945-46 season, though not an official one, started to inspire the fans again and huge crowds were attracted to the stadium.

Players were filtering back from their units and the 'Boro directors had already started to bring in new players to replace the older ones who were no longer good enough for the first team.

The ground was given another spruce-up and £400 was paid to Messrs McCreton for repairs to the East End embankment, which had partially collapsed during the war and become a general problem area.

It was a problem which would not go away for some time. The repairs made by McCretons proved to be unsatisfactory, as large cracks appeared in the concrete soon afterwards.

In 1946 the 'Boro board reluctantly accepted that the East End was unsafe and needed a total and very expensive overhaul.

Micky Fenton in the thick of the action against Stoke City on 23 January 1937. Fenton scored in a 1-0 victory.

Left: **A later picture of Charlie Cole, who spent most of his working life at Ayresome Park.**

Below: **This is the great 'Boro side of the late 1930s which many people believe would have gone on to win the championship but for the advent of World War Two. Back row (left to right): Cliff Chadwick, George Laking, Bobby Baxter, Dave Cumming, Billy Brown, Bobby Stuart, Charlie Cole (trainer). Front row: Ralph Birkett, Micky Fenton, George Camsell, Benny Yorston, Tommy Cochrane, Billy Forrest.**

A gathering of the greats with no less than seven internationals in their 1938-39 side. Left to right: Dave Cumming, Micky Fenton, George Camsell, Bobby Baxter, Benny Yorston, Duncan McKenzie and Jackie Milne.

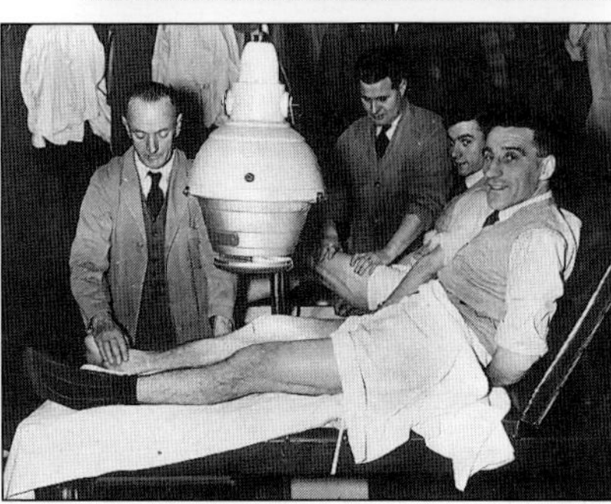

Don't worry, it's only a scratch. Trainers Tom Mayson (left) and Harold Shepherdson are busy in the treatment room. Jimmy Gordon is pictured in the foreground.

In September 1946, manager David Jack told the directors that Bobby Stuart had refused the captaincy for the reserve team at home to Spennymoor and when the team ran out, Stuart laid down near a goal post. The board transfer listed him at £3,500, and Stuart countered with a transfer request.

They accepted estimates of £16,675 from Jeffcocks to have the embankment and its staircases strengthened.

The work included: re-endorsing the concrete wall, constructing reinforced concrete columns and rakers, providing reinforced concrete stepping to the extended area, covering in with reinforced concrete the stepped ashed area and forming reinforced concrete barriers in place of the existing metal barriers.

There was a lot of work involved, even though it seemed straight-forward enough at the time. However, a lack of materials and skilled labour meant that it took several years for all the work to be completed.

Even before the work was finished, 'Boro made more alterations to the East End. In 1948 the boys' pen was made a separate entity with a special staircase installed at a total cost of £4,000. The terracing was also taken right round to the North Stand. The old scoreboard was dismantled and replaced by a new one, made of concrete.

On the field, 'Boro coped well with the problems of trying to blend a new team together. The two stars of the line-up were now George Hardwick and Wilf Mannion, both of whom had played in a number of wartime internationals. With normality restored, the duo continued their England careers in recognised internationals.

George and Wilf were the mainstays of a team which included full-back Dickie Robinson, half-backs Harry Bell and Jimmy Gordon and wingers Johnny Spuhler and Geoff Walker. Micky Fenton was still banging in the goals and who knows what scoring records he might have broken but for seven lost years during the war. George Camsell was still with the club and was appointed Colts coach at £4 a week.

Admission prices immediately after the war were set as: ground, East End 1s 3d; West End 2s; paddocks 2s 6d; stands, centre portion 4s 6d; wing seats 3s 6d.

The increased costs clearly didn't deter the fans. No less than 43,685 crowded into Ayresome Park for the first home League game against Stoke City on 7 September 1946 and as a result the chief constable wrote to 'Boro requesting a 42,000 limit, or 45,000 at the outside. The 'Boro directors not surprisingly agreed to 45,000.

However, it was not an easy limit to adhere to. On 1 March, a remarkable 53,025 fans paid to see the FA Cup sixth-round tie at home to Burnley. Thousands more were locked outside. It had not seemed possible that Ayresome Park could hold so many people.

Despite this terrific support, 'Boro showed patchy form in the early years after the war. They never managed to emulate the team of the late 1930s. As a result it made it difficult for established stars like Hardwick and Mannion to settle down.

Mannion first asked for a transfer as early as October 1946. He was told that he would not be transferred at any price. The following summer, Mannion refused to re-sign and the episode dragged on for several months.

In February 1948, Hardwick had a transfer request turned down, while Mannion again declined to sign in the summer. In fact he moved to Oldham with his wife, Bernadette, planning to take a business there and play for Third Division Oldham Athletic.

Unfortunately it was easier to break out of Alcatraz than it was to obtain a transfer from a club which didn't want to let a player leave. However, 'Boro did put a price of £25,000 on Mannion's head and might have been tempted to release him if Oldham had come up with the money. But Oldham were not a rich club and had very little chance of raising the cash.

Eventually Mannion realised that the move was not going to happen for him and returned to Middlesbrough on 14 January 1949.

Mannion recalls: "I stuck it out for a long time because I was determined to get away from Middlesbrough. The system was all wrong. You couldn't leave a club unless they wanted you to leave. It was a form of slavery.

"Obviously Middlesbrough paid you every penny that you were entitled to, but not a penny more. I knew from talking to other players from other clubs that there were ways and means of making more money and I felt that I had a right to try to take advantage of it. But 'Boro dug in their heels.

"I had nothing against Middlesbrough. This would have been a career move for me. I tried hard to stay in Oldham, but in the end I had no choice. I had to come back."

'Boro desperately needed Mannion back in the fold because they were struggling to avoid relegation. They had paid Charlton Athletic £10,000 for Scottish inside-forward Alex McCrae in the October of that season and also bought Newcastle United's reserve centre-forward Andy Donaldson for £17,000. But things were still not going well.

Donaldson scored a few valuable goals, but the return of the master, Wilf Mannion, proved to be the inspiration. Even so, it was a close run thing. 'Boro avoided the drop by beating Sheffield United by 3-1 in their last home game, thanks to the only hat-trick of his career by Jimmy Hartnett.

'Boro's form at Ayresome Park had been invaluable that season, because they were a poor side on their travels, winning only once and scoring only nine goals.

Mannion, of course, was a local boy and the Teesside area was still a tremendous spawning ground for talented young players. There was a need for 'Boro to harness this talent and on 5 May 1949, the first 'Boro Juniors game was staged at Ayresome Park, when they entertained Newcastle Juniors in a derby match.

The 'Boro Juniors was the brainchild of a local schoolteacher, Ray Grant, who had contacted 'Boro 12 months earlier and suggested that the team should be formed. Grant was prepared to put the team together and run it and asked permission to call the team 'Boro Juniors and play at Hutton Road.

The 'Boro directors jumped at the idea and it was the start of a long association with Mr Grant, who continued to scout for the club until modern times.

In April 1949, 'Boro transformed their training system by selling their War Stock to buy Hutton Road from the owners of the Middlesbrough Estate. It was a large open area, relatively close to Ayresome Park, with enough land for two training pitches and the erection of dressing-rooms. It also meant that 'Boro would be able to play practice games without the risk of damaging the pitch at Ayresome Park, particularly through the wet months.

'Boro commissioned Mr Wayman Brunton to carry out a full inspection of Hutton Road and he discovered that it had originally been a tip for furnace waste or slag. There was very little topsoil on top of the waste material.

Mr Brunton suggested that the area should be scraped and levelled and that a foot of topsoil should be laid on top. The

'Boro, pictured at Ayresome Park before a 3-0 win against West Bromwich Albion on 12 November 1949. Left to right: Peter McKennan, Alex McCrae, Wilf Mannion, Tom Blenkinsopp, Jimmy Gordon, Ronnie Dicks, George Hardwick, Bill Linacre, Rolando Ugolini, Dickie Robinson, Tom Woodward.

'Boro wrote to the BBC in October 1948 'protesting about the radio commentary of Mr Kenneth Wolstenholme after our game against Manchester City'. 'Boro had lost the game 1-0 at Maine Road.

'Boro board, who had forked out £4,100 to buy Hutton Road, agreed to have the work done at a cost of £1,985.

Work started immediately and two pitches were laid. 'Boro also paid an extra £500 for five inches of loose soil to be deposited on three sides of the outfield to prevent dust. Mr Brunton was then asked to engage six of his potato pickers to pick stones off the completed pitches.

However, not all new ideas won the favours of the 'Boro directors. In February 1949 they rejected an approach from Messrs H.Sproates Limited to provide floodlighting at Ayresome Park for £589.19s.

The erection of floodlights at this stage would have kept Ayresome Park at the forefront of English football, for lights were being introduced elsewhere. However, nobody had yet considered the possibility that the lights might one day be strong enough to light up League games on winter nights, so the 'Boro board were not partial to the idea. It was another seven years before floodlights were first used in a League game, when Portsmouth lost 2-0 to Newcastle United at Fratton Park.

The year of 1949 was still a momentous one. Mannion regained his England place, which had been put on hold during the Oldham saga and went on to win a club record 26 international caps. The 31-year-old genius also sparked a 'Boro revival.

On 27 December 1949, Ayresome Park somehow managed to cram in 53,802 fans for the 1-0 derby victory against Newcastle United, which set a new crowd record for the stadium. It was a figure which was never to be beaten.

'Boro went on to finish ninth in the First Division and maintained their progress the next season. They were in top spot at the end of 1950, but lost their way after the New Year – an all too familiar story – and had to settle for a respectable sixth position. The huge crowds were making things difficult for some of the eager spectators, particularly the small ones. Many diminutive fans had solved the problem of their being unable to see the action by hanging ropes from the corrugated sheeting at the top of the West End and watched the games by standing on pieces of wood which were suspended from the ropes.

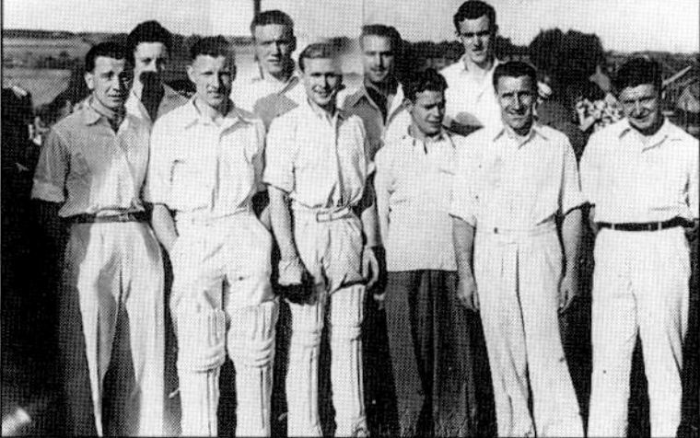

We can do anything! 'Boro line up for a charity cricket match in Crook in 1949. Harry Bell and Wilf Mannion are padded up and ready to open the innings. Bell was an accomplished batsman who played in 100 matches for Durham County, scoring 3,735 runs.

The 'Boro board wrote to the chief constable suggesting that this practice should be stopped in the interest of safety.

Meanwhile work on the East End embankment was continuing as the contractors struggled to get the safety work completed to the satisfaction of the directors. The board revealed that the ongoing cost of the repairs had now risen to £28,581 and that parts of the East End were still requiring attention.

In 1950, 'Boro said goodbye to one of their greatest players ever when George Hardwick moved to Oldham Athletic as player-manager. Ironically it was exactly the same route that Wilf Mannion had wanted to take in 1948, but had not been permitted. Hardwick, still only 30, had skippered 'Boro and was England's first post-war captain. 'Boro could have done with

'Boro prepare to go off on their travels by Bee-Line coach in 1950. Rolando Ugolini, wearing the straw boater, puts on the style which was later copied by Frankie Vaughan.

his experience in the ensuing seasons. In 1951, 'Boro hosted two Festival of Britain matches at Ayresome Park. The first was against Partizan Belgrade on 12 May. The Yugoslavs took the place of original opponents Akademisk from Denmark. 'Boro forked out for 20 tankards costing £2.10s (£2.50p) each to present to their visitors.

'Boro lost the match 3-2, with Neil Mochan scoring on his debut. Mochan had been signed for £14,000 from Greenock Morton a couple of days earlier. Geoff Walker grabbed 'Boro's other goal. After the match, everybody had dinner at the Corporation Hotel.

The second Festival of Britain match, on 15 May, was an amateur international between England and Norway.

More ground improvements were made the same year. 'Boro paid Mu-Ray Chrome Products 15s per seat to fit back-rests in the North Stand. Unfortunately the board took away one of Ayresome Park's attractive features by removing the trees behind the North Stand and resurfaced 2,500 square yards of land at a cost of 4s 6d per square yard. The directors had not heard of 'trees not tarmac' in those days.

There were lots of changes to the team in the early 1950s. New players coming into the club included Jamaican international forward Lindy Delapenha from Portsmouth and left-back Bobby Corbett from Newcastle United. Mochan was just one of a series of centre-forwards that 'Boro signed and then later moved on.

In 1952, manager David Jack resigned and his place was taken by Walter Rowley. It was a difficult time at Ayresome Park, because the team's fortunes were beginning to wane again.

When Rowley had to go into hospital for an operation in February 1954, he tendered his resignation at the same time. Alec Stock of Leyton Orient was offered a three-year contract of £2,000 a year in the March. He originally accepted it, but later turned it down.

'Boro then turned to Bob Dennison of Northampton Town. Dennison accepted a five-year contract at £2,250 a year, on the understanding that he had full responsibility for team selection. In the past the team was normally selected by the directors. However, the board agreed to Dennison's request even though two members, French and Hatfield, voted against.

However, Dennison first had to negotiate his release from Northampton. So it was a managerless 'Boro who won only six games at Ayresome Park all season, and were relegated along with Liverpool in the summer of 1954. It was the first time they had been outside the First Division since 1929.

That summer 'Boro carried out ground improvements by having the roof of the South Stand resheeted. They accepted an estimate of £2,615 from Dorman Long & Co and work started on 19 May 1954. The old sheets which were removed were sold to J.Hewitson of Pennyman Street, North Ormesby, for £100.

Meanwhile Dennison was negotiating his release from Northampton and one of his first jobs after arriving at Ayresome Park was to offer Wilf Mannion a new contract. However, Wilf was 36 by this time and decided to quit football.

In the September, he applied for his League Provident money, which would effectively bar him from playing League football again. However, few people wanted to see the maestro quit and Grimsby, Darlington, Colchester, Hull and Leeds all wanted to sign him. Eventually Mannion withdrew his application for the League Provident cash and signed for Hull on Christmas Eve, 1954. The Tigers paid 'Boro £4,500.

While Mannion was quitting 'Boro, the club made a very astute move by promoting Wilf Atkinson to head groundsman in place of Charlie Flintoff, who was retiring. Atkinson's wages were increased by ten shillings to £8.10s a week and he was given a £5 bonus.

It was one of the best moves that 'Boro could have made because Wilf went on to turn Ayresome Park into one of the best playing surfaces in the country. The days of a weed-infested pitch with bare patches were quickly dispatched. Within a few years, visiting teams were marvelling at the magnificence of the playing surface and Wilf kept it that way until his retirement.

Not that 'Boro's players excelled on Wilf's early pitches. In

Ayresome Park, as it was for the start of the 1951-52 season. Note the huge expanse of the open standing area of the East End. The bowling green behind Shaw's Club can also be seen.

David Jack, pictured shortly before his resignation in April 1952. He was manager of the 'Boro side which finished sixth in the First Division in 1950-51, which was the club's best ever post-war achievement.

The Young Christian Workers wrote to complain in 1952 that fans at Ayresome Park were not using the public conveniences. The club decided to post bills informing fans they must use the conveniences provided.

This was the South Stand in June 1954, when the roof was being resheeted.

'Boro were struggling to come to terms with life in the Second Division in 1955. Back row (left to right): Derek Stonehouse, Ray Bilcliff, Rolando Ugolini, Ronnie Dicks, Dickie Robinson. Front row: Lindy Delapenha, Joe Scott, Bill Harris, Ken McPherson, Arthur Fitzsimons, Bert Mitchell.

fact Dennison had a nightmare start to his career at Ayresome Park. 'Boro drew their first game back in the Second Division at Plymouth Argyle, but then lost eight in a row. A 2-1 home win against Lincoln City on 25 September got the team into gear and they recovered reasonably well to finish 12th.

At the end of the season there was another major development. A certain Brian Clough was demobbed from the forces and re-signed as a professional on a wage of £7.10s.

The Butlins Young Ladies Display took place at Ayresome Park on 27 November 1954.

Strong-willed, precocious and with a unique eye for scoring goals, Clough was to go on to become one of 'Boro's all-time greats. He scored an incredible 204 goals in 222 'Boro appearances.

With a goalscorer like Clough in their ranks, 'Boro could have gone on to achieve anything. But they never signed up the quality players to slot in around him and build a top-class side. In fact all of Clough's career at Ayresome Park was spent in the Second Division, which is probably the major reason why he gained only two England caps.

Another development in June 1955 provided 'Boro with the opportunity to increase their land holding at Ayresome Park. The Teesside Hospital Management Committee offered the club a 5ft strip of land, stretching for 185ft behind the West End. The offer was subject to 'Boro replacing the boundary wall on the hospital land.

The extra land was tempting, because it would have given 'Boro a lot of potential to rebuild the West End at some time in the future. However, the strip was relatively small, even though the Hospital asking price was only £941.2s.

Further discussions took place and the two parties negotiated on the possibility of extending the strip to 8ft at a cost of £1,177.5s. 'Boro's directors remained undecided and eventually the purchase plans were dropped.

In 1955, 'Boro suffered a body-blow with the tragic loss of secretary John Clifford Fairweather. The 38-year-old, who lived in Ayresome Street, was found dead at the foot of Huntcliffe at Saltburn. Earlier his hat and coat had been found at the top of the 325ft high cliff. The 'Boro board met the day after the death, on 22 June and reported: "a deficiency in the accounts of the club" which the chairman W.S.Gibson "regretted to say was reported by the auditors to be in the region of £1,300." The deficiency was later said to be £1,320 0s 5d and it was discovered that insurance cards had not been stamped for varying periods going back to the previous September.

Harold Shepherdson makes sure that Brian Clough – sporting a black eye – doesn't forget to pack his boots as he prepares to make his England international debut against Wales in 1959.

The following May, Clough handed in the first of his several transfer requests. However, the 'Boro board decided against taking any action. In those days you were tied to a club for life, unless the club decided otherwise. Clough must have thought it was a life sentence as he banged in the goals at one end and then watched as the defence shipped them at the other end.

Despite his set-back, Clough lost none of his zest for goals. In 1956-57 he scored 40 goals and then played for England 'B' and the Under-23 side. 'Boro finished the season strongly, but had to settle for sixth place in the Second Division.

The floodlight bug had now caught on all over the country and in March 1957, 'Boro took the plunge by awarding a contract to the General Electric Company. The plan was to erect four pylons, each 135ft high and each containing 36 x 1,500 watt lamps.

The erection work took place that summer and seven tons of steel was used in the construction of each pylon. 'Boro had to fork out almost £2,000 more than anticipated because the Electricity Board had to install a transformer and switchgear to cope with the extra electricity load. The final cost of installation was £18,209 2s 6d.

Unfortunately the new pylons didn't please everybody. Mr F.Smith of 64 Kensington Road, wrote to the club to say that the floodlights were an eyesore and would considerably lower the value of his property. 'Boro decided to take no action.

Clough continued to flourish under the lights and when Dennison brought in 18-year-old Alan Peacock alongside him in the December, the pair ended up with 55 goals between them. Even so, the team could finish no higher than seventh.

Dennison still made a £10,000 profit for the club and was rewarded with a new five-year contract. However, there was a desperate need to bring in a bit more experience to play alongside promising young lads like Billy Day, Derek McLean and Eddie Holliday.

The manager made strong attempts to sign Tommy Docherty from Preston North End, Don Revie from Sunderland and Ron Flowers from Wolves, but all his efforts failed. Eventually the void was filled by the ball-playing Willie Fernie from Celtic and the tough tackling Ray Yeoman from Northampton Town.

'Boro had the dressing-rooms modernised in 1958 as the team prepared for their fifth season in the Second Division. In the past they had never been outside the First Division for more than three seasons and there was a danger of a rot setting in. 'Boro started that season by crushing Brighton by 9-0 at Ayresome Park, with Clough grabbing five goals. However, 'Boro could not sustain the level of performance and in fact were gradually slipping towards the one of leanest periods in the club's history.

On 4 April 1959, Brian Clough and his wife Barbara were married at St Barnabas Church in Middlesbrough. They settled into a new club house bought specially by the 'Boro at 21 Newham Avenue. The house cost £2,675. Clough celebrated his forthcoming wedding by scoring 43 goals that season, but still England caps deserted him.

In September 1959, Clough scored all five goals for the Football League against Northern Ireland and finally made his full international breakthrough.

Along with teammate Eddie Holliday, Clough was called up for England's matches against Wales and Sweden. He failed to score in either game and never played for England again, though Holliday played in the next international against Northern Ireland.

Worse was to follow for Clough, because nine of the 'Boro

Welcome to Ayresome Park. 'Boro's new secretary, Harry Green, takes over the reins with help from manager Bob Dennison (left) and chairman W.S.Gibson (right).

players submitted a round-robin to the club's management saying that they were unhappy with Brian's captaincy. The team was split into factions and Clough's pompous attitude was bitterly resented in certain areas of the dressing-room.

It was an unfortunate affair for Clough, because all he ever wanted was to score goals and see success come to Ayresome Park. News of the round-robin reached the media and the arguments spilled over into the newspapers. Clough responded by handing in a transfer request, which typically was turned down.

However, the battle did not spill over into 'Boro's very next game. They crushed hapless Bristol Rovers by 5-1 at Ayresome Park and Clough grabbed a hat-trick in 34 minutes.

Unfortunately there were few indications that things were going to get better. In fact the first half of the 1960s was one of the darkest periods in 'Boro's history.

The squad was allowed to get weaker as good young players were sold on and inferior replacements were brought in. Clough was sold to Sunderland for £55,000 and it signalled the start of a five-year slide. Peacock was Clough's replacement at centre-forward and did a great job. He top scored with 24 goals and then hit 31 the following season, winning four England caps in 1962. But the club's lack of ambition remained and Peacock was sold on to Leeds United.

Another one in the onion bag. Brian Clough, whose goals per game ratio was better than that of any other 'Boro striker, celebrates another goal for the club.

The 'Boro board acted to try to improve results by dismissing Dennison on 10 January 1963, when his contract still had 19 months to run. Dennison took the club to court as a result and received a settlement for £3,200 with costs at York Assizes.

In the February, 'Boro announced plans to redevelop the South Stand by installing changing rooms, club offices and a two-storey social club. There were also plans for a new gymnasium under the North Stand. However, the cost was to prove prohibitive, though the social club was eventually built. At the end of that season 'Boro announced losses of £47,697, which was the heaviest in their history.

In the meantime Raich Carter had taken over the hot seat at Ayresome Park. Carter was a great player in his time and an England international, but he did not have the managerial know-how to arrest the gradual slide.

No doubt Carter was also under instructions to sell. Peacock moved to Leeds in February 1964, for £50,000 and Cyril Knowles moved out to Spurs for £42,500 a few months later. Then Mick McNeil went to Ipswich for £14,300. 'Boro were selling their best players without replacing them and it was a recipe for disaster.

The apparent lack of ambition affected the gates and the fans gradually started to drop away. As a result 'Boro's financial problems increased, despite the outgoing sales. 'Boro did have triers like Bryan Orritt, young talent like Bill Gates, Gordon Jones, Billy Horner and Frank Spraggon and real quality in the 21-year-old Scottish inside-forward Ian Gibson. But, overall, the squad was very weak.

In the summer of 1964, 'Boro received a letter which tended to overshadow events on the football field for the next two years. 'Boro were informed that they had been placed on the short list for games in the 1966 World Cup, which was being staged in England for the first time.

Naturally the news was very well received in the boardroom, because it promised to bring 'Boro great prestige. However, there was no point in resting on their laurels. The directors quickly decided that they had to do everything within their power to bring the World Cup games to Teesside. A series of plans was drawn up and the board set about securing the backing of the Government and the Football Association.

On 29 July 1964, sports minister Denis Follows visited Ayresome Park to inspect the stadium. In the meantime 'Boro had been working hard and had commissioned plans for extensive alterations to the North and South Stands, which were presented to Mr Follows during his fact finding visit.

The minister later informed the 'Boro directors that they would have a good chance of being awarded World Cup

This is the squad which carried 'Boro's hopes into season 1963-64, minus full-back Gordon Jones, who was ill with glandular fever, and goalkeeper Arthur Lightning, who was still in South Africa. Back row (left to right): Rodgerson, McPartland, Orritt, Smith, Appleby, Gibson, Walker. Second row: Fenton (assistant trainer), Yeoman, Bryan, Neal, Harris, Nurse, McNeil, Marshall, Knowles, Chapman, Peacock, Shepherdson (trainer). Third row: Kelly, Braithwaite, Kirk, Stonehouse, Horner, Brass, Raich Carter (manager), Kaye, Wright, Horsfield, Spraggon, Heath. Front row: Kinnaird, Masson, Butler, Lawson, Lakey, Povey.

Harold Shepherdson, one of 'Boro's all time great servants, was made a Member of the British Empire in July 1969.

matches if they could provide another 3,000-3,500 seats. 'Boro made inquiries and discovered that they could have seats installed at 35s each. So they decided to install them in the terraced areas in front of both the North and South Stands.

The board's determination to upgrade Ayresome Park led to a host of ideas being thrown into the melting pot. For a start, they discussed the possibility of replacing the famous old roof of the North Stand with a cantilever.

It would have been a sacrilegious destruction of one of the stadium's unique features. However, the idea was quickly discarded. Mr Smart of T.J.Newton & Co Structural Engineers was called in and explained that the uprights in the North Stand could be removed at a fraction of the cost of installing a cantilever roof.

The cheaper method was to erect one or two supports in the line of the present seating limit and run a lattice type girder longitudinally along the full length of the stand. Mr Smart estimated that the total cost would not exceed £5,000. The idea was taken up the following year.

The directors naturally expected the World Cup games to attract huge crowds and so concentrated on finding ways of revamping the stadium and still retain a capacity of 50,037. So most of the early plans revolved around spectator quantity rather than comfort and quality.

In August 1964 came the marvellous news. 'Boro had officially been selected as a venue for staging three World Cup group games. They were to share one of the groups along with neighbours Sunderland. It was a huge boost for the club and for the town. They had faced opposition from Newcastle United, but the Geordies had failed to gain the support of their City Council and so the FA decided to weigh in with 'Boro and Sunderland as the North-East venues.

With the World Cup games in the bag, the 'Boro board had to start making serious decisions. It quickly became clear that they would be unable to redevelop the whole of Ayresome Park because of the oppressive costs of such a major project.

So, in the November, the board dropped their plans to redevelop the South Stand which had been pending for 18 months. However, they did press ahead with plans to extend the Social Club, which had been opened in September 1963 and was proving popular with the fans. A contract of £7,131 5s 7d was later awarded to W.Taylor and Son (Builder) Limited to carry out the extension work.

'Boro decided that they would need a new entrance to the Warwick Street side of the stadium, which would back on to the North Stand. The building would contain a directors' room, a board room, a small kitchen and a gymnasium or conference hall.

The directors also applied to the Shaw's Club in Warwick Street to buy a strip of land at the west end of the ground to enable the club to extend their turnstile facilities. In fact the board also inquired about the possibility of buying Shaw's Club in its entirety.

The following month 'Boro made an official offer of £10,000 to buy Shaw's Club from the owners, W.Shaw & Co Limited, steel founders. 'Boro were willing to buy the club and lease it back to the club's officials, subject to the 'Boro being allowed to undertake any developments they required.

Shaws replied that they were willing to sell a strip of land at the west end of the ground, measuring 16ft by 83ft, for £600. This was on condition that the football club was responsible for the re-erection of fences and the reinstatement of any portion of the bowling green which may be used.

The Shaw's Club entrance was just outside the stadium gates in Warwick Street and the club land stretched parallel to the stadium as far back as the West End. The club premises were at the forefront with the bowling green at the back.

At the beginning of 1965, the 'Boro directors got their heads together and discussed a whole host of potential ground improvements. They knew that a lot of the cost would be met by grants and were keen to take advantage of the opportunity to upgrade Ayresome Park. It was an opportunity to bring about changes to the stadium which would previously not have been considered because of the oppressive costs.

Eventually it was settled that seats would be installed in the North and South Terraces and the East End. At the same time the East End would be covered, meaning that all four sides of the stadium would be roofed.

Ayresome Park was lagging behind when it came down to providing facilities to entertain guests and so there was a vital need to build a reception lounge for the use of FA officials and representatives of the national teams which were due to play on Teesside.

While grants would be made available, 'Boro still had to find the rest of the cash to finance these grandiose alterations in preparation for the World Cup. So, in May 1965, the 'Boro directors arranged an interest-free loan of £25,000 from the FA. It was to be repayable over five years.

The same month the directors held a special meeting with Denis Follows, who offered financial assistance from the Government. Follows said that the Government was prepared to pay roughly half the cost of the improvements.

Eventually 'Boro provided Follows with the costings of the planned work and he came back later with a list of grants made available by the Government.

The installation of seating in the North and South Terraces would cost £9,000, of which a grant of £4,500 would be made. The removal of the North Stand supports and general strengthening work was likely to cost £5,800, for which the Government would pay £3,000.

The provision of 4,500 permanent seats in the East End would cost £10,500 and the grant would be £5,000. The roof for the East End was costed at £28,000, with the Government paying 50 per cent.

The expenditure on the new roof was comfortably outstripped by the new lounge, catering and reception facilities which were to be built at the back of the North Stand. These would cost £35,000 and once again a 50 per cent grant was available.

Alterations to the turnstiles and toilets were costing £6,500 with a grant of £3,000 forthcoming, while the Government was also prepared to pay £900 for the erection of flag poles.

Overall, if 'Boro were to carry out all the work to the letter they would qualify for a Government grant of £48,400, of which £1,000 was being deducted for an undisclosed reason leaving a balance for the club of £47,400.

Follows said that the Government was prepared to pay £38,100 in cash, plus a loan of £9,300 repayable in five years "unless the work was not profitable". It seemed to be a piece of typical Government business, but the 'Boro directors were happy to accept it.

The Government grant and the FA loan came to £72,400 combined, so 'Boro estimated that they would need to find £20,900 in the short term in order to finance the alterations. It was still a lot of cash to find, especially considering that the club was not paying its way on the playing field at the time.

Fortunately they received a boost seven days later when Follows rang to say that there had been a change of heart by the Government and the grant would be upped by £6,600 to £54,000.

Clearly 'Boro had all the incentives they could have needed to get on with the work and turn Ayresome Park into one of the top stadiums in the country. From the seating point of view alone, they were taking a huge step forward by increasing the seats capacity from a mere 4,500 to almost 13,000. It was a figure which many First Division clubs could not match.

In addition to all the grant-assisted work, 'Boro decided that the 30-year-old South Stand would need a spruce-up as well. So they awarded a contract of remedial work for £1,120 to W.Latimer & Co Limited in the summer of 1965.

'Boro were also advised that they could rearrange the turnstiles at the West End of the ground without buying a strip of land from Shaw's Club. So they informed the social club that they were no longer interested in a deal. There was a pressing need to start the work on the East End, because it was likely to take most of the 1965-66 season, to complete. So the contract was awarded to T.P.Dunn and Sons Limited and work was quickly under way.

The last thing that 'Boro needed were worries on the field as well. But they were getting them. The team was struggling at the wrong end of the Second Division virtually from the off. On 18 November 1965, 'Boro made an astute signing when Stan Anderson was snapped up from Newcastle United for £11,500. The former England international had a great football brain and was a valuable new addition to the side. Anderson joined as player-coach on wages of £50 a week, with a £1,000 signing-on bonus.

In the same month, 'Boro accepted the offer of a £10,000 loan from the FA repayable over five years at four and a half per cent interest. They had been forced to turn to the FA for this second loan because the Midland Bank would not increase their overdraft facilities.

The financial situation became even more difficult when the architects informed the 'Boro directors that the North Stand alterations would cost almost £10,000 more than the original predictions. The new estimate was £44,500, consisting of £33,000 for the main building, £7,000 for the ground floor alterations including the dressing-rooms and offices and £4,500 for professional charges. It was a blow to the directors because it seriously hit their budget and they decided to hang fire for the moment.

There was great excitement leading up to the World Cup draw on 6 January 1966. 'Boro were allotted the following games: 12 July, North Korea against Russia; 15 July, North Korea against Chile; 19 July, North Korea against Italy. There was no loss of prestige, but the matches were not exactly what Teesside football fans might have hoped for. The least attractive group of all was due to be staged in the North-East and North Korea, one of the World Cup extreme outsiders, were playing in every game at Ayresome Park.

However, the most important consideration for the directors was that the stadium was fully updated for the World Cup matches. The North Stand extension continued to be the major bugbear because the rest of the work was being undertaken as planned and to the satisfaction of the board.

'Boro invited tenders for the North Stand improvements and were quoted £48,231 7s 8d by experienced local builders Messrs C.W.Athey and Sons. This was beyond the board's budget. However, the situation was finally resolved when director Charles Amer offered to do the work through his own Parkway Estates company for only £34,000. Amer told the board that he would not be asking for any professional charges. It was the answer to the club's prayers and the board were delighted to accept Amer's offer.

It came at a time when 'Boro's financial situation was getting worse by the month. The club had to continue to produce the money to pay for the World Cup work and, as the strain began to tell, they wrote to the FA requesting another loan of £20,000. However, the FA wouldn't agree to make the loan without security and for a while there was an impasse. Fortunately the Government was determined to make sure that nothing went wrong in the build-up to their showpiece World Cup and so they stepped in to provide the funds.

Problems were cropping up all along the way. 'Boro suffered another hiccup when an underground sewer was found unexpectedly during the North Stand extension work. It proved to be a nuisance and held up the work.

On the playing field, 'Boro were going from bad to worse, Raich Carter was sacked on 12 February 1966, after three disappointing years at the helm. Anderson was put in charge of the team with loyal club servant Harold Shepherdson carrying out most of the office duties.

Wembley song leader Frank Rea led community singing at Ayresome Park on 13 May 1967, as a prelude to the FA Cup Final. Most of the 32,500 crowd for the game against Peterborough United joined in the singing, though the Ayresome Angels sang their own versions of the songs. 'Boro won the game 2-1 with a brace from John Hickton.

Top man, Stan Anderson, the 'Boro manager, receives the club's Player of the Year trophy from Len Harton, managing director of the *Evening Gazette*, in 1967. Stan received it on behalf of the team. Looking on is skipper Gordon Jones.

However, the new partnership faced the near impossible task of keeping the struggling team in the Second Division. They held on until the very last match, when a 5-3 defeat at fellow strugglers Cardiff City sealed their fate. It was the first time that 'Boro had faced Third Division football in their history.

The situation was particularly embarrassing to the 'Boro directors as they prepared to host the World Cup. On the plus side, the World Cup had given Teesside, a fully refurbished and modern football stadium which was a match for the best in the country.

Even so, 'Boro lost £21,897 in the relegation season and it was going to take a lot of hard work to turn the club around.

The capacity of Ayresome Park had been reduced to 42,000 as a result of the alterations and any hopes the directors cherished of three full houses of the World Cup were to be dashed. Only 57,200 watched the three games, though 'Boro could not have tried harder to ensure that everything was up to scratch and they were highly praised afterwards for their facilities.

True to tradition, 'Boro's supporters got behind the underdogs, the North Koreans and played a huge part in the Asians going through as the surprise quarter-final qualifiers. They finished second in the North-East group behind Russia.

Off the pitch Anderson was now the 'Boro's fully fledged manager and he began the task of trying to turn everything around. There was not much cash in the kitty, but 'Boro decided to sell their stylish midfielder Ian Gibson and use the cash for team strengthening.

In June Anderson agreed a joint fee of £17,500 with Newcastle for his former United teammates Willie Penman and Ron McGarry, but the deal fell through because the players could not agree personal terms at Ayresome Park.

The first move for Gibson came from Southampton, who offered 'Boro £40,000 plus winger David Chadwick for the Scottish midfielder. 'Boro were prepared to accept, but the deal broke down. It worked in the club's favour because at the beginning of July, Gibson was sold to Coventry City for £57,500.

Anderson celebrated the cash boost by promptly going back to Southampton and signing Chadwick for £9,500. He then made another very astute move by paying Luton Town £18,500 for a free-scoring 21-year-old striker called John O'Rourke.

After the publicity from the World Cup had died away, 'Boro announced their admission charges for Third Division football. The centre stands were 9s, the wing stands 7s 6d, the North and South terraces 6s 6d, the East End 5s and the East and

'Boro in 1967-68. Back row (left to right): John O'Rourke, Ray Lugg, Bill Gates, John Hickton, Des McPartland, Willie Whigham, Bob Worthington, Peter Wilson, Arthur Horsfield, Dickie Rooks. Front row: Geoff Butler, Billy Horner, Eric McMordie, Gordon Jones, David Chadwick, Derrick Downing, Don Masson.

West standing 4s. 'Boro didn't make the best of starts to life in the Third Division. In early October Anderson made further moves to strengthen his squad by paying Sheffield Wednesday £20,000 for utility player John Hickton and Falkirk £9,500 for goalkeeper Willie Whigham. Both players were to prove to be crucial signings, just like Chadwick and O'Rourke before them.

The directors were happy to support the signings, especially as there was a grave threat of another financially disastrous relegation. There was no talk of promotion as 'Boro entered the December near the foot of the table and all the directors, coaches and players took part in clear-the-air talks.

The talks paid immediate dividends. 'Boro went from strength to strength as the players suddenly knitted together and started to pick up points. An 11-match unbeaten run sent the team shooting up the table by the end of February.

O'Rourke went on to grab 30 League and Cup goals, while Arthur Horsfield gave valuable support with 23 and Hickton notched 17. 'Boro secured promotion by winning five and drawing one of their last six games, culminating in a remarkable May night when they crushed Oxford United by 4-1 at Ayresome Park to secure second spot behind runaway champions Queen's Park Rangers. The Londoners compiled 67 points, while 'Boro were second with 55, Watford third with 54 and Reading and Bristol Rovers both on 53. It had been very close.

However, 'Boro had deservedly done the business and a season which started on such a black note became an important turning point in the history of the club. It also created a general reawakening of interest in the 'Boro by the club's supporters and generated the formation of the Ayresome Angels.

The only sad part of the season was the announcement of the death of that great club servant Charlie Cole in early 1967. Cole's connections with 'Boro went back to before World War One. He quickly progressed to head trainer and was responsible for training all the great 'Boro sides between the wars.

Charlie was one of the old type trainers, who had the players running around the track to maintain their fitness levels. But he was also one of the best. Charlie was 'Boro through and through and was respected by everybody he worked with.

His retirement came after World War Two and followed more than 35 years service. In 1964, 'Boro sent Charlie and his wife £25 to celebrate their golden wedding. Naturally the club was heavily represented at his funeral.

In the summer of 1967, 'Boro awarded a contract to the North of England Electrical Engineering Company Limited to renew the lamps in the floodlights. They had been in place only ten years, but several were reported to be badly corroded. 'Boro also gave Hutton Road a spruce-up and accepted an estimate of £252 6s 7d from Parkway Estates to erect training circuits at the training ground.

The same summer, 'Boro bought a house at 62 Kensington Road for future use as a players' hotel. The directors were determined to redevelop their youth programme, which had been so successful in previous years.

'Boro went back into the Second Division with high hopes. A return to the First Division was the ultimate target and Stan Anderson didn't intend to hang about. He knew what he was looking for, but it didn't work out for Anderson. In the first three seasons after the World Cup, 'Boro finished sixth, fourth and fourth in the Second Division. The team seemed to get gradually stronger, but somehow promotion wouldn't come.

In April 1970, 'Boro forked out £5,000 to have tip-up seats installed in the areas of the stands which did not already have them. It was a significant upgrading of the Ayresome Park seating.

At the same time, 'Boro began to take an interest in Shaw's Club again. They opened negotiations with W.Shaw & Co for the purchase of the social club. Shaw's Club still had a very high membership, but was not attracting enough customers during the week. As a result the bar was no longer making a profit.

A regular feature of the Stan Anderson era, as John Hickton heads another goal for the club. Hickton was top scorer for six seasons in a row.

W.Shaw & Co were happy to enter into negotiations. 'Boro initially offered £20,000 for the social club and the bowling green behind it. After several discussions, the fee was settled at £21,250.

'Boro's plans were to knock down the old club and apply for planning permission for a single-storey building fronting on to Warwick Street. This would be used to house a shop, the development association offices, match-day police headquarters and other ancillary rooms.

Behind this building, 'Boro had plans to install an all weather pitch and general training area, with the possibility of erecting a gymnasium there one day. These latter plans did not bear fruition, because the area was eventually tarmacked and used as a car-park by the directors.

'Boro showed interest in Rotherham defender David Watson in May 1969. They shied off when quoted £70,000, a huge fee at the time. However, it would have been money well spent. Watson went on to win an FA Cup winners' medal with Sunderland and played for England 65 times.

Ayresome Park was already a top-class stadium, but in January 1971, the directors discussed revolutionary plans which would have made the ground all-seater. They were to start by installing seats throughout the Holgate End. The matter received serious consideration, but in the end the plans were shelved.

At the same time, the directors inaugurated a thorough inspection of the Holgate End and discovered that it was in a relatively poor state of repair. The major problem concerned the roof. It had been given a 25-year guarantee when it was resheeted in 1962, but British Steel engineers examined it and reported that the sheets were in a very bad condition. As a result the whole roof needed to be resheeted.

'Boro didn't want too much unnecessary expenditure because, five years after the World Cup, they were still struggling to pay back the money they had borrowed to upgrade Ayresome Park. They were informed by Mr Robinson, the FA's finance committee chairman, that the initial £25,000 loan – which had been free of interest until 1970 – would now carry an interest rate of four-and-a-half per cent for the next five years.

The news was eased by on-the-field events, for 'Boro had finished the season with an unbeaten run and there was great optimism in the summer of 1971 that the following season could bring promotion. As a result 'Boro announced a record £43,293.50p in season ticket sales. 'Boro indicated their ambitions by spending all of this cash and more on a new centre-back. They bought Stuart Boam from Mansfield Town in a move which was to pay great dividends over the years.

It was at this stage that 'Boro officials were first starting to become unhappy with the condition of the Hutton Road training ground. 'Boro had bought Hutton Road just after the war and the ground had given useful service over the years. The players trained there and the juniors used it for their Northern Intermediate League fixtures.

However, Hutton Road was starting to deteriorate. The playing staff had expressed their dissatisfaction over the condition of the playing surfaces. In addition, vandalism to the changing rooms and shower block was becoming an increasing problem, not to mention the trouble caused by dogs wandering over the pitches.

'Boro were made aware that a Stockton sports ground was

available and they opened discussions with the owners of the Middlesbrough Estate with a view to a possible move. However, the directors suffered a blow when they were later informed by Middlesbrough Corporation that there was an agreement regarding Hutton Road which stated that if it was sold, it must be offered back to Middlesbrough Corporation for the fixed sum of £4,312 11s.

The 'Boro board could not possibly sell Hutton Road for this lowly price, especially if they wanted to finance the purchase of the land at Stockton. They approached the town clerk and offered to exchange Hutton Road for the Stockton land, but this offer was turned down.

The situation then became more frustrating when the land owners at Stockton officially made it available for purchase to the football club. But the 'Boro directors had their hands tied behind their backs, because they could not consider proceeding with the purchase unless Hutton Road was first sold. And the fact that they had to sell Hutton Road for only £4,312 11s meant that they would be virtually giving it away.

Even so, the 'Boro board continued to think positively about the future of the club. Average attendances at Ayresome Park were just below the 20,000 mark and the club was paying its way, even if 'Boro couldn't compete on the same level as the country's élite. As a result the directors decided to investigate the cost of drawing up a master plan for the future development of Ayresome Park.

However, within another 12 months, the promotion dream had still not been achieved and there was a belief that the fans might start to desert the club following so many near misses.

Perhaps it was time to switch things around in the first team. 'Boro turned down an offer of £80,000 from Ipswich Town for promising utility player Willie Maddren, but decided to listen to offers for John Hickton. The bustling striker had made a couple of transfer requests in the past, but they had been turned down. Now 'Boro were prepared to release Hickton if the right offer came along.

The first club to show interest were Huddersfield Town, who offered their own striker Frank Worthington plus a cash settlement. The 'Boro board decided to hold out for £100,000 clear for Hickton. Eventually Queen's Park Rangers entered the scene and agreed to pay the asking price. But the board got cold feet. They decided they couldn't sell their biggest asset until they had a ready-made replacement lined up and so the offer stayed on the shelf.

In the summer of 1972, 'Boro reported a huge financial loss of £49,640. The team had slipped to ninth position in the Second Division, though attendances had held up at just under 18,000.

Despite the financial worries, there was still room for optimism. Stan Anderson was still working hard to develop his team and astute signings like Stuart Boam, John Craggs and Jim Platt had settled into the side alongside some terrific home-grown talent like Willie Maddren, David Mills and David Armstrong.

Anderson did not have a lot of cash to spend in the close season, but he spent it wisely by snapping up Alan Foggon from Cardiff City and promising youngster Graeme Souness from Spurs. Foggon cost £10,000 and Souness £30,000.

The 'Boro board still retained every faith in the manager and in November 1972 Anderson was offered a three-year contract at £6,500 a year, backdated to July. It was a good deal and most managers would have jumped at the offer.

But Anderson was a man of great integrity and it was hurting him that 'Boro were so close season after season without seeming to come up with the winning formula. He also felt that he should be getting more from one or two of the players. So Anderson did not want to commit himself, nor the club, to a three-year contract. Instead, he went back to the board and asked for a one-year contract.

Two months later, bitterly disappointed with the results and some of the performances Anderson resigned. A 1-0 defeat away to Third Division Plymouth Argyle in the FA Cup was the straw which broke the camel's back. Anderson left with his head held high. Nobody could argue with the quality of the squad of players he had put together. All they needed was the spark to ignite the fuse.

Harold Shepherdson, still an important figure at the club, took over as caretaker-manager and did a great job. In fact 'Boro lost only three League games until the end of the season and went on to finish in fourth place. In modern times it would have brought 'Boro a place in the Play-offs.

However, as far as the fans were concerned it was another season of what might have been. The fans had stayed away in their thousands and the average attendance plummeted dramatically to 10,418. At the same time, 'Boro's loss of £27,099 was less than the previous year, despite gate receipts dropping over the 12 months by a staggering £42,226 to only £55,131. It left 'Boro with an accumulated deficit of £83,237.

Naturally the 'Boro board realised that they needed to do something to turn the club around. They achieved it with one fell swoop, though whether it was by good luck or good fortune will never be fully appreciated.

'Boro took the gamble of giving former England international centre-back Jack Charlton his first stab at football management. The Ashington-born player, brother of Bobby, had just finished his illustrious playing career with Leeds United, having won all the major honours, including a World Cup winner's medal.

At the time, some of the club's supporters might have preferred to see an experienced manager come in. But Charlton took to management like a duck to water. He was to prove to be exactly the catalyst that 'Boro were looking for.

That same summer, there were changes in the boardroom. Charles Amer took over as chairman from George Winney. One of Amer's ambitions was to see Ayresome Park given a complete overhaul and several plans were drawn up to bring about improvements and a general upgrading of the facilities. The first job was to have the South Stand roof resheeted and this was duly carried out. In addition, the guttering on the North Stand was leaking and was repaired.

Amer then offered £10,500 on behalf of the club for Ayresome Street Methodist Church, which stood behind the north-east corner of the stadium. The church was no longer in official use and had been put up for sale by the trustees. It was valuable land which might prove useful to the club in the future.

Negotiations with the trustees proved fruitful and two months later 'Boro signed the contract to buy the church. Initially the building was made available to the supporters club. But 'Boro quickly discovered that there were practical difficulties in maintaining the building and it was demolished in April 1974.

More work was needed that season on the floodlights, which needed a complete overhaul. 'Boro accepted an estimate of £24,390 from Christy Electrical and Thorn Electrics for the installation of new lights.

Meanwhile Charlton's team had been sweeping all before them in the Second Division. The team was heads and shoulders above any other side in the Division and 'Boro sailed to the championship, winning it by the huge margin of 15 points.

'Boro secured promotion as early as 23 March, when a goal from David Armstrong was enough to beat Oxford United at Ayresome Park. Seven days later the title was in the bag when David Mills scored in a 1-0 win at Luton Town. At that stage of the season 'Boro had lost only two League games.

Ironically, the team which was promoted consisted largely of players who had been brought to Ayresome Park by Stan Anderson. However, Charlton, in addition to signing former Scottish international Bobby Murdoch to play a key role in

Class of '74, though it's dubious whether this team actually won the Northern Intermediate Cup, which is pictured. Back row (left to right): Bobby Murdoch, Terry Cooper, Frank Spraggon, Peter Brine, David Armstrong, Willie Maddren. Middle row: Alan Willey, Keith Varley (director), Brian Taylor, Pat Cuff, David Mills, Malcolm Smith, Kevin Amer (director), Alan Foggon. Front row: Jack Charlton (manager), Harry Green (secretary), John Hickton, George Kitching (director), Stuart Boam, Charles Amer (chairman), Graeme Souness, Ernest Varley (director), John Craggs, Jack Hatfield (director), Harold Shepherdson (coach).

midfield, had given the side a decisive playing pattern and new sense of purpose.

The fans responded in traditional fashion. Attendances soared by an average of more than 12,000 to over 22,000. The gate receipts rocketed from £55,131 the previous season to a healthy £148,298. Even so, 'Boro's costs were increasing all the time and, despite spending not a penny on incoming transfers, 'Boro lost £2,470 over the year. Much of the profits had been spent on ground improvements

It was still a giant step in the right direction for the club, who were still paying off the World Cup loan, eight years after the event. In March 1974, another cheque for £2,273 as part payment was dispatched.

The following month Denis Howell, the Minister of Sport, arrived at Ayresome Park to discuss ground safety. 'Boro revealed to the minister that they were toying with the idea of ripping out the East End seats and restoring that part of the stadium to all-standing. However, Howell stressed that the seats should remain in the best interests of safety. Even at that time, the Government was thinking in terms of seats rather than standing at football stadia. So 'Boro went along with the minister and dropped the idea.

An era ended in August 1974, when head groundsman Wilf Atkinson retired after 28 years with the club. The high class condition of the Ayresome Park pitch was revered throughout the game and Wilf was the reason why. He had toiled long and hard to generate the lush turf which was the trademark of the playing surface.

Wilf, 66, was also the lord and master of the pitch. Woe betide any player who stepped on it without permission outside of match times. It was a labour of love, which 'Boro did not want to see lost forever, so he was offered and accepted the job of ground maintenance consultant at £12 a week.

'Boro secretary Harry Green went on the record by saying in the *Evening Gazette*: "Wilf must be the finest groundsman in the whole of the Football League. We are glad not to be losing him altogether."

With First Division football finally back at Ayresome Park for the first time in 20 years, 'Boro fans were asked to pay for the privilege of watching top-class games. Season ticket prices were increased to £25 for the centre stands, £20 for the wing stands and £18 for the North Terrace and East End. The increases were justified because the club's costs were higher. After all Jack Charlton had to be rewarded for his remarkable achievement! His salary was increased to £10,000 a year.

'Boro wasted no time in making a big impact in the First Division. At one time they held title aspirations, but eventually fell away and had to settle for a highly creditable seventh place.

It was a great season for the club and for the fans. The average attendance soared to a magnificent 28,605, which was

Wilf Atkinson, groundsman supreme at Ayresome for more than 30 years, receives a cheque for £3,000 from 'Boro chairman Charles Amer to mark his retirement.

more than 6,000 up on the previous season. It was the highest average since 1951-52 when football was still basking in the joys of post-war fervour. The result was a mammoth record profit of £140,000, which enabled 'Boro to comfortably wipe out their £80,000 deficit.

The extra cash came mainly through the turnstiles, which at £229,000 was £83,000 up on the previous year. Season ticket sales had zoomed, doubling to £146,000, while £88,000 came from cup revenue and £63,000 from the shop and development association.The club's lack of transfer activity had once again made a big contribution to the profit. The only incoming signing was former England international Terry Cooper, who was secured from Leeds for £45,000.

However, not everything was sweetness and light during 'Boro's first season back in the First Division. In fact 'Boro suffered a black-out on the night of 24 September 1974. The newly-refurbished floodlights failed after 29 minutes of the match against Leicester City at Ayresome Park.

Staff were unable to solve the problem and so the match was abandoned. Engineers were called in later to inspect the lights and a design fault was identified. New equipment and switchgear had to be purchased in order to complete the repairs.

In the November, 'Boro unveiled their new £12,000 television gantry, which was suspended above the South Stand. The gantry was supported by a main girder weighing five-and-a-half tons and was erected by the engineering firm of Wilson and Walton.

The gantry was soon tested by the BBC, whose sports producer Alec Weeks said: "This is one of the finest gantries in the whole of the First Division. It gives us height, width and depth – and that's everything we need."

However, Weeks was soon back at Ayresome Park to complain about the quality of the floodlights. He maintained that the lights had deteriorated to the point where television coverage of 'Boro's games could be in jeopardy next season. 'Boro were in good company because Manchester United, Manchester City and Leeds United had all received similar warnings. 'Boro's response was to go back to the firm who had installed the lights and request tests to be carried out.

The 'Boro board were continually looking at ways to improve Ayresome Park and early in 1975 they announced that they were considering plans for a £1 million face lift.

The idea was to pull down the North Stand and replace it with a brand new one, including a gymnasium for use by the players during the day and the public on an evening and a licensed social club to house a youth club and a businessman's club. 'Boro did not know it at the time but the plans were eventually to lead to the construction of the sports hall at the end of the 1970s.

The 1975 plans also included luxury dressing-rooms, with comprehensively equipped medical, treatment and physio rooms.

The North Stand was to be pulled down in three sections, according to the *Evening Gazette* and a new one erected in three parts so that there was minimum inconvenience to the spectators. The club hoped to increase the number of seats by another 2,000 and was planning to start work in the summer of 1975. It was a grand idea, but it never did get off the ground.

Plans were also put forward to demolish Shaw's Club and build a new shop, development association offices and police control rooms in its place. These plans did bear fruition.

At the same time, 'Boro announced in the March that they had purchased the Medhurst Hotel in The Avenue for £37,500. This was a major investment in the club's youth system, because the main purpose of buying the hotel was to provide the young players with a permanent home which could be closely monitored by the club.

Cleveland County Council had also been keen to buy the hotel for use as an adult probation centre, which had led to a storm of protests from local residents. They were much happier when they discovered that 'Boro's young players would be using it instead.

'Boro celebrated their centenary in 1976 and everybody realised that it would be wonderful to cement those celebrations by winning a major trophy. The team did manage to win something in the 1975-76 season, but it was not exactly what the board of directors or indeed the fans might have been looking for.

The trophy in question was the Anglo-Scottish Cup. 'Boro won the competition as a result of the dubious distinction of beating Second Division Fulham by 1-0 in the two-legged final. The only goal was an own-goal, scored by the unfortunate Fulham defender Les Strong in the first leg at Ayresome Park.

Unfortunately the Anglo-Scottish Cup was completed before Christmas in the 1975-76 season, shortly before the Centenary Year was due to start officially. There was still genuine hope of a major trophy coming to Teesside over the next 12 months because 'Boro made a big impact in the Football League Cup.

They beat Bury, Derby County, Peterborough and Burnley, all at the first attempt, to qualify for a two-legged semi-final against fellow First Division side Manchester City. There was reason to believe that this would be 'Boro's big breakthrough at long last.

'Boro entertained City in the first leg at Ayresome Park and won 1-0 thanks to a goal from John Hickton. But they were crushed 4-0 in the second leg at Maine Road and thus another dream was crushed. 'Boro's First Division form was not too good afterwards and they had to settle for 13th place in the First Division.

However, 1976 was still a milestone year for the club because they finally paid off the balance of their World Cup loan when sending off a cheque for £236.38 as the final settlement. The loan had taken 'Boro fully ten years to repay. At the same time 'Boro were justified to take the World Cup when it was offered to them, because it's hard to imagine what would have happened to Ayresome Park if 'Boro had not been given the World Cup catalyst to carry out the improvements.

Now that the 'Boro had re-established themselves as a First Division force, the club's directors were regularly visiting the country's top stadia again. They could see at first hand all the modern new facilities which the big clubs were introducing.

Executive boxes had become the latest rage and the 'Boro wanted to install boxes of their own. The first thought was that the South Stand was the most suitable place to erect the luxury boxes and a feasibility study was commissioned. The study showed that the boxes would be a winner and the club produced a handsome, illustrated brochure which was sent around local companies.

The plan was to install 22 boxes, including ten immediately and a further 12 later. There would be 16 eight-person boxes with an annual rental of £2,000 and six six-person boxes at £1,750. The boxes were to be erected in between the South Terrace and the main part of the South Stand.

However, it was another plan which did not get off the ground. A further feasibility study showed that it would be impractical to build luxury boxes in that particular area. So the plan was shelved. With it went the plan to knock down the North Stand.

Even so, the directors were right to look at ways to bring in improvements to the stadium. Business was booming and 'Boro were happy to announce a profit of £99,177 in the 12 months which ended 31 May 1976. It was a tidy profit and reflected the way in which the club was being run on careful financial lines.

Not everybody was happy. There was a growing feeling among the fans and many of the players, that the time had come

Testimonial games can be a gamble. But not for 'Boro defender Billy Gates. He attracted a crowd of 31,643 to his match against Leeds United at Ayresome Park immediately after Jack Charlton's team had won promotion to the First Division in 1974. Billy invested the money into sports shops, later sold out, and is reported to be a millionaire.

One of the special memories. Queen's Park Rangers players Ian Gillard and Stan Bowles were snapped by *Gazette* cameraman Brian Robinson having a quiet read of the 'Boro programme while they wait for a corner to come across. Rangers won the match 2-0 in September, 1978.

for the 'Boro to invest money in new players. There was a widely held belief that 'Boro were only two big signings away from a possible championship side. However, Jack Charlton was reluctant to ask for the cash to finance a major swoop in the transfer market. The club was doing well and was a formidable side in the First Division. Yet there was always room for improvement and the fans felt that this would only come about if the 'Boro bought and bought big. The most pressing need was for a top quality striker, because the goals had been drying up.

The players were ambitious, but they felt that their ambitions were not being matched by the club. The first signs of frustration in the dressing-room came in the summer of 1976 when Graeme Souness requested a transfer. The request was turned down. Souness was now a Scottish international and wanted to start winning honours within the domestic game. But there were no indications that his ambitions would be realised at Ayresome Park.

In February 1977, 'Boro discussed the possibility of removing the first nine or ten rows of seats from the front of the East End and convert the area to standing positions for family viewing. The directors were also looking at plans to install executive boxes again, but this time in the North Stand.

The following month 'Boro announced that 1,210 seats were being taken out of the front portion of the East End. Some 599 of the seats were to be refitted under cover at the rear of the north-east corner. This would create space for 2,000 standing at the front of the East End. 'Boro also looked into the possibility of installing a tunnel for families to enter this section for the stadium.

Another innovation was the provision of a sprinkler system on the pitch, which was laid into the turf by Pipecraft Limited during June.

At the end of the season, in an interview with Cliff Mitchell in the *Evening Gazette*, Charles Amer revealed that £270,000 had been spent on improvements and safety work at Ayresome Park over the previous four years.

Amer also announced in the *Gazette* that the club was still hoping to push through its plans to erect luxury boxes in the North Stand. Nineteen boxes could be built in the stand, accommodating an average of ten people per box. The plan was to install fridges and telephones in every box and link them all to a restaurant.

The chairman commented on the work which had already been completed. Tin sheets and rotten wooden fencing had been replaced by brickwork and all the main gates had been renewed with steel stanchions surrounded by brickwork replacing wooden pillars. Extra gates had been installed as well and every toilet had been rebuilt.

Shaw's Club was now no more. It had been knocked down and replaced by a modern new building incorporating a shop and the development offices.

The changing times were encapsulated by the resignation of manager Jack Charlton in the summer of 1977. It was not unexpected, for Charlton had always maintained that he did not intend to stay at Ayresome Park for more than four years.

Meet the other top team. 'Boro's directors entertained a dozen of their 14 scouts at Yarm's Tall Trees Hotel in the late 1970s. The scouts, back row (left to right) are Ray Grant (Middlesbrough), Jack Pinder (York and West Riding), David Lloyd (Newcastle), Cyril Siviter (Barnsley), Billy Brown (Northumberland), Jack Watson (North-West Durham), George Wardle (Durham), Alan Keen (London), Bobby McAuley (Northern Ireland), Don Cowan (Newton Aycliffe), Denis Sheriffs (Aberdeen), Neville Chapman (Cleveland). Front row: Harold Shepherdson, Keith Varley, John Neal, Charles Amer, Mike McCullagh, Ernest Varley, Kevin Amer.

However, it was still a disappointment for many fans, because Jack had achieved so much in establishing the club as a major force in the First Division again.

On the other hand, 'Boro's playing fortunes had more or less stood still over the past two seasons. The base had been built, but there was a great need to continue to move forward.

So it was an important time for 'Boro and it was clear that the directors needed to find the right man who could develop Charlton's platform. They plumped for John Neal, a soft spoken North-Easterner who had developed a much-admired footballing side at Third Division Wrexham. The Welshmen had missed out on promotion to the Second Division by only one point.

Neal was not content simply to carry on things in the Charlton way. He quickly decided to change it around and signings like Welsh international John Mahoney and striker Billy Ashcroft, from Neal's former club, were the beginning of a new look first-team squad. Micky Burns, Northern Ireland international winger Terry Cochrane and the Yugoslav Bosco Jankovic followed in Neal's second season at the helm.

Certainly Neal had arrived at a financially healthy club. Shortly after Charlton's departure, 'Boro announced club record profits of £142,196. It was the third big profit in a row, though 'Boro now had a bank overdraft of £190,083, largely as a result of safety work which was continually going on at Ayresome Park. It left 'Boro with current net liabilities of £316,002, which was not a problem considering the club's huge financial turnover.

While Neal was bringing in new senior players, he was also keen to encourage the kids to come through. Home-grown lads like Mark Proctor and David Hodgson forced their way into the side, along with Craig Johnston, the Australian lad who had paid his own fare to England to make the grade in this country.

It was a big transition stage, because the stars of Charlton's side gradually began to filter away. Graeme Souness was the first to go when he completed a £320,000 move to League champions Liverpool in January 1978.

He was eventually followed by Stuart Boam, who moved to Newcastle, David Mills, who went to West Bromwich Albion for a British record £500,000 and then Johnston's £450,000 move to Liverpool, which was the forerunner to Neal's departure from Ayresome Park.

However, despite these changes, Neal kept the club shipshape and never really received the credit he deserved, bearing in mind later events. In his time in control, 'Boro never finished below 14th place in the First Division and fully maintained their status.

In the summer, of 1979, Neal invested a club record £475,000 in Newcastle defender Irving Nattrass. 'Boro were still operating as a big club.

The changes on the field continued to come hand in hand with a determination to make improvements off it. In 1979, 'Boro announced major new plans to build a sports centre on the old Shaw's Club land behind the club shop and development offices.

It was a grandiose £1 million-plus plan designed to dramatically improve the club's training facilities and at the same time cement a bond with the local community. 'Boro stressed that they were willing to make the sports centre facilities available for public use in evenings. The plans received planning approval from Middlesbrough Council and work started almost immediately.

The sports centre had replaced the earlier plans of 1975, when most of the facilities envisaged were to be incorporated in a rebuilt North Stand. At the time that the plans were announced

Coming on nicely. The new sports centre at Ayresome Park was quickly taking shape in 1979. If the directors had known the problems the building would cause, they would have suspended work immediately.

for the sports centre there were no dissenting voices, certainly not through the pages of the *Evening Gazette*.

At that time, nobody could have imagined that the sports centre would quickly begin to tie a noose around the club's neck and would not be officially opened for ten years, during which time the club was to go into liquidation. In fact the sports centre was named as the chief cause of 'Boro's liquidation in 1986.

When the plans were first announced, however, 'Boro were in a relatively healthy state of affairs, financially. They could have comfortably absorbed all the costs of the sports centre if the team had continued to be successful on the football field.

Work was already under way on the sports hall when 'Boro announced that they were throwing in the towel yet again on plans to install private boxes in the North Stand. They conceded that a series of problems were insurmountable and this time the plans were postponed indefinitely. Unless the North Stand was totally rebuilt, it was not possible for Ayresome Park to incorporate luxury boxes.

'Boro did fork out on improvement work that summer underneath the North Stand, when £35,000 was spent to upgrade the dressing-rooms.

The following season was Neal's best, for 'Boro finished a very healthy ninth in the First Division. However, the whole season was overshadowed by the double tragedy which hit Ayresome Park on the Saturday afternoon of 12 January 1980.

The tragedy occurred immediately following a home draw against Manchester United, which was watched by 30,587 fans, which turned out to be the biggest crowd of the season at Ayresome Park.

Thousands of fans thronged the streets outside the stadium as they made their way home after the final whistle. But two of those fans, Mr Norman Roxby, 51 and his 52-year-old wife Irene, from Beechwood Road in Eaglescliffe, tragically died

A poignant moment as the 'Boro squad act as coffin bearers at the funeral of Mr and Mrs Roxby, who were killed when a wall collapsed on them outside Ayresome Park. Pictured, left to right, are Jim Platt, David Armstrong, John Craggs and manager John Neal.

when a brick pillar and the two gates it was supporting collapsed under pressure outside the south-east corner of Ayresome Park.

The gates were normally locked and used only as a service entrance during the week. They caved in under the pressure built up as the Manchester United fans tried to get out of the ground. The United fans were being held back until the streets had cleared of 'Boro fans.

In addition to the two deaths, J.Mills from Levick Crescent and A.Allison from Marton Grove Road, both from Middlesbrough, were injured.

Mr and Mrs Roxby were season ticket holders who had been standing outside the gates while they were waiting to be picked up by their 33-year-old son Colin. Ironically 'Boro did not possess a safety certificate at the time for that part of the ground, though Cleveland County Council stressed that they

Goodbye old friend. The famous Longines clock, which seemed to have stopped permanently at ten minutes to five forever, is finally removed from the roof of the North Stand in 1980.

had been in the process of issuing the certificate. An inquest was not held until the following year, though no blame was apportioned to the club. The verdict was 'misadventure'.

The funeral, which took place on 17 January at All Saints' Church in Eaglescliffe, was attended by directors, players and staff from the football club, in addition to supporters club representatives.

In March 1980, 'Boro announced that the sports hall brickwork was completed. The club added that they hoped to complete the internal work by September. The sports hall was 180ft long and 62ft wide and plans for the interior included a gymnasium, medical room, sauna, solarium, squash courts and a spectator viewing area.

However, the club quickly ran into problems gaining planning permission for the installation of squash courts and afterwards the project seemed to totter from one major problem to another.

'Boro attracted more unwanted publicity in September 1980, when supporter Craig French from Billingham was attacked and suffered a fatal stab wound. The incident took place at the corner of Costa Street and Crescent Road. Craig died in hospital that night.

The stabbing took place on 6 September, when 'Boro played a goalless draw against Nottingham Forest. Craig was reportedly attacked by a crowd of people, one of whom administered the fatal knife wound.

The stabbing was part of a national wave of violence from which football was suffering at the time. 'Boro could in no way be criticised for the incident, which took place a reasonable

'Boro fans Brian Threadgill from Percy Street and Pat Foy from Keith Road were so confident that the team would win their FA Cup sixth-round replay at Orient in 1978 that they postponed their wedding because it clashed with the date of the Final at Wembley. The 18-year-olds decided to get married a week later. However, it was all a waste of time, because 'Boro lost the Cup replay 2-1.

At the same time Middlesbrough-based pop group D Plus 3 announced that they had made a demo tape entitled 'Middlesbrough FC' which would be made into a record if 'Boro beat Orient. More wasted effort!

A battle for possession between Crystal Palace goalkeeper John Burridge and Craig Johnston, 'Boro's England Under-21 international. The transfer of Johnston in 1981 was significant in the history of the club in that it precipitated the club's gradual slide towards liquidation.

distance from the confines of the ground. However, it was another unwanted occurrence in a year when things were starting to turn sour for the club.

In March 1981, 'Boro kept up with the times by having a new electric clock erected on the Main Stand – nearly five years after the old one had ceased to function. The new clock was sponsored by Scottish and Newcastle Breweries.

It replaced the Longines model, which was originally put up for the World Cup in 1966. The old clock had stopped at 4.50pm in June 1976, only weeks after the ten year guarantee ran out.

The new clock was activated 15 minutes before the start of 'Boro's FA Cup sixth-round tie at home to Wolves. It was a bright start to the proceedings, but the clock was the last thing on the supporters' mind by the end of the afternoon.

'Boro went into the game against their struggling opponents as strong favourites to reach the semi-final for the first time in their history. No less than 36,382 fans crowded into Ayresome Park to witness the event. But 'Boro never looked like repeating their form from earlier in the season, when they had beaten Wolves by 2-0 at Ayresome in a First Division game.

Wolves forced a 1-1 draw in the sixth-round clash and then won the replay by 3-1 at Molineux. The defeat had a crushing effect on the 'Boro players' morale. In fact several of them failed to recover from the defeat and the club started a downward spiral. That disastrous night at Wolverhampton proved to be turning point in the history of Middlesbrough Football Club.

Manager John Neal parted company with the club soon afterwards and youth team coach Bobby Murdoch, who was the fans choice, was elevated to the hot seat. It was a huge step up for the former Scottish international and he was unable to deliver the goods.

The turmoil within the club had started to boil over after the Wolves defeat, when Craig Johnston was sold to Liverpool. Mark Proctor moved on soon afterwards to Nottingham Forest for £440,000 and David Armstrong went to Southampton for £600,000. 'Boro also lost striker Bosco Jankovic, who moved on to France.

Of these, only Johnston's transfer fee was included in the annual report for the 12 months ending in the summer of 1981. Johnston's move ensured that 'Boro made a profit of £370,000 on the period, which also brought in another £805,000 from the transfers of Jim Stewart to Rangers and Alan Ramage to Derby and Peter Johnson to Newcastle United.

There was a further £1 million to come in the next year's accounts from the sale of Proctor and Armstrong, though this was spent in bringing Heine Otto, Mick Baxter, Joe Bolton and Bobby Thomson to Ayresome Park.

'Boro had done very well as far as the bank manager was concerned and the overdraft was reduced from £714,861 to £265,592. But it only served to paper over the cracks. Things were not well within the club and this was reflected by the events of the following season, when 'Boro hurtled towards relegation.

The huge surge of cash into the club's coffers had been frittered away on players of inferior quality and Murdoch was powerless to halt the slide. Attendances crashed to an average of only 13,000, which was well below budget. It was a nightmare season both on and off the field.

Chairman Charlie Amer came in for a lot of criticism from the supporters and resigned midway through the season. He stayed on as a director, but handed the chairmanship to George Kitching.

In a statement to Paul Daniel in the *Evening Gazette*, Amer said: "Because I do not wish to be the cause of any person being injured in a demonstration I have decided to resign as chairman.

"This has not been caused by the chanting, but by physical attacks at the end of last season and threatened physical attacks during the course of the last ten days on myself and, the attack on one of my grandchildren who was knocked to the ground by

A view of the rear of the East End of Ayresome Park, taken in 1981.

a boy three times his size and then kicked on the head has caused me to take this action."

Relegation came hand in hand with a record £300,000 loss and the club's overdraft at the end of the financial year had zoomed up again to £850,000. So, despite the prospect of having to watch Second Division football, 'Boro's fans were asked to dig deeper into their pockets for the privilege.

Secretary Harry Green, in announcing the increases, said: "Continuing rising costs and the fact that for many years we have not increased our prices in proportion to inflation have forced this decision upon the club."

Centre stand seats were increased by 50p to £3.50, wing stands by 50p to £3 and East End seats by 30p to £2.50. The Holgate End admission also increased by 30p to £1.80 and the South Terrace by the same amount to £2. Season ticket prices were increased roughly by £5, with the Centre Stand costing £60 and the wings £47.

All the time, the sports centre was becoming an increasingly painful thorn in the club's side. 'Boro had already received £325,000 in grants towards completing the complex, but had to find the rest of the estimated cost of £1.2 million themselves.

By the summer of 1982, the sports centre was still not open to the public, even though it had been in use for club purposes for 18 months. The problem was that every time the club tried to make progress in certain areas they met problems, part of which was due to the fact that certain work had not been done correctly in the first place.

For example, there was a massive problem with the central heating system, which added a lot of expense to the projected cost because it created much extra labour, in addition to the parts.

Members of the board were split about the viability of the complex. Some were not convinced that the sports centre could ever run at a profit if it was opened to the public. They did not want to take the risk of putting an extra burden on the club's finances.

Mike McCullagh, 'Boro's financial director, revealed the unease in the boardroom when he said in the *Evening Gazette* that the investment in a modern leisure centre, instead of players, appeared with hindsight to have been misjudged.

He inferred that the centre would not be opened to the public in the near future because similar council owned leisure centres were losing money at a fast rate.

McCullagh also announced that 'Boro were in the process of drawing up a survival plan for the future. It was the first official indication from the club that things were in a bad way. It had all come about very quickly and needed drastic action.

And when things aren't going well, you don't seem to have many friends. That's how 'Boro found it when they applied to build 100 homes on the Hutton Road training ground.

The application was thrown out by 11 votes to eight at a meeting of Middlesbrough Borough Council's development services committee, despite a recommendation from the chief planning officer and architect Tony Noble that the plan should be approved subject to a list of conditions. These conditions included the number of houses being reduced to around 75.

While the application was rejected, Councillor David Ross also launched a public attack on the club for its 'cheek' and 'gall' for 'making a few quick bucks to try to keep them solvent'. It was a very strong attack, which in the cold light of day seems a little unfair, but it was an indication that the council did not regard the football club as one of the town's major assets.

Not until 'Boro went into liquidation in 1986 did the council come in with a genuine offer of support.

No doubt Councillor Ross was representing the views of the 70 residents who lodged letters of objection over the club's plans, which threatened to take away the stretch of open land near their homes.

It still represented a huge blow to the football club. They had been a major force in the 1970s, when they generated a strong band of regular supporters and had a squad of top quality players. They had a huge turnover and a high expenditure, particularly on wages.

When it all fell apart in a matter of 12 months, the directors were faced with mammoth problems because it was impossible to trim the expenditure at one stroke to match the dramatic loss of income.

They had been accused of lack of ambition by selling their big name players, but most of the players were determined to leave in any case. Most of the transfer cash was made available to buy replacement players, but 'Boro bought badly and the slide was both sudden and seemingly irreversible.

'Boro might have had a chance if the directors had been able to raise more cash for yet more signings, but there was nothing left in the kitty for transfer signings and valuable money had to be directed towards the sports centre.

In two seasons, 'Boro's average attendance dropped from more than 16,000 to 10,018 and the club just couldn't cope. The attempts to sell Hutton Road for housing represented one of the last throws of the dice, yet the community at large did not seem prepared to help, nor apparently did it care.

The slide gathered momentum after relegation from the First Division. 'Boro made a dreadful start to their Second Division programme by failing to win any of their first nine games. It was inevitable that Bobby Murdoch would be relieved of his duties. Murdoch deeply loved the club and was desperate for success. But he had not bought well and could not stop the slide.

Murdoch was a fledgling manager, so 'Boro decided to go for experience in his place and the job was offered to 55-year-old Malcolm Allison, one of the biggest names in football. Allison, a cockney with a penchant for high living, had tasted success at top level by winning the League championship with Manchester City in 1968.

He joined 'Boro shortly after returning to this country from Portugal, where he had won the League and Cup double with Sporting Lisbon before being controversially sacked.

Allison quickly discovered that he had not only taken on one of the hardest tasks of his career, but one of the hardest tasks in the Football League. The big name players of 'Boro's immediate past had now all moved on and the fans had left with them.

'Boro were in deep financial trouble and reported to be losing £12,000 a week. So there was to be very little cash available for new faces in the squad. Allison's expertise was needed as badly in the boardroom as it was in the dressing-room.

The same month that Allison took over the reins, there was a change at the helm of the boardroom as well. Mike McCullagh took over as chairman from George Kitching, who had suffered a traumatic eight months in charge. McCullagh had already started to get heavily involved in the running of the club and was largely responsible for bringing Allison to Teesside.

McCullagh told the *Gazette*: "The club, without doubt, is at the crossroads. It is in a very severe financial state, nevertheless it is a big club with big assets and provided modern business management is applied at the moment, there is no reason to worry about the future of the club.

"But it is a very big challenge at the most difficult time in the club's history. Many difficult decisions will have to be faced almost immediately. I want to see a great deal of change."

McCullagh's optimistic statement about the future of the club proved to be wrong, though at the time it was unthinkable that the aging dinosaur could possibly cease to exist one day.

The new chairman was still in no doubts about the severity of the situation. The first task was cost cutting. In the November 15 employees were sacked in order to trim the heavy wages bill. These included coach Micky Burns.

In 1984, former teacher Florence Bosomworth, a 74-year-old spinster from Adcott Road in Acklam, handed over her £3,000 life savings to 'Boro on the condition that the cash was spent 'solely for the players'. Her former pupils at Archibald Junior School included 'Boro duo Garry Macdonald and Mick Angus.

In McCullagh's first six weeks in charge, the club's weekly loss was cut by £2,000 to £10,000, made through redundancies and further stringent economies. It was a step in the right direction, but it was still not enough.

The chairman made it clear that the club could not continue to absorb the losses and that more help was needed from the community. However, his comments fell largely on deaf ears. The quality of football had hardly improved under Allison and the fans were not prepared to return until there were distinct signs of improvement.

Toward the end of the year 'Boro attempted to offload one of their biggest headaches by offering the problematic sports centre for sale to Middlesbrough Council. The hope was that the council would take the sports centre as a public facility, carry out the internal remedial work and open the centre to the public.

However, the sports centre didn't present a very attractive proposition to any potential owners in its present state. Many thousands of pounds needed to be spent to install all the necessary facilities and meet safety standards. So the council decided to take no action.

End of an era. Harold Shepherdson is pictured at his retirement in 1983, which marked the end of 51 years' service with the 'Boro. The former England coach is receiving a set of cut glass goblets from 'Boro skipper Irving Nattrass.

Laughing, but not all the way to the bank. 'Boro chairman Mike McCullagh welcomes new manager Malcolm Allison to Ayresome Park. There was little for both men to smile about as they battled against an impossible financial situation.

The one that got away. This miss by 'Boro striker David Currie against Carlisle United is regarded as one of the worst ever seen on the ground. Look at the reaction of the supporters. However Currie had an excellent goalscoring record with 'Boro, and went on to increase his prolific record when he moved away from Ayresome Park.

Early in 1983, shortly after the resignation from the 'Boro board of former chairman Charles Amer and his son Kevin, the club revealed that the sports centre could not be opened in its present state because it did not meet building and fire regulations. It was an honest admittance of some of the many problems concerning the building.

Fire protection work on the main steel framework had not been completed, the fire exit doors adjacent to the squash courts were unsatisfactory and wood panelling in the reception area needed to be treated against fire spread. This time there was a distinct threat that grants which had been made for the erection of the sport centre might be withdrawn by the Sports Council, so 'Boro dug deep and set the work into motion to remedy the faults.

However, the club did not have the cash to complete the squash courts and other planned facilities. So the spectator viewing gallery was scrapped, leaving the sports complex as a mere sports hall with a gymnasium. The project was now reduced to the bare bones and still not officially opened to the public. Eventually the sports centre was opened, but it was a hollow gesture because the lack of facilities ensured that it could not possibly be a success.

The only chance of reviving the club's fortunes rested firmly on the shoulders of the team. However, there were no signs that results were going to get any better. It was just one long battle to stave off relegation and now average attendances had dropped to below 9,000 which was the lowest in living memory.

Gradually a rift began to emerge between the board and Allison. It reached a head when Allison publicly stated that the financial situation was so bad, that liquidation might be the club's best course of action. So, following a home defeat by Fulham, Allison was dismissed on 28 March 1984.

'Boro quickly turned to one of their greatest managers of the past as Allison's replacement. They secured an agreement with Jack Charlton to return in a caretaker capacity.

There was still a battle against relegation to be won and only nine games left in which to achieve it. When Charlton came back, he was astounded by the state in which the club had got itself. He didn't have a lot to work with, but the players responded to the challenge and the club stayed out of the Third Division.

However, Charlton had no intentions of taking his second coming a long way and he departed at the end of the season. Big Jack handed over the reins to his assistant, Willie Maddren, who was the choice of Charlton himself, the board and the fans. Maddren was one of 'Boro's great players of the past and a crowd favourite.

Maddren had some idea what to expect at Ayresome Park. He had already learned how to operate on a shoe-string as a result of his coaching spell at Hartlepool, where he helped the club's junior side win the Northern Intermediate League.

However, nothing could have prepared the 33-year-old new manager for the situation he inherited on his return to Ayresome Park. If he had thought that the job was going to difficult, he soon discovered that it was nigh on impossible.

At the end of the financial year in the summer of 1984, 'Boro reported a huge loss of £300,00 which increased their overall debt to £1.2 million. The situation was becoming dire. Without success on the pitch, 'Boro had little chance of turning it around.

In the previous 12 months 'Boro had lost only £16,987, but that was because the annual accounts included the £400,000 from the sale of striker David Hodgson to Liverpool.

This season there was no pot of gold. 'Boro's only outgoing transfer in the financial year was the departure of Ray Hankin to Peterborough United for only £7,000. Cuts of £100,000 had been made in operating and administrative costs, but they were not enough to offset the huge losses.

At the start of the next financial year, 'Boro boosted their income by selling Mick Kennedy to Portsmouth for £100,000 and also received £50,000 from Chelsea for Darren Wood, with Tony McAndrew returning to 'Boro as part of the deal.

However, the outgoing transfers did not make it any easier for Maddren to obtain results, even if they were crucial to the day-to-day survival of the club. The situation was hopeless. There was no money, few spectators and a poor squad of players, who were just able to keep their heads above water in a tough Division.

In February 1985, only 3,364 fans turned up at Ayresome Park to watch a 1-0 defeat by relegation threatened rivals Notts County. The previous month 'Boro had suffered a humiliating defeat in the FA Cup by neighbours Darlington, who won 2-1 at Feethams following a goalless draw at Ayresome Park.

A change of chairman offered a ray of hope for a while. Mike McCullagh, having worked hard without any success, handed over the reins to Alf Duffield, a self-made businessman who was involved in the oil industry. One of Duffield's first tasks was to make some money available for new signings.

It wasn't a great deal, around £50,000, but Maddren spent it wisely by signing full-back Brian Laws from Huddersfield Town and striker Archie Stephens from Bristol Rovers for £30,000.

The duo added a bit of vital spark and 'Boro won three of their last six games to beat the drop again. Laws scored one of the goals in the 2-0 win at Shrewsbury Town on the last day of the season which guaranteed 'Boro's Second Division survival.

The victory against the Shrews led to defiant comments from club officials that it must be used as a platform for taking the club forward again. Duffield made more cash available for team strengthening in the summer and Maddren made another important swoop when paying £80,000 to Manchester United for goalkeeper Steve Pears. The Brandon-born keeper had previously been on loan at Ayresome Park during Malcolm Allison's time and was a quality player.

In the wake of the tragic fire at Bradford City, stringent safety checks were held at Ayresome Park that summer by Cleveland County Council surveyors. They discovered that many parts of the stadium were in a state of disrepair, particularly the North Stand. The council refused to issue a full safety certificate and as a result the capacity was slashed from 42,000 to 10,658.

In the short term it did not affect 'Boro because they were attracting crowds of less than 6,000. This was mainly because there was no sign of any improvement on the pitch. In fact 'Boro won only two games in the first three months of the new season. Maddren made what turned out to be arguably his most significant signing in October 1985, when paying Scottish Second Division side Albion Rovers £25,000 for striker Bernie Slaven. The 24-year-old had been top scorer in the whole of Scotland the previous season with 31 goals.

Slaven was eventually to play a major part in the club's dramatic revival after liquidation. However, in his first season at Ayresome Park, Slaven needed time to find his feet. He had been plucked out of part-time football and had been working as a park gardener in Glasgow immediately before joining 'Boro.

'Boro staged a mini-recovery towards the end of the year by winning five games out of eight. It looked as though the players were finally starting to gel together. The run included a stirring 2-0 derby win against Sunderland in front of 19,701 fans at Ayresome Park which was three times the average crowd.

How do you like my socks? Brian Laws is embraced by Ayresome Park's one and only streaker in its 92-year history. It happened on a very cold New Year's Day in 1986, when 'Boro lost 1-0 to Huddersfield.

Naturally, in order to stage the derby, 'Boro had been forced to carry out the list of remedial work which had been set down by Cleveland County Council. Otherwise they would have been limited to a crowd of less than 11,000.

Engineers who inspected Ayresome Park had discovered faults with all four sides of the ground and with the floodlight pylons. The engineers reported corroded gable columns and unsafe walls in the North Stand, undermined floodlight pylons in the north-west and south-west corners, corroded columns in the South Stand, unacceptable concrete supports in the Holgate End and problems with the East End roof.

It was a nightmare list, but 'Boro had no choice but to spend cash to have the work done. In the end it turned out to be a race against time because the council threatened to close the sections of the stadium where any of the pressing work was not carried out.

Fortunately 'Boro made it on time, completing the alterations just before Christmas. It was a relief because the cash generated by the derby against Sunderland was absolutely vital to help pay the bills.

However, any hopes of a revival on the pitch soon disappeared. 'Boro were unable to build on their good run at the end of the year and failed to win a single match in January. Enough was enough for Alf Duffield when 'Boro lost 3-1 at home to Charlton Athletic on 1 February and Maddren was relieved of his duties. It had been an onerous 18 months in

Crisis time. 'Boro chairman Alf Duffield addresses a shareholders' meeting less than three months before liquidation. Left to right are Jack Hatfield, David Thorne (secretary), Duffield, Dick Corden and Steve Gibson, who was later influential in the club's successful battle for survival.

The social club at Ayresome Park, pictured around the time of the football club's liquidation.

charge for Maddren, who was always working with one hand tied behind his back.

Maddren recalled: "I knew that we desperately needed new players, but I was always conscious of the threat of liquidation. Perhaps I should have asked for more money, but I did not want to do anything which might have taken the club out of existence.

"When I first came back to the club, I had only 12 players but I accepted the situation and tried to make the best of it. I compromised, but I compromised too much.

"I worked all the hours possible and so, too, did David Mills. We did the coaching through the day and went off looking at players on a night. For much of the time there was only the two of us. It was very, very hard.

"If we were to turn the corner, we needed that little bit of luck to go our way. But luck was the one thing I didn't get. I can remember a home game against Stoke City when Steve Pears went to save a routine 30-yarder, but it slipped through this hands and ended up in the net.

"Nine times out of ten he would have saved it. I knew then that I was not going to be lucky enough."

Bruce Rioch, the former Scottish international captain, who had arrived at Ayresome Park as new first-team coach in the January, was made caretaker manager when Maddren departed. Rioch had previously managed Torquay United and had worked in the United States.

Bad weather forced Rioch to wait more than a month before taking charge of his first game for 'Boro, though the delay was useful because it gave him the chance to develop a new team pattern and get his ideas across to the players.

'Boro responded well following the enforced rest by recording a resounding 3-1 victory against Grimsby Town at Ayresome Park, with Bernie Slaven grabbing two of the goals.

The team continued to show great promise, even if points were still hard to come by. In fact Rioch was awarded the manager's job on a permanent basis after a 2-1 home defeat by Sheffield United. Despite the scoreline, 'Boro had pounded United and on another night might easily have won 6-2.

Unfortunately time was not on Rioch's side and neither was it on the side of the club. Away wins at Huddersfield and Blackburn and a 1-0 home win against Portsmouth courtesy of a goal from defender Tony Mowbray, kept 'Boro's slim survival hopes alive.

In the end, they found themselves in the repeat situation of having to go back to Shrewsbury for their final League game of the season, once again needing to win to stay in the Second Division.

This time there was to be no escape act. It was a sad afternoon, especially as the match was marred by persistent crowd trouble which must have made it difficult for both sets of players to concentrate on their football.

'Boro went down to a 2-1 defeat, their goal coming from Archie Stephens. The day was a double disaster for 'Boro's 20-year-old central defender Gary Pallister, who was sent off.

The defeat signalled the end of Second Division football at Ayresome Park. It was also the end of Middlesbrough Football and Athletic Club (1892) Ltd.

Record Attendances

NOTHING sets the adrenalin running more freely before a big kick-off than the prospect of a football stadium thronged to full capacity, full of anticipation, noise and atmosphere.

The sight of Ayresome Park absolutely packed to the rafters was enough to send a shiver of excitement down the backbone of the most hardened supporters. The sense of belonging made it a very special occasion for those lucky enough to be inside before the gates were closed.

Unfortunately new generations of 'Boro fans will not have the opportunity to experience the thrill of being tightly packed together on the terraces, carried along by the relentless swaying of the crowd and sometimes spending several minutes without your feet touching the ground in a frenzied sea of excitement.

These scenes were repeated over and over again for the big games – the derbies, FA Cup-ties, promotion matches and even the First Division title battles.

However, gradually decreasing capacities at football stadiums all over the country have led to a situation where the huge crowds and heaving masses will never be repeated.

In fact it is 30 years since Ayresome Park was bursting at the seams for a First Division match. On that occasion, on 22 February 1975 a packed crowd of 39,500 watched Leeds United beat Jack Charlton's 'Boro side by 1-0.

That particular season was 'Boro's first back in the top flight after an absence of 20 years. The average attendance of 28,605 was the highest at Ayresome Park for 24 years and 'Boro never ever went close to matching it again.

Even so, there were many more big games at the stadium throughout the 1970s and early 1980s, but crowds and capacity figures were falling all the time and 'Boro never again promised to pack in a near-40,000 gate.

'Boro's Rumbelows Cup semi-final first leg at home to Manchester United on 4 March 1992, was as big a game as the stadium could ever hope to stage. Yet it attracted only 25,572 fans, mainly because of crowd limits. Young fans who enjoyed the electric atmosphere of the Rumbelows semi-final can hardly start to appreciate what it must have been like when more than twice as many supporters were roaring on the 'Boro.

However, 50,000 crowds occurred on only a few occasions, even though 40,000-plus was commonplace. Ayresome Park didn't realise its first 50,000 attendance until just before World War Two and it was for only a few years after the end of the hostilities that the stadium was able to repeat the feat.

In terms of support, the years from the late 1930s to the early 1950s was very much Ayresome's halcyon period. What a pity that the war intervened in the middle.

Ayresome Park attracted its first big crowd to the opening game in 1903, when up to 30,000 fans packed the new stadium for the First Division derby battle against Sunderland, which the Rokermen won 3-2. Estimates of the crowd vary, ranging from 25,000 upwards, though 30,000 has been accepted as nearer the mark.

The attendance against Sunderland was bettered the same season, when 34,000 watched the FA Cup quarter-final replay against Manchester City, which was played on a Wednesday afternoon. 'Boro lost that game as well.

This record survived for more than 16 years until over 35,000 fans watched a First Division derby against Sunderland in 1920.

By the end of the 1920s, 'Boro's record crowd had zoomed to 43,754. By the end of the 1930s it was more than 51,000.

Ayresome attracted more than 53,000 fans for the first time in the momentous FA Cup sixth-round clash with Burnley in 1947. Many thousands more were locked outside. Two years later, 500 or so more fans squeezed into the stadium for the all-time record of 53,802 for the Christmas holiday derby against Newcastle United. 'Boro won it 1-0 thanks to a Peter McKennan goal.

The following season, 'Boro attracted another massive crowd when 52,764 fans watched a 1-1 draw with Sunderland on 14 October, 1950. 'Boro had beaten Huddersfield Town 8-0 at Ayresome at the end of September and then went to Molineux and beat the mighty Wolves 4-3. The Sunderland derby came next, hence the big crowd, but Ayresome never again witnessed support of such magnitude.

By the time that 'Boro had a good enough team to attract the fans back in big numbers, Ayresome was no longer capable of holding 50,000 crowds. The installation of seats in the East End for the 1966 World Cup put paid to all that. In fact the capacity of the old Linthorpe Road End had been more than halved.

However there were still many big games after the World Cup. Many modern day supporters can recall the remarkable night of 16 May 1967, when a John O'Rourke hat-trick helped 'Boro to beat Oxford United 4-1 and guarantee promotion back to the Second Division. A terrific crowd of 39,683 watched the game and it is still fondly remembered by everybody who was fortunate to be there.

The stadium has been packed to capacity on several occasions since, but that record attendance against Newcastle was impossible to beat – unless the Ayresome Park stands had been extended to three tiers.

One of the great things about Teesside is that football is a way of life and the potential support to pack the stadium has never gone away. These are the stories behind the games which packed them into Ayresome Park in the past, from the initial record attendance of 1903 to the wonderful Christmas 46 years later.

Saturday, 12 September 1903
Middlesbrough 2 Sunderland 3
Attendance: 30,000

THE people of Middlesbrough had a great sense of civic pride at the turn of the century. The town was growing rapidly, with major construction work taking place virtually everywhere and generating prosperity for a good part of the community.

The official opening of any new building was enough to attract huge crowds, but the opening of a magnificent football stadium was extra special. 'Boro had already created a whole new generation of football fans by establishing themselves in the hallowed First Division of the Football League the previous season. There was great hope that the team could challenge for championship honours with the benefit of the modern new stadium at Ayresome.

So the first League game at the new Ayresome Park was both a civic and footballing occasion rolled into one. A day of speeches and celebrations was arranged and the great crowd swarmed

Joe Cassidy, scorer of the first ever League goal at Ayresome Park, in the 3-2 home defeat by Sunderland. Cassidy, who was captain, was inside-left and so, had shirts been numbered in those days he would have worn the number-ten shirt – the same number worn by John Hendrie when he scored the very last goal at Ayresome Park.

Andy Davidson, 'Boro's left-half in the first game against Sunderland.

Abraham Jones, 'Boro's centre-half in the first game against Sunderland.

David Smith, 'Boro's right-half in the first game against Sunderland.

John Hogg, 'Boro's right-back in the first game against Sunderland.

Andy Ramsay, 'Boro's left-back in the first game against Sunderland.

into the stadium very early to soak up the atmosphere.

'Boro took the field to a terrific clamour and were roared on throughout a hectic first half. They finally broke through to take the lead six minutes before the interval through skipper Joe Cassidy.

Sunderland, who were by far the more experienced of the two teams, gradually settled in the second half. And when Gemmell equalised the large contingent of travelling Wearside supporters made their vocal chords heard for the first time.

However, 'Boro regained the lead within a minute. Cassidy received the ball from the kick off and played it through for Sandy Brown to score. Unfortunately 'Boro could not maintain the momentum. Hogg equalised in the 70th minute and Robinson netted Sunderland's winner two minutes from time.

At the end of the game, the sense of occasion overshone the disappointment of a derby defeat. Both teams were warmly applauded off the pitch and the celebrations at the stadium carried on long into the night.

Middlesbrough: Williamson; Hogg, Blackett, Smith, Jones, Davidson, E.Gettins, White, Brown, Cassidy, Atherton.

Sunderland: Doig; Watson, McCombie, Jackson, McAllister, Farquhar, Bridgett, Gemmell, Hogg, Robinson, Craggs.

Wednesday, 9 March 1904
FA Cup third-round replay
Middlesbrough 1
Manchester City 3
Attendance: 34,000

FA CUP fever on Teesside was no less evident in the early 1900s than it is now. Everybody wanted to see 'Boro make their mark in the English Cup, as it was known at the time.

So when 'Boro cruised through to the quarter-finals, thanks to away wins at both Millwall and Preston North End, Cup fever was running very high.

'Boro were once again drawn away from home in the last eight. However they maintained their clean sheet in the competition so far by forcing a goalless draw against Manchester City at Hyde Road. 'Boro travelled home by train and an ecstatic crowd of 2,000 fans were waiting at Middlesbrough railway station to welcome the team back.

The mouth-watering prospect of the Wednesday afternoon replay had the whole town buzzing. Manchester City were challenging for the championship, but 'Boro had beaten them 6-0 at Ayresome Park earlier in the season. Everybody wanted to be there to witness a repeat win. In a move to avoid mass truancy, schools in Middlesbrough gave their pupils the afternoon off. Many works also closed their gates at lunchtime.

Unfortunately the Cup-tie turned out to be a huge let down for the massive crowd, which had Ayresome Park bursting at the seams. Influential wing-half Sam Aitken was forced to miss the match to attend his brother's funeral in Scotland and 'Boro never got going. Sandy Brown scored for 'Boro, but City were the better side on the day and the packed crowd witnessed the first of the many FA Cup frustrations they were to suffer over the years.

Middlesbrough: Williamson; Hogg, Blackett, Page, Jones, Davidson, Gettins, Atherton, Brown, Cassidy, Carrick.

Manchester City: Edmundson; McMahon, Burgess, Frost, Hynds, Holmes, Meredith, Booth, Livingstone, Gillespie, Turnbull.

Saturday, 6 November 1920
Middlesbrough 2
Sunderland 0
Attendance: 35,703

'BORO made a disappointing start to the 1920-21 season, but suddenly struck a rich vein of form in October which pulled them into the middle of the First Division table. They beat Arsenal, Bradford City and Bolton Wanderers at Ayresome Park and won 1-0 at Bradford.

A heavy 6-2 defeat at Bolton prior to the big derby at home to Sunderland failed to deter the 'Boro faithful, who packed into the Ayresome ground in anticipation of another home win. The Rokermen had been struggling of late, with only five points coming from their last six games and 'Boro started strong favourites.

It was quickly apparent from the terrific amount of noise from the terraces before the kick-off, that this was no average crowd. In the event, it was no surprise to discover that a new ground record had been set.

'Boro were given plenty of backing from the terraces and attacked Sunderland from the start to create several good chances. However the ball would not go into the net. Winger Tommy Urwin hit a post and then had another effort superbly saved by Sunderland goalkeeper Scott, while 'Boro wing-half Stewart Davidson missed a good chance when heading over the bar.

As a result the first half was goalless and 'Boro were fortunate not to fall behind just after the restart when Charlie Buchan missed a great chance to score for the Wearsiders.

As the second half progressed, a goalless draw looked the most likely result. However 'Boro's England international centre-forward George Elliott had other ideas. Twelve minutes from time Elliott finally broke the deadlock when heading in a corner from Urwin.

It was all over for Sunderland with 90 seconds remaining when Elliott scored his second goal when converting a centre from Jacky Mordue. At last a record 'Boro crowd had witnessed a home win.

Elliott, writing in the *Daily Mail*, said: "It was the fastest game of the season and the fastest game I have engaged in for some years. No roughness crept into the contest, which was rather contrary to my experience of local derbies.

"I think our victory was mainly due to our intermediate line being such a real live wire both in attack and defence. Then again the centres from both Mordue and Urwin were the acme of perfection."

Middlesbrough: Williamson; Marshall, Holmes, Davidson, W.Carr, Ellerington, Mordue, J.Carr, Elliott, Tinsley, Urwin.

Sunderland: Scott; England, Hobson, Poole, Parker, Mitton, Martin, Coverdale, Travers, Buchan, Best.

Bank on 'em. 'Boro's Jackie Carr (right) and W.Turnbull of Bradford City proudly wear their England shirts after playing against Ireland in Belfast in October, 1919. Both men are from South Bank. Carr played in front of three record attendances at Ayresome Park.

Tommy Urwin was described as the 'acme of perfection' following his performance for 'Boro in front of a record crowd of 35,703 against Sunderland in 1920.

Most 'Boro fanatics know that George Camsell set a new Football League scoring record with 59 goals in season 1926-27 – only for Dixie Dean of Everton to break it 12 months later with 60 goals. However, what isn't generally known is how near the story came to never taking place. In fact Dean might have achieved his goalscoring feat in a Middlesbrough shirt.

In November 1924, 'Boro sent a deputation to watch Dean playing for Tranmere and were very impressed. In fact they continued to monitor his progress. Then, in March 1925, 'Boro asked Tranmere to name their price for Dean. However, 'Boro were not prepared to go up to £2,000, and after several weeks of negotiations the proposed transfer fell down.

Later that year, in September 'Boro decided to negotiate for Camsell's transfer from Durham City. The deal went through on 7 October with Camsell accepting wages of £5 a week. The transfer fee was £810, but only £650 changed hands because 'Boro also cancelled a £160 loan made to Durham City more than three years earlier.

Saturday, 3 February 1923
FA Cup second round
Middlesbrough 1
Sheffield United 1
Attendance: 38,070

THE FA Cup competition took on a new coat in 1923 as Wembley Stadium neared completion. The magnificent project, on the outskirts of London, had grabbed the imagination of football supporters everywhere. So everybody was lifted by the prospect of watching their team play in the inaugural Cup Final at the grand new national stadium.

'Boro's fans had been boosted by the team's 1-0 win at Oldham Athletic in the first round, thanks to a goal from Billy Birrell.

The previous best attendance at Ayresome Park was comfortably beaten as a record crowd paid receipts of £3,060 for the match against Sheffield United. 'Boro had already beaten United 3-2 at Ayresome in a League game, thanks to a hat-trick from George Elliott and so confidence was high.

It was a bright, sunny day, but windy and 'Boro had to face both of the elements in the first half. They did well, therefore, to hold the visitors to 0-0 at the interval.

Scottish international Andy Wilson scored the equaliser from the penalty spot in front of 'Boro's record crowd of 38,070 for the FA Cup-tie against Sheffield United in 1923.

However 'Boro made a bad start to the second half when Fred Tunstall crossed for Tommy Sampy to put United ahead. Worse was to follow, for 'Boro full-back Jack Marshall was hurt trying to prevent the goal and became a limping passenger for the rest of the game.

'Boro kept plugging away and were rewarded when centre-forward Andy Wilson equalised from the penalty-spot. The home side went in search for the winner, but they could not break through United's spirited defence a second time.

Athletic News said: "Middlesbrough were pursued by the same old malignant fate which has made their lack of progress in the national competition a byword – in comparison with the reputation they have made in other walks of life."

The *Daily Mail* reported: "The Sheffield forwards were slightly more dangerous in front of goal but the outstanding exponent was J.Carr, whose great dribbling and magnificent centres should have been made more of by his colleagues."

Unfortunately 'Boro were unable to make use of their second bite at the cherry and lost 3-0 at Bramall Lane.

Middlesbrough: Williamson; Marshall, Fox, Davidson, Webster, Pender, J.Carr, Birrell, Wilson, Murray, Urwin.

Sheffield United: Blackwell; Cook, Milton, Pantling, Waugh, Plant, Mercer, Sampy, Johnson, Gillespie, Tunstall.

Monday, 27 December 1926
Middlesbrough 2
Manchester City 1
Attendance: 43,754

THIS marvellous game was arguably the greatest day in the club's history outside

This great side which won the Second Division championship in 1926-27 played in front of a record crowd of 43,734 against Manchester City on 27 December 1927. Back row: Twine, Mathieson, Smith, Freeman. Middle row: R.Ferguson, McKay, Miller, Birrell, Ashman, McClelland, Cole (trainer). Front row: Pease, Camsell, J.Carr, Williams.

George Camsell, one of the all-time 'Boro greats, who scored a record 59 goals in season 1926-27. Two of them came in front of a record crowd against Manchester City.

of the First Division and the FA Cup. Herbert Bamlett's clever blend of youth and experience had recovered from an uncertain start and were sweeping all before them in the Second Division.

'Boro had won 13 and drawn one of their 16 previous games, having hit seven goals against both Portsmouth and Swansea and six against Fulham, in the last five home games. On Christmas Day, they won 5-3 away to fellow promotion contenders Manchester City, with the irrepressible George Camsell scoring all five goals.

It was only natural, therefore, that 'Boro's officials were expecting a huge crowd for the return holiday fixture. The ground limit at Ayresome Park was set at 42,000 and a new record attendance was almost inevitable. In the event, 1,754 more fans squeezed into the stadium and many more were locked outside.

Pathfinder, writing in the *Evening Gazette*, said: "At 1.30pm, scores of disgruntled regular supporters stood outside the big stand – locked out. Their chagrin was pathetic.

"Inside, the grandstand was chock-full, whilst thousands were streaming into the popular ends."

'Boro skipper Billy Birrell won the toss and elected to attack the Linthorpe Road End with a dazzling sun at 'Boro's backs.

The excitement was intense and midway through the first half the crowd, struggling for air on the packed terraces, surged over the barriers and sat around the touch-line. An estimated eight to ten thousands crowded around the pitch and the police had to deal with some spectators who encroached on to the playing surface. Around 100 fans climbed the supports of the North Stand and were sitting on the roof.

There was a mini-invasion in 32 minutes when 'Boro took a deserved lead, Camsell scoring after City goal-keeper Goodchild had parried a low drive from Billy Pease.

At the start of the second half, referee J.Baker from Crewe made a tour of inspection of the crowd around the pitch before giving his permission for the match to restart.

Within two minutes 'Boro had doubled their lead, Camsell scoring again when he glanced in a header from a Pease cross.

The crowd were going wild and there was still a danger that Mr Baker might call a halt to the proceedings. 'Boro's reserve centre-forward Jimmy McClelland played his part by leaving his seat to help keep the crowd back.

In 71 minutes City reduced the arrears with a spectacular goal from Roberts and suddenly 'Boro were put under intense pressure. It was a nervous final 20 minutes for players and fans alike, but 'Boro held on. At the final whistle the crowd swarmed on to the pitch and carried off Camsell shoulder high.

Pathfinder said: "Memorable scenes were witnessed to the finish. The police had been busy stemming back the good humoured holiday crowd while the match was in progress, but at the conclusion there was a rush on to the field.

"While the happy members of the 'Boro team were struggling through the vast pack of admirers, a section seized Camsell and carried the young centre-forward shoulder high into the pavilion.

"It was an amazing exhibition of enthusiasm and a great spontaneous tribute to the spirit of the men who have so worthily carried the 'Boro colours from success to success in the first half

The rest, as they say, is history. But not quite. Because 'Boro were willing to sell Camsell within 12 months, Burnley wanted to sign him and were told to submit an offer. The board 'decided to part with Camsell if a suitable offer be received'. Fortunately Burnley's offer was not enough. Then Barnsley entered the scene. They were told to make a 'substantial offer'. The best they could come up with was £500. The 'Boro board said it was not enough. Four games into the next season, 'Boro's regular centre-forward Jimmy McClelland was injured. It seemed a blow at the time because McClelland had scored 32 goals in 38 appearances the previous season. 'Boro had to call up Camsell, the 23-year-old reserve centre-forward for the home game against Hull City. This time the rest was history. Camsell scored 59 goals in 37 appearances and 'Boro won the Second Division championship.

of the season." Camsell's brace moved him on to an incredible 33 goals from 17 appearances and well on target to beat Blackburn Rovers' Ted Harper's record of 43 goals in a League season, set the previous term.

'Boro's win took them to top spot because previous leaders Hull City lost 1-0 at home to Chelsea. 'Boro were to stay at the top, losing only two more games in the rest of the season.

Middlesbrough: Mathieson; Smith, Freeman, Miller, Ferguson, Ashman, Pease, Birrell, Camsell, J.Carr, Williams.
Manchester City: Goodchild; Cookson, Bennett, Barrass, Thompson, Benzie, Austin, Cowan, Roberts, Johnson, Hicks.

Saturday, 27 March 1937
Middlesbrough 1 Arsenal 1
Attendance: 44,773

A pageant of youth was held at Ayresome Park in 1937 to celebrate the Coronation of King George VI.

THE possibility of the championship coming to Teesside brought the crowds flooding back to Ayresome Park in the late 1930s. 'Boro were developing a bright, young crop of local lads to supplement the established big name stars and the Middlesbrough fans were inspired by this exciting blend of talent.

A 3-1 home win against Birmingham City on Good Friday had made 'Boro genuine title contenders and Saturday's visit of fellow challengers Arsenal sent Teesside wild. The Gunners were the team of the 1930s and if you saw only one game a season, you saw this one.

Just under 25,000 supporters watched 'Boro beat Birmingham, but double that number attempted to squeeze into Ayresome the following day. Eventually, a new record attendance made it through the gates.

Before the kick-off, spectators were sitting on the roofs of all three stands, with many more clinging to the iron supports. There were huge gasps from around the stadium when one man slipped from the top to the bottom of the North Stand roof. Miraculously he managed to avoid falling off and recovered his position to cheers from the crowd.

Shortly after the start, the crowd overflowed on to the grass around the pitch and were sitting ten rows deep.

Eddie Rose reported in the *Evening Gazette*: "The scenes when the second half restarted were the most remarkable on this ground for many years. The spectators around the turf were now standing up, forming a human wall all the way round the pitch and a few disappointed spectators, unable to get the view they desired, were scrambling up the framework of the grandstand like monkeys, a height of more than 30 feet."

Micky Fenton, who scored a dramatic equaliser against Arsenal in front of a 'Boro record crowd in March, 1937.

'Boro had the better of the game, yet could not break through the well-organised Arsenal rearguard. Eventually the Gunners opened the scoring against the run of play. Denis Compton crossed the ball into the goalmouth and 'Boro goalkeeper Dave Cumming was impeded by one of his own defenders as he came to collect it. As a result Ray Bowden was presented with an empty net and fired home.

The heading prowess of Micky Fenton. The goal ace played in front of no less than five record 'Boro crowds, both before and after World War Two.

With George Camsell hobbling injured at outside-right and Tommy Cochrane hobbling at outside-left, there seemed no way that 'Boro could force themselves back into it.

However, with many spectators on their way out of the ground, 'Boro finally broke through two minutes from time. Camsell crossed from the right and Micky Fenton hurled himself at the ball, getting there just ahead of Arsenal goalkeeper Frank Boulton to head into the top corner.

The goal generated great scenes of hysteria and there was a huge pitch invasion, mainly from the hundreds of fans standing around the touch-lines.

Eddie Rose said: "They all wanted to congratulate Fenton and the player bolted, apparently in sheer terror. Camsell was on the verge of collapse under the shoal of congratulations which he received for his share."

It was a long time before the match could be restarted and at the final whistle it seemed that every remaining fan in the ground raced on to the pitch. Fenton, Billy Forrest and Camsell were all carried shoulder-high to the dressing-room.

Eddie Rose said: "The battle was great, without being superlative. Middlesbrough did three quarters of the attacking but they never dominated a super Arsenal defence.

"The Arsenal's famous system of covering was never seen to better advantage and Boulton, a fine goal-keeper, was wonderfully protected."

Fenton's late goal preserved 'Boro's unbeaten home record and kept their championship hopes alive. Unfortunately they were to win only one of their final six games and eventually finished seventh, four places and six points behind the Gunners.

Middlesbrough: Cumming; Laking, Stuart, Brown, Baxter, Martin, Chadwick, Fenton, Camsell, Forrest, Cochrane.

Arsenal: Boulton; Male, Hapgood, Crayston, Joy, Copping, Kirchen, Bastin, Bowden, Davidson, D.Compton.

Saturday, 1 January 1938
Middlesbrough 2 Sunderland 1
Attendance: 45,858

THIS was one of the great Ayresome Park derbies, full of atmosphere and excitement and bringing the 'Boro both a record crowd and record receipts.

The 45,858 fans, including 5,000 from Sunderland, paid receipts of £3,509. It beat the previous best, set almost eight years earlier when a 42,080 crowd paid £3,104 to see 'Boro lose an FA Cup fifth-round tie at home to Arsenal.

The huge crowd was to be expected for this derby because both clubs had top quality sides and there were a fair sprinkling of internationals on view. The fans also turned up in good numbers despite the inclement weather. It was a cold day, with continuous drizzle.

The groundstaff and a few volunteers had arrived at five o'clock in the morning to start removing ten and a half tons of straw from the pitch. It had been put there to keep out the frost and ensure the game went ahead.

The *Evening Gazette* said: "Middlesbrough was the mecca of North-East football fans today. They poured into the town by train, bus, car, cycles and on foot.

"Shortly after noon – the gates were opened at 12.30pm – the march to the ground began. The spirit of the New Year and the occasion gave the impression that it was a Cup-tie; rattles and favours were in evidence and partisans good-humouredly engaged in seasonable and pointed verbal exchanges."

The match was played very soon after the death of Phil Bach, one of the father figures of the 'Boro and a great former club chairman through some of the golden years. The *Gazette* described him as 'perhaps the most outstanding figure in football the North-East has ever known.'

The flags were at half-mast and the players, wearing black armbands, walked out in twos before lining up in the centre of the field for an emotional two-minute silence.

'Boro manager Wilf Gillow was just starting to blend together his great side of the late 1930s. The team included 17-year-old George Hardwick, the youngest full-back in the First Division and 19-year-old inside forward Wilf Mannion, who had scored in a 2-0 win against Leeds United the previous Boxing Day Monday. Both players were making their fourth appearance for 'Boro.

The match started at a hectic pace, but Sunderland shook the large crowd by taking the lead through Bobby Gurney after 11 minutes. The Rokermen held their advantage until the interval, but 'Boro came out bombing in the second half and took the points with goals from Mannion in the 50th minute and Jack Milne five minutes later.

There was controversy over the result because Sunderland claimed that a shot from Len Duns had crossed the line in the second half. 'Boro goalkeeper Paddy Nash had lost possession from Duns' shot but recovered to gather it. The Rokermen claimed he had pulled it back from across the line. 'Boro full-back George Laking told the *Gazette* afterwards that it was at least a yard out and the referee obviously agreed.

After the game, several 'Boro players personally congratulated groundsman Charlie Flintoff for the excellent state of the turf.

Middlesbrough: Nash; Laking, Hardwick, Martin, Baxter, Forrest, Birkett, Fenton, Camsell, Mannion, Milne.

Sunderland: Mapson; Gorman, Hall, Thomson, Johnston, McNab, Duns, Carter, Gurney, Gallagher, Burbanks.

In February 1938, 'Boro made the second of two failed attempts to prise away Stanley Matthews from Stoke City. They offered £4,000 in cash plus a player.

Saturday, 12 March 1938
Middlesbrough 2 Arsenal 1
Attendance: 46,747

'BORO'S record attendance was broken for the third time inside 12 months as Teesside fans flocked to see this championship battle.

'Boro were absolutely flying at the time, having won their previous six games and taken 17 points out of 20 since Christmas Day. Those wins included a crushing 6-1 win at Manchester City only three days earlier, when Tommy Cochrane had scored four goals.

For the first time for many years, 'Boro had genuine title chances and everybody wanted to see this enthralling showdown. All seats were taken half-an-hour before the start and, as the terraces began to pack shortly before the kick-off, several supporters climbed on to the top of the West End stand.

The weather conditions were ideal. 'Boro made only one change, with Jack Martin replacing Billy Brown at right-half. The Gunners, who had stayed at York overnight, were late in arriving because a goods train had been derailed on the line.

'Boro were in fine fettle and had the

better of the exchanges. Micky Fenton, who had scored in each of his last two appearances, made it three in a row by striking both goals. Cliff Bastin replied for the visitors 15 minutes from time. It was 'Boro's first home success against Arsenal for 15 years.

Captain Jack, writing in the *Evening Gazette*, said: "It was a triumph for 'Boro's skilful teamwork, fast, exhilarating and suggesting great possibilities of the first League championship coming to Ayresome Park in the history of the club."

However 'Boro had youngsters like Wilf Mannion in their side and probably needed another year's experience. Captain Jack wrote: "It was a big ordeal for Mannion against those big Arsenal chaps and sometimes he was over-shadowed, but was always a grand little trier."

'Boro carried on where they left off against the Gunners by drawing at Everton and winning at Wolves. But then the pressure began to tell. Home defeats by Brentford and Huddersfield paved the way for a disastrous run-in and 'Boro finished fifth. Arsenal had the last laugh by going on to carry off the title.

Middlesbrough: Cumming; Laking, Stuart, Martin, Baxter, Forrest, Milne, Mannion, Fenton, Yorston, Cochrane.
Arsenal: Swindin; Hapgood, Male, Crayston, Sidey, Copping, Griffiths, Jones, Drake, Drury, Bastin.

Saturday, 21 January 1939
FA Cup fourth round
Middlesbrough 0
Sunderland 2
Attendance: 51,080

IT TOOK an FA Cup home tie against Sunderland to fire the Teesside footballing public into topping 50,000 for the first time at Ayresome Park. Not only did 4,000 more fans enter the ground than ever before, but club officials reported afterward that more could have been accommodated.

In the media build-up, the *Gazette* described the match as the derby of derbies. Captain Jack said: "It is the most magnetic Cup-tie in the history of Middlesbrough Football Club."

Queues started to form at the turnstiles from 9am and when the gates opened at 12.45pm there was a terrific rush. It was estimated that 25,000 fans entered the stadium in the first half-hour alone.

An hour before the start, George Camsell appeared in the North Stand where he received an ovation. The *Gazette* reported that "he had come up for the purpose of seeing that Mrs Camsell and their sturdy looking boy, Billy, were comfortably seated".

The 'Grandstand Full' notices appeared before 2pm. Several fans fainted before the kick-off and needed treatment. One man escaped the crush by climbing on to the West End roof and there were many more on the stanchions. The total receipts of £3,997 were a record.

'Boro were going well in the First Division and the fans were starting to believe that this was the club's Cup year at last. 'Boro had earned the right to entertain the Rokermen following a remarkable three-match third round-battle with Bolton Wanderers. After goalless draws in the first two meetings, the second replay was finally settled in the very last minute with a goal from Micky Fenton.

'Boro were expected to comfortably beat Sunderland. Captain Jack said: "All concerned with and interested in the 'Boro had thought that the team had hit the Wembley trail and surely had reason to think that Sunderland would not turn them off it." Earlier in the season, goals from George Camsell and a Benny Yorston penalty had given 'Boro a 2-1 win in a League game at Roker Park.

Unfortunately the Cup-tie didn't go to plan. The game was played in a steady drizzle, which made the surface slippery. 'Boro couldn't finish, but Sunderland could and sent their estimated 12,000 travelling fans home delighted. One of the Roker goals, from Smeaton, involved a great build-up and finish which knocked the stuffing out of 'Boro. The Cup dreams were over for another year and, as it turned out, seven.

Captain Jack said: "The 'Boro played some great football in midfield. Their approach work brought promise of something tangible time after time. Unfortunately there was too much short passing and the finishing was not decisive.

"Not much luck came 'Boro's way at any time during the game. And frequently the ball ran unkindly."

At the end of February, 'Boro beat Sunderland 3-0 at Ayresome Park in the return League game with two goals from Micky Fenton and another from Cliff Chadwick. Less than half the fans that had watched the Cup-tie – 23,882 – witnessed the League game.

Middlesbrough: Cumming; Brown, Stuart, Forrest, Baxter, Murphy, Milne, Mannion, Fenton, Camsell, Chadwick.
Sunderland: Mapson; Gorman, Hall, Housam, Lockie, Hastings, Duns, Carter, Thompson, Smeaton, Burbanks.

Saturday, 1 March 1947
FA Cup sixth round
Middlesbrough 1
Burnley 1
Attendance: 53,025

IN TERMS of the remarkable fervour which it created, this momentous match was 'Boro's biggest FA Cup-tie of all time. It was played in the first season after the war, at a time when football stadiums were packed all over the country.

However, more than ever, the Teesside fans believed that 'Boro's name was at last etched on to the Cup. On the way to the sixth round they had beaten Queen's Park Rangers, Chesterfield and Nottingham Forest. Wilf Mannion had hit a hat-trick as Forest were dispatched by 6-2 in a fifth round replay.

Now 'Boro were expected to make home advantage count against Burnley. The visitors had a very good side, but they were in the Second Division, from which they were destined to win promotion at the end of the season. Nobody on Teesside could possibly entertain the thought of 'Boro losing.

As a result, it was a game that everybody desperately wanted to see. And it was not only the whole of Teesside that was buzzing. The *Gazette* reported that hundreds of coaches from Manchester, Burnley, Nelson, Oldham, Richmond, Darlington, West Hartlepool, Halifax and Durham, among others, were making their way to Ayresome Park. The result was huge traffic jams everywhere. Around 1,000 cars were said to be parked on the Recreation Ground before the kick-off.

There had been a lot of recent snow and it was very cold. But it didn't prevent around 58,000 leaving their firesides. When the gates were closed at 2.30pm, there were an estimated 5,000 fans still outside the ground including many from Lancashire who had been held up on the way because of the difficult driving conditions. As soon as the gates were locked, there was pandemonium outside.

Thousands charged around to the main entrance in Warwick Street and demanded admission. The police, fearful of a riot, called the fire brigade. Eventually a fire tender arrived and forced its way through the massed ranks, before positioning itself right in front of the main gates.

The water cannon on top of the tender was turned around to face the crowd in a menacing manner. The supporters claimed afterwards that the firemen had threatened to turn on the water, though

Newcastle here we come. 'Boro's beauties keep in trim on Saltburn beach prior to playing in front of the club's record crowd of 53,802 against the Magpies in December 1949.

this was denied officially by the fire brigade.

The fire tender ensured that there was no riot, but the fans refused to budge during the whole course of the match. Unfortunately there was no live commentary on the radio in those days, but Chief Constable Edwards came to the rescue. He stayed at the main gates to announce the story of the game to the fans locked outside. His act of devotion was a godsend to the supporters.

Inside the atmosphere was electric. There were thousands of Burnley supporters spread throughout the stadium, but the red and white was dominant both in terms of numbers and in song. Before the kick-off, a little boy dressed in the 'Boro colours went on to the pitch and shook hands with the players.

There was snow lying on the pitch, but it didn't bother the 'Boro, who forced the early pace. They were rewarded with the opening goal just before the interval when Micky Fenton created the opening for Geoff Walker to score.

With the tie seemingly in control, 'Boro continued to push forward in the search for the clinching goal. They thought they had done it when Fenton scored from a free-kick, but Johnny Spuhler had drifted inches offside and the 'goal' was disallowed.

Burnley gained heart from this slice of luck and began to create openings. They were rewarded with an 81st minute equaliser which sent an uncanny silence over the 'Boro fans. Centre-half Norman Robinson lost his footing on the slippery turf and Billy Morris netted.

It was a set-back, but the 'Boro players still believed that they would finish the job in the replay at Turf Moor. In the event they went down 1-0 to a hotly-disputed goal by Morris and the Cup dreams were over for another year. Burnley went on to beat Liverpool in the semi-final before losing the Wembley Final by 1-0 to Charlton Athletic in extra-time.

However, while 'Boro were out of the Cup, the fans who both watched and missed the first game against Burnley were still burning with anger. In fact the *Evening Gazette* postbag was flooded with letters from complaining fans.

J.H.E. of Middlesbrough said: "I was at the south-west corner of the ground and was forced by the pressure behind me from near the top of the steps adjacent to the end of the West Stand, right through a seething mass of humanity until I finally landed on the ground.

"It was an experience I will never forget. The danger will remain until the semi blind spot at the end of the South Stand is eliminated. The pressure comes from the people gathered there in an endeavour to follow the game and there is no resisting it."

G.A.Herbert of Whinney Banks said: "I and several hundred supporters saw a police constable who, by his action of leaving his post on the field and going among the crowd which was entering the ground at the 1s 3d end, averted a disaster."

A.Evans of Middlesbrough said: "I would like to voice my disapproval at the number of spectators admitted to the ground. At the 1s 3d enclosure, a portion of the crowd were as near to disaster as to warrant that steps be taken to improve this part of the ground."

'Never Again' from York said: "The failure to close the gates before 53,000 had secured admission was criminal. It was a miracle that there was not a serious accident. The condition in the 2s stand was appalling."

W.Joyce of Burnley said: "I wish to register strong disapproval over the shabby treatment which I and thousands of other Burnley supporters received at Ayresome Park. Hundreds of us were left outside the ground. Yet we were in the queue at 1.45pm.

"The only sympathy we got from the police was for them to send for the fire engine, which threatened to give us a shower bath."

Middlesbrough: Cumming; R.Robinson, Hardwick, Bell, N.Robinson, Gordon, Spuhler, Mannion, Fenton, Dews, Walker.

Burnley: Strong; Woodruff, Mather, Attwell, Brown, Bray, Chew, Morris, Harrison, Potts, Kippax.

'Boro failed to get into the Central League by one vote in July 1947. Barnsley were elected in their place.

Tuesday, 27 December 1949
Middlesbrough 1 Newcastle United 0
Attendance: 53,802

IT IS quite remarkable that the game which attracted the biggest-ever attendance at Ayresome Park passed by virtually without incident.

Supporters who have attended matches in recent years must wonder

Peter McKennan, who scored the only goal of the game against Newcastle in front of Ayresome Park's biggest-ever crowd.

This is a scene at the East End during 'Boro's game against Newcastle United in 1949 which attracted the biggest ever crowd to the stadium. Newcastle are pictured on the attack, with Jackie Milburn holding off a challenge from Ronnie Dicks before shooting over the bar. Goalkeeper Rolando Ugolini, Bill Whittaker and Harry Bell look on.

how so many could possibly have been packed into the stadium. But the vast open terraces of the East End could comfortably hold around 20,000 spectators, provided they didn't want any breathing space!

The terraces in front of the two grandstands were also standing areas and supporters everywhere were prepared to put up with any amount of crush to see the big games.

So it was during the Christmas of 1949. Local derby matches were terrific occasions and this one enjoyed a better build-up than most because 'Boro had won their two previous games and were starting to find a rich vein of form following a poor start to the season.

'Boro beat Huddersfield by 3-0 at Ayresome Park on Christmas Eve in front of 33,424 fans and then followed up with one of the sweetest victories of all when a goal from Alex McCrae earned a 1-0 win at Newcastle on Boxing Day. That match was watched by no less than 61,184 supporters.

Many Geordies travelled to Teesside for the return fixture, which was played on a surprisingly warm afternoon for the time of year and they were packed in together alongside the home fans.

Wilf Mannion recalls: "You could always tell if it was a big crowd when you were still in the dressing-room. But, even though they were tightly packed, the fans were always good humoured.

"They could come to watch a game of football and enjoy themselves. If anybody was suffering in the crush, like the young lads, they used to pass them over their heads down to the front."

Ironically, few of the players who took part in this momentous game can remember specific incidents.

Peter McKennan was the main man for 'Boro. In the early stages he brought two fine saves from Newcastle goalkeeper Jack Fairbrother before heading what proved to be the winning goal from a corner.

Unfortunately Cliff Mitchell, the *Evening Gazette*'s doyen of sports writers, missed the game. He had been rushed to hospital in Newcastle the previous day with a perforated appendix.

'E.L.T.', taking Cliff's place in covering the derby for the *Gazette*, wrote: 'Without being vastly superior to the Tynesiders, Middlesbrough deserved their two points.

"Mannion was the finest inside-forward on view, his ball manipulation being a joy to behold."

'Boro were the only team in the top two divisions to record a 100% record over the holiday programme and went on to finish the season very strongly.

There were more big crowds for the visit of Manchester United, who attracted 46,702 fans and Sunderland, who were watched by 44,260. But the record attendance against Newcastle was to stand for all time.

Middlesbrough: Ugolini; Dicks, Hardwick, Bell, Whitaker, Gordon, Linacre, Mannion, McKennan, McCrae, Walker.
Newcastle United: Batty; Brennan, Crowe, Dodgin, Fairbrother, Graham, Hannah, Milburn, Mitchell, G.Robledo, Taylor.

EVERYBODY has a favourite game. Some might be remembered for producing a glut of goals, others for toe-to-toe battles which had the fans on the edges of their seats throughout. Some were mouth-watering encounters that had been eagerly awaited for weeks, others were run-of-the-mill matches which became memorable for the events on the pitch.

The common denominator is that they all provided a feast of entertainment and memories to last a lifetime.

Naturally it would be impossible to go into detail about all the favourite games. There were enough fantastic battles at Ayresome Park in its 92-year history to fill many volumes. However, there are many great games which deserve to be recorded and preserved for posterity. And there's a complete mixture across the board.

Some consist of 'Boro goal blitzes, often unexpectedly. Others are terrific team performances, or contained devastating individual displays. A few were memorable simply because they were huge games, whether 'Boro won, drew or lost.

There are special games, like the Mannion Match, when Wilf turned on his magical skills against Blackpool. There's the Hughie McIlmoyle match, when 'Boro hit Queen's Park Rangers for six. And the Graeme Souness match, when Sheffield Wednesday were handed an 8-0 drubbing on Teesside.

Games like these are constantly recalled in the pubs and clubs throughout the region. So, too, is the Zenith Data Systems Cup semi-final second leg against Aston Villa when 'Boro reached Wembley for the first time.

This is a selection of the great games which helped give Ayresome Park and football on Teesside its charm and charisma. These are the games that dreams are made of.

The Great Games

Saturday, 3 December 1910
Middlesbrough 1
Sunderland 0
Attendance: 27,980

FEW Ayresome Park games have caused the virtual cancellation of local league programmes on Teesside. However, it happened on this occasion, when everybody who had any interest in the sport whatsoever was desperate to witness this big derby clash.

It was no ordinary derby, for Sunderland were still unbeaten fully three months into the season. In fact they were the only unbeaten side in the country.

So, fearing a mass exodus of players to Ayresome Park, the local leagues postponed their games. It was a popular decision and the stadium was packed.

For the very first time, 'Boro's officials made an attempt to count the exact crowd, instead of sticking to the usual policy of making an estimate. This official attendance was one of the biggest recorded at Ayresome in the first ten years at the stadium.

While Sunderland were going well, so were 'Boro. They were unbeaten at home, having dropped only one point from a 2-2 draw against Liverpool the previous month.

However, 'Boro still faced a mammoth task against the much vaunted Rokermen, especially as influential Scottish centre-half Andy Jackson and young inside-right George Elliott were both out injured. On the plus side, right-back Don McLeod was fit to return.

The weather was cold and showery, but it failed to dampen the enthusiasm of the fans. More than 20,000 were present more than half an hour before the kick-off, including 1,600 who had travelled by train from Sunderland.

The Rokermen, wearing

James Weir, the left-back signed by 'Boro from Glasgow Celtic in 1910, was a consistent performer in some great games in the years following his arrival on Teesside.

In August 1913, 'Boro's directors turned down a request from the players for boxing gloves to be provided in the club gymnasium.

white shirts and black knickers, were the first to take the field, followed by a huge roar as they were joined by the 'Boro.

'Boro took the game to their illustrious neighbours from the start and were rewarded with a goal after 25 minutes. Sammy McClure, deputising for Elliott, crossed from the right, though there seemed little danger when Sunderland right-back Troughear went to clear.

Unfortunately for Sunderland, Troughear miskicked. The visitors' defence was caught flat-footed and the ball screwed towards the far post where 'Boro outside-left James Nichol was left unmarked to score with a short sharp shot.

Urged on by a vociferous crowd, 'Boro went in search of a second goal, though Sunderland finished the half stronger and 'Boro were indebted to skipper and goalkeeper Tim Williamson for making fine saves from Bridgett and Mordue.

Most of the second half was dominated by Sunderland, but some magnificent defensive work kept the Rokermen out. As full-time approached, the excitement was intense. In the gathering gloom, Mordue had a late chance to equalise but Williamson pulled off a brilliant save. The final whistle was greeted by a deafening roar.

Old Bird, writing in the *Evening Gazette*, said: "I venture to assert that the result of no previous game at Ayresome Park has given such unqualified delight to the home club's supporters.

"Considering the positions the clubs hold and the keen rivalry, a more attractive or sporting contest could not have been desired. It was a battle of giants and will rank as one of the most memorable contests in the 'Boro's first League experience."

The hero of the day was Williamson, who was described by Old Bird as 'magnificent'. McLeod is said to have come back 'a giant', while left-back James Weir also earned accolades.

Middlesbrough: Williamson; McLeod, Weir, Barker, Wardrope, Verrill, Gibson, McClure, Pentland, Cail, Nichol.

Sunderland: Allan; Troughear, Forster, Tait, Thomson, Lowe, Mordue, Coleman, Cowell, Gemmell, Bridgett.

Saturday, 11 November 1911
Middlesbrough 1 Newcastle United 1
Attendance: 32,986

FIRST Division leaders Newcastle attracted the record League attendance to Ayresome Park as football fever began to take a hold on Teesside. The match produced record receipts of £1,357 5s.

The Geordies were two points ahead of 'Boro at the top of the table, though 'Boro had a game in hand and were naturally keen to consolidate their championship challenge at the expense of their North-East rivals.

In the event, the large crowd was sent home happy with the performance but disappointed with the result because 'Boro could and should, have won the match.

Old Bird said in the *Evening Gazette*: "The 11th day of the 11th month of the 11th year of the 20th Century ranks as the greatest day in the history of Middlesbrough Football Club.

"Football of the highest standard was produced by the club's representatives against a team which is generally acknowledged as the finest in the country.

"On the run of play, the 'Boro richly deserved the full spoils, but they were not in luck. All things considered from a Teessider's point of view, there is every reason to be grateful for the great exhibition which the 'Boro players gave."

'Boro were at full strength with left-back James Weir and centre-half Andy Jackson back to bolster the defence. The gates were opened at 1.15pm and the ground was packed within an hour.

Twelve special excursion trains came down from Newcastle. Before the game two little tots wearing Tyneside colours walked around the pitch. The boy was wearing a top hat and suit and the girl wore a bonnet and carried a parasol. They were given many coppers by the appreciative fans.

The ground was soft after overnight frost, though the sun was trying hard to break up the morning fog. From the kick-off it was a gruelling battle, with both sides giving nothing away in a goalless first half.

At the start of the second half the fog began to thicken, though there was never any threat that the fixture might not be completed. The defences were still on top, though 'Boro finally broke through with the opening goal in 65 minutes. Ninty Eyre crossed from the left and inside-right George Elliott gleefully slammed home his ninth goal of the season.

Soon afterwards there was amusement on the terraces when a cat ran across the pitch. But it failed to bring 'Boro good luck, for the Magpies dashed upfield to equalise almost immediately.

Tim Williamson seemed certain to save a shot from Hibbert, but despite knocking the ball up into the air, the goalkeeper failed to get it over the bar and Stewart won the race to get there first and force the ball home.

Both sides battled hard for the winner, but despite a late flourish by 'Boro, they had to settle for a draw.

Middlesbrough: Williamson; McLeod, Weir, Barker, Jackson, Verrill, Stirling, Elliott, James, Cail, Eyre.

Newcastle United: Lawrence; McCracken, Whitson, Willis, Low, Hay, Duncan, Stewart, Hibbert, Higgins, Watson.

Saturday, 13 February 1915
Middlesbrough 7 Tottenham Hotspur 5
Attendance: 7,000

NOT ALL great games are watched by great crowds. This match was extra special because of the glut of goals which produced the highest aggregate score in Ayresome Park's first 30 years.

It was a thoroughly entertaining and absorbing game which could have gone either way. The disappointing crowd was largely due to a dropping off of interest because 'Boro had failed to continue their terrific form from the previous season when they finished third in the Football League, which is their highest-ever placing.

In addition, of course, it was the first year of World War One and some supporters had other matters to attend to. A 4-0 defeat at Burnley the previous week also did little to boost the attendance.

There might have been more goals in this extraordinary game, for Spurs were awarded an early penalty when 'Boro left-half George Malcolm handled a Middlemiss cross. However, Spurs' right-back Clay hammered his spot-kick over the crossbar.

The first of the 12 goals did not come until the 25th minute when 'Boro inside-right Jackie Carr headed in from a Tom Storey corner. Spurs equalised virtually from the kick-off when centre-forward Cantrell stormed through the middle to shoot home.

However, outside-right Storey restored 'Boro's lead when he netted after Spurs goalkeeper Eadon had parried a shot from George Elliott, while Carr and inside-left Walter Tinsley made it 4-1 before the interval.

In 55 minutes Cantrell reduced the arrears and five minutes later 'Boro were left hanging on when Bliss scored again for Spurs. However, Elliott turned the tide with the best goal of the game, striking home a left-foot shot and outside-left John Cook set up another goal for Tinsley.

Two goals from Cantrell, taking his personal tally to four, again put 'Boro under pressure, but the home side made sure of the two points when Tinsley completed his hat-trick from the penalty-spot.

Middlesbrough: Williamson; Haworth, Walker, Davidson, Jackson, Malcolm, Storey, J.Carr, Elliott, Tinsley, Cook.

Tottenham Hotspur: Eadon; Clay, Pearson, Weir, Steel, Lightfoot, Walden, Lowe, Cantrell, Bliss, Middlemiss.

Saturday, 9 January 1926
FA Cup third round
Middlesbrough 5
Leeds United 1
Attendance: 29,000

SCOTSMAN Jimmy McClelland may be best known as the man who lost his place to George Camsell in the momentous season when Camsell scored a record 59 League goals.

However, it would be unfair to McClelland not to recall that he was a quality centre-forward in his own right. In fact, in the season immediately prior to Camsell's record-breaking feat, McClelland rammed in 32 goals in 38 League appearances for 'Boro.

Yet McClelland's finest moment that season came in the third round of the FA Cup, when Yorkshire rivals Leeds United were completely bamboozled by the man from Fife. What made it all the more remarkable was that Leeds were riding high in the First Division, while 'Boro were in Division Two.

As ever, the attraction of a possible David and Goliath result pulled in the fans to Ayresome Park. The 29,000 crowd paid receipts of £2,134. Pathfinder, writing in the *Evening Gazette*, said: "Cup tie fervour everywhere was in evidence for Leeds had brought four special train-loads of be-ribboned supporters, whilst the legions of Teesside seemed to have marked the occasion for a rally. Lowering rain clouds were in the skies when the teams received a great welcome from 29,000 spectators – a splendid gate."

Leeds won the toss, leaving 'Boro to play into the wind towards the Workhouse End. But it was Leeds who were up against it from the start. Pathfinder reported: "Within 60 seconds, 'Boro had scored – amid scenes of indescribable excitement."

Don Ashman started the move, playing the ball through for Jackie Carr to nip past right-back Allen and put McClelland away. The Scot coolly fired into the corner of the net.

'Boro were lifted by the early goal and controlled the tie towards the interval. They were rewarded with a second goal shortly before the interval after Leeds left-back had punched away a George Jones cross which was intended for the head of McClelland. Jimmy got his revenge by crashing home the resulting penalty with such force that it rebounded back into play from a goal stanchion.

Jimmy McClelland, the 'Boro centre-forward who scored all five goals in a 5-1 thrashing of Leeds United in the FA Cup in 1926. Jimmy's feat remains a club record in the Cup.

The start of the second half was littered with rough play, which has been a feature of 'Boro-Leeds games. The needle became more intense when Leeds reduced the arrears in the 68th minute. Ashman handled as Whipp tried to send Jennings clear and Armand scored from the penalty-spot.

The large crowd was then treated to some great end-to-end football as both teams battled for the crucial next goal. The grandstand roof was almost lifted when 'Boro made the breakthrough six minutes from time. Billy Birrell worked his way downfield and crossed to the far post, where Carr knocked it down for McClelland to complete his hat-trick from close range.

Leeds then fell away completely. Two minutes later McClelland threaded his way through several half-hearted tackles before leaving the goalkeeper helpless. The visitors' agony was complete when McClelland rammed home his fifth goal from 25 yards with two minutes remaining.

The 'Boro fans were ecstatic. "One-two-three-four-five" they chanted. And at the final whistle they stormed the pitch, seized McClelland and carried him shoulder high to the dressing-room. Jimmy's magnificent nap hand had beaten Leeds out of sight.

Pathfinder said: "It was the most brilliant success of any centre-forward in the 'Boro colours – not excepting the famous nap hand of Andy Wilson against Nottingham Forest in a League match.

"Clough, Freeman and Holmes have never been seen in such form simultaneously, Freeman literally astonishing everybody.

"At one time Leeds looked like snatching a draw, but that was all. They provided, until their ultimate collapse, however, probably the best Cup tie fight which 'Boro supporters have ever been privileged to see."

Middlesbrough: Clough; Holmes, Freeman, McAllister, Webster, Ashman, Jones, Birrell, McClelland, Carr, O.Williams.

Leeds United: Johnson; Allen, Menzies, Edwards, Townsley, Atkinson, Turnbull, Whipp, Jennings, Armand, Jackson.

'Boro took a 'small but lusty contingent' of supporters to Second Division strugglers Clapton Orient in the fourth round and they made their presence felt by singing "one-two-three-four-five" before the kick-off. However, 'Boro were unable to repeat their third-round feat and went down 4-2, with McClelland grabbing one of the goals.

Saturday, 9 February 1929
Middlesbrough 8
Wolverhampton Wanderers 3
Attendance: 14,636

THIS was the Camsell and Pease Show – both players going goal crazy as 'Boro rammed home their highest score so far in the Football League.

The duo were virtually unstoppable and thrilled a host of civic guests, for the respective Mayors of Middlesbrough, Darlington, Redcar, West Hartlepool, Thornaby and Richmond were all sitting in the grandstand to watch the rout.

George Camsell's hat-trick took his League and Cup tally for the season to 25, while wily winger Billy Pease grabbed four to move on to 23.

There was no surprise about the manner of 'Boro's victory. They were already well on their way to winning promotion and securing the Second Division championship.

Peter McWilliam's men had lost only once in the League since the end of November and that was a narrow 5-4 defeat in a thrilling game at home to Chelsea three weeks earlier.

For the visit of Wolves, 'Boro welcomed back right-half Joe Miller and inside-left Bobby Bruce to the team which had drawn 1-1 at Southampton the previous week.

The weather was spring-like and the ground was soft. However, there was a dream first half for 'Boro, despite falling behind after only eight minutes when Wolves' outside-right Ferguson beat home goalkeeper Jimmy Mathieson from three yards.

'Boro levelled nine minutes later when Camsell set up Bruce for the equaliser. Three minutes later 'Boro were ahead when left-half Kay brought down Camsell in full flight and Pease scored from the spot.

In 28 minutes Pease and Camsell combined for the latter to score. This was the signal for 'Boro to step up a gear and they thrilled the home crowd with 60 minutes of virtual non-stop attacking football.

Wolves had no answer before the interval. They had two let-offs when Pease hit the foot of a post and Owen Williams missed an open goal, but then Pease scored twice in quick succession to complete his hat-trick and make it 5-1 at the interval.

'Boro increased their lead after the restart after Camsell had been sandwiched by the Wolves backs and Pease scored his second penalty and fourth goal overall.

Camsell then headed in from a Pease corner to make it 7-1, though Wolves centre-half Pritchard reduced the arrears while his opposite number Maurice Webster was off the field having treatment for an injury.

Pease then crossed for Camsell to head in and complete his own hat-trick and at the same time give 'Boro their best-ever score in a League game. The scoring was completed by Wolves, when inside-left Chadwick scored from the spot after he had been fouled by Jarvis.

Erimus, writing in the *Evening Gazette*, stressed: " 'Boro simply toyed with the opposition and Bruce was a veritable box of tricks."

But it was the partnership of Camsell and Pease which did the damage. By the end of the season Camsell had scored 33 goals and Pease 28 and First Division football was back at Ayresome Park.

Middlesbrough: Mathieson; Jarvis, Smith, Miller, Webster, Peacock, Pease, J.Carr, Camsell, Bruce, O.Williams.

Wolves: Lewis; Watson, Shaw, Richards, Pritchard, Kay, Ferguson, Green, Weaver, Chadwick, Baxter.

In October 1929, 'Boro turned down a request from Herbert Chapman of Arsenal asking for support for the Gunners' bid to get the Football Association to switch England internationals from Saturdays to midweek. Yet only two weeks previously 'Boro had failed to secure George Camsell's withdrawal from the England v Ireland match, even though he was selected only as a reserve.

Saturday, 15 February 1930
FA Cup fifth round
Middlesbrough 0
Arsenal 2
Attendance: 42,073

'BORO'S FA Cup record was as bad as ever in the period between the two wars. Every time they had a chance of putting a decent run together, they went and lost unexpectedly.

However, 'Boro were going well in the First Division and there was genuine hope of success on two fronts when they reached the fifth round of the Cup. 'Boro had already beaten Chesterfield by 4-3 at Ayresome Park in a third round replay and then needed four attempts to overcome Charlton Athletic in the fourth round. John McKay scored the crucial goal in extra-time in the second replay at Maine Road.

They were favourites to beat Arsenal in the fifth round because they were seventh in the First Division – nine places above the Gunners. Arsenal were just starting to put together their all-conquering side of the 1930s.

'Boro warmed up in style by crushing Birmingham City by 5-1 in a League game at Ayresome Park and Cup fever took hold of the town. Despite the difficult social and economic times, queues began to form at 10am, which was a full two hours before the gates were due to open. The grandstand was full at 1pm, while the stadium was absolutely packed thirty minutes before the kick-off. The crowd of 42,073 was 'Boro's record for a Cup-tie.

As usual there were spectators on the stand roofs and there was an alarming incident when a man fell from the roof of the grandstand. At first it was thought he was badly injured, but he was later reported to be all right after treatment for shock and bad bruising.

Teesside had never seen a Cup-tie like it and Erimus reported in the *Evening Gazette*: "Scenes unprecedented in the history of the 'Boro club were witnessed at Ayresome Park.

"Casualties were frequent owing to the packed character of the enclosure, members of the local ambulance brigades being kept busy reviving spectators, old and young, who had fainted."

Unfortunately for 'Boro, another casualty was star centre-forward George Camsell. The ace goalscorer was forced to miss the game and 'Boro took a gamble by playing John Elkes in his place.

It was a gamble which failed to pay off. Elkes had a nightmare match and was heavily criticised by the fans during the game and by the media afterwards. It was claimed that Bert Hall, who scored one of the five goals against Birmingham but was then left out, should have led the line against the Gunners.

However, even if Camsell had played, 'Boro might not have fared any better. Arsenal went ahead after only four minutes through Lambert and then were in full control from the moment that Cliff Bastin netted number two on the half-hour. The star of the game was the Gunners' lively inside-forward Alex James, who was described as a constructive genius.

In the last five minutes 'Boro raised the hopes of their fans when Bobby Bruce moved from inside-forward to centre-forward, swapping places with Elkes. 'Boro pounded the Arsenal defence and Bruce went close to scoring on a couple of occasions. But it was not to be 'Boro's day.

Middlesbrough: Mathieson; Smith, Ashman, Watson, Webster, Forrest, Pease, McKay, Elkes, Bruce, Warren.

Arsenal: Lewis; Parker, Hapgood, Barker, Roberts, John, Williams, Jack, Lambert, James, Bastin.

Saturday, 18 November 1933
Middlesbrough 10
Sheffield United 3
Attendance: 6,461

'BORO had hit Stoke City for six in their previous home game, so Sheffield United had every right to expect a tough game. But not as tough as this.

Despite the romp against Stoke, this game failed to attract the fans to Ayresome Park on a damp, cold afternoon and 'Boro's only ever double-figure score in a Football League game was witnessed by the second- lowest crowd of the season.

Ironically, United were first to score when Baines netted after only three minutes. The fans had to endure another 20 minutes of cold before 'Boro warmed them up with a magnificent solo goal from George Camsell, who proved that

'Boro are on the attack during their 10-3 drubbing of Sheffield United in 1933. It was the only time 'Boro ever reached double figures in a League game at Ayresome Park. George Camsell, who scored four times, is pictured second right.

he was still as strong as an ox at the age of 30 by powering his way through four tackles to crash home the equaliser.

After that it was a case of blink and you missed it. 'Boro led 6-2 at the interval with Camsell scoring again, Bobby Bruce adding two, including one from a free-kick and wingers Charlie Ferguson and Fred Warren also netting. Pickering replied for United.

Camsell completed his hat-trick in 53 minutes, Bobby Baxter scored six minutes later and Baines netted his second to make it 8-3 after 74 minutes. Bruce completed his hat-trick four minutes later and with the crowd wondering whether 'Boro could finally make it to ten, up popped the indomitable Camsell with his fourth goal two minutes from time.

Writing in the *Evening Gazette* was E.L.T. He stated " 'Boro were the perfect scoring machine. There was no weak link in the attack, Baxter and Ferguson both playing splendid football and fitting into the scheme of things in style.

"No centre-forward in the game can take a ball through like Camsell and his first goal was one of the finest he has ever scored."

The four-goal haul took Camsell's tally for the season to 14 and increased calls for him winning another England cap.

Middlesbrough: Gibson; Jennings, Stuart, Brown, Griffiths, Martin, Ferguson, Bruce, Camsell, Baxter, Warren.

Sheffield United: Smith; Robinson, Hooper, Jackson, Holmes, Green, Oxley, Killourhy, Baines, Pickering, Williams.

Saturday, 15 February 1936
FA Cup fifth round
Middlesbrough 2 Leicester City 1
Attendance: 42,214

AT LAST – 'Boro reached the sixth round of the FA Cup for the first time in their history thanks to this thrilling victory against Leicester City, which attracted a Cup record crowd of 42,214 to Ayresome Park.

The tie had everybody on the edge of their seats throughout, with Billy Forrest grabbing the winning goal with only a couple of minutes left on the clock.

'Boro had been at home in every round of the competition. They were fortunate to win the third-round tie at home to Southampton, when a bad mistake by Saints goalkeeper Light gifted the winner to winger Arthur Cunliffe. 'Boro finished the game with Eric Wightman and Jack Martin limping badly at the end.

In the fourth round 'Boro played a lot better in beating Clapton Orient by 3-0, with George Camsell scoring twice and Cunliffe netting again.

The scene was set for an enthralling fifth-round tie at home to Second Division Leicester, which naturally 'Boro were expected to win. However, it didn't go according to plan. Leicester were comfortably the better side in the first half and it was no surprise when the visitors took the lead through centre-forward McNally shortly after the restart.

At first it seemed as though 'Boro's Cup hoodoo would strike again, but fortunately McNally's goal stirred them into action. They grabbed the equaliser through Camsell and then poured forward in the search for the winner.

The excitement grabbed the imagination of the crowd and there was a state of pandemonium when a wall collapsed around the pitch.

Eddie Rose, writing in the *Evening Gazette*, said: "During a tense period the closely packed spectators surged forward, snapped a wooden barrier and then broke like a huge tidal wave on the concrete wall surrounding the ground. The wall shuddered under the terrific pressure before collapsing for fully 40 yards."

Miraculously there was only one serious injury. Twelve-year-old Joseph Mohan from Spencer Street in

Middlesbrough was picked out of the mêlée suffering from a broken thigh.

With order restored, 'Boro continued to press for the winner, but Leicester defended with grit and threatened to hang on for the replay. However, 'Boro forced a late corner and Forrest, standing only three yards out, hammered home the winner to a deafening noise from the terraces.

Eddie Rose said: "It was one of the most stirring finishes which any of us had seen for a long time. Fortunate, perhaps, but inspiring by its drama. As soon as the whistle blew the crowd invaded the field in their thousands. One might have thought it was Wembley itself. The players were patted and slapped with delight until their ribs must have ached."

Forrest said: "That's my favourite spot for shooting. I always prefer them about three yards out."

Middlesbrough: Gibson; Brown, Stuart, Yorston, Baxter, Forrest, Birkett, Fenton, Camsell, Coleman, Cunliffe.

Leicester City: McLaren; Frame, Jones, Smith, Sharman, Ritchie, Carroll, O'Callaghan, McNally, Maw, Liddle.

'Boro received only 300 tickets out of a crowd of 30,000 for the sixth-round clash at Grimsby Town. They lost 3-1.

It cost 'Boro £18 10s to have the wall rebuilt, plus £3 for every new crash barrier which was installed.

Safety standards were different in those days and 'Boro officials were able to claim that the wall collapse was due to the frost, rather than the pressure of the crowd.

However, they did agree to pay £2 to the parents of Joseph Mohan as compensation for his injury.

Chelsea defender Dowd clears a dangerous situation in a muddy goalmouth watched by George Camsell and visiting goalkeeper Woodley.

These three 'Boro stars featured in plenty of great games in the 1930s. Left to right: Benny Yorston, George Camsell and Bobby Baxter.

Saturday, 17 October 1936
Middlesbrough 5 Sunderland 5
Attendance: 36,030

IN TERMS of goals alone, this was the greatest derby played at Ayresome Park. It produced the highest aggregate of goals ever in a derby and was a storming match which swung one way and then the other.

Sunderland were the reigning League champions, so it was not surprising that the clash attracted easily the biggest crowd of the season to Ayresome Park.

They were not disappointed with the action and the *Evening Gazette*'s Eddie Rose described it as: "One of the most remarkable matches ever played at Ayresome Park."

A fierce rainstorm broke out just before the kick-off but it failed to dampen the enthusiasm of the packed crowd. Both sets of supporters were, as usual, mingling together, but the good natured banter was as strong as ever.

'Boro made one change, giving a debut to new right-back George Laking, just signed from Wolves. Billy Brown moved to right-half in place of Jack Martin.

'Boro, defending the Linthorpe Road End in the first half, were given a dream start. Benny Yorston, playing against his former club, knocked the ball over to winger Ralph Birkett, who cut inside before playing the perfect pass for George Camsell to fire home in the fourth minute.

Three minutes later bubbling 'Boro made it 2-0. This time Camsell was the provider, creating the opening for inside-left Tim Coleman to score.

Any hopes the home fans held that 'Boro might build on their lead were dashed on the quarter-hour when the Rokermen reduced the deficit. Raich Carter tried an angled shot, Dave Cumming saved but couldn't hold it and Len Duns pounced to score.

This remarkable game continue to see-saw with 'Boro restoring their two-goal advantage in 21 minutes when Camsell scored from a narrow angle, the ball spinning off Sunderland goalkeeper Johnny Mapson into the net.

'Boro were still unable to dominate despite their two-goal lead and it was the champions who took control in the final 15 minutes of the half to score three goals without reply and turn around 4-3 ahead. First Bobby Gurney broke clear from a long ball from Feenan to score, then Duns levelled from a corner. The Rokermen went ahead when Connor headed in from a Duns cross.

'Boro were well and truly on the rack two minutes after the restart when Sunderland scored their fourth goal in a row. This time Carter scored when heading in from a Duns corner.

However, the irrepressible Camsell brought 'Boro back to life when reducing the arrears four minutes later. Urged on by the excited crowd, 'Boro took the game to their visitors again and were rewarded with the equalising goal in 64 minutes. Camsell had a shot pushed out by Mapson, but only as far as Ralph Birkett, who promptly volleyed it back into the net.

There was still almost half an hour for both sides to try to find the winner, but defences finally took control for the first time and the teams had to settle for a point apiece.

Middlesbrough: Cumming; Laking, Stuart, Brown, Baxter, Forrest, Birkett, Yorston, Camsell, Coleman, Cochrane.

Sunderland: Mapson; Feenan, Collin, Thomson Johnston, McNab, Duns, Carter, Gurney, Gallacher, Connor.

Saturday, 10 December 1938
Middlesbrough 9 Blackpool 2
Attendance: 17,166

IT would be easy to confuse this one-sided game with the famous Mannion

Benny Yorston gets in a shot goal for 'Boro in 1936 watched by Micky Fenton, far left.

In 1936 the 'Boro board was quoted £27 10s for the erection of concrete posts to chain off the land in Ayresome Park Road where cars were parking. They decided it was too expensive. A 'No Parking' sign was erected instead and the directors decided to rope off the land once a year.

Match, which also came against Blackpool.

After all, wonderful Wilf scored no less than four times in this pre-war clash and produced some lethal finishing for a 20-year-old. However, on this occasion Blackpool were taken apart by a Mannion-inspired 'Boro team performance. After the war, Wilf was to beat Blackpool single handed.

In the build-up to Christmas, 1938, 'Boro were in need of a pick-me-up after a lacklustre few weeks. They had won only one of their previous five matches and were in danger of wasting a bright start to their championship aspirations.

Against Blackpool, 'Boro were presented with a perfect afternoon for football. It was a bright, sunny day, without any wind and the turf was wet following overnight rain.

Unfortunately the match attracted 'Boro's lowest crowd of the season so far. They voiced their disappointment before the start when Cliff Chadwick was named on the left wing in place of the popular Tommy Cochrane. But they need not have worried, for Chadwick went on to become a leading light behind the big win.

'Boro were ahead in only four minutes, Mannion picking up a throw-in from Duncan McKenzie and scoring with a left-foot drive. Ten minutes later Wilf did it again, receiving a pass from Jack Milne and hitting a stinging drive which Blackpool goalkeeper Wallace got a hand to but allowed to slip into the net.

It was the signal for an all-out assault on the Blackpool goal. A Milne pass was driven in by Chadwick, Mannion completed his hat-trick from close range and then Wilf picked up a throw-in from Chadwick and slipped it through for Micky Fenton to score from close range.

With a five-goal lead at the interval, the points were in the bag. However, 'Boro relaxed after the restart and inside-left Eastham reduced the arrears in the 47th minute.

'Boro came back to life and Mannion collected his fourth goal when he fired in off a post following a pass from Milne. Then Fenton made it seven when he shot home from a miskick by Benny Yorston, after Chadwick had split open Blackpool's right flank.

Just in case Blackpool had any doubts about the score, the crowd was chanting "One-two-three-four-five-six-seven". That chant was extended to eight seven minutes from time when Fenton completed his hat-trick, scoring from close in after Chadwick had dribbled his way to the near post and set him up.

Three minutes later it was 9-1, Fenton repaying the compliment by sending Chadwick away to score his second goal. 'Boro's determination to try to reach double figures cost them a second goal at the back, when a mix-up allowed Blackpool outside-right Munro to score.

However, there was a golden opportunity of a tenth 'Boro goal when Milne broke clear in the very last minute, only to disappoint the crowd by firing wide.

It was Mannion who earned all the accolades. Captain Jack, writing in the *Evening Gazette*, said: "Standing out in this 'Boro victory, whirlwind like and leaving us all breathless, was four-goals Wilfred Mannion.

"More than once I have expressed the wish that Mannion would shoot harder and more frequently. The boy has proved his value and class in the open. It was emphasised in unmistakable fashion and he proved that he can shoot.

"He shared in movements which led to most of the goalscoring, particularly in the first half when the lads gave a positively dazzling exhibition. But it wasn't a one-man show. It was easily one of Milne's best games for 'Boro, while Yorston worked incessantly."

The victory was missed by manager Wilf Gillow, who was at Horden Colliery to watch the FA Cup-tie against Newport County. After the game, Gillow signed Horden's 19-year-old outside-left Sam Armes. The teenager went on to make

A determined Micky Fenton gets up high to win this aerial dual against Derby County at snowbound Ayresome Park. Watching the action are Raich Carter, second right, and Wilf Mannion.

'Boro offered £6,000 to Sunderland for Raich Carter in December 1945. The Roker club were not interested in selling their star to local rivals and instead he moved to Derby County for whom he had been guesting since 1942. However, 'Boro eventually got their man almost 20 years later, as manager.

three appearances for 'Boro before the onset of the war.

Middlesbrough: Cumming; Brown, Stuart, McKenzie, Baxter, Forrest, Milne, Mannion, Fenton, Yorston, Chadwick.

Blackpool: Wallace; D.Blair, Sibley, Farrow, Hayward, Jones, Munro, Buchan, Finan, Eastham, J.Blair.

Saturday, 7 September 1946
Middlesbrough 5 Stoke City 4
Attendance: 43,685

SEVEN Football League seasons were lost as a result of World War Two. So the football starved British public were desperate for a taste of the action when competitive football returned to stadiums in the summer of 1946.

There were huge crowds everywhere and Ayresome Park was no exception, where 'Boro were attempting to regenerate the immense promise the team had shown in the late 1930s.

'Boro started the new season with two away games and won them both. A lone goal from Wilf Mannion produced a 1-0 win at Aston Villa on the opening day and then 'Boro won a mid-week fixture at Liverpool thanks to a Laurie Hughes own-goal.

The scene was set for 'Boro's triumphant return to Ayresome. It was a game which everybody on Teesside wanted to see, even though there was great disappointment that Stanley Matthews, Stoke's England winger, was unable to play because of injury.

Thousands of fans thronged Ayresome Park and Police Superintendent McDonald made a special broadcast appeal to the crowd to close ranks so that more fans could be admitted to the stadium.

Finally, 15 minutes before the kick-off, the police decided to close the gates with hundreds of fans locked outside. It had been nine long years since there had been similar scenes for a League fixture at Ayresome.

The weather was cricket-like, with a pleasant breeze blowing from the West End. 'Boro ran out to a great ovation on their homecoming and put Stoke under heavy pressure from the start.

They were rewarded with the opening goal after 11 minutes. Harry Bell played the ball out to outside-right Johnny Spuhler whose remarkable cross from near the corner flag was stabbed home by Micky Fenton from virtually on the goal-line.

Sixteen minutes later, Stoke silenced the crowd's celebrations by equalising when George Mountford fired in off a post following a free-kick from inside-left Baker. The goal sparked an amazing tit-for-tat game in which 'Boro were never behind, but never able to relax.

Two minutes later 'Boro restored their lead when Mannion set up Fenton to score with a left-foot drive. The lead lasted only six minutes before lively Stoke centre-forward Fred Steele scored with an angled shot. In the 41st minute Fenton completed a first-half hat-trick to restore 'Boro's advantage after Geoff Walker had beaten two defenders and crossed from the left. However, 'Boro could not hold on until the interval, Steele levelling in the 44th minute shortly after he had hit the bar from an earlier attempt.

The pace began to drop in the second half especially when 'Boro settled down after Mannion had restored their lead when shooting in off a post. 'Boro held on comfortably until ten minutes from time when Steele completed his hat-trick after Baker had hit the crossbar.

It looked a draw all over, but the elusive Fenton had other ideas. In the 89th minute the 32-year-old goal ace produced the winner out of nothing to send the packed stadium into raptures.

Captain Jack, in the *Evening Gazette*, described the goal as 'a breathtaking individual effort'. The Stockton-born forward showed that he was as deadly as ever. Who knows what scoring feats Fenton might have achieved and records he might have broken if his career had not been affected by the war.

Middlesbrough: Cumming; R.Robinson, Hardwick, Bell, Shepherdson, Gordon, Spuhler, Mannion, Fenton, Dews, Walker.

Stoke City: Herod; Brigham, Meakin, F.Mountford, Franklin, Kirton, G. Mountford, Poppitt, Steele, Baker, Ormston.

'Boro maintained their bright start to the season and held genuine championship aspirations until the end of February. However, only one win in the final three months of the season told an all-too familiar story.

The Mannion Match
Saturday, 22 November 1947
Middlesbrough 4 Blackpool 0
Attendance: 38,936

THE greatest individual display by any 'Boro player at Ayresome Park came from the all-time great himself, Wilf Mannion, in this drubbing of hapless Blackpool.

Mannion dictated every aspect of the play to such an extent, that the match became christened the Mannion Match both by the media and by the near-39,000 spectators who were fortunate to be there.

Remarkably, Wilf failed to score any of 'Boro's four goals. But he had a hand in virtually every attack and left

Action from a Tees-Wear derby just after the war as Harry Bell gets in a shot at the Sunderland goal.

Blackpool, one of the First Division's top sides, in tatters. It was an unforgettable virtuoso performance by the maestro.

Cliff Mitchell, writing in the *Evening Gazette*, said: "Behind almost every 'Boro attack – and there were plenty of them – was the guile, the incomparable craft of a brilliant Mannion.

"Wilf was the consummate football artist.

"He moved his body a couple of inches and had three defenders running the wrong way. He balanced the ball on his head, let it run slowly down his body to trap it on the move. He drew a net around him, to come waltzing out of it, the ball at his feet. He split open one of the most formidable rearguards in the League to flash a goal pass to an unmarked colleague."

In a letter to the *Gazette* 'SOS' of Billingham wrote: "Having been a supporter of the 'Boro for more years than I care to remember, I cannot recollect, even in the days of Jackie Carr or Alex James, such an exhibition of football as that given by Mannion.

"I am sure that for years to come it will be talked about on Teesside. It was truly the sort of football craft that has earned Wilf his place in the great English team and I feel that if he had scored we would have had a demonstration of hero worship probably never seen before at the Park."

It's only recently that Wilf has explained the reasons behind such a phenomenal individual display. He said: "It's simple. I played for me. I had just got engaged to Bernadette and she was sitting in the stand watching me.

"Naturally I wanted to impress her. So I produced all the skills and all the tricks I knew. It was like putting on an act, if you like. The only problem was that Bernadette came away thinking that I played like that every week!"

'Boro would have beaten any team in the country that day and it was just Blackpool's bad luck that Wilf had got engaged. Amazingly, Blackpool had not conceded more than two goals in any previous match that season.

Cliff Mitchell wrote: "Blackpool never gave up the fight and Stan Mortensen's exhilarating burst of speed always held danger. But there was never any doubt about this game. From the kick-off it went to a Middlesbrough team which, on this form, is good enough to account for the best there is."

Cec McCormack scored two of 'Boro's goals, while the others were netted by Micky Fenton and Johnny Spuhler.

Middlesbrough: Goodfellow; R.Robinson, Hardwick, Bell, Whitaker, Gordon, Spuhler, McCormack, Fenton, Mannion, G.Walker.

Blackpool: Wallace; Shinwell, Suart, Farrow, Hayward, Johnston, Nelson, Mortensen, McIntosh, McCall, Munro.

'Boro and Blackpool weren't the only clubs impressed by Mannion's pulsating performance. Leeds United offered £15,000 for Wilf's signature in the week following the game. But 'Boro turned it down.

'Boro followed up that win with a crushing 7-1 victory at Blackburn Rovers, with McCormack netting a hat-trick and Fenton and Geoff Walker scoring twice apiece.

At that stage of the season, 'Boro had scored 42 goals in 18 games with Fenton the top scorer in the First Division on 16.

Saturday, 14 October 1950
Middlesbrough 1 Sunderland 1
Attendance: 52,764

'BORO'S second-highest League crowd of all time packed into Ayresome Park expecting to witness a comfortable victory against struggling Sunderland.

Rampant 'Boro were riding high in second place in the First Division and went into the game on the back of an 8-0

It's Wolves on the attack at Ayresome Park in January, 1950, as Chatham wins a header against Bill Whittaker, while Smythe and 'Boro's Harry Bell look on. 'Boro won the match 2-0 in front of 41,000 fans.

annihilation of Huddersfield Town, including hat-tricks for Wilf Mannion and Alex McCrae and a 4-3 victory at Wolves.

However, it didn't go as expected and a good section of the mammoth crowd were already on their way home when McCrae spared 'Boro's blushes by grabbing the equaliser 30 seconds from the end.

'Boro had started the game without the injured Jimmy Gordon, with the ever reliable Ronnie Dicks taking his place at left-half. Sunderland entertainer Len Shackleton was also out through injury, though skipper Willie Watson returned for the Rokermen.

'Boro attacked from the kick-off, though the home fans were silenced when Sunderland took the lead against the run of play in the 19th minute through centre-forward Dicky Davis.

Despite this set-back, 'Boro continued to hold the balance of play and missed a chance to turn the game around in the last minute of the first half when Wilf Mannion hit the Roker crossbar. As the second half progressed, 'Boro became more and more ragged as the game threatened to slip away from them. However, they finally salvaged a point in the dying seconds with a goal created by Johnny Spuhler against his former club. The winger raced down the right and crossed for McCrae to shoot first time past goalkeeper Johnny Mapson for his 12th goal of the season.

He flies through the air... Rolando Ugolini shows remarkable agility to punch clear during a match against Everton.

Cliff Mitchell, writing in the *Evening*

Heads I win! Wilf Mannion, the man with the golden boots, illustrates his heading ability in a match in the early 1950s.

Goal! Johnny Spuhler beats Chelsea goalkeeper Collins and centre-half Greenwood with a fine header. However the match finished all-square at 3-3 in March 1954.

Gazette, said: "Before McCrae's winner, the Middlesbrough forward had been guilty of a series of outstanding lapses.

" 'Boro failed to find their men with any consistent degree of accuracy: they fell victim too often to the admittedly robust tackling of their opponents and, most important, their shooting lacked fire, accuracy and frequency."

Middlesbrough: Ugolini; Robinson, Hardwick, Bell, Whitaker, Dicks, Delapenha, Mannion, Spuhler, McCrae, Walker.

Sunderland: Mapson; Stelling, Hudgell, Watson, Walsh, A.Wright, Duns, T.Wright, Davis, Broadis, Cunning.

Going down... Wilf Mannion and Danny Blanchflower watch the action in the home game against Aston Villa in April 1954. 'Boro won 2-1, but it was their last victory before relegation to the Second Division.

Hotshot Lindy Delapenha demonstrates his shooting prowess at home to Notts County in 1954, while Joe Scott looks on.

Wednesday, 17 October 1957
Middlesbrough 2 Sunderland 0
Attendance: 27,241

THIS friendly midweek derby is notable because it was the first ever floodlit game played at Ayresome Park.

However, it will be better remembered by some fans as the game in which 'Boro scored the famous penalty goal which was not given – because it escaped through a hole in the net.

'Boro had been awarded the spot kick by local referee Kevin Howley when Brian Clough was brought down while in full flow.

Cliff Mitchell, writing in the *Evening Gazette*, explained: "Lindy Delapenha took the kick and crashed the ball past goalkeeper Routledge. It ploughed into the corner and crept through a hole there – and Sunderland's players thought they might as well try to bluff their way back into the game.

"Gamesmanship of the highest order – and incredibly it worked. Referee Kevin Howley of Billingham allowed himself to be talked out of his original and correct, decision."

In an *Evening Gazette* interview with Neil Abbott more than 20 years later, Kevin finally got to put his side of the story.

He said: "A lot of people fail to remember that in those days floodlights were quite a novelty. Games were played with a white ball, white nets and white walls.

"However, for a start, there was no hole in the nets, which were brand new and in perfect condition, though I have yet to see a net without a hole in it.

"And I certainly wasn't conned by Stan Anderson, the Sunderland player who picked the ball up and put it down for a goal kick. I've no doubt that he tried it on but I did not see what he was doing because at that time I was walking towards the Boys End to speak to Peter Baldwin, who was the linesman on that side.

"It took some courage not to give the goal but I couldn't because I did not see the ball enter the net.

"After the match it was established that the pegs securing the net were not holding the pull. They were put in wrongly – instead of riding the pressure the nets just slipped out of the hook.

"Any powerful shot could conceivably have gone under the net. I am not saying it did, but that seems to be what happened.

"I still think I did right, though. As with justice in the High Court if there's any room for doubt you don't give – and as there was room for doubt I didn't give

The goal ace himself. Brian Clough, pictured in a typical shooting pose. Clough was top scorer for 'Boro five seasons in succession.

The world famous Harlem Globetrotters made their debut at Ayresome Park on 17 July 1957. Prices ranged from 7s 6d in the grandstand to 3s on the terraces. They appeared again the following June.

Kevin Howley, the Billingham referee who disallowed a goal by Lindy Delapenha in 'Boro's first floodlit match at Ayresome Park, against Sunderland. It is thought the ball went through a hole in the back of the net. Howley was a top rated FIFA referee, who was respected throughout the country.

a goal. I thought Lindy had shot wide."

In the event, the disallowed goal hardly mattered because 'Boro, wearing their new fluorescent strip, won this otherwise friendly match quite comfortably in front of a large crowd. Arthur Fitzsimons opened the scoring in the 34th minute and Clough struck home a second in 68 minutes.

Cliff Mitchell said: "It might have been 5-0, so superior was a Second Division side to a First Division side that started brightly, faded and was finally outplayed."

And the floodlights? Sunderland skipper Don Revie admitted: "They are the best floodlights I have ever played under. And the pitch is as good as Wembley."

Middlesbrough: Taylor; Bilcliff, Stonehouse, Mulholland, Phillips, Dicks, Delapenha, McLean, Clough, Fitzsimons, Burbeck.

Sunderland: Routledge; Graham, McDonald, Anderson, Robson, Elliott, Bingham, Revie, Fleming, O'Neill, Goodchild.

Saturday, 23 August 1958
Middlesbrough 9
Brighton 0
Attendance: 32,367

'BORO had been expecting a tough game against newly-promoted Brighton and Hove Albion at the start of the new season – but it turned out to be a rout.

Brian Clough celebrated his elevation to captain at the ripe old age of 23 with five goals as 'Boro recorded their biggest-ever winning margin at Ayresome Park.

Alan Peacock also netted twice and Bill Harris scored two from the penalty-spot as Brighton were run ragged.

Cliff Mitchell wrote: "Ayresome Park was set alight by a brilliant display of power football. It was a baptism of fire for Brighton. They fought bravely enough but were outplayed and outclassed in every aspect of the game.

"The score might well have been greater, so completely in command was this sparkling 'Boro side."

He added: "If Clough is overlooked by the England selectors this season then a lot of people from Middlesbrough – and Brighton – will want to know why."

The game was a rough experience for Brighton's teenage goalkeeper Dave Hollins. Cliff said: "At the end of a nightmare match for young Hollins, Clough went up to the young goalkeeper and offered his sincere sympathy."

Clough went on to score 43 goals that season, but the marvellous season which the fans might have expected failed to materialise as 'Boro went on to finish 13th.

'Boro fielded their famous home-grown forward line of the 1950s against Brighton, while new signing Ernie Walley from Spurs also made his debut.

Middlesbrough: Taylor; Bilcliff, Robinson, Harris, Phillips, Walley, Day, McLean, Clough, Peacock, Holliday.

Brighton: Hollins; Tennant, Ellis, Bertolini, Whitfield, Wilson, Gordon, Shepherd, Sexton, Forman, Howard.

Saturday, 10 October 1959
Middlesbrough 1
Sunderland 1
Attendance: 47,297

THIS gruelling derby was memorable because it attracted the last 45,000-plus crowd to Ayresome Park to create one of the last truly great Tees-Wear atmospheres.

The fans were attracted by 'Boro's fine start to the season and the chance to get one over on the Rokermen. In recent games Brian Clough had hit four goals in the 6-2 hammering of Plymouth Argyle at Ayresome Park, while Alan Peacock scored four in a 7-1 win at Derby County.

'Boro's superb attacking play had not gone unnoticed. Clough and outside-left Edwin Holliday were both called up for their England international debuts against Wales in the week following this derby.

So the large crowd was also partly attracted by the news of the double call-up, in addition to the unusually warm sunny weather. Both sides received huge ovations when they took to the field, with Sunderland kicking off towards the Linthorpe Road End with the sun on their backs.

It was 'Boro who forced the early pace and they deservedly took the lead in the 19th minute. Billy Day, the provider for so many goals for Clough and Peacock, slipped the ball into the middle but at first it looked as though the chance had gone when the ball went behind Clough. Fortunately Holliday had cut in from the wing and blasted the ball home for a great boost before his England debut.

Roared on by the happy crowd, 'Boro continued to force the pace. But they paid the penalty for missed chances when the Rokermen broke upfield to equalise in the 59th minute.

Ernie Taylor and Ian Lawther did the spade work for Amby Fogarty to finish off the move by shooting past 'Boro goalkeeper Peter Taylor. 'Boro, well marshalled by Willie Fernie in midfield, still held the balance of play, but had to settle for a share of the spoils.

Middlesbrough: Taylor; Bilcliff, McNeil, Harris, Phillips, Yeoman, Day, Fernie, Clough, Peacock, Holliday.

Sunderland: Wakeham; Nelson, Ashurst, Anderson, Hurley, McNab, Bircham, Fogarty, Lawther, Taylor, Grainger.

Monday, 11 March 1963
FA Cup third round replay
Middlesbrough 3
Blackburn Rovers 1
Attendance: 39,596

THE winter of 1962-63 had been a very bad one, with weeks and weeks of snow, ice and frost. It was not until 5 March, therefore, that Second Division 'Boro were finally able to play their FA Cup third-round tie away to First Division giants Blackburn Rovers.

The wait was worthwhile, for 'Boro pulled off one of the shock results of the round by forcing a 1-1 draw on a mudbath. Bryan Orritt netted for 'Boro, equalising an early goal by Blackburn centre-forward Fred Pickering.

Naturally the replay grabbed the imagination of the success-starved 'Boro fans, who paid receipts of £7,122 on a bitterly cold night at Ayresome Park.

The famous Ayresome roar was witnessed for the first time for some years as 'Boro attacked from the start. They were rewarded with the opening goal in the 23rd minute. Arthur Kaye took a corner and Ronnie Burbeck hit a first-time shot which hit Blackburn goalkeeper Fred Else and rolled along the line. Alan Peacock was on it in a flash to shoot home.

Eight minutes later it was 2-0. A great cross from Kaye had the Rovers defence at sixes and sevens and Peacock stabbed it home.

Shortly after the interval, Rovers silenced the home crowd for a while when Byrom reduced the arrears. However, 'Boro were not to be denied and the outcome was never in doubt from the 56th minute when Orritt was brought down by McGrath and Kaye blasted home a great free-kick.

Two-goal Peacock said: "The crowd was the best that I have ever played in front of – and that includes internationals and representative matches and Tees-Wear and Tees-Tyne derbies. The roar that went up from the terraces acted like a tonic to all the 'Boro players, myself included."

Cliff Mitchell said: "The return of the Ayresome roar must have brought a chill touch of fear to the hearts of even the bravest Blackburn players. The 'Boro players earned a fat crowd and win bonus. They were worth every last penny."

While Peacock and Kaye grabbed the goals, the man who was the greatest thorn in the side of Blackburn all night was 'Boro's 19-year-old Scottish inside-forward Ian Gibson.

Brian Douglas, Blackburn's England international, said: "Ian Gibson gave the finest inside-forward display I have seen this season. It was a fantastic performance and he must be a certainty for a Scottish cap."

Unfortunately Gibson spent his four years at Ayresome Park in a struggling side and, despite occasional spells of sheer brilliance, that Scottish cap never did come his way.

Middlesbrough: Emmerson; McNeil, Jones, Yeoman, Nurse, Horner, Kaye, Gibson, Peacock, Orritt, Burbeck.

Blackburn Rovers: Else; Bray, Newton, England, Woods, McGrath, Ferguson, Douglas, Pickering, Byrom, Harrison.

Tickets for 'Boro's fourth-round tie against Leeds United were sold out by noon the following day. However, 'Boro's FA Cup runs are invariably short ones and they lost 2-0 to their fellow Second Division opponents.

Tuesday, 16 May 1967
Middlesbrough 4
Oxford United 1
Attendance: 39,683

THE last really great League game at Ayresome Park, certainly as far as crowd noise and fervour was concerned, was the highly-charged clash with Oxford United which earned 'Boro promotion back to Division Two.

The atmosphere created by that seething crowd of more than 39,000 which packed into the stadium that night were never overtaken again and neither were the scenes of ecstasy and jubilation which the crushing victory generated on the terraces.

Only three days earlier a brace of goals from John Hickton had earned 'Boro a crucial 2-1 victory against Peterborough United in front of 32,503 fans at Ayresome. This win meant that Stan Anderson's enthusiastic side needed to beat midtable Oxford in their final match to be certain of promotion.

So, a mere 12 months after the club had rightly been severely criticised by fans and media alike for ending up in Division Three in the first place, Middlesbrough was awash with promotion mania.

Hundreds of fans had queued for stand tickets in pouring rain the previous morning. However, only 420 seats had been made available and these were snapped up very quickly. The rest of the 4,050 seats for the Centre Stands, North Terrace and Holgate Wings had been selling steadily over the previous two weeks.

The remaining 8,500 seats for the South Stand and the East End were available through the turnstiles on the night. It led to huge queues all around the stadium for several hours before the kick-off as supporters took no chances in the battle for admission.

The atmosphere was simply electric long before the kick-off and the mood was the same in the dressing-room. As soon as the game was under way it quickly became evident that 'Boro were not going to lose. In fact the crowd were chanting "Easy, Easy" long before terrace idol John O'Rourke headed 'Boro in front in the 29th minute.

After that, it was all too easy. O'Rourke headed another before the interval, Hickton scored ten minutes into the second half and O'Rourke completed his hat-trick ten minutes later. All the 'Boro goals came from headers.

Oxford reduced the arrears five minutes from time through Colin Harrington, but it was academic. The celebrations on the terraces were already in full swing and had been for a long time. In fact there were three celebratory pitch invasions during the game and at one time in the first half there was the fear that it might be abandoned.

However, there were no major problems until the final whistle when 50 feet of restraining wall collapsed by the players' entrance under the pressure of the swaying ground. It was a mere three feet high wall, but it fell to pieces when the crowd swayed forward as the 'Boro players threw their shirts into the crowd in a victory salute.

Children at the front were trampled and with 10,000 fans surging on to the pitch at the same time, there was a sudden emergency situation for the already overworked ambulance staff and 150 police and specials.

A potential disaster was averted by quick-witted secretary Harry Green, who raced to a microphone and bellowed the order "Stand still everyone": over the loudspeaker system.

His pleas were heeded, though many fans were injured in the incident. An ambulance shuttle service was set up to take the injured to Middlesbrough General Hospital.

Fourteen young fans needed treatment at the hospital, though only two were detained. They were 13-year-old Stephen Smith from the Woodmans Arms in Normanby and 15-year-old Ann Connor from Sefton Road in Thorntree.

However, even these unfortunate injuries failed to sour the evening for the vast majority of spectators.

Cliff Mitchell said in the *Evening Gazette*: "Middlesbrough marched majestically back to the Second Division on a wave of emotion and goals in a drama-charged match.

"Before the baying, chanting, fantastically partisan crowd of 39,683 – a good thousand more than we thought the ground would hold – 'Boro won 4-1."

Billy Horner recalled: "Our build-up was so relaxed. We knew that we were going to win it. We played golf the day before and spent the night before all together, at the Grand Hotel in Scarborough. When the time came for the kick-off we couldn't wait to get on with the job. We knew that we had to do the business. It was a great night."

Middlesbrough: Whigham; Butler, Jones, Masson, Rooks, Horner, Chadwick, Hickton, O'Rourke, McMordie, Downing.

Oxford United: Sherratt; Beavon, Lloyd, R.Atkinson, Kyle, Clarke, Harrington, Kerr, G.Atkinson, Hale, Shuker.

Stan Anderson was rewarded for his achievements in turning the club

around by signing a new two-year contract.

However, 'Boro fans had to pay through their pockets for the club's return to the Second Division. Almost immediately 'Boro announced new season ticket prices. The Centre Stand season ticket was increased to £9 10s from £7 7s, the Wing Stands from £6 to £7 and the North Terrace from £6 to £6 10s.

Match-day prices were increased to 10s for the Centre Stand, while in future it would cost 4s to stand in the Holgate End.

When 'Boro entertained Manchester United in the FA Cup sixth round in 1970 they were watched by 87-year-old season ticket holder William Harding, who could remember seeing Middlesbrough Ironopolis in action. William, from Albion Terrace, Saltburn, had been a fan of both Middlesbrough clubs since 1891.

The McIlmoyle Match
Saturday, 26 September 1970
Middlesbrough 6 Queen's Park Rangers 2
Attendance: 16,788

VERY few players have their names permanently attached to one particular game, but this six-goal drubbing of Queen's Park Rangers will forever be known as The McIlmoyle Match.

The 30-year-old Hughie McIlmoyle, who was deceptively agile in the air, was an enigma. At times the immensely talented Scot flattered to deceive – at other times he was an unstoppable match-winning centre-forward.

Such was the case in September 1970, as 'Boro battled to recover from a disappointing start to the season in a tough test against an attractive Rangers line-up. On the day, McIlmoyle was a revelation. He scored twice, had a hand in all the other 'Boro goals and single-handedly tortured the hapless Londoners.

Cliff Mitchell wrote: 'The magical Hugh McIlmoyle turned the smell of defeat into the sweet taste of success.

" 'Boro trailed 2-0 after only five minutes through goals from Rodney Marsh and Dave Clement. From then on Mighty Mac mesmerised the Rangers defence with his total command in the air and brilliant passing.

"He scored two himself and had a hand in all the others. He was taken off eight minutes from time but by then the damage was done. 'Boro ripped Rangers' defence wide open time and time again with a memorable display of powerful, lethal soccer that packed a real punch."

McIlmoyle, who was remarkably a shade under six feet yet gave the impression of being much taller because of his aerial ability, revealed that the secret of his success was a training stint the previous day.

He said: "Our coach, Jimmy Greenhalgh, took me on to the pitch and crossed at least 50 balls into the goalmouth. Some I headed for goal, but the others I directed towards imaginary teammates in the box. You've got to like that sort of training. I do and it is worthwhile."

It could have been a different story if McIlmoyle had not been playing, because Rangers took command from the kick-off with Clement putting the visitors ahead after two minutes and Rodney Marsh heading in an Ian Morgan cross three minutes later.

'Boro did not pull back a goal until the 23rd minute, when McIlmoyle got up high to meet a cross from left-back Gordon Jones and headed in. Five minutes later it was 2-2. Jones crossed again and this time McIlmoyle headed back into the goalmouth for John Hickton to head in.

With the crowd roaring them on, 'Boro began to pour forward and took the lead in 35 minutes. This time McIlmoyle headed down for Derrick Downing to score. Then one minute before the interval, 'Boro scored again when McIlmoyle was brought down in the area and Hickton scored from the spot.

The fun continued immediately after the restart. In 48 minutes Frank Spraggon passed out to the right, where McIlmoyle controlled the ball and left Hunt standing before flashing home a great right-foot shot.

'Boro continued to dominate, but Rangers goalkeeper Phil Parkes needed to pick the ball out of the net on only one further occasion. In 65 minutes McIlmoyle broke down the right and gave a great cross-field pass to Downing, who crossed back into the middle for Hickton to score at the second attempt.

Middlesbrough: Whigham; Maddren, Jones, G.Smith, Gates, Spraggon, Downing, McMordie, McIlmoyle (Mills), Hickton, Downing.

Queen's Park Rangers: Parkes; Hazell, Clement (Watson), Venables, Hunt, Sibley, Morgan, Francis, Saul, Marsh, Ferguson.

Tuesday, 5 January 1971
FA Cup third round replay
Middlesbrough 2 Manchester United 1
Attendance: 40,040

MANCHESTER United had a great side, full of internationals and world-renowned players, in the late 1960s and early 1970s. In 1971, the bulk of the United team which had won the European Cup three years earlier were still in their line-up. So they presented a fearsome test for all opponents.

As a result, nobody could overstate the terrific performance of Second Division 'Boro when they not only forced a goalless draw in the third round of the FA Cup on United's home territory at Old Trafford, but were also the better side on the day.

Even so, United were just as formidable away from home and the replay was one game that everybody on Teesside wanted to see. In fact 'Boro officials could have sold out Ayresome Park twice over.

There was a late boost for the ticketless section of Teesside because United returned 8,000 unsold tickets. 'Boro fans who had missed out first time around queued from 2am on the morning of the match to snap up the returned tickets.

The main reason why so few tickets were sold to Manchester United followers was because of the appalling weather. It had been intensely cold for some time and there was snow everywhere. In fact fans on both sides of the Pennines doubted whether the replay would take place.

There was one-and-three-quarter inches of snow on Ayresome Park on the morning, but most of it was cleared during the course of the day. However, there was still snow on all parts of the pitch when match referee Gordon Hill from Leicester made his inspection, but he deemed it to be fit for play.

The evening turned out to be bitterly cold, but it failed to weaken the enthusiasm of the huge crowd, or the determination of the 'Boro players.

'Boro attacked strongly from the start and almost brought the stands down when they took a seventh-minute lead. Left-back Gordon Jones crossed towards the far post and the United defence was left standing as Hugh McIlmoyle got up high to head a great goal.

'Boro made no attempt to sit back on their lead. Eric McMordie hit a post and John Hickton fired against the angle of the upright and the bar as 'Boro fought hard to increase their advantage.

United never looked relaxed in the extreme cold and it was no surprise when 'Boro increased their lead in the 72nd minute, thanks to a tremendous solo goal from Derrick Downing. McMordie played a brilliant pass out to the right and Downing cut in along the goal-line to score from the narrowest of angles.

Downing said: "I saw the goalkeeper moving out, expecting me to cut the ball back to Alan Moody. I toe-ended it the other way and it went in."

With 'Boro's twin spearhead of McIlmoyle and Hickton continuing to leave the United defence at panic stations, there was never any way back for the visitors. In fact the ecstatic 'Boro fans were chanting "Easy, Easy" and "Let's Have Another"

Not until the last couple of minutes did 'Boro ease off and George Best nipped in for an 89th minute consolation headed goal.

'Boro left the field to a standing ovation and there were no complaints from the United camp. Manager Sir Matt Busby admitted: "'Boro played well. We didn't play so well."

Middlesbrough: Whigham; A.Smith, Jones, Moody, Gates, Spraggon, Downing, McMordie, McIlmoyle, Hickton, Laidlaw.

Manchester United: Rimmer; Fitzpatrick, Dunne, Crerand, Edwards, Sadler, Morgan, Best, Charlton, Kidd(Gowling), Law.

All 'Boro Cup stories end on a sad note. They crashed 3-0 to another First Division side, Everton, at Goodison Park in the fourth round.

Saturday, 21 April 1974
Middlesbrough 8
Sheffield Wednesday 0
Attendance: 25,287

'BORO received the Second Division championship trophy and their individual medals from Football League chairman Len Shipman before the start of this one-sided romp.

Wednesday never had a chance from the kick-off, as rampant 'Boro proceeded to tear them to shreds. The game began with a carnival atmosphere, which continued all the way through. The shirt-sleeved crowd were treated to slaughter in the sunshine.

Manager Jack Charlton said: "The lads did us proud and showed the sort of spirit we want them to show. The one thing they must learn to be is ruthless and they went a long way towards that against Wednesday. But I did feel sorry for Wednesday."

Charlton's talented team was just moving into top gear at that time, having matured tremendously during the all-conquering season in which they stormed away to the title. Defensively they were very strong and never looked like losing once in front.

In fact this game against Wednesday got better and better from the moment that John Hickton headed in an Alan Foggon cross after only five minutes.

Graeme Souness, one of 'Boro's all-time greats who scored a hat-trick in the 8-0 drubbing of Sheffield Wednesday.

David Mills grabbed a second goal nine minutes later when lobbing goalkeeper Peter Springett, while Bobby Murdoch added the third ten minutes before the interval, Foggon having created all three.

In the second half Graeme Souness, the linchpin of the side, scored what turned out to be his one and only hat-trick for 'Boro. It was a fitting reward for his performance on the day because he was virtually unstoppable, winning everything, threading though perfect passes and beating defenders at will. Foggon, another who had a great game, scored the other two.

Afterwards the crowd would not leave the stadium until the players had re-emerged from the dressing-room with the championship trophy, to receive warm applause.

David Mills recalled: "We knew that we were capable of giving somebody a right going over and it was just unfortunate for Wednesday that it was them.

"It was one of those days when everybody clicked and the longer the game went on the more we enjoyed ourselves. Souness had a great game. Wednesday couldn't handle him. But everybody played well. We had a good side and when we played like that, nobody in the Second Division could live with us."

Middlesbrough: Platt; Craggs, Spraggon, Souness, Boam, Maddren, Murdoch(H.Charlton), Mills, Hickton, Foggon, Armstrong.

Sheffield Wednesday: Springett; Rodrigues, Shaw, Mullen, Holsgrove, Coyle(Eustace), Potts, Prudham, Joicey, Craig, Cameron.

Saturday, 25 January 1975
FA Cup fourth round
Middlesbrough 3
Sunderland 1
Attendance: 39,400

ALL derby victories against Sunderland are memorable, particularly in the FA Cup, but this tie was notable because it was one of the handful of dwindling occasions that Ayresome Park would be filled to full capacity before safety regulations drastically reduced the crowd limit in the early 1980s.

Naturally, as ever, 'Boro could have sold many more tickets for this mouth-watering Cup clash. All the tickets, except for a few in the Boys End, had been snapped up by the previous Monday. Sunderland fans had also sold their 10,000 allocation.

The Rokermen's FA Cup Final victory of 1973 was still strong in everybody's minds and so it was vital to the Teesside faithful that 'Boro made no mistakes against their Second Division opponents.

However, at first things threatened to go wrong. Sunderland had a gale behind them in the first half and took an 11th minute lead when Pop Robson fired them ahead.

The Rokermen continued to run the game, but Bobby Murdoch popped up with a 39th minute equaliser which

The goal which won 'Boro a trophy. Fulham defender Les Strong, running back, chests a flying header from David Armstrong into his own net to give 'Boro the lead in the first leg of the Anglo-Scottish Cup Final. It turned out to be the winning goal, because the teams drew the second leg 0-0 at Craven Cottage.

proved to be crucial. It gave 'Boro the platform to control the second half and they went ahead in the 55th minute when John Hickton scored from the penalty-spot after David Mills was tripped by Sunderland goalkeeper Trevor Swinburne.

Fifteen minutes from time Mills was upended again and Hickton scored his second penalty to give 'Boro a thoroughly merited victory.

Manager Jack Charlton said: "I was delighted with the way the lads buckled down in the conditions. They showed character because the early goal might have flattened some sides in a derby."

Middlesbrough: Platt; Craggs, Spraggon, Souness, Boam, Maddren, Murdoch, Hickton, Mills, Foggon, Armstrong.

Sunderland: Swinburne; Malone, Bolton, Moncur, Watson, Ashurst, Kerr, Hughes, Halom, Robson, Towers.

'Boro, who had beaten non-League Wycombe Wanderers after a replay in the third round, needed another replay to beat Third Division Peterborough United in the fifth round. They were drawn away to Birmingham City in the quarter-final, but lost disappointingly by the only goal of the game.

'Boro might have become the team of the 1960s and 1970s – instead of Liverpool – if they had made the right decision in June 1952. Their three-man short list to replace manager David Jack included a certain Bill Shankly, who was then in charge of Grimsby Town. Shankly seemed to be top of the list, because the 'Boro directors contacted the chairmen of both Carlisle United and Grimsby for information about Shankly's character. The information clearly was not good. Not only did 'Boro not appoint Shankly, they also ignored the other two men on the original list, F.Hill and L.Paige. Shankly eventually went on to manage Liverpool in 1959, and the rest is history. 'Boro finally took the plunge with Walter Rowley, who was offered the job for £1,250 a year on condition that 'he agreed to coach Harold Shepherdson as future manager'. That didn't happen either, although Harold became a very good caretaker manager on several occasions.

Tuesday, 13 January 1976
League Cup semi-final first leg
Middlesbrough 1 Manchester City 0
Attendance: 34,579

'BORO failed to sell out Ayresome Park for their very first appearance in a major Cup semi-final, which was an indication of changing times and the fact that the League Cup was still regarded as very much secondary to its big brother the FA Cup.

However, hopes remained very high that 'Boro could reach Wembley for the first time. One fan, Tommy Coulton from Teesville, was so confident that he had already provisionally booked a coach and a London hotel for the Final. Forty-five hopefuls had enrolled for the trip.

'Boro warmed up for the first leg with a rehearsal against Manchester City in the First Division. A goal from David Armstrong gave 'Boro a 1-0 win, also at Ayresome Park. It was an improved performance following 'Boro's shock FA Cup defeat at the hands of Third Division Bury. Naturally 'Boro lacked nothing in commitment in the battle to forge a healthy first-leg lead against Manchester City though they struggled to create openings in a competitive first half.

However, they did suffer some bad luck just after the interval when City defender Colin Barrett knocked a header from John Hickton on to the underside of his own crossbar. Terry Cooper's follow-up shot looked to be over the line when goalkeeper big Joe Corrigan pounced on it, but play was waved on.

David Mills said afterwards: "It was definitely a goal. The ball had to be over the line."

'Boro finally started to create chances in the second half, urged on by terrific vocal support. They broke through in the 66th minute following great work by central defender Stuart Boam.

He broke out of defence and passed to Cooper, who sent a high cross into the middle. Boam continued running forward and won possession again, before chipping the ball over for Hickton to hammer it into the net.

'Boro then threw everybody forward in the search for the second goal which would have given them breathing space, but it would not come.

Middlesbrough: Platt; Craggs, Bailey, Souness, Boam, Maddren, Murdoch, Mills, Hickton(Foggon), Cooper, Armstrong.

Manchester City: Corrigan; Barrett, Donachie, Doyle, Booth, Oakes, Barnes, Power, Royle, Hartford, Tueart.

Six thousand Teessiders made their way to Maine Road for the second leg but it turned out to be a night of disaster. The 'Boro coach was held up in traffic on its way to the stadium and the players were forced to change on the coach.

They got off the coach straight on to the pitch and were two goals down before they could settle. City went on to win 4-0 with goals from Ged Keegan, Alan Oakes, Peter Barnes and Joe Royle.

It ended hopes of an all-North-East Wembley Final against Newcastle United.

Willie Maddren recalls: "I was annoyed with the preparation. You could sense something was going to go wrong. We left the Pennine Hotel in Huddersfield and got stuck in horrendous traffic.

"I liked to be at a ground early, but there was no chance of that. We were totally disorganised. We had one pair of pliers between us to change boot studs and when we ran out, our minds were still in the dressing-room.

"On the morning I felt that we could have held them, especially as Dennis Tueart was out injured. But our plans were blown to smithereens within minutes. I was as sick as a parrot, especially as I felt that one or two players bottled it on the night. I had desperately wanted to get to Wembley."

Saturday, 26 February 1977
FA Cup fifth round
Middlesbrough 4 Arsenal 1
Attendance: 35,208

THIS great FA Cup win was marred by violence and thuggery – which was a tragedy because 'Boro were producing some of their best post-war football in the build-up to this match.

Jack Charlton had the lads absolutely buzzing and they were unbeaten in any competition from November until mid-February.

Ironically 'Boro had come unstuck the week before entertaining the Gunners, when they were stuffed 4-0 at Sunderland. It was the Rokermen's youthful exuberance which brought about 'Boro's downfall, but then Big Jack's men already had one eye on the Cup-tie.

The showdown with Arsenal was a big game both on Teesside and in London. The Gunners fans purchased 3,250 tickets and 2,500 of those supporters travelled to the North-East in four special trains. A 119-seater aeroplane was also chartered from Luton Airport. It was no surprise, then, that the tie brought 'Boro record gate receipts of £29,652.

Unfortunately the tie was marred by violence which started early on the morning and carried on during the match. Gangs were fighting before the kick-off and the players emerged to see a line of police in front of the South Stand in a bid to establish order.

However, 42 fans had to be arrested on charges ranging from possessing offensive weapons, obstructing the police, being drunk and disorderly and causing a breach of the peace. Twenty-five of those arrested were from London. A further 45 fans were ejected.

The worst problem came from dart-throwing. One young Arsenal supporter was taken to North Riding Infirmary with a dart lodged in the corner of his eye. In fact the fighting continued among injured fans at Middlesbrough General Hospital and police reinforcements had

David Mills, pictured here in action against Queen's Park Rangers, scored a magnificent FA Cup hat-trick against Arsenal in 1977.

to be sent to the emergency department to quell the trouble.

Altogether, 26 fans were treated at the hospital and a further 46 at the ground. Superintendent George Potter of the St John Ambulance Brigade said: "Bottles are stones were flying all over the place."

It was tragic that all this fighting took place, because the football served up was exhilarating. In the end the scoreline indicated an emphatic 'Boro win but, while Charlton's men fully deserved their success, Arsenal had played a full part in a spellbinding game and created plenty of chances of their own.

The major difference between the sides was the quickness and brilliance of David Mills, who grabbed a hat-trick. The transfer-listed striker put 'Boro in control when opening his account after only four minutes and 18 seconds.

Ten minutes later Mills added another after Liam Brady had stopped a shot from Phil Boersma on the line. The goal sparked a chant of "What a load of rubbish" by the 'Boro fans, who were quick to goad Arsenal's star-studded side.

However, the match was thrown wide open for a spell when Malcolm Macdonald scored with a header after 28 minutes. 'Boro did not regain control until after the restart when David Armstrong netted in the 51st minute.

The tempo never slackened in the second half with 'Boro making certain in injury-time when Mills completed his hat-trick after goalkeeper Jimmy Rimmer had parried a shot from Terry Cooper.

Charlton said: "We are not pretty, but we are effective when we do the job right. The game is all about how you play to your strengths. Arsenal showed that they are better at keeping possession and passing the ball around – but in the end they had to thump it into the box to try to get something.

"The game is not just about possession. There's more to it than that. All Arsenal's possession came to nothing. It was a 50-50 game but we were more effective the way we played. So we won."

On Mills, Charlton added: "He had four chances and he stuck three of them in the back of the net. That's not bad."

Middlesbrough: Cuff; Craggs, Cooper, Souness(McAndrew), Boam, Maddren, Boersma, Mills, Brine, Wood, D.Armstrong.

Arsenal: Rimmer; Rice, Nelson, Ross, O'Leary(Matthews), Simpson, Brady, Hudson, Macdonald, Stapleton, G.Armstrong.

'Boro's Cup dreams came to an end in the next round. They were drawn away to reigning champions Liverpool and lost 2-0 in front of almost 56,000 fans.

Wednesday, 3 February 1988
FA Cup fourth round replay
Middlesbrough 2 Everton 2
Attendance: 25,235

'BORO made a huge mistake in not making this big FA Cup replay all-ticket. As a result, thousands of fans were locked outside the gates and there were some ugly scenes as the disappointed supporters vented their frustrations on police and officials.

The gates were locked 50 minutes before the kick-off, which naturally came as an unexpected shock to the many regular fans who had stopped for their usual pie and pint on the way to Ayresome Park.

In the event several people were arrested and a policeman was taken to

Bosco Jankovic was a popular 'Boro striker in John Neal's reign. The Yugoslav was top scorer in 1980-81 with 13 goals.

Peter Shilton shows his world class goalkeeping in blocking this close-range effort from Micky Burns. This late season match against Nottingham Forest in 1980 ended goalless.

Middlesbrough General Hospital after being attacked outside the stadium. It was difficult for the ambulance to get through to him in the first place because the streets were packed solid with thousands of locked out fans.

The reason for the wave of excitement was that Bruce Rioch's talented young side had just earned a battling 1-1 draw at Goodison Park against one of the top sides in the country. There was no fluke about the scoreline and everybody had good reason to believe that 'Boro were capable of finishing the job.

In the event the replay was an absolute classic. The *Evening Gazette* reported: "The thousands locked outside the gates of Ayresome Park were robbed of the chance to witness one of the truly great 'Boro games. "The game had everything, with agony followed by ecstasy and then agony again as 'Boro had the most memorable of victories snatched away from them in extra-time injury time."

'Boro forced the pace in the first hour but it was Everton who took the lead against the run of play in 66 minutes when Dave Watson headed in a cross from Alan Harper.

With time gradually running out, 'Boro's efforts to retrieve the tie seemed in vain. However, skipper Tony Mowbray brought 'Boro back from the brink when storming in to head home a corner from Gary Hamilton in the second minute of injury-time.

The crowd, very few of whom could drag themselves away before the end of the 90 minutes, erupted. And they were dancing on the terraces again in the ninth minute of extra-time when 'Boro took the lead.

Alan Kernaghan, who had come on as a substitute for the concussed Gary Pallister, reacted superbly on the ground to hook home a rebound from his own diving header.

Now it was 'Boro's turn to try to hang on. It seemed they would do so as the tie moved into injury-time again – but then disaster struck. Adrian Heath's flick was met by Trevor Steven and took an unfortunate deflection off Colin Cooper to sneak inside the left-hand post. Thirty seconds later came the final whistle and with it tears for the 'Boro players as they left the field. Rioch revealed the next day that he had been inundated with calls from family and friends to say what a great game it had been.

He said: "Many of them said they couldn't sleep afterwards, which is a tribute to the amount of excitement and adrenalin which flowed.

"I thought it was a game which had everything. It had competitive, good football, chances at both ends and so many highs and lows. We had chances in regular time to win it but it needed our skipper to pop up at the death with an equaliser.

"In extra-time we were absolutely excellent and it was a pity to concede such a late equaliser. But at the end of the day we can look back and say that we have played our part in a great game – and we are still in the Cup."

Middlesbrough: Pears; Glover, Cooper, Mowbray, Parkinson, Pallister (Kernaghan), Slaven, Ripley, Hamilton, Kerr, Laws.

Everton: Southall; Stevens, Pointon, Van den Hauwe, Watson, Reid, Steven, Heath, Sharp, Snodin, Harper(Clarke).

Gary Pallister was detained in hospital overnight after suffering double vision from a fifth minute knock on the head picked up in a collision with Everton goalkeeper Neville Southall.

Pallister returned for the second replay six days later. 'Boro lost the toss for venue and 5,000 accompanied them back to Goodison Park. On a dreadful cold and windy night, 'Boro went down 2-1 with Tony Mowbray unfortunate to score an own-goal six minutes from time to give Everton a fifth-round derby tie at home to Liverpool.

Tuesday, 6 February 1990
Zenith Data Systems Cup Northern Final second leg
Middlesbrough 2 Aston Villa 1
Attendance: 20,806

WEMBLEY hysteria was witnessed only once at Ayresome Park – and it came on an emotional night in early February when 'Boro finally made it through to the hallowed Twin Towers.

In many respects, qualification for Wembley via the Zenith Data Systems competition was no great achievement. After all, it was known locally as the Mickey Mouse Cup.

However, on this eventful night in 1990, nobody would have minded if it was the Girl Guides Cup. 'Boro had finally made it to Wembley – and they did it in style in front of more than 20,000 deliriously happy fans.

'Boro had moved to within 90 minutes of Wembley thanks to a 2-1 win in the first leg at Villa Park in a torrential downpour. The achievement was no mean feat because Villa were challenging for the championship, whereas 'Boro were struggling to keep their heads above water in the Second Division.

The full extent of the task facing 'Boro when they went into the first leg was that the bookies rated them only 9-1 against to win on the night. But they won their fans a few bob thanks largely to Mark Brennan, who scored a late winner at a time when the pitch more resembled a boating lake than a football pitch.

Unfortunately Brennan was suspended for the second leg, but midfielder Trevor Putney returned to the side. It proved to be a nightmare return because Putney was stretchered off after only a few minutes after breaking his leg from a rash tackle by Gordon Cowans.

Young Owen McGee came on as replacement as the 'Boro side went on to battle hard, without looking like producing the verve and confidence from their first-leg victory.

In any case, a draw was enough to send 'Boro to Wembley and they looked like getting one – thanks to a couple of crucial saves from agile goalkeeper Steve Pears.

However, just when it was starting to look as though 'Boro were going to go through, Villa substitute Stuart Gray fired the visitors ahead from a corner with only 13 minutes of normal time

Moment of agony for 'Boro as Stuart Gray forces home the goal at Ayresome Park which levelled the aggregate scores for Aston Villa in the Zenith Data Systems Cup semi-final.

Delight for 'Boro as Bernie Slaven slams home the crucial goal in extra-time which put the home side back in front on aggregate against Aston Villa in the Zenith Data Systems Cup semi-final.

remaining. It was enough to send the match into extra-time. If there were no more goals in the extra half-hour then the tie would have to be decided by penalties. It was the finish that nobody wanted.

In the event, 'Boro's best was yet to come. And it was crowd favourite and goal-grabber extraordinaire Bernie Slaven who sent 'Boro on the road to Wembley with a marvellous goal 12 minutes into the first period of extra-time. Slaven swivelled on a sixpence before ramming the ball high into the net after Peter Davenport's shot had been blocked.

It looked all over for the Villa and it was, four minutes into the second period. Paul Kerr struck a low drive through a sea of legs which beat everybody and ended up in the back of the net. There was no way back for Villa and everybody knew it.

The celebrations began immediately and there were scenes of joy among the supporters which had not been equalled in the previous 20 years. Not surprisingly, the rejoicing continued long into the night.

Manager Bruce Rioch said: "We witnessed a terrific team performance out there and we finished the stronger side. I'm proud of every single player and I'm delighted for everybody connected with the club.

"You can't underestimate the value of Bernie's goal. It was world class. You had to be out there in the heat of the moment, with the ball dropping at your feet in a crowded goalmouth, to appreciate the brilliance of the finish."

Skipper Tony Mowbray said: "The lads were absolutely fantastic. It's a great day. When Villa scored I thought it was a case of here we go again. But Bernie's goal turned it around. His finish was a flash of brilliance."

Slaven said: "We had to work very hard for it. We were up against it when Villa scored but we kept plugging away and we got the win."

Kerr, who grabbed the vital clinching goal against his former club, said: "The ball came over Kent Nielsen's head. I caught it well but it had to go a long way before ending in the net. It was unbelievable."

Middlesbrough: Pears; Parkinson, Mowbray, Coleman, Mohan, Putney (McGee), Proctor, Kerr, Slaven, Ripley (Davenport), Kernaghan.

Aston Villa: Spink; Price, Mountfield, Nielsen, McGrath, Gage, Ormondroyd(Gray), Platt, Cowans, Daley, Olney.

Wednesday, 4 March 1992
Rumbelows Cup semi-final first leg
Middlesbrough 0
Manchester United 0
Attendance: 25,572

MANAGER Lennie Lawrence reckoned that nothing would be decided in the first leg and he was perfectly right – with battle-hardened 'Boro from the Second Division proving a match for their erstwhile opponents from the top flight.

'Boro had already played four times at Ayresome Park and six times altogether in a hard-fought Cup campaign in which they had squeezed through all the previous rounds by no more than one goal.

They reached the semi-final by overcoming battling Third Division side Peterborough United after a replay, a flash of brilliance from Stuart Ripley gave 'Boro victory in the match at Ayresome Park.

Naturally the prospect of seeing 'Boro test themselves against the re-emerging Manchester United – and the knowledge that Wembley was on the horizon – sparked great interest on Teesside. 'Boro sold all their tickets quickly, while United sold all but a few of their 6,000 allocation and the eventual crowd was just short of the 26,000 maximum.

It turned out to be a tense game, rather than a thriller. The tie was highly competitive, but there were few clear-cut

Battle royal... Bernie Slaven gets to the ball first, shadowed by Paul Ince and Bryan Robson, in the Rumbelows Cup semi-final first leg at Ayresome Park in 1992.

More action from the Rumbelows Cup semi-final first leg against Manchester United as Bernie Slaven evades a challenge from Bryan Robson, while Stuart Ripley and Jamie Pollock look on.

chances at either end. Steve Pears made a great reflex save to deny Paul Ince in the second half, while Gary Parkinson brought two fine saves from Danish international goalkeeper Peter Schmeichel.

Lawrence said: "We were patient and gave nothing away. But we also had a couple of chances in the first half from Paul Wilkinson headers.

"That's all you are ever going to get against United, a couple of chances and a couple of half chances. We didn't put one away, but then we are still very much in it. Nobody could write us off after that."

Of Pears, Lawrence added: "Steve was marvellous. We've come to expect that sort of thing from him. But Schmeichel was superb as well."

Wilkinson said: "It was a close game but I thought we just shaded it in the first half."

Middlesbrough: Pears; Parkinson, Phillips, Kernaghan, Mohan, Mustoe, (Proctor), Slaven, Pollock, Wilkinson, Hendrie, Ripley.
Manchester United: Schmeichel; Parker, Irwin, Donaghy(Phelan), Webb, Pallister, Robson, Ince(Sharpe), McClair, Hughes, Giggs.

The thrills and spills of the semi-final were reserved for the second leg at Old Trafford, where the action was fast and furious and there was a lot of goalmouth activity.

'Boro could not have played better, but were pipped 2-1 and it was United who went to Wembley. Bernie Slaven grabbed the 'Boro goal and but for a remarkable save by Schmeichel from a Willie Falconer header, it could have been 'Boro heading for the Twin Towers.

Goal ace Micky Fenton is in the thick of the action in this FA Cup third round tie against Bolton Wanderers in January, 1939. After two goalless draws, Fenton grabbed the winner in the second replay.

'Boro's record win in the FA Cup at Ayresome Park was 9-3 against Goole Town on 9 January 1915. Jackie Carr, George Elliott and Walter Tinsley all scored hat-tricks.

The FA Cup Jinx

IF MIDDLESBROUGH fans ever need confirmation that Ayresome Park was forever jinxed they should look no further than the club's FA Cup performance.

Five times 'Boro were at home in FA Cup quarter-finals and quarter-final replays and five times they failed to reach the semi-final.

On four of those occasions 'Boro were drawn out of the hat first and thus had first bite at the cherry. It's uncanny how something always seemed to go wrong in the big Cup-ties at Ayresome Park when 'Boro started to get a sniff of Wembley.

It has been proved many times in the past that the effects of big Cup defeats can have far-reaching effects.

The last occasion when 'Boro reached the sixth round at Ayresome Park was in 1981 when, as usual, they were comfortably expected to win. They were drawn at home to Wolverhampton Wanderers, who were struggling to avoid relegation from the First Division. 'Boro, on the other hand, were in a fairly strong position higher up in the League.

However 'Boro were held to a 1-1 draw at Ayresome Park and then lost the replay 3-1 at Molineux. It was a shattering blow for the club for both the players and the supporters.

In fact the team failed to recover from that defeat and it is regarded by many people as the catalyst when led to 'Boro going into liquidation five years later.

In virtually every season following a sixth-round defeat, 'Boro's Football League form has fallen away dramatically. After losing a sixth-round replay to Burnley at Turf Moor in 1947, 'Boro won only one of their 13 remaining League games. In 1904, after going down 3-1 in a quarter-final replay at home to Manchester City, 'Boro won one out of eight in the League.

However, none of the Cup reverses have been as painful as the Wolves defeat. Within a few weeks of the defeat, a chain of events started which was to lead to the eventual break-up of both the team and the club.

Yet 'Boro could hardly have approached the tie with more optimism. They had opened their Cup campaign that season with a scintillating 5-0 win away to Second Division Swansea City and then overcame a good West Bromwich Albion side in a tight game at Ayresome Park thanks to a goal from left-back Ian Bailey.

Cup fever was rising when 'Boro were paired at home to Third Division side Barnsley in the fifth round. The Yorkshiremen were going well in their own Division, but it was anticipated that they would not have enough strength to resist 'Boro.

Micky Fenton scores with a header as 'Boro beat Queen's Park Rangers by 3-1 in an FA Cup third-round replay at Ayresome Park in January 1946. 'Boro reached the sixth round that year, before losing in controversial circumstances to Burnley.

So it proved. A huge crowd of 37,557 packed into Ayresome Park to see goals from Mark Proctor and Bosco Jankovic record a 2-1 victory. It was closer than it should have been because 'Boro seemed to suffer from Cup nerves in the second half. But they were good value for the victory in the end.

Now only Wolves stood between 'Boro and a first-ever appearance in the semi-finals. It looked as though their time had finally come. Earlier in the season John Neal's men had comfortably beaten the Midlands club by 3-0 in a League game at Ayresome.

Everybody tipped a 'Boro win. However there was a chilling forecast from Bertie Mee, Watford's general manager, in a special article in the *Sports Gazette*. He said: "Wolves have no rhythm and no consistency, but beware Andy Gray."

They proved to be prophetic words indeed, even though Mee did tip 'Boro to win the tie. He said: "Boro should win because they are the much better balanced side."

Before the match, there was trouble between rival supporters in the town. A huge fight broke out in The Trooper in Waterloo Road and staff said that "Broken glass was flying like snow". Many fans tried to escape from the fracas through the pub's narrow windows.

There was also trouble in Clive Road. Thomas Solan, 21, from Moortown Road in Middlesbrough, suffered a nasty gash on his head and was taken to hospital.

Inside, the *Match of the Day* TV cameras were present to record the event. The Wolves party was surprisingly led by manager John Barnwell, who had not been expected to attend after falling and suffering concussion after hitting his head on a building brick the previous day. Another surprise was that the crowd of 36,382 was lower than for the fifth round against Barnsley.

Naturally the atmosphere inside the stadium was one of great excitement and anticipation, with 'Boro's supporters in tip-top shape vocally and comfortably outshouting the few thousand visiting fans from Wolves.

However the home fans were thrown into silence in the eighth minute when Mee's warning came true. Mel Eves sent over a good cross and Gray, just back from injury, headed home to put the underdogs ahead.

'Boro suffered another blow when influential midfielder David Armstrong limped off with a badly-gashed ankle. He was off the field for a full ten minutes, but returned to set up the 'Boro equaliser.

Armstrong exchanged passes with Northern Ireland international winger Terry Cochrane, who crashed the ball past Wolves goalkeeper Paul Bradshaw into the corner of the net.

The goal left 'Boro with more than an hour's play still remaining in which to grab the winning goal. However they looked out of sorts and rarely looked like breaking through again. The jinx which caused 'Boro to play within themselves in big games at Ayresome Park had struck again.

Middlesbrough: Platt, Nattrass, Bailey, Johnston, Ashcroft, McAndrew, Cochrane, Proctor, Hodgson, Jankovic(Shearer), Armstrong.

Wolves: Bradshaw, Palmer, Parkin, Clarke(Bell), McAlle, Berry, Hibbitt, Carr, Gray, Richards, Eves.

Afterwards, Neal admitted: "We didn't get the balance right at all. You can get away with three or four players struggling a bit, but when you have so many below par, you generally get beaten. I'm just grateful to have a second chance."

Goalscorer Cochrane looked forward with new belief to the replay. He said: "I don't think Wolves can play as well again.

No way through for Alan Ramage and Stuart Boam as Orient clear a corner in the FA Cup sixth-round tie in 1978.

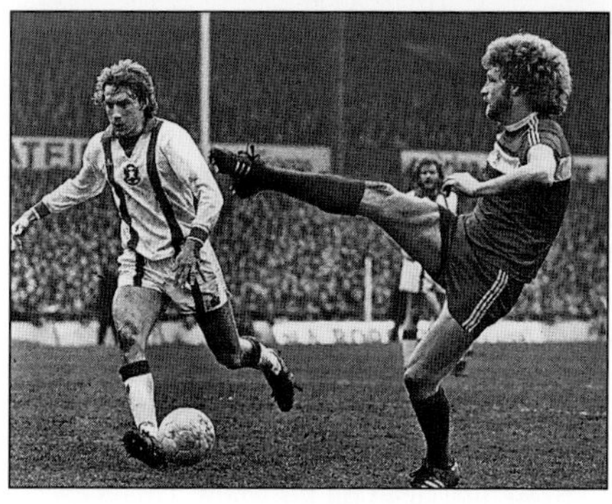

This is the one which got away. Billy Ashcroft misses the best chance of the FA Cup sixth-round tie at home to Orient, while defender Nigel Gray races back.

We had them worried when we ran at their defence. They were a bit afraid when we started to commit them."

'Boro's optimistic fans felt the same way. This tie was still winnable. So several thousand hopeful supporters made the long journey to Molineux for the replay and gave the team magnificent support. But it was not to be.

Wolves again took an early lead, this time through Mel Eves. It took 'Boro a long time to get into the game, but they broke through with the equaliser in 71 minutes when David Hodgson headed in a cross from Bosco Jankovic. For a while 'Boro looked the more likely winners, but they could not grab the winner before the end of normal time.

Extra-time followed, which took 'Boro nearer to the semi-finals than ever before. However they were up against it from the 97th minute when John Richards converted a Gray cross. Wolves were in no mood to lose it and Norman Bell wrapped up victory with the their third goal two minutes from the end.

Once again the dreams of thousands of 'Boro fans had been dashed and, for many, their spirit was broken. There were many fingers pointed in different directions and the club and the players were accused of not being ambitious enough. The defeat signalled the end of a successful 'Boro era, which had been started by Jack Charlton eight years earlier. It was also the prelude to a rapid slide into oblivion.

Under the circumstances it was quite remarkable that the scene of utter dejection following the defeat by Wolves was even worse than that which had been felt from 'Boro's last sixth round defeat only three years earlier.

On that occasion 'Boro suffered the humiliation of being knocked out of the quarter-final by lowly Second Division side Orient. It was a defeat which simply should not have happened. However it was par for the course. Once again 'Boro were drawn out of the hat first and once again they were beaten in a replay.

If 'Boro are to look for a likely reason for the unexpected defeat by Orient, it is that over confidence may have crept in – and once the players realised that they were in a hard battle, they were not in the right frame of mind to turn things around.

The 'Boro players were absolutely certain beforehand that they were going to win and they had the support of the bookmakers. Ladbrokes opened with 'Boro 9-4 on to win and later shortened the odds to 11-4 on. The draw was 3/1, with Orient 6-1, eventually lengthening to 7-1. Ladbrokes reported that they had taken £1,500 alone in bets backing Stan Cummins to score the first goal at odds of 7-2.

The 'Boro players enjoyed a sunny build-up in Jersey where David Armstrong, about to play his 242nd consecutive game for the club, said: "We've got to fancy ourselves. If we don't beat Orient at home we don't deserve to win."

Full-back John Craggs said: "We'll win. We'll go out there and do a good job and that is going to be too much for Orient."

Cummins, who had scored one of the goals in the 2-0 home win against Bolton Wanderers in the previous round, said: "We'll win 2-0. I haven't been wrong yet in my prediction of a match."

You couldn't blame the players for this super optimism. They were an experienced First Division team with lots of quality players and it was reasonable to assume that they wouldn't have any problems winning at the first attempt.

All the seats were sold out a week in advance, while the South Terrace standing area was sold out five days before the tie. However 25,000 standing £1 tickets were on sale on the day.

Orient were followed by 3,000 travelling fans. Most of them came by rail or by car, though the club also brought 18 coach loads. The attendance of 33,426 was slightly disappointing, even taking into account the fact that people thought it was a foregone conclusion. 'Boro had drawn bigger crowds in both the fourth and fifth rounds, when they had beaten Everton and Bolton at Ayresome.

The mistake everybody made was in writing off Orient. They may have come from the lower reaches of the Second Division, but they had proved their Cup-fighting ability by overcoming Blackburn Rovers and Chelsea in the two previous rounds.

The game turned out to be a nightmare for 'Boro. They rarely did anything right and never looked like penetrating Orient's defensive shell. Cummins headed against the bar and Billy Ashcroft had an effort kicked off the line, but they were rare chances.

Orient's 35-year-old goalkeeper John Jackson was hardly threatened until the closing minutes, when he made a miraculous save to keep out a pile driver from 'Boro substitute Craig Johnston. It finished goalless at the final whistle and it was Orient and their fans who were doing all the celebrating.

Middlesbrough: Platt, Craggs, Bailey, Mahoney, Boam, Ramage, Mills, Cummins, Ashcroft, McAndrew(Johnston), Armstrong.

Orient: Jackson, Fisher, Roffey, Grealish, Headley, Roeder, Godfrey, Gray, Mayo, Kitchen, Payne.

Just as they were to do against Wolves, 'Boro's players genuinely believed that they could win at Brisbane Road. They knew that they probably couldn't play as badly again and were expecting to create more chances in the replay because they believed that Orient would be forced to come out of defence.

David Mills admitted in the *Evening Gazette*: "We were terrible but we are still in the Cup. We are not worried about the replay because we can't play any worse and they can't play any better."

Alan Ramage added: "Our team spirit is still great and we'll win tomorrow. If Orient want to get a result they will have to come at us and that will mean openings for us."

'Boro completed their build-up for the Tuesday replay on a red shale pitch at Highbury, but it didn't do them much good. They were virtually dead and buried in the first 12 minutes at Brisbane Road as Orient went two up with goals from Peter Kitchen and Joe Mayo.

It took 'Boro until the 84th minute to reduce the arrears when David Armstrong netted. Three minutes later Armstrong almost set up the equaliser, but his fine cross was missed by Mills virtually on the goal-line. So it was Orient who went forward to meet Arsenal in the semi-final.

Mills recalled: "We had our chances in both matches. Billy Ashcroft missed a great chance at Ayresome Park and I missed one in the replay. It was another case of Middlesbrough failing to live up to the expectation in a big game."

The match against Orient brought to an end the most successful FA Cup decade in the 'Boro's Ayresome Park history because they reached the sixth round on no less than four occasions in the Seventies.

In 1977 they lost a tough tie at Liverpool 2-0 and in 1975 went down 1-0 at Birmingham City in a tie where winning had been well within their capabilities. At the start of the season 'Boro had won 3-0 at St Andrew's in a First Division game.

The best performance 'Boro ever gave in the sixth round came at the start of the decade against Manchester United in 1970. At the time 'Boro were pushing for promotion near the top of the Second Division, while United were First Division giants who were the first English club to win the European Cup when crushing Benfica 4-1 at Wembley in 1968.

United's star players like Pat Crerand, Bobby Charlton and the irrepressible George Best were household names everywhere.

'Boro had worked very hard to qualify for a home plum against United. They had beaten West Ham United, York City and Carlisle United at the first time of asking and were brimming with confidence.

'Boro's reward for their Cup run, a tie against the best club side in Britain, sparked a Cup fever on Teesside the likes of which had not been witnessed for more than 20 years.

Secretary Harry Green announced that it would be a 40,000 all-ticket match. Prices were increased to the following: ground 6s; boys 3s; South Terrace 8s; East end and North Terrace seats 10s; wing stands 15s; centre stands £1.

Not that the high prices would deter any fans from scrambling for a ticket. Writing in the *Evening Gazette*, Cliff Mitchell described the game as "Ayresome's Match of the Century" and nobody was going to argue with that statement.

The tickets went on sale on the Monday afternoon before the match and sold out in three hours. The fans included Edgar Burns, a 'Boro supporter for 50 years, who travelled all the way from Leeds in an invalid carriage to buy his ticket. The tickets realised all-time record receipts of £15,755.

In the event, thousands were turned away without tickets. Even some of those who were near the front of the queue were unlucky. Jane Tibbett, 22, a telephonist from Harrogate and schoolboy Peter Waller from Clements Rise in Norton collapsed in the queue. They were allowed home after treatment at Middlesbrough General Hospital.

There was snow on the pitch on the day of the match, but it didn't bother 'Boro. They took the game to their more illustrious opponents and forced the pace throughout. However 'Boro had to do it the hard way after conceding an unlucky goal after 11 minutes when a shot from Brian Kidd was diverted into the net off Carlo Sartori.

However 'Boro levelled in 35 minutes with a great goal from John Hickton, who powered his way down the left before hammering an unstoppable shot past United goalkeeper Alex Stepney. 'Boro continued to dominate the game but couldn't grab the winning goal they deserved.

'Boro went very close on two occasions to settling the issue. United left-back Tony Dunne made two goal-line clearances to keep out a header from Bill Gates and a shot from Hickton. United eventually held on for a replay, but had been given the fright of their lives.

Middlesbrough: Whigham, A.Smith, Jones, G.Smith, Gates, Spraggon, Downing, McMordie, Hickton, Laidlaw, McIlmoyle.

Manchester United: Stepney, Edwards, Dunne, Crerand, Ure, Sadler, Morgan, Sartori, Charlton, Kidd, Best.

There was justification in assuming that Second Division 'Boro might struggle in the red-hot atmosphere at Old Trafford. In fact they were far from overawed on the night. Urged on by a vociferous following of 15,000 travelling fans, 'Boro again took the game to United and were the better side for long spells.

Charlton settled the home side by giving them a 26th minute lead, but 'Boro refused to lie down and eventually forced a 74th-minute equaliser through John Hickton.

However, before 'Boro could lay the foundations for a renewed assault, they once again fell behind when Willie Morgan scored from the penalty-spot. That's how the scoreline remained and another sixth-round battle had ended in defeat.

However 'Boro had covered themselves in glory. If it had been 'Boro and not United, who were going on to meet Leeds United in the semi-final, then nobody could have argued. Pat Crerand told Willie Whigham: "You outplayed us twice and we are still in the Cup."

'Boro's other post-war quarter-final came in 1947, when they were drawn at home to Second Division Burnley.

It was not as easy as it looked, because several sides were better than their League situations suggested after the war. Personnel changed dramatically at many clubs during the seven-year absence of League football and Burnley were one of those clubs whose players were much better than Second Division status. In fact they not only went on to win promotion at the end of that season, but finished third in the First Division the following year.

Even so, with home advantage, 'Boro were hot favourites to end their Cup bogey and finally reach the semi-final. They had a very good side themselves, with internationals like Dave Cumming, George Hardwick, Wilf Mannion and Micky Fenton.

The tie attracted a huge crowd of 53,025, which was a ground record at the time and remains an FA Cup record for Ayresome Park. When the gates were closed at 2.30pm, there

Happy chimes for Stephen Bell as he puts 'Boro ahead against Bishop's Stortford in the FA Cup third-round tie in 1983. Bell scored the other in 'Boro's 2-2 draw.

Dutch courage from Heine Otto as he flicks the ball past Pat Jennings to give 'Boro a deserved late equaliser in the FA Cup fifth-round tie against Arsenal in 1983. The Gunners edged home in the replay by 3-2.

was an estimated 5,000 fans still outside the ground, many of them from Burnley.

'Boro enjoyed the best of the first half and when Geoff Walker put them ahead amid tumultuous noise just before the interval, the home side had the platform they needed to go on and win it.

The noise was even greater in the second half when Fenton scored from a free-kick and the referee pointed to the centre-circle. However the referee's attention was diverted by the Burnley players to a linesman, who was standing with his flag raised. The referee went over to consult him and ruled out Fenton's goal. The linesman had spotted Johnny Spuhler standing fractionally offside on the other side of the pitch when Fenton crashed home the free-kick. Spuhler was not interfering with play and the 'Boro players protested strongly – but the referee awarded a free-kick to Burnley.

'Boro were still capable of winning the tie, but it's hard when you have to contend with an FA Cup jinx as well as the referee and 'Boro were left with a replay when Billy Morris grabbed the equaliser for the visitors.

'Boro's England captain George Hardwick said: "Twenty minutes from time we were 1-0 up and murdering Burnley. We won a free-kick 25 yards out and in front of goal. The Burnley defensive wall had left a tiny gap and Micky Fenton blasted through it and into the net.

"The stadium erupted as the referee pointed to the centre

line. Two-nil up and only 17 minutes from an historic occasion. But a lone figure on the right touch-line standing erect with his flag raised high silenced the celebrations.

"At first, not even the Burnley players had noticed that linesman, but he stood firm and eventually they brought it to the attention of the referee, who went to have words with him. The linesman had given Johnny Spuhler offside standing only eight to ten yards in from the touch-line.

"How on earth he could have judged Johnny to have interfered with the play, standing way out there, I will never know. But the goal was disallowed." He added: "Before we had even recovered our composure the free-kick was taken and Burnley came to our end and scored the equaliser, about the only time they had been in our half in the second period.

"'Boro's luck ran out again with that linesman's diabolical decision. But we didn't know that there and then because the team was confident we could win the replay at Turf Moor."

Middlesbrough: Cumming, R.Robinson, Hardwick, Bell, N.Robinson, Gordon, Spuhler, Mannion, Fenton, Dews, Walker.

Burnley: Strong, Woodruff, Mather, Attewell, Brown, Bray, Chew, Morris, Harrison, Potts, Kippax.

'Boro's fans also believed that the team was capable of winning the replay. Hardwick said: "Half of Teesside followed us to Turf Moor on the Wednesday."

The longest round in FA Cup history was concluded on Monday, 11 March 1963, when 'Boro beat Blackburn Rovers 3-1 in a third-round replay at Ayresome Park. Due to the big freeze that year, the replay took place two days after the arranged date for the sixth round. The original tie at Ewood Park was postponed no less than ten times from 6 January to 5 March.

It was a tricky drive over the Pennines because of the icy conditions and the supporters arrived to find that Turf Moor was icebound as well. Surprisingly the referee decided that it was fit for play and a near-50,000 crowd greeted the two teams on to the pitch.

Neither side really managed to exert any control over the 90 minutes, partly due to the difficult playing conditions and the match ended goalless, forcing extra-time.

Then came the drama. In the very first minute of extra-time 'Boro goalkeeper Dave Cumming came off his line to gather a free-kick from Burnley outside-left Peter Kippax. But Cumming took a blow on the chin from a boot as he went low to gather the ball and, concussed, he lost possession.

The ball bobbled about in the goalmouth as 'Boro struggled frantically to boot it clear. Then Harrison, lying on the ground, pushed the ball with his hand towards Morris, who was standing unmarked. Morris instinctively knocked the ball into the net, but was probably as amazed as anybody when the referee awarded a goal.

'Boro's angry players, who had been laughing and joking with their opponents over the handball, immediately surrounded the referee to voice their protests. Once again he would not listen. He did, however, consult his linesman before making it clear that the goal would stand.

Fenton went agonisingly close to grabbing the equaliser in the second period of extra-time, but his lobbed effort sailed just past the post. The semi-finals were not to be. The jinx had struck again and it was to be another 23 years before 'Boro were back in the last eight.

'Boro reached the quarter-final of the FA Cup on only two occasions before World War Two. Otherwise they seemed to meet one disaster after another and were nationally renowned as a poor Cup team.

However they had a great run in the competition in 1935-36, winning three home games in a row to qualify for the quarter-final.

In the third round 'Boro had pipped Southampton with a goal from outside-left Arthur Cunliffe. Another goal from Cunliffe and two from goal-machine George Camsell then earned a comfortable 3-0 victory against Clapton Orient in the next round.

The fifth round clash at home to Leicester City attracted a huge crowd of more than 42,000 to Ayresome Park and 'Boro won 2-1 thanks to a late winner from Billy Forrest. Camsell scored the other.

'Boro were then drawn away to fellow First Division side Grimsby Town, the club which was previously managed by 'Boro boss Wilf Gillow. It was a game which 'Boro were well capable of winning and they warmed up with a 1-0 win at Leeds United in the League, thanks to a goal from Benny Yorston.

The game at Grimsby attracted plenty of interest on Teesside and there was a lot of ill feeling when 'Boro were given only 300 tickets for the 21,000 capacity match.

In the event, 'Boro were fortunate to have a full contingent on the pitch. The *Evening Gazette* reported that the 'Boro team had to change trains at York on the way to Grimsby, but that three players missed the connection and were left behind by the rest of the party.

Unfortunately the *Gazette* does not name the trio, who caught a later train to Hull, crossed the Humber on the ferry to New Holland, caught a cab to Grimsby and got to Blundell Park before the rest of the party!

A disaster was averted in this respect, though the match was still a nightmare for 'Boro. They lost 3-1 and two of the Grimsby goals were hotly disputed. 'Boro's goal came when a cross from George Camsell was knocked into his own net by Grimsby full-back Kelly. To complete an afternoon to forget, 'Boro's inside-forward Tim Coleman was sent off along with Grimsby's Betmead.

So 'Boro's players fell foul of the FA Cup jinx which had been there since the very first season at Ayresome Park. 'Boro suffered huge disappointment in the Cup in 1903-04 and it never got any better.

On 6 February 1904, 'Boro went to Millwall for a first-round tie believing that the English Cup must eventually come their way. They knew they faced a stiff test at North Greenwich, because the Lions had lost only one Cup-tie at home in the previous 12 years.

However on a damp day and in front of 12,000 spectators, 'Boro finished comfortable 2-0 winners. It was 'Boro's first away win of the season in any competition. Sandy Brown put 'Boro ahead five minutes before the interval and the same player added another in the second half. The win might have been even greater, but Joe Blackett had a penalty saved by goalkeeper Joyce.

'Boro were drawn away from home again in the second round. However on this occasion they fared even better, winning 3-0 away to future Second Division champions Preston North End. Two hundred Teessiders travelled by train to join the 15,000 crowd, most of whom had to stand in the pouring rain.

'Boro were in the driving seat from the start when Brown put them ahead after only three minutes. The same player added the second on the half-hour and then Bob Atherton put 'Boro well in command with the third goal just after the restart.

So 'Boro had reached the third round of the FA Cup, which was also the quarter-final in 1903-04. Unfortunately 'Boro were drawn away from home yet again. This time they had to travel to Hyde Road to tackle fellow First Division side Manchester City.

A huge crowd of 30,000 turned out to watch the tie, which was played on a boggy pitch which reportedly contained not a single blade of grass. However the conditions didn't trouble 'Boro, who battled their hearts out to earn their third consecutive clean sheet away from home in the FA Cup.

The outcome was a goalless draw, which cheered the huge crowd of supporters which had gathered outside the *Evening Gazette* offices in Zetland Road. The news of the result was greeted with boisterous enthusiasm and hundreds of supporters went to Middlesbrough Railway Station to greet the team off the train from Manchester later that evening.

The replay was set for the Wednesday afternoon of 9 March and the whole of Middlesbrough went Cup crazy. It quickly became obvious to civic officials and local businessmen that life could not continue as normal on the cup day, so schools closed down and many works gave their employees the afternoon off.

It's a goal for Paul Sugrue as he slots the ball past Arsenal goalkeeper Pat Jennings and defender Tommy Caton on the way to 'Boro's terrific 3-2 revenge winning victory in the FA Cup third round in 1984.

No way through for Mark Burke as he tries to spark an attack in 'Boro's nightmare FA Cup defeat by struggling Grimsby Town in 1989.

The moment of agony for 'Boro as Marc North prepares to celebrate his second goal for Grimsby Town in the FA Cup third-round clash at Ayresome Park in 1989. Tony Mowbray is kicking the ball after it had rebounded out of the net. Goalkeeper Steve Pears and Colin Cooper are also pictured. The Mariners won 2-1.

Gotcha... 'Boro old boy Peter Beagrie storms in to make a lunging challenge on Bernie Slaven during the FA Cup third-round clash with Everton in 1990 which ended goalless.

When 'Boro were building up to their FA Cup sixth-round tie against Orient in 1978, they went to Jersey – and took along Malcolm Allison. The former Manchester City manager was invited by 'Boro boss John Neal as a goalkeeping coach for Jim Platt. Four years later Allison was back with 'Boro, this time as manager.

As a result, a ground record crowd of 34,000 crammed into Ayresome Park for the replay. The atmosphere was incredible. 'Boro had already beaten Manchester City by 6-0 at Ayresome Park earlier in the season and everybody expected that 'Boro would comfortably reach the semi-final for the first time.

However it did not go as planned. 'Boro could not pull off the victory. In fact they failed to do themselves justice on the day and City were by far the better side. Even the normally reliable Tim Williamson was caught well out of position for one of the goals as City won 3 -1. Sandy Brown scored 'Boro's consolation.

City went on to win the Cup, beating Bolton Wanderers by 1-0 in the Final at the Crystal Palace. But it was scant consolation for 'Boro, whose disappointment was reflected by the fact that they won only one of their remaining eight League games. It was also a blow for the fans, though Cup shocks are something they have become used to over the years.

Middlesbrough: Williamson; Hogg, Blackett, Page, Jones, Davidson, Gettins, Atherton, Brown, Cassidy, Carrick.

Manchester City: Edmundson; McMahon, Burgess, Frost, Hynds, Holmes, Meredith, Booth, Livingstone, Gillespie, Turnbull.

Not all of 'Boro's Cup shocks have been reserved for the sixth round of course. In fact the worst FA Cup defeat in the club's history came in the third round in 1989.

On that occasion 'Boro looked to have a simple task when paired at home to Fourth Division Grimsby Town. Bruce Rioch's young 'Boro side had swept all before them in the previous two seasons, winning consecutive promotions to reach the First Division. They were sitting in the top half of the First Division.

Offside! Stuart Ripley slams the ball past Manchester City goalkeeper Tony Coton in this third-round clash in 1992, but the goal was disallowed. Robbie Mustoe and Bernie Slaven are also in the thick of the action. Despite this set-back, 'Boro won the match 2-1.

However, it did not go as anticipated. 'Boro were not playing well, even though they took the lead through top scorer Bernie Slaven. Grimsby substitute Marc North then came on to score two second-half goals which gave the Mariners a fully deserved success. It's the only occasion when 'Boro have been knocked out of the Cup by a team three full Divisions below them.

Another humiliating defeat came in 1985, when 'Boro were knocked out of the third round by Fourth Division neighbours Darlington. 'Boro were struggling in Division Two, but were still expected to be too strong for the Quakers. Unfortunately Darlington had other ideas. They drew 0-0 at Ayresome Park and won the replay by 2-1 at Feethams, with Tony McAndrew netting for 'Boro.

Jack Charlton's renowned side also suffered an embarrassing defeat by Third Division Bury in 1976. Bury forced a goalless draw at Ayresome Park and then won 3-2 at Gigg Lane.

In 1952 'Boro lost 4-1 at home to Second Division Doncaster Rovers in front of 41,560 fans. Two years earlier they had gone down away to Third Division Chesterfield shortly after winning a great three-match battle against Aston Villa.

A bad defeat just before the war came with a 1-0 reverse at Third Division North outfit York City. Ralph Birkett recalls: "We had reached the fifth round and we really thought it was going to be our year. But York gave us a big shock. The lads couldn't believe it. We were very embarrassed when we made our way home."

But there have been some great FA Cup-ties as well. The fourth round trilogy against Everton in 1988 attracted 94,000 fans, including more than 25,000 for the replay at Ayresome Park. 'Boro drew 1-1 at Goodison Park, 2-2 at home and then lost 2-1 in the second replay back on Merseyside.

More than 40,000 fans saw Second Division 'Boro beat Manchester United by 2-1 at Ayresome in 1971 and FA Cup-ties in general attracted huge crowds to the stadium.

Sports Minister Denis Howell is shown the finer points of Ayresome Park by 'Boro chairman Eric Thomas as a top level FA deputation inspect the stadium's facilities before the World Cup.

The World Cup 1966

IN 1966 the World Cup finals were hosted by England and Ayresome Park was selected as one of the venues to stage three of the group games.

Middlesbrough was handed the Group Four games between the USSR and North Korea, Chile and North Korea and finally Italy and North Korea. At the time, it was a surprise that North Korea had to play all their group games at the same venue, though it turned out to be a huge bonus for the Asians.

Group Four was shared between Middlesbrough and Sunderland. The initial choice by the Football Association to host the North-East group was St James' Park at Newcastle, in addition to Roker Park. However an unresolved dispute between Newcastle City Council, the owners of St James' Park, and Newcastle United regarding the lease and use of the ground, led to Ayresome Park being selected in its place.

'Boro were informed in August 1964, that they had been chosen as replacement venue. It was a massive shot in the arm for the club, which was struggling in the Second Division, and for the town, which was suffering the effects of the post-war industrial and economic slide of the early 1960s.

The benefaction of the World Cup led to a major redevelopment of Ayresome Park, largely as the result of grants and loans from both the Government and the Football Association.

'Boro's directors were able to turn the stadium into one of the best in the country. They installed seating in the East End and the North and South Terraces which increased the overall seats from 4,500 to almost 13,000. Few of the leading clubs in the country could provide more than 10,000 seats for their supporters.

In years to come, the additional World Cup seating was to make it much easier for 'Boro to cope with the demands of the Taylor Report, particularly with the provision of seating. It's impossible to imagine Ayresome Park being improved on such a scale at any other time, was it not for the World Cup.

In addition to the extra seating, 'Boro also erected a roof over the East End, which meant that all four sides of the stadium were covered for the first time.

'Boro also carried out a major refurbishment of the reception area behind the North Stand which, remarkably, turned out to be the most expensive individual item of all the work undertaken.

The total cost of the redevelopment was around

Another delegation at Ayresome Park, this time from North Korea. The Korean officials are shown around the stadium by 'Boro secretary Harry Green (right). Construction work is well under way to erect a roof on the East End.

£100,000, which was a huge sum at the time, specially considering that 'Boro were a cash strapped club with little money coming through the gates. However, three-quarters of the money came from the grants and loans, which made it much easier for 'Boro to pay the bills. Even so, the directors would not have been too happy if they had known that they would still be paying off the loans ten years later.

The work on the alterations got under way in the summer of 1965 and took most of the next 12 months to complete. Naturally the fans had to put up with the inconvenience as the contractors carried out the work – though this inconvenience was suffered only by a miserable average of 13,000 fans as 'Boro continued to struggle on the pitch.

In fact the World Cup eventually arrived with 'Boro having suffered the ignominy of relegation to the Third Division for the first time in their history. It was a major embarrassment for the directors, though they could not have worked any harder to make sure that the World Cup games were successful and reflected well on the club.

The 'Boro board had hoped for three full houses for the World Cup, but in the event around 57,000 people watched the three games, which was less than 50 per cent of the capacity. In fact – the attendances were the lowest at any ground in the tournament, though 'Boro fans could be excused for their non-attendance as many were still in a state of deep depression following relegation.

Even so, the fans who did go along to Ayresome Park made their presence felt, particularly in their support of the North Koreans, who were one of the underdogs in the competition. As a result, Teesside played a large part in one of the biggest upsets of the tournament and, indeed, any World Cup, because the North Koreans progressed to the quarter-finals despite all predictions.

North Korea had arrived on Teesside amid great secrecy and stories of two years' dedicated training. However all the experts reckoned that the Asians were physically too small and too inexperienced to be taken seriously at this level of competition.

Their headquarters were at the St George Airport Hotel at Middleton St George, and the first thing they did was to make sure that their eating preferences were properly catered for.

The list for breakfast was: bowl of rice, boiled beef and spaghetti soup, cabbage, cucumber and onions with soya sauce, tomatoes and cucumber, beef and eggs (the main course), apples, bread and butter, and coffee.

Lunch was: rice, chicken, fish, eggs, apples, cucumber, carrots, tomatoes, pork, mushrooms, cabbage, onions, bars of chocolate, cider and soda water.

The next step was to get a haircut. John Hunter and his staff were dispatched to the hotel to give 30 haircuts.

The North Koreans then quickly decided that they were unhappy with the training ground at the airport, and so they were offered 'Boro's facilities at Hutton Road, which they found more to their liking. The Italians and Russians were based in Durham City and used the university facilities, while Chile were billeted in Gateshead.

'Boro staged the first match at Ayresome Park on the evening of Tuesday, 12 July though it was touch and go whether the stadium would be ready. Twenty four hours earlier, 50 workmen were working flat out to complete the reception rooms and carry out alterations to the stadium entrance.

North Korea's first opponents were the USSR, who were second favourites in the group behind Italy. A very inquisitive 22,568 Teessiders came to cheer the underdogs and immediately took the North Koreans under their wing. No doubt the red shirts had a lot to do with it.

Russia were without regular goalkeeper Lev Yashin, who was injured, but the match still went true to form. The North Koreans made a lively start, but never recovered from a double blast when Eduard Malafeev put the Russians ahead after 31 minutes and Anatoliy Banishevskiy added another 60 seconds later.

In the final minute Malafeev made it 3-0, though there was a suspicion of offside, which was ignored by Spanish referee Juan Gardeazabalk. The crowd made it absolutely clear that they disagreed with the decision.

The Times reported: "For half an hour these little men from the Land of the Morning Calm showed the Russians to be somewhat lacking in providing entertainment. One might have expected the North Koreans to take time to find their feet, but instead they fizzed around the bigger Russian defenders, making them look square and often flat footed.

"But the proverb of more haste less speed really applied to these little orientals. The Russians, helped by their opponents' lack of finish, began to come into the game and the contest was over when they scored twice just after the half-hour."

The North Koreans were beaten, but not downhearted. Team manager Myung Rye Hyun said: "We were beaten by giving away goals. Our goalkeeper came out too far for the first one. There was another mistake for the second and we are positive that the third goal was offside.

"Still, it is all good experience for us. It's the first time we have played against opponents of Russia's class and I am sure that we can do much better."

Teams: North Korea: Chan-myung, Li-sup, Yung-kyoo, Zoong-sun, Bong-chil, Seung-zin, Seung-hwi, Bong-jin, Do Ik, Byong-woon, Seung-il.

USSR: Kavasashvili, Ponomarev, Shesterniev, Khurtsilava, Ostrovski, Sabo, Sichinava, Chislenko, Malafeev, Banishevski, Khusainov.

The following night Italy, who were third favourites to win the World Cup, comfortably beat Chile by 2-0 at Roker Park with goals from Sandro Mazzola and Paolo Barison.

Chile, who had finished third in the 1962 World Cup in their own country, were hot favourites to beat the North Koreans when they met at Ayresome Park on Friday, 15 July.

However the Asians went into the game in a positive frame of mind. Hyun said: "The football against Russia was rougher than we are used to but the team were pleased with the pitch at Ayresome Park and were absolutely delighted with the way the Middlesbrough crowd cheered them on. It was almost as good as a home match and we hope we can play well enough to justify similar support against Chile."

It looked plain sailing for Chile when they took a 27th minute lead. Pedro Araya was brought down by Lim Zoong-sun and Ruben Marcos crashed the penalty kick into the roof of the net.

The whole Ayresome Park World Cup story might have taken a different turn if Chile had tied up the two points in the 64th minute, but Honorio Landa screwed the ball wide when left with only goalkeeper Li Chan-myung to beat.

Lifted by that let-off and the terrific backing from the terraces, North Korea began to take control and pounded the Chilean defence. Even so, it looked all over for the Asians, until Pak Seung-zin shot through a crowded goalmouth to grab the equaliser with only two minutes left on the clock.

The boys in red and white. North Korea salute the Ayresome Park crowd before one of their World Cup games.

The crowd of 15,887 was ecstatic and was reported to have "given itself up in delirious acclaim to celebrate the goal".

At the final whistle many of the North Korean players walked off Ayresome Park in tears, such was the emotional end to the match. Hyun acknowledged the importance of the crowd's involvement by saying: "Thanks to the peoples of Middlesbrough very much for their support."

Cliff Mitchell, writing in the *Evening Gazette*, said: "The crowd was as much responsible for the goal as the jubilant little Korean forward Pak Seung-zin."

Teams: North Korea: Chan-myung, Li-sup, Yung-kyoo, Zoong-sun, Yoon-kyung, Seung-zin, Seung-hwi, Bong-zin, Do Ik, Dong-woon, Seung-il.

Chile: Olivares, Valentini, Cruz, Figueroa, Villanueva, Prieto, Marcos, Fouilloux, Landa, Araya, Sánchez.

Referee: Ali Kandil (Egypt).

A goal from Igor Chislenko gave the USSR a surprise 1-0 win against Italy at Roker Park the following day and threw group four wide open. It was now possible for the North Koreans to qualify for the quarter-finals, but only if they could emulate the Russians by beating the vastly experienced Italians at Ayresome Park on Tuesday, 19 July. Most of the experts believed that it was beyond the bounds of possibility, though the Koreans had not read the script.

In the build-up to the match, the Asians booked their quarter-final accommodation at Liverpool. It was probably done to comply with the World Cup rules rather than through self-belief, though it was to prove to be a useful move.

The Italians were somewhat dispirited by the Russian defeat, but still anticipated a comfortable win against North Korea. They had dropped the gifted, if inconsistent, Giovanni Rivera for the game against the USSR but reinstated him against the Asians.

The match did not start well for Italy because they lost Giacomo Bulgarelli, carried off on a stretcher with torn knee ligaments midway through the first half. As there were no substitutes allowed in the tournament, they had to play for the best part of an hour with only ten men.

The Italian team now became very anxious. The Ayresome crowd sensed their apprehension and urged on the men in red. A groundswell of support had developed on Teesside for the North Koreans, and the crowd were fully behind them.

Once again the Koreans were lifted to new heights and they played with flair, nimbleness and athleticism, consistently outjumping the Italians and effectively utilising their mobility.

They had visibly grown in confidence since their first match against the Soviet Union and Pak Seung-zin, the tiny link man, again imposed himself on the game. The Koreans, with the benefit of the extra man, harried the Italians until they became uncertain and unsettled.

Then, four minutes before half-time, the unbelievable happened. The Koreans scored. Pak Do Ik controlled a pass on the right edge of the penalty area. Unchecked, he burst forward and shot across goalkeeper Enrico Albertosi into the right-hand corner of the Holgate End goal.

The Ayresome Park crowd roared their approval, fully aware that the chance of their adopted team reaching the next stage of the tournament was now a distinct possibility.

The match was developing into a melodrama or tragedy, depending on which team you supported. As a result the second half was to be one of cliff-hanging suspense. Could the North Koreans hold on to their lead or would the Italians save themselves?

There were more than 3,000 Italians inside Ayresome that night and, fearing a national embarrassment, they tried to lift their team at the start of the second half.

In fact for a quarter of an hour it looked likely that Italy could retrieve the situation. Rivera's passes dangerously probed the hard-pressed Korean defence and he went close to scoring when his firm shot was acrobatically turned around the post by the gymnastic Li Chung-myung.

However the Koreans remained resolute, working tirelessly to preserve their slender lead. When Romano Fogli headed a good scoring opportunity over the bar from Rivera's corner, the crowd began to realise that this might not be Italy's night after all and that footballing history was about to be made at Ayresome Park.

The Koreans gradually regained their composure and,

The goal which sunk every heart in Italy. Pak Do Ik scores the goal at the Holgate End which put Italy out of the World Cup and North Korea into the history books.

They shall not pass. Determined defending from the North Korean defenders clears their lines against Italy in their shock 1-0 win.

backed by vociferous support from the locals, held on to record a famous victory.

When the final whistle was blown by French referee Pierre Schwinte, the Koreans were accorded the type of ecstatic standing ovation usually reserved for the 'Boro on promotion nights.

The Koreans jubilantly hugged and kissed each other while the Italians heads bowed, trudged disconsolately off the Ayresome Park turf, no doubt already contemplating their impending mauling by the Italian Press and the tomato throwing reception committee of supporters awaiting their return to Genoa airport.

Once again the contribution of the Ayresome Park crowd to the Korea performance was highlighted by Hyun, who said: "Our success is due to the support given by the citizens of Middlesbrough and because our players fought so hard for the fatherland."

Cliff Mitchell said: "Italy lost their composure in the second half and what limited assurance they had boasted. In the end the Koreans richly deserved their fantastic victory."

The crowd of 18,727 had learned how to get behind a team again and play a apart in its success – something which was to rub off the following season when 'Boro marched back into the Second Division.

Teams: North Korea: Chan-myung, Zoong-sun, Yung-kyoo, Yung-won, Yoon-kyung, Seung-hwi, Bong-jin, Do Ik, Seung-zin, Bong-hwan, Seung-kook.

Italy: Albertosi, Landini, Facchetti, Guarneri, Janich, Fogli, Perani, Bulgarelli, Mazzola, Rivera, Barison.

North Korea were still not in the quarter-finals. They had to await the result of the final group game the next night, when Chile met the USSR at Roker Park. Chile could still win through to the last eight by winning the game.

In the event, it looked as though the Russians had played a dirty trick on North Korea by making no less than ten changes. They had already qualified and so gave the fringe members in their squad the chance of a run-out. It was virtually a Russian reserve team.

Chile were the better team on the night and put the Russian defence under heavy pressure. But they paid the penalty for missed chances and then lost the match when Valeri Porkujan broke away to score the winning goal four minutes from time. North Korea had made it through to the quarter-finals despite all predictions.

Their reward was a match against Portugal at Goodison Park. The Portuguese, who had beaten Brazil in their last match, were on £500 a man to win a place in the semi-finals. The North Koreans had been promised a certificate of merit.

Another upset looked on the cards when North Korea took a three-goal lead in no time at all. But Portugal gradually asserted themselves and went on to win 5-3, with the great Eusébio scoring four of the goals. The fairy-tale was over. But then the Koreans switched to white shirts for the quarter-finals. It must have been their undoing.

OVER the years the reporting of football at Ayresome Park changed radically in its style, content and presentation. Initially without the benefit of television or radio, early football coverage was the exclusive domain of the local and national newspapers and it was to these columns that supporters turned for information about their team's performances.

The often idiosyncratic styles of the anonymous writers, with names such as Erimus, Spectator, Old Bird, Tom of Tees, Arneton and Ranger provided the reader with very graphic and detailed match reports. Their accounts of all the major incidents had a certain colourful naïve charm, that is sadly lacking in today's frantic search for the sensational tabloid headline.

In an effort to recreate the atmosphere of football reporting in those bygone days, all the press comments have been carefully researched from authentic sources.

Internationals, Representatives and Amateur Cup Finals

Full Internationals

Ayresome Park was the venue for three full England International matches during the 20th century.

Saturday, 25 February 1905
England 1, Ireland 1

The prestigious honour of staging their first international match was conveyed on Middlesbrough FC 18 months after the opening of Ayresome Park and was without doubt a just accolade for the completion of their fine, modern stadium facilities.

A reporter at the time was fulsome in his praise. He said:

"The ground proved to be in perfect condition for the game. The arrangements at Ayresome Park were excellent in every way and the 23,500 spectators found every accommodation." The crowd paid receipts of £1,070.

Middlesbrough goalkeeper Tim Williamson made his England debut in the match, but was unfortunately responsible for gifting Ireland their goal. Williamson allowed a corner to drop from his grasp and cross the line.

A critical observer noted:

"The ball came rather high and the Middlesbrough goalkeeper seemed to beat it down. Unfortunately he failed to hold it and the leather cannoned against the upright and rolled over the line. Tim looked none too pleased for an instant and did not seem to realise what had happened, until the referee Mr Robertson tootled his whistle and pointed to the centre. Tim ought really to have saved it. I have seen him clear many much more difficult shots. It was practically the only serious thing he was called upon to do during the match."

England equalised almost immediately when Steve Bloomer – later to sign for 'Boro from Derby – scored. "It was a beauty; one of the Derby crack's very best," said the reporter.

This was a match England should have won but chance after chance went begging and the journalistic advice was not slow in pin-pointing the apparent deficiencies in the home side.

He said: "This latest display by England's internationals indicates that considerable target practice is necessary. It was simply extraordinary that a side so much superior to their opponents as England were at Middlesbrough could not win the match."

Nothing seems to have changed with the passage of time!

England: Williamson (Middlesbrough), Balmer (Everton), Carr (Newcastle), Wolstenholme (Everton), Roberts (Manchester Utd), Leake (Aston Villa), Bond (Preston NE), Bloomer (Derby County), Woodward (Tottenham Hotspur), Harris (Corinthians), Booth (Manchester City).

Ireland: Scott (Linfield), McCracken (Newcastle Utd), McCartney (Everton), Darling (Linfield), Connor (Belfast City), Nicholl (Belfast City), Sloan (Bohemians), Sheridan (Stoke), Murphy (QPR), Shanks (Brentford), Kirwan (Tottenham Hotspur).

Saturday, 14 February 1914
England 0, Ireland 3

THIS memorable match proved to be a depressing second international for 'Boro centre-forward George Elliott, as Ireland completely swamped a poor England side. So well did the Irish play that 3-0 was not a fair reflection of their supremacy.

The game was played at a time when there had been an upsurge of political tension between Ireland and England and whether this was the catalyst for the Irish team's performance one can only speculate.

However their endeavour certainly captivated one

'Boro legend Tim Williamson, wearing an England jersey with natty button down collar. Tim's England debut was notable mainly for the fact that he scored an own goal!

scribe. He wrote: "The Irish team snapped enthusiastically at every chance. Their first time tip top passing, their ready interchange of positions and the vigour and reliability of their finishing, had the English defence baffled from the very start."

The massed Ayresome Park enthusiasts, who had paid club record receipts of £1,247, were appalled and shocked by the dire England performance and vented their feelings on the players.

The report said: 'There were wild and disgusted vilifications of the England team by the spectators. They had never seen such rotten half-backs or forwards.'

The crowd of 27,439 was still kept very much entertained by the Irish side. The visitors scored through Lacey (twice), and Gillespie, while their skipper O'Connell was reported to be outstanding. In fact Ireland would have won by a much wider margin but for the brave goalkeeping of Hardy.

It was, however, his opposite number McKee, who caught the imagination of a local press reporter. He wrote: "The queerest man on the Irish side was McKee, the goalkeeper. He is a thin spindle-shanked young man and in the manner of dress seems to be a law unto himself.

'He played in his club sweater which has horizontal stripes of red and white and underneath his knickers he appeared to be wearing black woollen tights. He explained to me afterwards, however, that in Ireland the grounds are very rough and cindery and he is bound to wear some protection for his knees, so he prefers long black stockings coming up to his thighs rather than knee caps. He looked like a weird red striped wasp buzzing among the English forwards on the few occasions they got near him.'

George Elliott was dropped for England's next two games, their last for over five years due to the onset of World War One.

George Elliott, 'Boro's first great goal ace, who earned the second of his three England caps against Ireland at Ayresome Park in 1914.

How to relax before an international match. The England team are pictured playing snooker at the Zetland Hotel in Saltburn prior to the match against Wales at Ayresome Park in 1937. Pictured front centre is 'Boro trainer Charlie Cole, who trained the England side, with a young Stanley Matthews standing behind him.

England: Hardy (Aston Villa), Crompton (Blackburn Rovers), Pennington (WBA), Cuggy (Sunderland), Buckley (Derby County), Watson (Burnley), Wallace (Aston Villa), Shea (Blackburn Rovers), Elliott (Middlesbrough), Latheron (Blackburn Rovers), Martin (Sunderland).
Ireland: McKee (Belfast City), McConnell (Bohemians), Craig (Morton), Hampton (Bradford City), O'Connell (Hull City), Hammill (Manchester City), Rollo (Linfield), Young (Linfield), Gillespie (Sheffield Utd), Lacy (Liverpool), Thompson (Clyde).

Wednesday, 17 November 1937
England 2, Wales 1

THIS was the first international match played at Ayresome Park for over 23 years and was a just reward for the enterprise of the Middlesbrough directors, who had recently completed a major modernisation of the stadium.

The winning margin of 2-1 did not really reflect England's superiority over the Welshmen and this was due in part to the comparatively weak performance of Mills, the Chelsea centre-forward, whose efforts were analysed in these rather personal, destructive newspaper comments.

'Mills was on a ground where for many years centre-forward play of the highest quality has been seen. (A reference to 'Boro's George Camsell.) This was unfortunate for Mills because the crowd began to make comparisons and in the second half they made them audibly, probably to the discomfort of Mills, if he is a sensitive player. On this showing Mills is definitely not England class.' Blunt and to the point!

Wales had in their side that afternoon Bryn Jones, who was soon to become the most costly player in the country, when Arsenal paid Wolves £14,000 for his services in 1938. In complete contrast to the much admired Jones, the Wales goal was scored by Perry after 16 minutes, who was playing his football in the Third Division North for Doncaster Rovers.

The wizard of the dribble, Stanley Matthews, was certainly the player of the first half scoring England's equalising goal after 29 minutes and constantly teasing his marker Hughes with his close control skills.

The report said: 'The young Stoke man had a grand game

To-day's Teams.

England v. Wales.

PLAYED AT AYRESOME PARK, MIDDLESBROUGH.

NOVEMBER 17, 1937 KICK-OFF 2.30

Referee: W. WEBB (Glasgow).
Linesmen: A. Meadows (North Riding); J. A. Settle (Rhyl).

ENGLAND.
Colours: White Jerseys.

RIGHT LEFT

(1) Woodley, (Chelsea)

(2) Sproston, (Leeds United)
(3) Barkas (capt.), (Manchester City)

(4) Crayston, (Arsenal)
(5) Cullis, (Wolverhampton)
(6) Copping, (Arsenal)

(7) Matthews, (Stoke City)
(8) Hall, (Tottenham)
(9) Mills, (Chelsea)
(10) Goulden, (West Ham)
(11) Brook, (Manchester City)

(11) Morris, (Birmingham)
(10) Jones (B.), (Wolves)
(9) Perry, (Doncaster Rov.)
(8) Jones (L.), (Arsenal)
(7) Hopkins, (Brentford)

(6) Richards, (Birmingham)
(5) Hanford, (Sheffield Wed.)
(4) Murphy, (West Brom.)

(3) Hughes, (Birmingham)
(2) Turner (capt.), (Charlton Ath.)

(1) Gray. (Chester)

WALES.
Colours: Red Jerseys.

LEFT RIGHT

England Trainer: C. Cole (Middlesbrough).

This is the team sheet for the last international at Ayresome Park, between England and Wales in 1937. The picture was taken from the match programme.

and left the spectators in no doubt as to the wisdom of the selectors' preference for him on the right wing.'

The winning goal was scored by the Spurs forward Hall, who on the hour hit a magnificent left-foot shot past the stranded Gray, the chance having been created by the oldest player in the match, Manchester City's Brook.

This was a fine all round team performance by England, which was much appreciated by the Ayresome Park crowd of

How do you do! Welsh captain Turner, left, shakes hands with English skipper Barkas before the start of the international at Ayresome Park.

over 30,000. The positive contributions made by the officials to the absorbing spectacle, were also generously highlighted in print.

It read: 'It was altogether a capital contest rendered the more enjoyable because of the general effort of both teams to play football as it should be played and because of the refereeing of Mr Ebb who was never caught out of position.'

Since the end of World War Two in 1945, Ayresome Park never hosted another full international match for England.

England: Woodley(Chelsea), Sproston (Leeds Utd), Barkas (Manchester City), Crayston (Arsenal), Cullis(Wolves), Copping (Arsenal), Matthews (Stoke City), Hall (Tottenham H), Mills (Chelsea), Goulden (West Ham Utd), Brook (Manchester City).

Wales: Gray (Chester), Turner (Charlton A), Hughes (Birmingham), Murphy (West Brom A), Hanford (Sheffield W), Richards(Birmingham), Hopkins(Brentford), L.Jones (Arsenal), Perry (Doncaster R), B.Jones (Wolves), Morris (Birmingham).

Football League Representative Games

Saturday, 17 February 1912
Football League 2, Scottish League 0

NORTH-EASTERN players formed the backbone of the Football League side with Middlesbrough goalkeeper Tim Williamson and Sunderland's Buchan, Holley and Mordue chosen for this representative encounter.

The match was much praised at the time for the quality of its football. 'On the whole it was a game at which one could puff away with anonymity and enjoy the sterling work provided for you by the *crème de la crème* of English and Scottish football.'

By half-time, the game which had provided 45 minutes of excellent entertainment for the crowd of nearly 25,000 still remained scoreless. Buchan had gone close for the English and Williamson had saved, 'in some style', from Scotland's Quinn.

One report said: 'The struggle revealed what a glorious spectacle 22 skilled footballers can produce. I have no doubt that it is many years since the people who lined the Ayresome Park ground have ever experienced such enjoyment.'

After the interval 'there was only one team in it …England set the pace magnificently and the crowd cheered heartily.'

Ten minutes into the second half England opened the scoring when Buchan, who had a generally fine first representative match, passed accurately to Freeman whose shot from an oblique angle beat Scottish 'keeper Brownlie.

The Football League side from then on were totally dominant and contrived to waste many more goalscoring opportunities. Just on time however, Sunderland forward George Holley gave the result a truer reflection of the play when he converted a Freeman miss-kick and shot into the net with terrific force.

The Ayresome Park public who paid receipts of £950, had been privileged to witness a fine team display by the home side who, if they had accepted all their chances would have achieved a greater margin of victory. Charles Buchan making his debut at this level was the surprise packet with his accurate passing while 'Boro custodian Tim Williamson 'brought off two excellent saves and altogether gave the impression of soundness and reliability coupled with brilliance.'

A local correspondent was so captivated by the match that

Charles Buchan of Sunderland, who was the star of the match between the Football League and the Scottish League at Ayresome Park in February 1912.

he declared it: "A superb, glorious, thrilling and sensational encounter." So much for understatement.

Football League: Williamson (Middlesbrough), Crompton (Blackburn Rovers), Pennington (West Bromwich A), Duckworth (Manchester Utd), Boyle (Burnley), Fay (Bolton W), Wallace (Aston Villa), Buchan (Sunderland), Freeman (Burnley), Holley (Sunderland), Mordue (Sunderland).

Scottish League: Brownlie (Third Lanark), Blair (Clyde), McNair (Celtic), Galt (Rangers), McAndrew (Clyde), Mercer (Hearts), Brown (Celtic), Cunningham (Kilmarnock), Quinn (Celtic), McMenemy (Celtic), Bennett (Rangers).

Wednesday, 22 March 1950
Football League 3, Scottish League 1

THIS was a proud day for Middlesbrough FC as they staged their first representative match after World War Two. The match captured the imagination of the Teesside public and had been a sell out for days, with hotel accommodation in the town at a premium.

Both squads stayed at the nearby seaside resort of Saltburn but in different hotels, with the English players training at the local Saltburn Cricket Club and the Scottish team using Ayresome Park.

Unfortunately Tom Finney and Stanley Matthews had withdrawn from the Football League squad, but 'Boro favourite Wilf Mannion was chosen at inside-forward and with the forthcoming World Cup tournament in Brazil only a few months away, this encounter would be the perfect opportunity for both sets of players to stake their claim for inclusion.

After all the pre-match anticipation the game was generally a disappointment for the 39,352 crowd. 'The Football League team was undoubtedly the better combination but these were two largely unimpressive teams.'

Much to the locals pleasure the star of the match was Mannion. 'I would bank on Mannion as a certainty for the World Cup in Rio,' wrote one reporter. 'No other player used the ball more effectively or intelligently than the England international forward.'

Mannion was in fact instrumental in the making of all three of his side's goals. As early as the fifth minute he darted through the Scots' defence before passing to Hancocks, who crossed for Mortensen to head the opening goal with ease.

Then three minutes before the interval, he was involved in the movement which resulted in Mortensen scoring his second from close range.

The third goal was just reward for Mannion's persistence when after 78 minutes his defence-splitting pass to Baily saw the Spurs forward's shot strike the crossbar. Mannion retrieved the rebound only to see it scrambled away for a second time. Not to be denied the 'Boro player's determination was rewarded when his pass was easily converted by Baily with a bemused Scottish 'keeper stranded.

Much of the play in the second half was tedious, as the Football League team coasted to an easy victory. The Scots did however score a consolation goal through Young, with the help of a dubious penalty against Dickinson for a tackle on Mason. This however only served to give the final result a little more respectability than the outclassed Scots really deserved.

As a preparation for the World Cup the match solved few problems for either manager. In a few months time Walter Winterbottom and his England players would be on the end of one of the biggest upsets in World Cup history, when England lost 1-0 to the USA. The Scots had still to even qualify for the final stages.

Football League: Williams (Wolves), Ramsey (Tottenham Hotspur), Aston (Manchester Utd), Wright (Wolves), Franklin (Stoke City), Dickinson (Portsmouth), Hancocks (Wolves), Mannion (Middlesbrough), Mortensen (Blackpool), Baily (Tottenham Hotspur), Langton (Blackburn Rovers).

Scottish League: Brown (Rangers), Cox (Rangers), Young (Rangers), Hewitt (Partick T) Woodburn (Rangers), Egans (Celtic), Reilly (Hibs), Brown (East Fife), Bauld (Hearts), Mason (Hibs), Smith (Hibs).

Wednesday, 20 March 1968
Football League 2, Scottish League 0

IT WAS fortunate that Manchester United goalkeeper Alex Stepney was in such fine form in the early stages of this match, as the Football League team were comprehensively outfought by an adventurous, if over-anxious Scottish side who played with two raiding wingers.

Having survived the initial onslaught, the turning point of the match came in the 28 minute, when totally against the run of play Liverpool's Roger Hunt, who had been relatively anonymous until then, headed home a Geoff Hurst cross into the corner of the net. This goal seemed to deflate the Scots, resulting in Bobby Moore and company taking control.

The dreaded curse of the Scottish goalkeepers struck in the 49th minute, when Peter McCloy, attempting to recover his position, slipped and allowed a 35-yard shot by England full-back Keith Newton to scream into the net. This effectively ended the game as a contest.

Ex-'Boro full-back Cyril Knowles had an eventful return to his old stamping ground, receiving mild concussion in the first half after being struck full in the face by the ball and then in the second, acrobatically clearing off the line when a goal-bound header from Colin Stein for once evaded Stepney.

This representative match was extremely well supported by the Teesside public, with a fine attendance in excess of 34,000,

The great Bobby Murdoch, who played for the Scottish League against the Football League at Ayresome Park.

who obviously appreciated the decision of both managers to choose sides strong enough to grace a full international match.

In fact England manager Alf Ramsey, not known for his post match comments, displayed how seriously he was taking the game when he criticised his team's urgency in the initial period, "It has been a long time since I've seen an England back line as ragged as it was in the first 20 minutes," he commented pointedly.

The resounding success of the evening, however, certainly vindicated the choice of Ayresome Park as the venue for the fixture.

Football League: Stepney (Manchester Utd), Newton (Blackburn Rovers), Knowles (Tottenham Hotspur), Stiles (Manchester Utd), Labone (Everton), Moore (West Ham Utd), Ball (Everton), Hunt (Liverpool), Charlton (Manchester Utd), Hurst (West Ham Utd), Peters (West Ham Utd).

Scottish League: McCloy (Motherwell), Callaghan (Dunfermline), Gemmell (Celtic), Greig (Rangers), McKinnon (Rangers), D.Smith (Rangers), Johnstone (Celtic), Murdoch (Celtic), Stein (Rangers), Lennox (Celtic), J.Smith (Aberdeen).

Wednesday, 15 March 1972
Football League 3, Scottish League 2

SIR Alf Ramsey was unable to choose many of his current England squad because of FA Cup replay commitments and injuries. Although left with a somewhat makeshift side, the Middlesbrough public still had the opportunity to see Bobby Moore and Geoff Hurst while Malcolm Macdonald of Newcastle United and Jim Montgomery of Sunderland provided the local interest in the squad.

Scottish manager Tommy Docherty had few problems in comparison to his English counterpart, although Kenny Dalglish was 'physically tired' and unable to play.

The match officials, referee Pat Partridge and his linesmen Alan Jordan and Lol Douglas, all hailed from the Teesside area.

The closeness of the scoreline belied the Football League's superiority in this match. The Scottish side were comprehensively outplayed particularly in the first half when goals from the very impressive Tony Currie on 14 minutes and Mike Doyle after 24 minutes put the English players totally in control. Macdonald thought he had made it there but his arm-waving victory celebrations were curtailed by a flag for offside, much to the delight for some reason of the 20,000 Teesside fans.

After the interval Docherty managed to instil some fighting spirit into his side and their improved play was rewarded with a goal from McQuade. The fight-back was short-lived when Tony Currie took advantage of a glaring mistake by the Celtic centre-half George Connelly to restore the Football League's two-goal margin.

Having regained control, Alf Ramsey's side were then guilty of complacency, when they allowed Colin Stein to score after 72 minutes, thus making the final score a rather flattering 3-2.

Overall, the Football League were the more constructive side and carried the greater forward threat and in Currie of Sheffield United they had the game's most outstanding player.

Football League: Clemence (Liverpool), Lawler (Liverpool), Nish (Leicester City), Doyle (Manchester City), Blockley (Arsenal), Moore (West Ham Utd), Hughes (Liverpool), Macdonald (Newcastle Utd), Currie (Sheffield Utd) Hurst (West Ham Utd), Wagstaffe (Wolves).

Scottish League: Hunter (Kilmarnock), Brownlie (Hibs), Forsyth (Partick T), Jardine (Rangers), Connelly (Celtic), Blackley (Hibs), McQuade (Partick), Phillips (Dundee), Stein (Rangers), Hay (Celtic), Ford (Hearts).

The FA Amateur Cup

THE outstanding achievements of Bishop Auckland (ten times winners), Crook Town (five times winners) and Stockton (three times winners) reflects the remarkable success that North-Eastern clubs have had throughout the history of the FA Amateur Cup.

Over the years Ayresome Park played its part in that success by staging the following final matches.

Saturday, 13 April 1912
Stockton 1, Eston United 1

THIS closely contested match was recorded for posterity by a cinematographic operator who, 'Darted up and down the field with his camera, in the vain hope that play would concentrate itself on the same spot.' The whereabouts of his finished film footage is a mystery.

The game was a complete contrast of styles, with Eston United adopting the tactics of 'Kick and rush' while Stockton had the 'better ideas of scientific play'.

Several individual players' performances were closely scrutinised by the local match reporter, who certainly pulled no punches with his disparaging comments.

He said: 'Stamper the Stockton centre-half did not impress me very much. He was shaky and easily bustled off the ball. I did like Veitch however. His was a brainy game. He headed the ball nicely and used consummate judgement.

'The surprise of the match was the sterling Eston defence. Davidson and Roddam played like Trojans, while Hill rejected shots in a manner suggestive of Tim Williamson.'

Eston's goal was scored by Parsons with 'a lovely shot that beat Callaghan all the way', and was greeted with wild delight by the United followers. 'It was a wonder that Parsons' arm was not pulled from its socket', wrote an excited sports columnist.

Stockton's equaliser from Sutherland was the result of 'cleverly evading the backs and shooting past the Eston custodian Hill as he ran out of his goal.' This caused a similar crowd reaction to that of the Eston success. 'It was the turn of the Ancients' devotees to become hysterical. Their yells were deafening', recorded the enthused football writer.

Both sides strove hard for the winner and it was Eston who had the chance in the very last minute to lift the cup when 'Hollis had a splendid opportunity. The Stockton ranks were short, but instead of a swift low drive, he nearly booted the ball over the Ayresome Park shilling stand and the crowd moaned bitterly.'

There was no extra-time, and the match was to be replayed at Ayresome Park the following Thursday. The first match drew a crowd of 20,479, paying receipts of £705.

Stockton: Callaghan, Loney, Chapman, Evans, Stamper, Veitch, Bradford, Robinson, Sutherland, Davis, Callender.
Eston United: Hill, Roddam, Davidson, J.Smith, Housham, O'Hara, Allan, Parsons, W.Smith, Morris, Hollis.

Thursday, 18 April 1912
Stockton 1, Eston United 0

THIS rousing replay was settled after only five minutes by the Stockton forward Sutherland who capitalised on a tragic mistake when the Eston defender Roddam 'made a shocking miss and Callender bustled along with a clear field. Hill stopped his shot but Sutherland rushed up and with a swift drive gave Hill no chance.'

On the balance of play Stockton deserved their success, it was a triumph of 'method over dash'.

The match was played on a Thursday afternoon which meant that large crowds of workmen were unable to attend the game. They did however assemble anxiously outside the building of the local Stockton paper waiting for news of the match. The extraordinary outpouring of emotion that greeted the final result was witnessed by a reporter from an upstairs office window.

'When the result came through, proclaiming victory for the Ancients, it was greeted with a terrific outburst of cheering, which was renewed again and again. The High Street in the old borough of Stockton was a seething mass of humanity. Never, except on Mafeking night, has there been so much enthusiasm shown.'

This euphoric reaction by the residents of Stockton to their team's Amateur Cup success only serves to emphasise the social importance of the non-professional game at that time and underlines the civic prestige attached to the winning of this national competition.

The crowd of 12,531 paid receipts of £403. Both teams were unchanged.

Saturday, 16 April 1921
Bishop Auckland 4, Swindon Victoria 2

WITH this defeat of Swindon Victoria, Bishop Auckland won the Amateur Cup for a record fourth time, in their eighth final appearance.

Swindon were completely outclassed from the start and as a comparatively new club it was generally acknowledged by the pundits of the time that: 'They had not yet attained the high standard usually associated with the clubs who reach the final stage of this competition.'

Cook scored an early goal for the Bishops, but Roberts equalised from a free-kick for Swindon. The Northern League side then attacked 'pertinaciously' and established an unassailable lead with further goals, 'accurately registered' by Binks and Ward, 2. A much improved display in the second half by Swindon saw them reduce the arrears with a penalty converted by Poole, but Bishop Auckland easily held on for their record breaking victory. The game was watched by 21,097 fans.

In the evening the town's main streets were 'lined with thousands of people. Two bands preceded the triumphant Bishop Auckland team in a victory procession firstly to the Market Place and then on to the Durham Hotel where a celebration dinner was served. Mr Kit Rudd the popular club secretary exhibited the cup to the cheering crowd from the hotel window.'

Bishop Auckland: North, Wilson, Garbutt, Nattrass, Atkinson, Kasher, Brown, Cook, Binks, Ward, Wemsley.
Swindon Victoria: Weston, Saunders, Poole, Roberts, Cooper, Summers, Rees, Blumsdon, Eggleton, Dawson, Chivers.

Saturday, 1 April 1922
Bishop Auckland 5, South Bank 2 (after extra-time)

THIS game was undoubtedly one of the most dramatic Amateur Cup Finals ever played, not only at Ayresome Park but anywhere in the history of the competition.

After 86 minutes the Bankers were leading 2-1 and looking the more likely winners. Yet less than 15 minutes later they were a well-beaten side trailing by a three-goal deficit.

The 'Boys Own' turning point in the match proved to be the final minute of ordinary time.

Following a late Bishop Auckland equaliser by Mullen, South Bank were awarded a penalty when Wilson fouled Towse in the area and 'the referee pointed to the dreaded spot. Thompson the South Bank captain elected to take the kick himself.'

The tension of that moment was admirably recorded by an anxious reporter. He wrote: 'In a silence that could almost be felt, Thompson drove the spot kick hard and true for the net. It seemed a scorer all the way, but Potts dived at full length and diverted the ball safely out of the danger zone with a magnificent save.'

During extra-time the Bishops played like men possessed scoring three times while the Bankers fell to pieces.

Bishop Auckland, winners of the FA Amateur Cup against South Bank in 1922. The players are, back row (left to right): Wilson, Potts, Taylor. Middle row: Nattrass, Atkinson, Maddison. Front row: Burrows, Cook, Binks, Mullen, Goldsborough.

The final result was certainly very harsh on South Bank who had come within a penalty kick of victory, but in the end it was generally acknowledged that Bishop Auckland deserved their success, 'If only for their splendid late rally.'

Bishops' scorers were Binks (2), Cook, Mullen and Nattrass, while Peacock replied twice for South Bank. The 22,500 crowd paid a total of £1,638.

Bishop Auckland: Potts, Wilson, Taylor, Nattrass, Atkinson, Maddison, Burrows, Cook, Binks, Mullen, Goldsborough.

South Bank: Burns, Thompson, Thomas, Lloyd, Brighton, Tubb, Spencer, Peacock, Towse, Hepworth, Robinson.

Saturday, 14 April 1928
Cockfield 2, Leyton 3

GALLANT Northern League miners team Cockfield could not prevent Leyton from retaining the Cup, although they were very unfortunate to be beaten five minutes from time after twice holding the lead.

Nicknamed the Fellmen, their remarkable eight-month cup journey had begun in September 1927 and embraced a record 15 games, including three to beat the sixth Durham Light Infantry in the qualifying rounds.

In a wind affected match Cockfield captain Coates elected to play with the elements in the first half. The Fellmen took the lead after 15 minutes through their centre-forward Rutter. Leyton equalised when McKinley, who also appeared regularly in the Third Division for Charlton Athletic, headed home. But right on half-time Rutter restored Cockfield's lead.

In the second period Leyton made full use of the wind, securing their victory with goals from Smith and Cable. But they were at times fortuitous, particularly in the last 20 minutes when: 'Cockfield made a bold bid for the cup. There was however no disgrace in defeat, they played well and on the run of play they should not have gone down – a draw would have been a more fitting result.'

In complete contrast to contemporary press conferences, the post match comments congratulated the referee Mr Robert Brown of Newcastle for his control of the game and referred glowingly to 'this fine sporting contest free from all feeling, at the end of which, Cockfield could be proud of their achievements and enhanced reputations.'

Cockfield: Wedge, Dixon, Coates, Barker, Harrison, Oldfield, Longstaff, Pearson, Rutter, Thompson, Kirby.

Leyton: Grainger, Preston, Goldsmith, Graves, Cable, Margetts, McKinley, Hall, Avey, Smith, Hawkins.

Saturday, 13 April 1935
Bishop Auckland 0, Wimbledon 0

THIS was one of the most lacklustre FA Amateur Cup Finals played at Ayresome Park. The match certainly did not live up to expectations. Bishop Auckland were a disappointing side and in particular their forwards did not produce the goods.

Critical press comments suggested that 'There was none of the dash and elusiveness which had characterised the Bishops' display on the same Middlesbrough Ground against Dulwich Hamlet (semi-final 3-0), and it was difficult to realise that this was indeed the same team.'

So mundane was the football that the post-match headlines centred around the referee, whose navy blue blazer was undistinguishable from the shirts of the Bishop Auckland players. In fact some of the first-half incidents boarded on the farcical.

'Confusion among the Auckland players was very evident before the interval. They were leaving the ball, as they thought, for a colleague but it was in fact the referee. One of the best scoring chances of the first half was lost when Bryan left the ball to the official. At half-time a determined protest by the Bishop Auckland club representatives resulted in Dr Barton turning out for the second half without his blazer and wearing a white cricket shirt.'

The 23,335 crowd paid receipts of £1,552. Bishop Auckland went on to win the replay 2-1 at Stamford Bridge the following Thursday with goals from Wilson and Bryan.

Bishop Auckland: Hopps, Minton, Scott, Birbeck, Straught, Shield, Dodds, Bryan, Wilson, Stephenson, Hogg.

Wimbledon: Irish, Goodchild, Balkwill, Wright, Bridge, Reeves, Batchelor, Barnes, Dowden, Turner, Zenthon.

Thursday, 22 April 1954
Crook Town 1, Bishop Auckland 0

CROOK Town triumphed over Bishop Auckland in this second replay to win an epic Amateur Cup Final saga which was full of suspense, drama, fluctuating fortunes and mind-boggling statistics.

The three matches played over a fortnight at Wembley, Newcastle and Middlesbrough were watched by nearly 200,000 spectators and grossed a record £46,000. Amateur football in the 1950s certainly experienced a golden period, with many full houses at the Wembley showpiece.

The all important goal that settled this cup marathon was scored in the 40th minute by Ken Harrison, who took a pass from Ron Thompson and calmly shot past the advancing Sharratt.

Controversy however had surrounded an earlier incident in

Crook Town, FA Amateur Cup winners in 1954 following a second replay at Ayresome Park. Back row (left to right): J.Harvey (manager), Riley, Jeffs, Davison, Jarrie, Stewart, Taylor, C.W.Peart (trainer). Front row: Appleby, Thompson, Harrison, Williamson, Coxon, McMillan.

the tenth minute when Oliver, Bishop Auckland's international forward, headed home a Major corner only to have it disallowed by the referee for climbing. Many in the 36,727 at Ayresome Park were amazed by the decision. Oliver was adamant that he had scored a perfectly legitimate goal, declaring indignantly in a post match interview that: "I headed the ball and it was going in before I ever touched the defender."

In such a closely fought game this controversial refereeing decision proved crucial to the destiny of the cup, as once Crook had taken the lead their defence stood firm and 'an equaliser never looked like coming'.

This was Crook Town's second final win and it was greeted with wild enthusiasm by their supporters who ignored repeated loudspeaker appeals to stay on the terraces and swarmed on to the Ayresome Park pitch to congratulate their heroes. The receipts were £6,600.

Crook Town: Jarrie, Riley, Steward, Jeffs, Davison, Taylor, Appleby, Thompson, Harrison, Williamson, McMillan.

Bishop Auckland: Sharratt, Marshall, Stewart, Hardisty, Cresswell, Nimmins, Major, Dixon, Oliver, O'Connell, Watson.

Saturday, 14 April 1956
Bishop Auckland 4, Corinthian Casuals 1

THERE was high drama behind the scenes at Ayresome Park involving both teams before a ball was even kicked in this replay.

Casuals attempted to include in their side Surrey cricketer Mickey Stewart, who was on tour in the West Indies with England. After eventually securing his temporary release from the touring party, Stewart proceeded to miss his connecting flight to Prestwick airport and despite chartering an aircraft to fly him to Teesside he arrived too late to take part in the match.

A rib injury to half-back Bob Hardisty provided the pre-match drama for Bishop Auckland. Hardisty was declared unfit by the team doctor but an apparent plea from the other team members, resulted in a hastily convened club committee meeting 45 minutes before the kick off, which decided that Hardisty could play with strapping and injections.

Bishop Auckland, proudly parade the Amateur Cup in 1956 in front of the North Stand at Ayresome Park after beating Corinthian Casuals. Players, left to right, are: Oliver, Hardisty, Bradley, Lewin, Stewart, Sharratt, Cresswell, Marshall, O'Connell, McKenna, Edwards. Insets: Nimmins, Fryer.

It was a gamble that was to eventually pay off but not before Casuals had taken the lead against the run of play after 34 minutes with a 'grand goal' scored by their inside-left Citron. His powerful cross shot flashed into the net of a post, past the stranded Sharratt.

To their credit Bishops were level within just three minutes when Derek Lewin equalised to send the 29,099 crowd into raptures.

After the interval the North-Eastern side took complete control of the game when a fierce scoring shot by Hardisty from outside the penalty area was quickly followed by another from Lewin. The match had a rousing finale when right on time Tommy Stewart raced through from the full-back position to drive home the fourth goal and give Bishops a well-deserved, resounding 4-1 victory.

The post match analysis emphasised that: 'While this was essentially a team triumph, the No.1 hero was Bobby Hardisty, the central figure of a gamble that was an unqualified success.'

Bishop Auckland had now won the cup for a record ninth time. The receipts were £5,245.

Bishop Auckland: Sharratt, Marshall, Stewart, Hardisty, Cresswell, O'Connell, McKenna, Lewin, Oliver, Bradley, Edwards.

Corinthian Casuals: Ahm, Alexander, Newton, Shuttleworth, Cowan, Vowels, Insole, Sanders, Laybourne, Citron, Kerruish.

Saturday, 21 April 1962
Crook Town 4, Hounslow Town 0

AFTER a 1-1 draw at Wembley, Crook Town made it four wins in four finals with this comfortable, if slightly flattering win over Hounslow at Ayresome Park in front of 18,279 spectators.

The platform for the victory was based on a pulsating nine minute burst in the first half, when they scored three times through Coates, Sparks and McMillan.

Indeed one report hinted that their performance was down to scientific help. 'Despite the rainsoaked pitch the Crook players dashed about at a cracking pace and accepted and parted with the ball as if they were controlled by a radio beam.'

Hounslow rallied very strongly in the second half, 'carving out openings galore, but their shooting was pathetic.' Right winger Alder was singled out for specific criticism by an irate columnist.

'He side-footed over the bar, allowed the goalkeeper to make easy saves and hesitated when he should have been burning his way towards the Crook goal.' Obviously it was not his day.

The Northern League side won, according to one match reporter, 'because they had the know-how to score goals. For them, there was no hustle, bustle or panic shooting, and despite Town's best efforts to get back into the game it was Crook who scored a fourth goal through Coates' oh-so causal shot, ten minutes from time. Crook were certainly worthy winners of the trophy.'

Crook Town: Snowball; Gardener, Clark, Storey, Heatherington, Brown, Sparks, Garbutt, Coates, Peary, McMillan.

Hounslow Town: Rhodes, MacDonald, Creasey, Evans, Taylor, Digweed, Alder, Somers, McHattie, Dipper, Patterson.

The Players' Memories

AYRESOME PARK was fortunate to have been graced by some great footballers over the years.

For a start there were the goalscorers. Names like George Elliott, George Camsell, Micky Fenton, Brian Clough, Alan Peacock, John Hickton and Bernie Slaven just roll of the tongue.

All of these great finishers, with the exception of the indefatigable John Hickton, were internationals. And they scored almost 1,500 goals between them for the 'Boro.

There were the wingers. The goalscoring Billy Pease, Tommy Urwin, Ralph Birkett, and Terry Cochrane.

Ayresome has also seen its fair share of ball players in the middle of the park. There was the maestro himself, Wilf Mannion, who could take three men out of the game simply by moving his eyes. Don't forget 'Boro's first great ball player, Jackie Carr, or Bill Harris and of course, Graeme Souness and Bobby Murdoch.

And there were the iron men. Top defenders like the tower of strength Bobby Baxter, Maurice Webster, the uncapped telepathic twins Stuart Boam and Willie Maddren, Gary Pallister, Tony Mowbray, the great George Hardwick, Dickie Robinson and Gordon Jones.

Last but not least are the goalkeepers. The legendary Tim Williamson, who holds the club record number of appearances, Dave Cumming, Jim Platt and Steve Pears.

These are just a few of the top-quality players who wore the 'Boro shirt with pride. And there were many more, players of all shapes and sizes, of all levels of ability.

Together, they played a huge part in the story of Ayresome Park, for the game would be nothing without its players.

These are some of the memories of a selection of those players. Some were characters, others did their jobs with the minimum of fuss. Some have a lot of stories to tell, others cherish one or two moments from their career.

Middlesbrough Football Club and the rush of adrenalin sparked by putting on the red and white shirt at Ayresome Park is their common ground.

The dates in brackets after each player's name indicate the year in which they made their 'Boro debut, and the year when they played their final first-team game for the club.

Hugh McKay, one of the club's first professionals, applied to the 'Boro for financial assistance in January 1939. The directors sent him £2 on the understanding he didn't publish the fact in the Press.

STAN ANDERSON (1965-66)

STAN ANDERSON was a seasoned midfield player and England international who was extremely worldly wise to the ways of the game when he arrived at Ayresome Park as player-coach in November 1965.

He made his First Division debut with Sunderland as a teenager and went on to play more than 400 games for the Rokermen. Stan then moved to St James' Park and skippered Newcastle United to promotion before his switch to Teesside, where he completed the feat of captaining all three leading North-East clubs.

Stan was elevated to 'Boro manager in April 1966, following the departure of Raich Carter. He went on to guide 'Boro to promotion from Division Three in his first full season at the helm.

Despite several near misses, Stan battled without success to guide the club into the First Division. Even so, when he quit Ayresome Park in January 1973, he left behind a highly-talented squad which went on to walk away with the Second Division championship under Jack Charlton.

Anderson was delighted to have worked with some of Ayresome's most

Stan Anderson, pictured early in 1966, shortly after his arrival at Ayresome Park. Anderson was the first player to captain all three major North-East clubs.

exciting players. He said: "My most vivid memory was having a good set of players under me who eventually made the First Division when Jack Charlton took over.

"Willie Maddren, John Hickton, John Craggs, Dave Armstrong and Derrick Downing were wholehearted players who gave everything for the club. Stuart Boam was also an outstanding player in a side which always promised so much.

"Local lads such as Gordon Jones, David Mills and Bill Gates contributed a lot to the side without sometimes getting the credit they deserved. I count myself lucky to have worked with players who were a credit to the club."

Anderson reveals that his biggest disappointment was the inconsistent form of Hugh McIlmoyle, who could be a lethal match winner on his day.

Stan added: "I suppose the biggest disappointment, apart from failing to get into the First Division, was not getting the best of Hugh McIlmoyle. He was a very talented player who showed his true potential only in a few matches. He had everything to have played international football but lacked the will to achieve it."

David Armstrong, current holder of 'Boro's consecutive appearances record. He played in 356 League and Cup games in a row.

DAVID ARMSTRONG (1972-81)

DAVID ARMSTRONG was one of the mainstays of 'Boro's quality team of the 1970s. In fact he was virtually a regular feature, making a club record 356 consecutive League and Cup appearances.

David was a rare commodity – a cultured natural left-sided midfield player, with a great passing ability and an uncanny knack of scoring goals. In 416 first-team appearances for 'Boro, he netted 73 goals.

'Boro spotted Armstrong's talent at an early age. He was only nine years old when he started coming to Ayresome Park for coaching. 'Boro's junior coach, George Wardle, used to bring David in from his Durham home – and it was Wardle who was to make the biggest contribution towards David becoming a League footballer.

Armstrong said: "George knew more about football coaching in his little finger than anyone I have ever known. I don't think I would have been half the player I was if it wasn't for George.

"A lot of players made the grade because of George. Naturally he helped you develop your skills, but he also instilled in you the determination to succeed and self discipline. It was an investment for the future which paid off for a lot of young 'Boro lads."

David was ready for the first team by the age of 17 and was brought in by Stan Anderson. He was still a teenager when Jack Charlton arrived and became an immediate permanent fixture, helping 'Boro to win the Second Division championship.

David said: "Jack wasted no time in weighing up everybody's strengths and weaknesses. He got us to play to our strengths, and used the team as a whole to cover up our weaknesses.

"Nobody could live with us. We won the title with a month of the season still to go. Jack made sure that we never stopped working hard. He used to say that we were the best team at giving the ball away and the best team at getting it back.

"Jack was a terrific manager. He should have gone on to manage England. And I know now that he feels he could have done that little bit better at Middlesbrough. We finished seventh in our first season in the First Division and we needed a little bit more quality to take it forward again. He should have bought David Cross when he had the chance. Who knows what might have happened."

John Neal eventually took over from Charlton and began a gradual transition. Armstrong said: "John Neal was a good manager. He wanted us to express ourselves and he was also keen to bring the kids through. Craig Johnston, David Hodgson and Mark Proctor all came in and did well. It was a time of change at the club, but it was still a relatively successful period."

It was during Neal's reign that Armstrong's consecutive run of games finally came to an end when he missed a goalless draw at home to Nottingham Forest. David said: "I was carrying an ankle injury and then I strained my groin, so I couldn't play.

"To be honest I asked John Neal to drop me on a couple of earlier occasions when I didn't feel I was doing myself justice. He said he would leave me in the team if I was playing at only 50 per cent of my ability. But I was always disappointed if I couldn't play to the standards I had set myself."

In Armstrong's last season at Ayresome Park, 'Boro reached the sixth round of the FA Cup before losing in frustrating circumstances to Wolves. In the first meeting, at home, Armstrong was injured. He said: "I was tackled, and I gashed my ankle. I had to go off to have 18 stitches inserted. I came back on and made the goal for Terry Cochrane to equalise.

"Naturally everybody was disappointed that we didn't go through, but I don't look back with any regrets. I consider myself fortunate to have played for the club during that period."

IAN BAIRD (1990-91)

IAN BAIRD was the last signing made by manager Bruce Rioch, and was a strong, aggressive striker who linked well with regular front runner Bernie Slaven.

Baird was bought from Leeds United in February 1990, and his goals helped 'Boro retain their Second Division status.

The following season he was instrumental in helping 'Boro to reach the play-offs, and finished second top scorer with 15 League and Cup goals. Overall he scored 20 goals in 74 appearances.

Baird's favourite memory was the thrilling 4-1 victory against Newcastle United at Ayresome Park on 5 May 1990, which ensured that 'Boro avoided relegation.

He said: "I had recently signed from Leeds, who were already promoted and were playing at Bournemouth. We were playing Newcastle, needing to win to stay up.

"The first half was a tense affair with neither side really creating anything,

Ian Baird, whose double strike against Newcastle United helped keep 'Boro in the Second Division in 1990.

Robert Dawson McArthur died in North Ormesby Hospital in April 1938. He had complained of pains after being crushed in the 'Boro match at home to Liverpool on the Good Friday. An inquest, on 26 April recorded a verdict of 'accidental death owing to being crushed in a crowd'.

then in the second half Bernie Slaven did well on the left and squared the ball for me to tap in from two yards.

"Then we went two-up through Bernie, but my favourite moment came when a free-kick from Colin Cooper put me in and I scored with a left-foot volley from the edge of the box, beating John Burridge.

"It was fantastic for me personally and for the 'Boro supporters. Bernie grabbed another goal and we managed to stay up, and the 'Boro went on to bigger and better things."

Ian moved on to Hearts when Lennie Lawrence arrived at the club at the end of the following season. He added: "I thoroughly enjoyed my time at Ayresome Park. It would have been nice to win promotion, but I was pleased to see the lads reach the Premier League the following season."

HARRY BELL (1944-55)

HARRY BELL was one of a whole new wave of talented young players who swept into the 'Boro line-up immediately after the war.

The Sunderland-born wing-half joined 'Boro on amateur forms during the war, later became a pro, and went straight into the team when League football resumed in 1946.

Harry Bell, pictured left, was equally adept at football and cricket. He was a professional cricketer with Middlesbrough and Crook, and opened the batting for Durham County.

Harry went on to become a great club servant and stalwart. He played more than 300 games in the First Division for the club, and just a handful in the Second Division. Harry was a hard working, tough-tackling terrier type who was always totally committed in every game.

He was also a fine all-round sportsman, opening the batting for Durham County. He was also Middlesbrough's cricket professional for a spell.

Harry recalls: "We had a good side just after the war. We had a good blend of top-class experienced players, and young players, plus we signed some players to fill in the gaps.

"George Hardwick and Micky Fenton returned from the RAF and Wilf Mannion was demobbed from the Army, and we also still had Dave Cumming in goal and Bobby Stuart at left-back.

"David Jack was the manager, and he brought in Johnny Spuhler from Sunderland and Jimmy Gordon from Newcastle. They were both very astute signings.

"I played at right-half and Jimmy played at left-half. I was only 5ft 8in, and Jimmy was 5ft 6in. But we were both hard players. I like to think that the inside-forwards knew that they had been in a game after they had played against us. We certainly knew how to wind them up during the game."

'Boro played in front of huge crowds after the war. In fact the period is remembered by many as football's halcyon days.

Harry said: "We averaged around 40,000, Sunderland 50,000 and Newcastle 60,000. The North-East grounds were packed every week.

"Naturally there was no television then. People had been starved of football during the war and thronged to the grounds. But there were a lot of good footballers to watch as well."

Bell played in the First Division with 'Boro for eight consecutive seasons and, despite plenty of promise, the trophy that the fans yearned for evaded them.

Harry said: "We were going really well in 1950-51 and I thought we had a chance of the title. But then Alex McCrae was injured, and it made a big difference to us. Alex had been playing very well. We fell away a bit afterwards and eventually finished sixth."

Ironically, one of Harry's best memories comes from the season before League football started again – when 'Boro put together a great run in the wartime FA Cup. They had three mammoth fourth-round ties against Blackpool.

Harry also fondly recalls the great atmosphere in the dressing-room. He said: "We were a team, on and off the field. There was always somebody who would say something to get everybody laughing.

"Relegation was a terrible thing when

it came. The club had been in the First Division as long as anybody could remember. But it always seemed inevitable that season. No matter what we did, it didn't work out. We kept going. I didn't know how to play any other way.

"The fans stayed behind us. And we did our best to keep our spirits up. We lost 8-1 at Charlton and the dressing-room was a morgue afterwards. But then Wilf said to David Jack, 'Never mind boss, we were the best team kicking in'. Everybody laughed and it lifted the gloom.

"Towards the end of the season we were 5-1 down at Aston Villa and the Villa full-back scored an own-goal near the end. As Villa kicked off again, Wilf said: 'Come on lads, they are panicking'. We needed humour then. It lifted morale and enabled us to keep battling positively."

Despite his determination to play the game hard, Harry was always a fair player. In fact he was sent off just once in his career – and even then he failed to make any contact.

Harry said: "I got sent off playing against Len Shackleton in a Sunderland derby. Jimmy Gordon always used to intimidate Shack, who didn't like to get involved in the physical side of the game.

"In this game I tackled him. He went down, and I threatened him. Then I walked over him. It was right in front of the ref. Then the next time I went to tackle Shack, I lunged in, but he was too quick for me. The next thing, the ref came over and sent me off. I protested. I said that I never touched him. But the ref said: 'You meant to', and that was that.

"I got a one-match ban as a result. I missed the next game. You were supposed to stay away from the ground, but I came in late and watched it. I always hated missing any game."

RALPH BIRKETT (1935-38)

RALPH BIRKETT was a lively winger who played a big part in 'Boro's rise in stature in the late 1930s.

Although he was born in Kent, Ralph was the son of a Middlesbrough man. He started his League career in Torquay and had a short spell with Arsenal before joining 'Boro for £5,900 in March 1935.

He was capped for England against Ireland within seven months of his arrival on Teesside, and went on to score 22 goals in the 1935-36 season, finishing second top scorer behind George Camsell.

That international call-up remained one of Ralph's most vivid memories. He said: "I was having my tea at my digs in Redcar when I switched on the wireless and heard I had been picked to play for England."

That same season 'Boro beat Sunderland 6-0, with Birkett scoring twice. He said: "It was a terrific team performance, especially as Sunderland went on to win the League."

Ralph also recalls vividly recalls one early season double. He said: "We played Preston North End at Deepdale and won 5-0. Then we stayed at Buxton over the weekend, and on the Monday

Ralph Birkett, the son of a Middlesbrough man, he grew up in the south but returned to Teesside in a £5,900 transfer from Arsenal in 1935.

we played Aston Villa at Villa Park and won 7-2." Birkett made his mark in both games, netting twice at Preston and once at Villa Park.

His biggest disappointment as a 'Boro player came in the FA Cup in February 1938. 'Boro had beaten Stockport 2-0 and Nottingham Forest 3-1 to reach the fifth round. Ralph said: "We lost 1-0 at York City, who were in the Third Division North. It was my worst moment as a 'Boro player. With the team we had, I'm sure we would have won the Cup that year."

STUART BOAM (1971-79)

STUART BOAM was a £50,000 signing from Mansfield Town in the summer of 1971, and turned out to be yet another of Stan Anderson's astute buys.

A big, commanding centre-back, Boam attacked the ball and became the cornerstone of Jack Charlton's illustrious side of the 1970s. Boam also formed a great partnership with Willie Maddren, and together the pair became one of the top defensive duos in the First Division.

Boam went on to play 378 League and Cup games for 'Boro before moving on to neighbours Newcastle United for £100,000 in 1979.

He said: "When I arrived at Middlesbrough, the club had a reputation for scoring a lot of goals, and conceding a lot as well.

"We changed it around very quickly and became a lot tighter at the back. Those were the days when you got just two points for a win, so an away draw was very useful.

"But while the goals stopped going in at one end, they stopped going in at the other end as well. Alan Foggon had a couple of productive seasons, but during my time there we never had the prolific goalscorer that the team was crying out for."

'Boro's run of promotion near misses ended with the arrival of Jack Charlton, whose side romped away with the Second Division title in the 1973-74 season.

Boam said: "Jack knew how he wanted us to play and we worked at it until we got it right. The players were picked to fulfil a role, and nothing ever changed.

"And he only brought a couple of players in. His biggest investment was bringing in Bobby Murdoch. He had a dustbin full of medals. He was a great bloke and a great player. David Armstrong came through, and so, too, did Graeme Souness.

"When we went up we were a great force, but we needed to change things and bring in a couple of new players. But Jack wouldn't do it. He brought in Phil Boersma, but Phil couldn't do the job that Jack wanted him to do. We needed a big goalscoring centre-forward, but Jack wouldn't spend anybody else's money, never mind his own."

He added: "It was still a great time to be around. We had a lot of good players, and there were some great players around in the League. Great players like the Tony Curries, George Bests and Stan Bowles used to come to Ayresome Park. It was terrific entertainment for the fans, and it was great for us to play against them."

Boam was never regarded as a ball player himself – more of a stopper centre-half. But he liked to produce more than just basic skills from time to time.

He said: "Jack used to say to me 'You

'Boro's full first team were carpeted by the directors in October 1923, following a dressing-room bust-up. They were told to foster team spirit and settle all differences amicably. The next day they went out and beat Newcastle 1-0 at Ayresome Park. George Elliott scored the winner from the penalty-spot.

Stuart Boam, showing his heading prowess in this aerial duel against Manchester United. Boam was skipper of Jack Charlton's great side of the 1970s.

are a labourer, not a craftsman'. But I enjoying making storming runs down the right, dropping my shoulders and beating players.

"I made sure I always passed the dug-out, about two yards from where Jack was standing. The veins on his neck used to stand out about three and a half inches. But I loved it, and the crowd loved it too. And it was never a problem, because I only ever did it when we were in front, and there was never any danger of us losing in the situation."

He added: "Everybody knew what was going on and we used to laugh about it. We were always laughing. But we had a serious side. We all wanted to be successful.

"There was a great atmosphere in the dressing-room. Just the occasional fall-outs. We used to play five-a-sides, and the winners got a Mars bar. You would kill for a Mars bar, and it sometimes got rather heated. But all you could think of was eating that Mars bar at the end of the game."

Boam has terrific memories of his partnership with Willie Maddren. He said: "Willie was a great player. There were some great players around in our position, but he was one of the best. I think he would have won caps if he had been at a fashionable club.

"Willie developed into the best sweeper centre-half in the country. I always knew what he was going to do, and it made my job a lot easier. They used to all us the Telepathic Twins, and I think it was a fair description.

"But then Willie's knee started swelling up and it got harder all the time for him. His knee swelled up after every game. It reached the stage where for the last two years he never trained. He just turned up on the Saturday and played. He was magnificent. But the knee was always going to finish him in the end, and it was a crying shame."

After Maddren's enforced early retirement, Boam played on alongside Alan Ramage and Tony McAndrew at the back under the new regime led by John Neal.

Boam said: "John Neal came in and changed things around, but the spirit of the club remained. But I think I got stale after Jack left. It was never quite the same for me."

Even so, Boam did not want to leave Ayresome Park when Neal negotiated a deal with Newcastle boss Bill McGarry in 1979.

The 'Boro defender was settled in the town and was running a shop in St Barnabas Road, near to Ayresome Park.

He said: "I really wanted to stay. I had a testimonial coming up in a year and a half, and I had the shop. The shop used to be packed out on Saturday mornings and I just couldn't get away. I used to get more bollockings than enough because I had stayed in the shop too long talking to supporters.

"But then John Neal paid Newcastle £500,000 for Irving Nattrass and the deal was fixed up for me to go the other way. It broke my heart to leave. I had to sell the shop and forego the testimonial.

"Newcastle doubled my wages, but it was still hard work travelling up there every day. But that's football. I'll always remember the great times we had at Middlesbrough."

BRIAN CLOUGH (1955-61)

BRIAN CLOUGH was 'Boro's greatest post-war striker, averaging almost a goal a game throughout his career with the club.

George Camsell and George Elliott scored more goals for the club, but Clough's strike rate per game is better than any other player in the 'Boro's history.

In five consecutive seasons, Clough's haul of League goals was 38, 40, 43, 39 and 34. Despite his prolific feats, 'Boro could not use the goals as a springboard for promotion, and all of Clough's career at Ayresome Park was spent in the Second Division.

That's the main reason why the Middlesbrough-born player failed to win no more than two caps for England, and ultimately why he moved on to Sunderland in the search for personal success.

Clough broke into the first team at 'Boro in September 1955, playing in a 1-1 draw at home to Barnsley. It was the club's second season following relegation from the First Division, and the fans were itching to get back to the top flight.

Brian said: "We had a lot of talent in the team, particularly up front, and most of them were local lads.

"We had Billy Day, Billy McLean, Alan Peacock, Eddie Holliday, Arthur Fitzsimons. Most of those lads could play a bit, and they were desperate to get into the First Division.

"But we didn't win promotion because we couldn't defend. I found it staggering. I used to stick in 40 goals a season myself, and between us we banged in 80 or 90 a season. But we used to keep missing out and missing out. It was too daft for words."

'Boro never scored less than 83 goals in any of Clough's five fantastic seasons, and in four of those years were always among the promotion contenders. However, they had to settle for fifth place on two occasions, and also sixth and seventh.

The team was never very strong defensively, and got weaker in this

Brian Clough, seen in a battle with Charlie Hurley of Sunderland, had the best scoring record per game in 'Boro's history. He scored 204 goals in 222 appearances.

department towards the end of Clough's stay with the club.

He said: "We used to ask the manager and the directors to bring in good defenders, so that we had a good all-round team, but they never seemed to be able to put their fingers on the right men.

"It was very frustrating for the forwards. There's nothing worse than going two-goals up and failing to win the game.

"We had one game at Charlton where we drew 6-6. Can you imagine scoring six goals away from home and not winning the game? And if it had gone on another ten minutes we would have lost 8-6."

Clough was a natural goalscorer all his life, from the moment he started playing for Ray Grant's 'Boro Juniors side in the Northern Intermediate League.

When Brian was demobbed from the Forces in June 1955, he became a full-time professional on £7 10s a week. Five months later his wages were increased to £10 and £8. Brian had the gall to ask for a wage increase in the January, but his request was turned down.

In his first season Brian had to play second fiddle to the experienced Charlie Wayman, who went on to finish top scorer with 16 League and Cup goals. Clough scored three times in nine appearances, but clearly felt that he deserved better and asked for a transfer at the end of the season. It was the first of several transfer requests and, like the others, it was turned down.

Clough said: "I knew that I was the best centre-forward at the club, but I was stuck in the reserves. I needed to be in the first team where I knew I could do the job. It was through frustration that I put in the transfer request."

Brian was left out for the first match at the start of the new season, which 'Boro drew 1-1 at home to Stoke City. However, he was drafted in for the next match, at Bury, scored two goals, and never looked back. Bristol City tried to sign him in the September, but 'Boro turned them down. Clough responded by scoring twice against City in a 4-1 win at Ayresome Park the following month.

Clough went on to score goals for the club like turning on a tap. It quickly became evident that 'Boro did not have the ambitions to match those of his own, and further transfer requests followed in 1957 and 1958. But 'Boro stood firm.

Early in 1958, both Everton and Birmingham City made positive inquiries to try to prise away the goal machine. Clough might have got the talented defender he desperately wanted for 'Boro in October 1958, when 'Boro made a brave move to sign Ron Flowers from Wolves. However, their £20,000 offer was turned down.

Clough was made club captain in the summer of 1958 and celebrated by scoring five goals in the 9-0 annihilation of Brighton at Ayresome Park. Any hopes of a great season quickly disappeared and 'Boro went on to finish 13th, despite a remarkable 43 goals in 42 League games from Clough and 19 from his striking partner Alan Peacock.

Towards the end of season, on 4 April, Brian married his wife Barbara in St Barnabas Church. The club seemed to be helping him to put down roots by buying 21, Newham Avenue, for £2,675 for him.

Clough says: "It was the most important day in my life. But the speeches had to be short because I needed to be at Ayresome Park before two o'clock to play against Leyton Orient." Brian celebrated with one of the goals in a 4-2 victory.

The following season Clough's future at Ayresome Park was again up in the air when the players organised a round-robin against his captaincy. The petition was handed to manager Bob Dennison and the board. It contained nine signatures and complained of "Clough's harsh words on the pitch" and also made a reference to his sulking after defeats.

Clough was naturally hurt, and it didn't help when the matter reached the Press and received national headlines. However, Brian and the players did try to bridge the gap in training that week, and the result was an inspirational team performance in beating Bristol Rovers by 5-1 at Ayresome Park. Brian grabbed a hat-trick.

'Boro went on to join the promotion battle, but lost their way a little in February and March and finished fifth.

They were fifth the following season, too, and Clough eventually took advantage of the opportunity to complete a £55,000 move to Sunderland. He said: "It's always sad to leave a club you love. Middlesbrough was my club. It had been since I was a boy. But I couldn't see things getting any better, and I'm

Mr J.Woodhouse was struck in the face by the ball and had his spectacles broken prior to 'Boro's 1-0 win against Barnsley in March 1929. 'Boro offered to provide new glasses as long as the cost did not exceed ten shillings.

absolutely certain I would have won more international caps elsewhere. You wish things could have been different, but they weren't."

TERRY COCHRANE (1978-83)

TERRY COCHRANE was a club record signing at £238,000 when he was snapped up from Second Division Burnley, and became a big hit with the Ayresome Park fans.

A Northern Ireland international, Cochrane was a traditional right winger, with speed and guile, who could open up defences and create a goal out of nothing with a swish of his hips.

Terry played 128 games for 'Boro scoring 12 goals, and also won 19 of his 26 Irish caps while at Ayresome Park.

He said: "John Neal signed me, and I met him at the Cleveland Tontine. I didn't know the way to the stadium, so he said: 'Just follow the lights'. I tried to do that, but I got lost and ended up at Stockton railway station! It was a long time before I finally got to Ayresome Park."

Once at the ground, Terry quickly settled in and became an important part of Neal's new look side.

Cochrane said: "At the time we were called Boring, Boring 'Boro. It was a legacy of Jack Charlton's time.

"But it was an unfair tag. John Neal was trying to change things. We played with two wingers and we attacked teams. John Craggs and Ian Bailey, the full-backs, used to get forward all the time as well. We tried to entertain.

"In my first full season at Middlesbrough, we lost only three home games, and only three the following season. Teams didn't like to come here because they knew it was going to be difficult."

Cochrane enjoyed the luxury of long runs in the team on only a few occasions.

He said: "I played in flashes, but I could do things. The fans liked to see tricks and defenders put under pressure. I liked to entertain and I always talked to the crowd. They appreciated it and they were always very good to me."

In his first full season, 'Boro finished ninth in the First Division, but never threatened to challenge for honours.

Terry said: "We had a good side, but we probably needed to score more goals. We got Billy Ashcroft from Wrexham, and he wasn't as effective in the First Division and we got Bosco Jankovic, but he was never a prolific scorer.

"I used to hear people say that Jack Charlton's team was only two players short of a great team. Well the same applied to our team. Another two or three quality players and Middlesbrough would have held their own in the First Division for many seasons."

Terry Cochrane, pictured in action in a home win against West Bromwich Albion in 1979, was signed for a 'Boro club record £238,000 from Burnley the previous year.

There was still quality in the team. Terry said: "David Armstrong was the best left sided player in Britain of his time. You never saw him have a bad game. He used to know where to put the ball every time."

Cochrane was also a good ball player, and he grabbed the odd goal or two as well. He remembers his first goal at Ayresome Park as his best for the club.

It came in the 7-2 drubbing of Chelsea in December 1978. Terry said: "It was a bit special. I cut in from the right and hit it with my left, and it went into the bottom corner like a rocket."

Happy times, and Cochrane recalls that there was an excellent atmosphere at the club. He said: "There were lots of funny incidents, most of them unprintable.

"One of the best I can remember came in a reserve game against Barnsley at Ayresome Park. During the game, two lads were giving Alan Ramage a lot of stick. As soon as the final whistle went, Alan set off after them. They were up and away, and he ended up chasing them down the street outside the ground wearing his kit and his boots!"

The atmosphere began to change after the infamous Cup defeat by Wolves in 1981. Cochrane says: "That match broke our hearts. Perhaps John Neal should have gone out and bought somebody straight away to give us a bit of a boost. But we struggled to get going again.

"John Neal left at the end of the season, and the team started to break up. We lost quality players and didn't replace them with quality.

"The fans started to drift away and we struggled. I think Bobby Murdoch could have had more support from the club, and more from the players as well. Bobby was a lovely man, and everybody respected him. But some of the players let him down on the pitch."

The slide continued to gather momentum, and new manager Malcolm Allison allowed Cochrane to go on loan to Hong Kong side Eastern, where the coach was Bobby Moore. Terry added: "I enjoyed it there, but I was very sad to leave Middlesbrough. I've never lost the feeling for the club or the fans."

JOHN CRAGGS (1971-82)

JOHN CRAGGS was an institution at Ayresome Park throughout the 1970s. A strong overlapping right-back, he was a great favourite with the fans.

Signed for £60,000 from Newcastle United in 1971, Craggs established himself in the side immediately and made the full-back position his own throughout his 11-year career with 'Boro.

He was one of the mainstays of Jack Charlton's much renowned defence and continued to pile up the games during the John Neal era. John's final tally of 473 appearances was bettered only by other great club servants Tim Williamson, Gordon Jones and John Hickton.

Ironically, cash strapped 'Boro had to sell, before they could buy Craggs in the first place. He said: "Newcastle manager Joe Harvey told me that 'Boro were interested, but they had no money. They had to sell Hughie McIlmoyle first to get the money to buy me.

"Eventually McIlmoyle was sold, and I was signed a few weeks into the season. We had a good bunch of lads like Gordon Jones, Bill Gates, John Hickton and Derrick Downing. We had a good side, but sometimes the results were disappointing."

Players like Jim Platt, David Armstrong, Alan Foggon and Graeme Souness followed Craggs into the team as manager Stan Anderson tried to complete a promotion side. But Anderson eventually quit in the middle of Craggs's second season.

John said: "Stan had been there a long time and he had worked with some of the same players all that time. He had got the best out of them, and I think he thought he couldn't get any more.

John Craggs, a consistent and polished defender who made 473 appearances for the 'Boro.

"The club needed a fresh man in charge, and went for Jack Charlton. It was good decision. He was one of a new breed of managers who had just finished playing. He knew what he wanted and you had to do it his way or you were out.

"But I always got on well with Jack. He didn't change the way I played. I could defend and I liked to go on overlapping runs and cross the ball. I like to think that I could play a bit as well."

"We were criticised for being defensive, but Jack always believed that everything started from defence. When we attacked teams we could tear them apart. When Alan Foggon and David Mills were running through nobody could catch them."

John added: "We developed into a very good side. We were defensively as good as anybody in the country. It helped that the defence were all about the same age. We worked together and we got that blend.

"There was so much talent in the side that if Jack had brought in a couple more players, we could have been a championship side."

Charlton's departure left a void which was filled by new boss John Neal. Craggs said: "John did well for the club. He carried things on. Some players wanted to leave, but John let them go and replaced them.

"Graeme Souness was the first to go, then David Mills and David Armstrong, but John brought the kids through like Proc, Hodgy and Craig Johnston and he kept it going."

Craggs was also capable of banging in a goal or two, and it was under Neal's reign that he scored his best. John recalls: "It was against Bolton Wanderers. I got the ball on the right and cut inside before hitting it with my left. It absolutely flew into the top corner. It's brilliant when they go in like that."

John's only regret from his long career is that he never got to win anything with 'Boro.

He said: "The only thing we ever won was the Anglo-Scottish Cup and we got slated for that. We won the first leg with an own-goal and then played a goalless draw at Fulham.

"I was really disappointed to lose the FA Cup sixth-round tie at Birmingham when we were first promoted. People said we went there to defend, but really we just didn't play well. Birmingham were really hyped up and played out of their skins.

"But we had our chance a few years later when we played Orient at home. I remember Billy Ashcroft missing a great chance towards the end which would have put us in the semis.

"When we went down to Orient it was blowing a gale, but we still fancied our chances. Then one of their guys, standing with his back to goal, had a pot over his shoulder from 35 yards and it sailed in. We got back in it late on, but then Millsy missed one from about three yards and we went out. I'm a great believer that you must make your own luck, but we didn't do it against Orient.

"Overall I can't grumble. It would have been nice to play at Wembley but there are only so many winners. I'm pleased to have been a member of such a good side which won the Second Division championship."

LINDY DELAPENHA (1950-58)

LINDY DELAPENHA gave 'Boro sterling service in the 1950s. A stocky winger cum inside-forward, he scored 93 goals for the club. Signed from Portsmouth in April 1950, Lindy went on to finish top scorer for the 'Boro on three occasions.

One of Lindy's favourite memories comes from a 3-1 win at Ayresome Park against Pompey in December 1950. He said: "I scored a good goal and had a great game in the snow and ice."

However, Lindy's favourite goal was a cracking 25-yarder which absolutely belted into the back of the net against Derby County in 'Boro's Second Division days. 'Boro won the match 3-1.

Lindy, who was born in Jamaica, well remembers the famous 'Boro fan of the 1950s, Astor, whose booming voice could be heard all around the ground. His lively banter kept the fans just as entertained as did the players with their football.

Astor was a club comedian in his own right, and a big fan of Delapenha, who he used to refer to as 'Our Kid'. Lindy said: "Astor was a very humorous Jamaican who had a very big voice and kept

Lindy Delapenha, pictured scoring from the penalty-spot against Port Vale in 1956, possessed a rocket shot.

'Boro held a collection during their game against Clapton Orient in April 1929, for supporter Mr J.Hutchins of South Bank, who had been killed at Bradford railway station while going to watch 'Boro in action the previous month. The collection raised £8 16s 2d.

everybody in stitches with his wisecracks."

One of Lindy's most vivid memories will always be the Ayresome Park goal that never was. He scored from the penalty-spot against Sunderland in the first ever floodlit match at the stadium. But the ball went straight through a hole in the back of the net and referee Kevin Howley, believing that it had missed, awarded a goal kick.

Lindy said: "I hit a right-foot shot and it tore open the back of the net. It must have had a weak link."

Delapenha went on to play 270 League and Cup games for 'Boro before moving on to Mansfield Town. He thoroughly enjoyed his stay on Teesside, even though it took him a long time to settle in.

He added: "Middlesbrough was a bit of a let-down after Portsmouth. But I came to love the town. In fact my happiest memories were spent at the 'Boro, and I also married a Middlesbrough girl."

RONNIE DICKS (1943-58)

RONNIE DICKS was born in Kennington, but joined 'Boro as the result of a wartime posting to Marske, and became a great club servant over two decades.

He was the perfect utility player, having joined 'Boro initially as a right winger, and went on to play in every position for the club – including goal!

Ronnie Dicks, a hard working two-footed utility player, he gave 'Boro great service from during the war until his retirement in 1958.

Most of Ronnie's appearances were made at wing-half or full-back. He played 334 League and Cup games, scoring ten goals, and also made 22 wartime appearances.

Ronnie joined Dulwich Hamlet when he left school, but joined the Army during the war and, after basic training at Plymouth, was posted to Marske artillery training camp.

He said: "I didn't even know where Middlesbrough was. It was my first time in the North-East. But I came along to Ayresome Park for a trial. I must have done well because Wilf Gillow signed me on, and I was getting £1 10s 0d a match. It was marvellous. It was more than my wages in the Army."

Ronnie was later posted to Burma, where he saw active service. He was in Calcutta on VE night, and was posted to Barnard Castle on his return to England at the end of the war.

He said: "I played a few reserve games for 'Boro in the 1946-47 season, and was going to join one of the London clubs. But then David Jack, who was the new manager, told me that I had signed for 'Boro and if I wanted to play football, I had to play for them. So that was that."

Dicks quickly broke into the first team, where he alternated between inside-forward and the wing. It was an injury to George Hardwick, at Blackpool in September 1949, which changed

Ronnie's career. He said: "George was hurt, so I switched from the right wing to left-back. Stanley Matthews was Blackpool's outside-right, and it was the first time I had ever played in defence. But I had a good game against him, and we drew the game.

"I saw Tommy Blenkinsopp at 'Boro's last game at Ayresome Park against Luton, and he told me that it was the best performance he ever saw against Matthews. I appreciated that. I think 'Boro were impressed at the time as well, because I was always regarded as a defender after that. And I found it much easier there."

Ronnie's one appearance in goal came in an FA Cup-tie against Leicester City at Ayresome Park in 1954. He said: "Rolando Ugolini was hurt and Wilf Mannion went around asking the other players if they fancied going in, but nobody did. So I decided to have a go. I kept a clean sheet and we drew 0-0. But we lost the replay at Leicester by 3-2."

The lack of Cup success was one of Ronnie's regrets. He said: "We were known in the game as being a poor Cup side, and never did anything. I don't know why it was, because we had a good team in the First Division and could give anybody a hard game.

"We had some good players in the Second Division as well, like Alan Peacock and Brian Clough. But it was a hard division to get out of. There were some good teams around. And we never got the players we needed. I think it was purely monetary."

Injuries forced Ronnie to drop out of Football League and England 'B' games, and he also missed the chance of a World Cup trip to Brazil in 1950. He said: "Our director Harry French was also an England selector. He stopped me in Linthorpe Road and asked me if I was interested in going. I had just got married, so I was a bit non-committal and that was the last I heard of it."

Ronnie was a member of the 1950-51 'Boro side which finished sixth in the First Division, which is 'Boro's best post-war achievement. He said: "It was a very good season, and we could have finished as high as fourth. We went to Newcastle on the last day of the season knowing that a draw would put us fourth. But we lost it 1-0."

Dicks didn't score many goals in his career, especially as defenders rarely came forward at that time. But one goal, against Sheffield Wednesday at Ayresome Park in 1951 will always stick in his memory.

He said: "Jimmy James was a great fan of the 'Boro in those days. He came from Stockton and watched us whenever he could. And if we were away from home and he was appearing in the area, we went to see him on the Friday night.

"Jimmy always remembered that goal against Sheffield Wednesday and used to say to me 'Scored any good goals recently'? We had won a corner and I ran forward to get into position. The corner was knocked out to about ten yards outside the box. I never stopped running and just hit it. It flew into the net and back out off the stanchion. Everything about it was perfect, but unfortunately they don't happen too often. That's why you always remember them."

MICKY FENTON (1933-50)

MICKY FENTON was a great goalscorer and a great clubman. Lethal with both feet, the Stockton-born striker was a key member of the talented side in the late 1930s which many people believe would have gone on to win the championship but for the outbreak of World War Two.

Like his England contemporaries, George Hardwick and Wilf Mannion, Fenton lost seven years of his career because of the war. He still managed to score 162 goals, and was 36 years old when he made his final first-team appearance.

Those goals make him fifth on the 'Boro's all time goalscoring lists yet he would undoubtedly have been in the top two but for those seven lost seasons.

There may have been more England caps as well, though in the end Micky had to settle for his one solitary cap against Scotland. In his early years at Ayresome Park, Fenton was in the shadow of the great George Camsell. But he must have learned a lot from the Great Man, because he eventually took over his coveted number-nine shirt.

Micky lists Wilf Gillow as one of his early influences. He said: "When I first came to Ayresome Park the team was always struggling to avoid relegation. But Wilf turned things around. We had a very big staff of players. But most of them were old. Wilf cleared them out.

"At the same time there was a big influx of good young players. They all came through at the same time. They were helped along by the older players in the team and we got stronger every season.

"We scored a lot of goals. We had two good wingers in Ralph Birkett and Tommy Cochrane, we had inside-forwards like Wilf Mannion and Benny Yorston. Bobby Baxter was a great centre-half, and the wing-halves, Billy Brown and Billy Forrest were very important.

"Dave Cumming was also a brilliant goalkeeper. There was one game which we won at Derby 2-0. They hit him with everything. His hands were like puddings afterwards. The ball was not light, like it is today. It was all leather, and very heavy.

"Wilf's last big signing was Duncan McKenzie from Brentford. He was a wing-half. A marvellous ball player. He was a great addition to the side. I don't think there's any doubt that we would have won the title but for the war. We were just coming to our peak."

Fenton himself was not the biggest of

In March 1932, 'Boro circulated clubs to say that they had several players available for transfer. One of them was 21-year-old Scot Bobby Baxter. Fortunately there were no takers. The following month 'Boro decided to keep Baxter, initially for another year, and he went to play for Scotland and become a great club captain.

Micky Fenton, pictured in action against Brentford in 1936, was a prolific scorer who went on to join 'Boro's coaching staff. He spent over 30 years of his career at Ayresome Park.

centre-forwards, but it was his space and his shooting ability which terrified defenders. He said: "I was only nine and a half stones when I signed pro, but I was very fast. If I got away with the ball, there were very few who could catch me."

When he first left school, Micky became a butcher. But all he ever wanted to do was to play football for 'Boro. He was 19 when 'Boro eventually snapped him up on professional forms from South Bank East End. It was the days of the maximum wage, but Micky reckons that the money was not to be sniffed at.

He said: "I started off on £4 10s 0d a week, with £3 10s 0d in the summer. It was manna from heaven. I could live like a lord. Later, when I got into the first team I was getting £6, and then it moved up to £8, with £2 for a win and £1 for a draw. I felt like a millionaire."

Throughout his career with 'Boro, Micky was renowned as a bit of a practical joker. But then in the 1930s, the 'Boro dressing-room was full of good humour and japes. Just to make sure that the place was swinging, the players had their own gramophone and records.

A collection was held at the home game against Everton in January 1924, for the widow and family of William Henderson from Thornaby. He had been knocked down and killed by a charabanc on his way to watch 'Boro play Cardiff City at Ayresome Park on the New Year's Day.

Micky recalls: "We used to play the records a lot. One of them was called Red Hen. Maurice Webster started to get a bit tired of hearing it, so the players put it on to annoy him. One day he just picked up the gramophone when Red Hen was playing and threw it outside in the tunnel. So that was the end of that."

At the outbreak of war, Micky joined the technical training command of the RAF, and saw a lot of service in Egypt and North Africa. However, he saw very little of the action, for most of the time he was playing football. Micky played for a forces team called the Wanderers, which included several well-known players, including Tom Finney. He reckons he must have played hundreds of games during the war.

Towards the end of the war he was stationed at Blackpool, and returned to link up with 'Boro again. He was almost 33 when League football started again, yet in the second season after the war grabbed 28 goals in 40 appearances and helped keep the team in the First Division.

Micky said: "I was allowed to play for Blackpool during the war and they wanted me to join them after the war, but I wanted to come back to 'Boro. The side we had before the war had broken up. Most of the players were too old. Bobby Baxter had gone back to Scotland and was playing for Hearts. The team wasn't anywhere near as good."

Micky decided he wanted to turn his hand to coaching and took a ten-day course at Birmingham University for his coaching badge. He said: "They had professors running the course. One of them told me that he wanted me to shoot at the goal from a distance. The Portsmouth goalkeeper was in goal and I beat him and scored. This professor then came up to me and told me I hadn't kicked the ball right."

Fenton went on to play his final game for 'Boro in an emergency at Aston Villa in January 1950, when Peter McKennan was injured. 'Boro lost it 4-0, but the appearance ensured that Mick's playing career with 'Boro spanned three decades.

His coaching career was only just starting. Micky had special responsibility for the reserves, and was a club coach until the mid-1960s when he retired. Micky also took on a newsagent's after the war, and was successful in business.

GEORGE HARDWICK (1937-50)

GEORGE HARDWICK was one of the greatest ever players to wear the red shirt of Middlesbrough. As a competitive player, he has had few peers in the whole history of the club.

Every single match was a battle to George. Every game contained a one-against-one struggle to dominate his immediate opponent, which in George's case was normally the opposition outside-right.

Naturally George usually came out on top, and his opponent always knew that he had been in a physical game. George was no respecter of the reputations of the great wingers of his day, Stanley Matthews included.

The individual battle aside, George was also very much a team player, committed to winning every game. It's no surprise that he was England's first post-war captain, and that he also skippered the Great Britain side.

Not that George was on his own at Ayresome Park. In fact he was fortunate to be a member of one of the 'Boro's best ever teams in the late 1930s.

He said: "We had a great side, and some great players. I don't think there's any doubt that the club would have gone on to win the championship but for the outbreak of World War Two.

"We had Bobby Baxter, who was a world beating centre-half. What a man, what a football player. He used to throw dummies in his own penalty area and dribble the ball out.

"Bobby created a few nervous moments for our goalkeeper Dave Cumming. Dave was an excitable Aberdonian who used to scream at Baxter to get the ball away. But Bobby was a brilliant ball player who was always in control. Cumming was a top-class goalkeeper as well. One of the best.

"The best ball player of all time was Wilf Mannion. Like the rest of us he was denied the best part of his career by the war years. There was nothing that Wilf couldn't do with the ball and spectators paid their money just to see him play.

"And up front we had Micky Fenton. He was a great finisher. The ball was in the back of the net in a flash."

Despite all of these international stars, 'Boro never had the chance to make that big final push towards the championship.

Hardwick said: "Wilf Gillow was the manager and he knew he had a side with championship potential. When he signed Duncan McKenzie from Brentford he was the last piece in the jigsaw. Duncan wasn't a great tackler, but he stroked an immaculate ball.

"We finished fourth in season 1938-39, but never had the chance to build on it, because the war intervened. After the war, everything was different. Wilf Gillow had died, and players like Bobby Baxter had moved on. We still had a good side, but we were never championship material.

"But the years just after the war were a great time to be playing football. There were huge crowds everywhere you went. There was always a special atmosphere at Ayresome Park."

As he battled to break into the 'Boro first team as a teenager, Hardwick had to try to dislodge experienced left-back Bobby Stuart.

George said: "Bobby was a great tackler and ball winner. He could also hit a tremendous ball, which wasn't easy in those days when the heavy ball was saturated in the rain.

"Bobby was also a great fella to have around in the dressing-room. In fact we had a lot of comedians. Some days you were aching with laughter. Bobby took me under his wing. He was quick, and I needed quickening.

"Charlie Cole, the trainer, told me to run with Bobby all the time and I quickened. But that's all training consisted of in those days. You put your training gear on and ran around the pitch. Charlie made runners of us all. You never saw a ball. If you got a ball it was like getting gold dust.

"There were no tactics either. You learned them for yourself. You learned to measure up your opponent very quickly. And in those days you didn't sit down and analyse the opposition. You didn't really care who you were playing. In fact on many occasions I led the team out at Ayresome Park and had to look at the other end of the field to see who we were playing."

George Hardwick, centre, pictured in a pre-season practice game at Ayresome Park. Hardwick captained England 13 times immediately after the war. Also pictured are Wilf Mannion, Dickie Robinson and Rolando Ugolini.

Hardwick's career with the club started when he signed amateur forms in October 1935. Eighteen months later he became a professional, and had the misfortune of scoring an own-goal in the very first minute of his debut against Bolton Wanderers.

George didn't allow it to affect his game. He went on to play 166 peacetime games for 'Boro, most of them at left-back but some at centre-half, before being transferred to Oldham Athletic as player-manager at the age of 30 in November 1950.

He might have gone even earlier. During the war, Hardwick played for Chelsea while stationed in the South with the RAF, and when League football resumed, Chelsea manager Billy Birrell turned up at Ayresome Park with an open cheque book to sign George. 'Boro could have named their price, but they would not sell. Everton also later inquired, but were turned down as well.

In 1948, Italian club Juventus made an ambitious bid to sign George and Wilf Mannion. In fact Juventus's English agent came to George's house. But the move, which would have been the first taking English players to Italy, never materialised.

Financially, it would have been the making of the two players. However, they stayed tied to the maximum wage in England. Any extra cash they did make had to come from outside football, such as appearance fees at functions.

George said: "After the war, most of the top players were being helped by their clubs to develop business interests. I approached the club on behalf of Wilf and I for them to subsidise us in opening a petrol station in Normanby Road. But they wouldn't listen.

"The club was always run on very tight financial reins and was noted for its meanness. We had a change strip of white shirts and blue shorts, but the shorts were so old that the colour had washed out. It looked as though we played in all-white away from home.

"And we always had to have cold baths after training. We were each issued with a wafer thin piece of soap. The old soda type soaps were cut into strips. Once we started messing about in the baths we used to throw the pieces of soap at each other. When you asked Charlie Cole for a new piece he used to say 'What do you think this is, a millionaire's club?"

"We had a secretary Herbert Glasper, who was a nice man but he made Jack Benny look like a big spender. He was the meanest man in Britain. During the war, when you had to travel from your RAF base to play for the team, getting expenses was like drawing blood from a stone.

"I had to travel a long way. We once played in front of a full house and I asked for £10 expenses. Micky Fenton was based in Blackpool at the time and asked for £8. Herbert pointed out that he was too late, saying 'Hardwick's already taken the gate money'!"

George Hardwick wrote a weekly column for the *Evening Gazette* for 27 years.

JOHN HENDRIE (1990-1996)

JOHN HENDRIE was one of 'Boro's key players of the 1990s. Signed initially as a winger, the Scot was eventually switched to a striking role and proved highly successful in both departments.

He was snapped up from Leeds United by Colin Todd for £550,000, and helped the team reach the Play-offs, before winning promotion the following season under Lennie Lawrence.

It was Lawrence who switched Hendrie into the middle, and that's where he stayed, becoming a feared striker who topped the club's scoring charts along with Paul Wilkinson with 19 goals and led the way again under Bryan Robson. The only disappointment was that Hendrie never got the Scottish International call-up he deserved.

John was a hit with the fans virtually from the beginning, certainly after he scored what he believes is the best goal of his whole career in only his tenth League game for 'Boro at home to Millwall in October 1990.

He said: "Robbie Mustoe won the ball on the edge of the 18-yard box and played it square to me. I just ran and kept on running. Then, when I cut inside in the Millwall half, their defence opened up.

"I nearly stumbled at one time, but

John Hendrie, one of 'Boro's shrewdest signings of the 1990s, he was the club's player of the year in 1992-93.

when I got to the edge of the box and the 'keeper started to come out, I knew I was going to score, It was a wonder goal. The kind you dream about. I'd never score another goal like it."

That goal went on to win the Hennessy North-East Goal of the Year competition, and 'Boro ended the season in the Play-offs, before losing to in-form team Notts County in the two-legged semi-finals.

The same summer Colin Todd quit Ayresome after around 15 months in charge. Hendrie said: "I liked Toddy and always got on well with him. But he didn't seem to do as well without Bruce Rioch, and Bruce didn't do so well without Toddy. They were a partnership who worked best when they were together.

"But it was a weird summer. We had 11 players on the list and some of the players were upset by things that were being said.

"When Lennie arrived I thought I might have a problem at first. The previous three summers I had been transferred, and I wondered if the same thing was going to happen again.

"In 1988 I had gone from Bradford to Newcastle, in 1989 to Leeds and then 1990 to Middlesbrough. In fact I thought it was going to happen earlier when I saw Jim Smith drive into Ayresome Park with Keith Lamb. Jim had come to help out with the coaching, and he had sold me when I was at Newcastle.

"But I was able to settle down and I got on well with Lennie. That first season when he arrived was brilliant. Lennie bought well. Paul Wilkinson and Willie Falconer made a big difference to the side. I was on one wing and Stuart Ripley was on the other, and with Wilko, and Bernie Slaven and Andy Payton we were a good attacking side.

"And that was Steve Pears' best-ever season. He was magnificent. He won an England 'B' call-up before he was injured, and he was North-East Player of the Year."

The promotion success on the last day at Wolves, and the Rumbelows Cup semi-finals against Manchester United were the highlights of a great season, while 'Boro also had a good FA Cup run before losing 4-2 at home to Portsmouth in a fifth-round replay.

Hendrie said: "The main thing I can remember about that match was Darren Anderton taking a corner. Bernie was on the bench and was warming up. He went up to Anderton and called him a divvy. The next thing, Anderton takes the corner and it goes straight in the net. When Anderton turns around, Bernie is there holding his face in his arms in horror!"

Promotion to the Premier League brought big games, notably early in the season when Hendrie scored one of 'Boro's four goals in a hammering of champions Leeds United at Ayresome Park.

He said: "That was a bit special. It was the first time I had played against Leeds since I left them. It was a fantastic game to play in."

However, Hendrie remembers the 3-2 home win against Blackburn Rovers in the December as his personal peak, when he scored all three 'Boro goals. "It was my most special day personally. It was a big game, on *Match of the Day*, and to score a hat-trick against the team run by my boyhood hero, Kenny Dalglish, was unforgettable."

'Boro were unable to maintain that fine start, and ended up back in the First Division, despite finishing the season well with three wins in the last six.

There was still time for fun. John was responsible for an April Fool's Day jape, which involved writing on the dressing-room blackboard that training was at Norton that day. He said: "Half the team set off for Norton in two cars, but we were training on the pitch! It took ages for people going out to look for them and bring them back. I had to own up to that one eventually."

However, Nicky Mohan soon got his own back. John added: "I went to get in my car in the underground car-park to find that it was camouflaged by the contents of the rubbish bins. Everything was emptied on and around the car. It was stinking!"

Hendrie always seems to be in the thick of the pranks, one way or another. When Chris Kamara arrived on loan at Ayresome Park, he was walking around with a sign saying 'The Saviour' on his back, thanks to John.

But John was a serious character on the pitch. He scored 14 goals by October after relegation, but picked up an ankle injury which side-lined him for several months. The team suffered as well, and missed out on the Play-offs despite a bright finish to the season.

Lennie Lawrence moved on that summer, and the rest is history. Bryan Robson came in and took 'Boro back into the Premier League.

John said: "Lennie did a good job by marking Bryan's card, but he bought, and bought well. The bottom line is that the club was turned around by Steve Gibson when he got sole control.

"We were always up there, and I'll never forget that last home game against Luton when we virtually settled it. It's the best atmosphere I have ever known, and it was an emotional experience for me to score the goals. It's nice to think that you have scored the very last League goal at Ayresome Park."

'Boro's reward for winning promotion was a short break in Portugal, where the players were finally able to let their hair down following the pressures of a testing season.

It wasn't all celebrations for John, however. He said: "We were shattered after the journey there, and after a couple of drinks I fell asleep in the sun around the pool. The lads very kindly covered me up from the sun's ray, except for pulling my shorts down to the bottom of my backside.

"The result was third degree burns. The lads said they were barbecuing sausages on my backside. It made the rest of the holiday rather painful!"

John Hickton, showing the aerial power which made him a greatly feared striker. Hickton is 'Boro's most prolific goalscorer since Brian Clough.

JOHN HICKTON (1966-78)

JOHN HICKTON was one of 'Boro's greatest players. Most supporters can remember his terrific strength on the ball, his powerful running and his bullet-like shooting prowess.

He also joined 'Boro for an absolute snip. He was signed from Sheffield Wednesday for £20,000 in October 1966, in 'Boro's first-ever season in the Third Division. Hickton initially became one of three regular goalscorers in the 'Boro side, alongside John O'Rourke and Arthur Horsfield. But then he took over the mantel of chief goal grabber and went on to top the 'Boro goalscoring charts for six consecutive seasons.

Hickton recalls: "I had played in the First Division with Wednesday and been to the FA Cup Final. But Alan Brown wouldn't play me. He was prepared to sell me.

"I could have gone to Norwich or 'Boro. But I fancied 'Boro. Stan Anderson had a reputation for success in the North-East, and I thought it was the best move for me. I fell in love with the club and with the area. But it was in a mess when I got here. There were a lot of players whose hearts weren't in the club. Stan eventually sorted it out by having a clear-out, and we got better and better as the season developed.

"We played with two wingers at that time, and we had three strikers. We were capable of putting sides under a lot of pressure, particularly at Ayresome Park. That night when we clinched promotion against Oxford was unbelievable. The atmosphere inside the ground was tremendous. And there were a lot of fans locked outside."

Hickton went into the Second Division with 'Boro with high hopes, but over the next few years he felt that the club lacked ambition. He said: "I wanted to play in the First Division. It was my overriding ambition. I felt that everybody should think the same way, but I wasn't really convinced that the club's ambition was the same as mine. We were unbeatable at Ayresome Park, but we weren't good enough away from home. They wouldn't get the players."

The reply from Hickton was a series of transfer requests, which were turned down. He said: "Spurs were interested in me, but Stan told the directors that he would quit if they sold me. So I stayed. Burnley came in as well, and Sheffield Wednesday inquired about taking me back, but nothing came of it. I still loved the club. I felt sure at the start of every season that we would win promotion but it never happened. I don't think we ever got the blend right."

It was Jack Charlton who came in and got the blend right, and from then on everything was plain sailing. 'Boro stormed away with the Second Division championship in 1973-74 season, and went on to become a force in the First Division. Hickton, as ever, became one of the mainstays of the side.

He said: "We had a mixture of fear and respect for Jack. We knew he had done everything in the game. He had won the World Cup. He made it absolutely clear in pre-season training what he wanted. He got us playing his way, and it suited us.

"Jack brought in Bobby Murdoch, who was a great passer of the ball. He was made for players like Alan Foggon and David Armstrong. And we had Graeme Souness. You couldn't get the ball off him in training, but on match days he was a great team player. Jack's system was simple. David Mills used to drag the two centre-backs out wide and Alan Foggon came running into space through the middle.

"It wasn't just the system. We had a lot of good players. We got criticised by a lot of people. But it was just sour grapes. We played a lot of attractive football, particularly in the First Division.

"We could have gone on to win things, but we needed another couple of players. We probably needed a midfield player and another striker. We didn't get them, but we still had some great times. It was a good time to be part of the club."

All goals are memorable, and John scored with some great strikes in his

David Hodgson, seen here after receiving the Robinsons Barley Water Young Player of the Month award from England manager Ron Greenwood in 1981. He won six England Under-21 caps.

time. His final League tally of 185 make him 'Boro's fourth top goalscorer of all time, behind Camsell, Elliott and Clough. Hickton also made 482 appearances for 'Boro, and only Tim Williamson and Gordon Jones have done better.

The best goal of all, arguably came not in the League, but in the FA Cup sixth-round tie at home to Manchester United in February 1970. He powered forward in scything fashion, before crashing a blistering shot past United goalkeeper Alex Stepney to equalise an earlier goal from Carlo Sartori. John admitted: "You tend to forget a lot of your goals. But I still dream about that one against United, running down the left wing and hitting it perfectly right. In any case, scoring against United was a memorable goal at any time, because they were such a great side."

'Boro eventually lost to United in a replay, and it was to be one of several Cup disappointments in John's career. He said: "The worst was the sixth-round defeat at Birmingham City when Bob Hatton scored. I had scored at St Andrew's at the start of the season when we won there 3-0. I really thought it was going to be our year because there were not a lot of quality sides left in the Cup. But we didn't play well on the day.

"Obviously it's every player's ambition to play at Wembley. I had to settle for a Second Division championship medal but I had some great times in my career.

"You look back and you think of the big games, and the characters. Eric McMordie and Gordon Jones were always a couple of live wires together. They kept you on your toes."

International honours didn't come Hickton's way, though it's a shame that he never had the opportunity. The nearest he came was as a reserve for an England Under-23 international against Italy at Nottingham.

At the end of John's playing career, he still had all the experience necessary to go into coaching. But Hickton decided to quit while still at the top.

However, he did accept a two-year contract in the United States with Fort Lauderdale. His old pal David Chadwick was the coach there. It should have brought a happy ending to John's playing career, but a double fracture of his leg brought it to a premature end.

DAVID HODGSON (1978-87)

DAVID HODGSON was one of the most talented of several young players who were given an early baptism in the First Division by manager John Neal. A determined player, with a great turn of pace and a good crosser, Hodgson did a lot of the running up front and quickly became a crucial member of the side.

David was never a prolific goalscorer, grabbing 20 in almost 150 appearances, but he was the type of player who could prise open defences and he was the provider for many 'Boro goals.

The Gateshead-born player was picked up by 'Boro while playing for Redheugh Boys Club, and turned down the chance to sign for Bolton Wanderers in preferring the move to Ayresome Park.

He said: "When I came to 'Boro, I moved into the Medhurst Hotel, and that's the best thing that could have happened to me. A lot of young lads, like Craig Johnston, Peter Johnson, Billy Askew and Charlie Bell were in there. We developed a special relationship.

"A lady called Mrs P used to look after us. It was a marvellous set-up. It was a major factor in me becoming a professional player. I was very disappointed when the club later sold the Medhurst. It was bad business. They didn't realise what they had."

As an apprentice, Hodgy had to look after the boots and kit of professionals like Graeme Souness and David Armstrong. He quickly wised up to the art of football wind-ups, and became one of the chief instigators among the 'Boro kids.

He admitted: "I was the worst among the apprentices. I was forever playing tricks on people. Putting gunge in beds, loosening curtain rails. I did the lot.

"I got a bit of a name for it, and I can remember one FA Youth Cup-tie against Everton when Harold Shepherdson threw my boots at me and warned me that I had better play well in the match, because my conduct had not been too good. Harold warned me that my future might be on the line. He knew exactly what he was doing, because he got me fired up and I went out and covered every blade of grass."

David was 17 when he turned pro, and was quickly promoted to the first team, making his full debut in a goalless draw at home to Bristol City in November 1978.

He said: "John Neal brought in a lot of kids, but he had to. Several of the senior pros were coming to the end of their careers. The great thing about all the lads that John brought in was that we all had a gut feeling for the club. It was a natural reaction to go out there and run yourself into the ground for the club.

"I clicked on the field with Mark Proctor, because we were so used to playing together, and Craig Johnston and Peter Johnson linked in as well. The enthusiasm that we introduced rubbed off on the rest of the team and that was one of our strengths.

"We had a good side. We could give anybody a good game. But if we had bought a couple of top quality players to fill in the gaps, then we could have gone on to be anything."

Hodgson's first few goals for 'Boro were all scored away from home, and he well remembers his first goal at Ayresome Park – which came against Everton in a 2-1 win in March 1980.

He said: "I played a one-two with David Armstrong and then just seemed to stroke the ball, and it went into the corner. I can remember running back down the pitch with Craig Johnston and Mark Proctor hanging on my back. They were more delighted for me than I was!

"But I never really bothered that much about goalscoring. I wanted to play a major part in the game. We had two other men up front, Micky Burns and Billy Ashcroft, who weren't the fastest of players. I did all the running for them, and was in the side more for making goals than scoring them."

Like most players from that period, Hodgy looks back at the FA Cup defeat by Wolves in 1981 as a turning point for the club.

He said: "We played so well all the way up to Wolves. We had that great win at Swansea in the third round, and then had huge crowds when we beat West Brom and Barnsley at Ayresome Park. The atmosphere against Barnsley was the best I have ever known at the stadium.

"If we had beaten Wolves I'm sure that we would have gone on to reach Wembley, because we didn't have any fears about Tottenham in the semi-finals. We had already stuffed them 4-1 at Ayresome Park when I scored a hat-trick.

"We had so many chances to beat Wolves at Ayresome Park. If we had beaten them, I'm sure the club's fortunes would have gone the other way. In the event, everything fell apart.

"It was hard on Bobby Murdoch because it happened so quickly, It was his first step into management, and no disrespect to him, but it was not easy for him to deal with it when it was collapsing around him.

"A lot of players wanted to be away, and most of the players who came in had no feeling for the place. Eventually I left as well, and it was so sad to see the club struggling."

David did return to Ayresome Park, when he joined the club on a month's loan from Norwich City in 1987. But he was sent off in his second game, at home to Bristol City, and Bruce Rioch brought the loan deal to a premature end.

However, Hodgy will always be remembered fondly for his commitment and determination during one of 'Boro's best modern periods.

BILLY HORNER (1961-69)

BILLY HORNER was a stalwart of the club throughout the 1960s, and had the distinction of playing a big part in Stan Anderson's memorable Third Division promotion winning side.

Cassop-born Horner was a strong ball-winning wing-half who was a good guy to have around in a battle. He went on to play more than 200 games for the club.

He was an inside-forward when he was picked up by 'Boro and brought to Ayresome Park in 1957, signing professional forms two years later.

Billy said: "There were a handful of apprentices when I arrived and I got the job of cleaning the professionals' boots, along with Gordon Jones. It was a privileged job, because the other lads had to work outside on the ground, putting divots back and things. We had a little wooden boot room with a one-bar electric fire, which used to send sparks flying off it."

Jimmy Gordon ran the Northern Intermediate League side at that time, while Micky Fenton was in charge of the reserves in the North-Eastern League.

Billy recalls: "They were totally different personalities. Jimmy didn't swear, but he was a hard man, and fair.

Billy Horner, who played for 'Boro throughout the 1960s, was an important part of Stan Anderson's promotion team in 1966-67.

When I moved into the reserves, I got a shock with Micky. I'd never heard language like it. He had a way with words and used to frighten players. If he gave you a rollicking you were shaking like mad. But it was what you needed. It toughened you up."

Horner made his first-team debut in a 1-1 draw at Orient in March 1961. He said: "It was fabulous just to be playing alongside players like Brian Clough and Alan Peacock. We were always an entertaining side. We played with wingers and we used to push forward and attack teams.

"We never had any coaching. Bob Dennison was the manager, but you never saw him in a track suit. He always had a collar and tie and a suit on. He used to come into the dressing-room before the game, look around at everybody, and just tell you to get stuck in. But we were all individual players. We knew our jobs."

He added: "We had more international players than any club in the North-East. We had McNeil, Holliday, Peacock, Jones, Fernie, Harris and Fitzsimons. The problem was that we had no leadership. We went close to promotion a couple of times, but never got it all harnessed together to be successful."

Dennison eventually moved on, and was replaced by Raich Carter, who was a great player in his own right in his day. However, 'Boro did not enjoy a successful period during Carter's reign, and Horner in particular didn't see eye to eye with him.

Police, acting on a tip-off in 1963, questioned 'Boro centre-half Mel Nurse as he left a local cinema with his wife, on suspicion of being one of the Great Train Robbers. The flabbergasted Welsh international said: "I thought they wanted to talk to me about my car tax. It took quite a while to convince them who I really was."

Billy said: "We were at loggerheads a little bit. He used to keep us waiting in the dressing-room sometimes and then we'd get a phone call from Redcar and had to go over there. You'd find him walking the dog on the beach. I asked for a transfer, but he wouldn't let me go."

Horner was back in the frame when Stan Anderson took over at Ayresome Park. Billy said: "Stan could handle people, and all the players played for him. He brought one or two new men in, and once we got to know each other it all gelled together.

"It was the first time I had ever seen a track suit manager and it made a big impression on us. Stan was still a very big name in the game. He bought John Hickton as a centre-half, but when he pushed Hickton up front he was a different class. We were also strong in defence with Dickie Rooks and Billy Gates and we had our fair share of goalscorers, because we had John O'Rourke and Arthur Horsfield as well."

Horner helped 'Boro re-establish themselves in the Second Division but then suffered a knee ligament injury. He said: "That's when I took my coaching badge, and I took the reserves. We had some good lads coming through like Webb, Laidlaw, Maddren and Mills, and went on to win the League. I could have stayed on with Stan, but once I was fully fit I missed playing first-team football so I moved to Darlington."

Billy scored few goals for 'Boro, though one for the most memorable was his first – in a 3-3 draw at home to Sunderland. 'Boro were 3-0 down at the time, and the goal sparked the fight-back. Horner said: "Ian Gibson went into a tackle on Jimmy McNab and the ball broke to me, 20 or 25 yards out, and I hit it past Jimmy Montgomery into the bottom corner. It was one to remember."

Horner rates Gibson as one of the best players he ever played alongside, but not the best. He added: "Willie Fernie was probably the most talented and gifted player I have ever seen. We used to play 25-a-side in the car-park on a morning and you just couldn't get the ball off him. Every part of his body seemed to move.

"He only needed to turn it on for 20 minutes and he could win a game on his own."

GORDON JONES (1961-73)

GORDON JONES was a remarkable club servant who went on to make 528 League and Cup appearances for 'Boro, which stands as a post-war record. In fact only legendary goalkeeper Tim Williamson, with 602, played more games for the club.

Jones was the perfect left-back, strong into the tackle, and keen to get forward at every opportunity, where his deft left foot was the provider for many a goal.

Gordon won nine England Under-23 caps and was reputed to be on the verge of winning a place in the England squad for the World Cup Finals in 1966. It didn't happen, but he was always regarded as one of the top left-backs in the country.

Remarkably, Jones was signed by 'Boro after one of the briefest trials of all time.

He said: "I was living in Sedgefield at the time and I wrote asking for a trial. The club were holding trials at Hutton Road and the coaching staff of Jimmy Gordon, Harold Shepherdson, manager Bob Dennison and Mick Fenton were running the rule over the triallists.

"I'd only been playing for ten minutes when Jimmy Gordon shouted, 'Come off number three'. I went into the bath and thought that was it.

"Then Jimmy Gordon and Bob Dennison came in and said they wanted to talk to my father because they wanted to sign me. I couldn't believe it, but of course I was delighted.

"I asked Jimmy Gordon later how he could sign me after just ten minutes and he said he saw that I had a good left foot, and the way I knocked a ball in was different to that normally expected of a 15-year-old. He said he knew I had something different immediately."

'Boro had a tremendous record in picking up players with great potential at that time, and Jones was another gem.

Gordon's first match on the groundstaff was 'Boro's 9-0 crushing of Brighton at the start of the 1958-59 season. He said: "I remember it for two things. First of all I was stuck in a long queue of traffic going to the match because the Newport Bridge was raised. It's the first time I'd ever seen it up.

"And then it was awe inspiring to be in the same dressing-room as players like Brian Clough and Bill Harris. They were stars. Then I couldn't believe the atmosphere when 'Boro won 9-0. I thought it was always going to be like that."

Gordon learned quickly that being a footballer is not all about playing football – you have to be able to stand up and be counted when it comes to being worldly wise.

He said: "On my very first day I walked into the dressing-room with Billy Horner and a lad called Arthur Proctor, who was also on the ground staff. We were there before the pros, and we got changed, and started cleaning boots.

"At ten to ten Billy Horner told me that Brian Clough was shouting for me. I couldn't imagine why he wanted me, but I went into the dressing-room.

"Brian looked angry. He pointed to Arthur's clothes hanging on the peg and said 'If I see those clothes on my peg again I'll see to it that you are kicked out of this club by the first door'.

"Of course I was terrified at the time and I didn't like Brian for a long time. But when I got to know football I realised that it was just part of the way of things. And I changed my opinion of Brian."

Gordon went on to make his 'Boro first-team debut as a 17-year-old, at right-back in a 3-2 defeat at Southampton in January 1961. Immediately he became a regular member of the squad.

The breakthrough came 14 months after the famous Round-Robin incident against Brian Clough. Jones said: "I can remember Willie Fernie coming into the dressing-room, taking his shirt off, throwing it at Bob Dennison's feet and saying that he wouldn't wear it again as long as Brian was centre-forward. Willie left the club soon afterwards.

"But it was a rare incident. There were no factions, and no back-biting. The players got on well together and they were always helpful. Brian was always approachable. He could be a bit bombastic at times, but he was happy to help and give advice. I think we had a pretty good atmosphere at the time."

Cloughie was grabbing all the headlines for his goal feats, but Jones reckons the best player he ever saw wear a Middlesbrough shirt was the Welsh international wing-half Bill Harris.

Gordon Jones, right, made 528 appearances for 'Boro, more than any post-war player. He spent 12 years at Ayresome Park, winning nine England Under-23 international caps.

He said: "Bill was a great player. He was one of the best passers of a ball I have ever seen. He could place it exactly where he wanted it, time and time again. The forwards got most of the praise, but Bill was the provider."

Jones's early career was spent under Bob Dennison, but when he left the club, Raich Carter took over. It coincided with 'Boro gradually sliding towards the Third Division.

He said: "I learned a lot from Bob Dennison. I was sad when he left. Raich did well for a while, but then the team found it difficult. Raich was a great, great player. Football came naturally to him and he thought some players were capable of playing better than they did. But it wasn't like that."

Despite 'Boro's poor results on the pitch, Jones still earned a place in the England Under-23 team and was talked about as a possible full international – without ever breaking through.

On the other hand, he became a Third Division player when 'Boro were relegated in 1966. Gordon said: "We were relegated in the last game when we lost 5-3 at Cardiff. Dickie Rooks scored a hat-trick from centre-half and we still lost. Without accusing anybody, some of the players were very disappointed that night. We felt that something was not right."

Fortunately good times were around the corner. Stan Anderson had replaced Carter and 'Boro's fortunes were transformed.

Jones said: "Stan was great for this club. He weeded the rubbish out and turned the club around. He brought in players like John O'Rourke and David Chadwick and set out to achieve something. He made me captain as well, so I had to be pleased about that.

"Naturally people look at John Hickton and say he was the best signing, but to be honest I feel that the best of all was Willie Whigham. He wasn't the greatest goalkeeper in the country but he was an excellent shot stopper, and he instilled a confidence in the team that we hadn't had for a long time."

Anderson's first full season in charge culminated in promotion, thanks to that 4-1 win at home to Oxford United in the last game of the season at Ayresome Park.

Gordon said: "Later in my career, I played in front of 100,000 people for Crook Town in India, but I never ever experienced an atmosphere like the one that night against Oxford. I don't think there has been an atmosphere like it since at Ayresome Park.

"Obviously it was a bit special because we won easily and gained promotion. But I always felt that we were going to do it. It was a much harder match the previous Saturday when we beat Peterborough United by 2-1 at Ayresome Park. We knew we had to win both games and that was the pressure one."

In the few years following their return to the Second Division, 'Boro went agonisingly close to reaching the First Division on a number of occasions.

Gordon said: "We had a good side. Stan continued to make improvements and he would have made more if we had gone up. It annoyed me to miss out on all those occasions because I believed we were good enough. But we were always let down at the end of the season.

"I know we were good enough because Jack Charlton came in and took virtually the same side up. Big Jack got the best out of Graeme Souness, who was a great player with a bit of self arrogance, and he brought in Bobby Murdoch, who had great experience."

ALAN KERNAGHAN (1985-93)

ALAN KERNAGHAN arrived at Ayresome Park as a striker, had a spell in midfield, and eventually developed as a quality defender which brought him Republic of Ireland international honours.

In many respects he was a late developer, struggling to hold down a regular place in Bruce Rioch's young side, and as a result going on to make more than 50 appearances as substitute for the club – which is a club record. However, perseverance paid dividends, and Kernaghan's determination to succeed finally brought stability, a regular place in the team, and eventually the club captaincy when Tony Mowbray moved on to Celtic. Alan went on to make more than 250 League and Cup appearances for the club.

He made his first-team breakthrough in February 1985, when 'Boro were hurtling towards liquidation. Kernaghan said: "The club was obviously in a bad way at the time, but the young players couldn't appreciate it at the time. It was just great to be part of the first-team squad of a Football League club, which is all we had ever wanted to do.

"I'm sure the older players were aware of it, but I didn't think about the slide. It's only now that I can look back and understand."

Alan Kernaghan, who proved himself a useful utility player, before settling down at centre-back and going on to win Republic of Ireland international caps.

Joy riding is not just a contemporary problem. In 1956, 'Boro winger Sam Lawrie was fined £35 for taking a car without the owner's consent, driving without a licence or insurance and was disqualified for one year.

Alan was brought to Ayresome by Malcolm Allison, and played under three more managers in Jack Charlton, Willie Maddren and Bruce Rioch before the 'Boro went into liquidation.

He said: "Once again, I think the players were able to handle liquidation because we were so young. Even though the gates were locked, we just felt we were carrying on as normal. The only difference was that we didn't get any wages for a long time.

"I was in digs and paying £30, but my landlady was understanding. She knew I wasn't getting any money. Eventually I got some money off the receiver to pay her; then later we got money from the PFA and the consortium. Fortunately most of the lads were local and were living at home, so it wasn't too hard for

Brian Laws, pictured scoring against Millwall in April, 1986. It was the last goal at Ayresome Park before liquidation.

The three Carr brothers from South Bank, Jackie, George and William, played together 26 times for 'Boro. This is a unique record as no other Football League club has ever had three brothers turning out in the same fixture.

them." 'Boro survived the crisis, and swept to two consecutive promotions in the following seasons.

Kernaghan said: "We knew almost immediately that there was something good there. We were so well drilled. Everybody was fighting for each other. We didn't have any stars who felt they should be somewhere else.

"Everybody knew what to do. We used to call it 'The Script'. It was a pattern of play that we worked on to the training ground and then carried on in matches. It became a habit.

"In that season in the Third Division we murdered some teams. They just couldn't handle us. We played for each other and were like a group of mates. That's why we had so many clean sheets. There was never any danger that we would fail to win promotion.

"We kept it going the following season, but it was touch and go. When Bruce signed Trevor Senior it was the final piece in the jigsaw. Trevor's goals got us promoted.

"He was also such a great lad to have around. He was so funny. We were always laughing the things he came out with.

"I can remember one occasion at Maiden Castle when Colin Todd was really laying into us. Trevor started giggling, and when Toddy yelled at him 'Why are you laughing', Trevor replied: 'I'm not laughing, I've just got big teeth'. Everybody fell about. Trevor kept a smile on our faces."

'Boro's second promotion took them into the First Division, where the pressures were so much different for Rioch's young side. They did well in the first half of the season, but then struggled and were relegated at Sheffield Wednesday on the last day of the season.

Kernaghan said: "If we had stayed up, who knows what might have happened? But we just needed a couple more players. Bruce spent all his money on Peter Davenport, and it didn't really work out for him.

"Once we started losing, we couldn't stop it. It snowballed. When Bruce Rioch came down to Maiden Castle and called us all together to say he was leaving, it shook everybody up. He was a hard man at times, but we respected him for what he had achieved. Our success was all due to him. It was strange."

Colin Todd took over the helm, and 'Boro just managed to avoid a second successive relegation when crushing Newcastle 4-1 at Ayresome Park at the end of the 1990-91 season. Kernaghan said: "It was a boiling hot day and we needed to win to stay up, and they needed to win to go up. In the end we murdered them. Newcastle had Mick Quinn and Mark McGhee up front but Simon Coleman and me didn't give them a kick."

The following season Alan was a regular under Todd, but began to become the brunt of terrace criticism. Kernaghan said: "The crowd started to hammer me, and once when Toddy brought me off, I told him that he had just bowed to the crowd. That was me out of the team."

Alan spent three months on loan at Lennie Lawrence's Charlton Athletic, and was preparing to make the move permanent. He said: "I was on my way to London to sign, but I popped into Ayresome Park because Toddy had left and 'Boro were revealing the new manager.

"Nobody would tell me who it was. They told me to go and look on the pitch. I couldn't believe it when I saw Lennie Lawrence. He talked me into staying, and I achieved a lot of consistency. I had my best spell for the club under Lennie."

Kernaghan achieved his success despite being diagnosed as a diabetic, following a goalless draw at Queen's Park Rangers in the First Division in 1989. It was also the day of the Hillsborough disaster.

He said: "To be honest it was a relief when it was diagnosed. I had lost a stone in two weeks and I couldn't sleep.

"Once I started injecting the insulin I started to feel a lot better. I've never had a problem with the diabetes and the great thing is that it never affected my career. In fact it got better afterwards."

BRIAN LAWS (1985-88)

BRIAN LAWS was one of Willie Maddren's prudent buys, when snapped up for just £30,000 from Huddersfield Town.

He went on to score the vital first goal at Shrewsbury which kept 'Boro in the Second Division in 1984-85, and was the only ever-present the following season.

Laws said: "That goal at Shrewsbury was very important to the club, because it kept us up. We were hopeful of doing better the next season, but it didn't happen for us. We struggled again.

"That's why we were grateful for a bit of fun. It was a cold New Year's Day at home to Huddersfield when a streaker ran on the pitch with only his socks on. He made a bee-line for me and gave me a hug. I couldn't help but laugh when I saw the size of it. It must have been very cold that day!"

Relegation was followed by liquidation, and it was a difficult summer for the 'Boro players. Laws said: "It was a bit worrying being locked out of the ground and not getting paid.

"But then we really got it together in the following season. Bruce Rioch brought in the kids and pushed me into midfield. I moved there reluctantly, but I scored ten goals within a couple of months, and so that was very pleasing.

"Unfortunately, I then snapped my cruciate ligament and was out of football for a year. It was then I realised how much I would miss the game if I had to quit, so I took my coaching and management courses. These led me to being awarded the Grimsby manager's job."

Laws came back after injury the following season and vividly remembers the three epic FA Cup-ties with Everton in January and February 1988, which were watched by 94,000 fans.

He said: "All three games were classics. Everton were in the First Division at the time but we were as good as them. Then, at the end of the season we were promoted to the First Division, to complete a second successive promotion."

Laws did not play for 'Boro in the top flight, instead electing to join Brian Clough at Nottingham Forest under freedom of contract and going on to make several Wembley appearances with the Midlands club.

JIM LAWSON (1966-68)

JIM LAWSON was a home-grown midfielder who never really established himself as a youngster at Ayresome Park.

However, he matured into a quality League player after being sold to Huddersfield Town, for whom he played for nine seasons and played at top level in Division One.

Jimmy Lawson, a home produced midfield man who played 37 games for 'Boro before moving on to Huddersfield.

The South Bank lad had the best possible tutor – Wilf Mannion. Jim said: "As a 15-year-old with Middlesbrough, I can remember knocking on Wilf's door with my father to ask him for his help and guidance."

Five years later Jim moved on to Huddersfield, but it was at Ayresome Park where he gained one of his most vivid memories while playing for the Terriers.

Lawson said: "I came to Ayresome with Huddersfield needing a point to be certain of promotion to Division One. This was attained when we drew 1-1. TV and media were in abundance after the game and all my family were there, making it the most memorable night I can remember."

TONY McANDREW (1973-86)

TONY McANDREW was a typical Ayresome Park crowd favourite, a thoroughly committed and aggressive player who always made his presence felt on the field of play.

Born in Lanark, Tony was picked up by 'Boro as a youth and went on to make more than 350 appearances for the club, playing in a variety of positions. However, the vast majority of his games were played in the 'Boro defence.

McAndrew had two spells at Ayresome Park, moving on to Chelsea in 1982, but returning two years later to play another two seasons, before retiring as a player.

One of Tony's most vivid memories was playing alongside the great Scot Bobby Murdoch. He said: "It was a marvellous experience for me because

In 1979 'Boro opened negotiations with Manchester United to buy David McCreery for £150,000. However, the negotiations for the Northern Ireland international broke down. McCreery eventually came to Cleveland 15 years later as manager of Hartlepool.

Tony McAndrew, pictured in action against Birmingham City in 1977, made over 350 appearances for 'Boro in two different spells at Ayresome Park.

Bobby was a legend in Scotland. There was nothing he couldn't do with the ball."

Another memory came from off the field. He said: "I always thought it was unusual that the clock on the stand never moved! It was stuck at the same time. Nobody tried to fix it."

Despite his popular appeal, Tony occasionally had to endure abuse from the crowd. He said: "I will always remember the comments from the Chicken Run, which was the South Terrace. There was constant abuse at times.

"But a happier moment was my hat-trick against Sheffield United in 1976. It was a great feeling for me. Even the Chicken Run kept quiet that day.

"And another memory was Terry Cochrane's great home debut against Norwich City. He had a marvellous game and tore them apart."

After moving to Chelsea, Tony had the dubious distinction of returning to Ayresome Park with the London club and scoring against his former club. He admitted: "It was a very strange feeling."

When Tony returned to 'Boro, times were hard. The club was struggling against relegation, and crowds had dipped dramatically. McAndrew became a cornerstone of the side, and this difficult period still produced a notable memory. He said: "I scored my very last goal for 'Boro in a Christmas derby at home to Sunderland. That was a bit special."

The pitch at Ayresome Park was lengthened by one yard to 115 yards in 1966 to meet World Cup requirements.

ALEX McCRAE (1948-53)

ALEX McCRAE was a strong left-footed striker who was the key player in 'Boro's best post-war season. The Scot top scored with 21 goals as 'Boro finished sixth in the First Division in 1950-51.

McCrae spent five years at Ayresome Park after being signed from Charlton Athletic, where he had never really settled following a move from Hearts.

Alex became popular with the 'Boro fans and went on to score 49 goals in 130 appearances for the club before returning to Scotland when joining Falkirk in March 1953.

He said: "My time at Ayresome Park was the best of my career. We had a very, very good side, and the team spirit was marvellous.

"Players like Mannion, Hardwick, Spuhler and Ugolini were among the best in the country. And in the season we finished sixth, we were as good as anybody until we fell a way a little towards the end of the season."

Alex McCrae, pictured centre, along with Jimmy Gordon, left, and Lindy Delapenha, was top scorer with 21 goals in season 1950-51 when 'Boro finished sixth in Division One, their best post-war achievement.

In that season, McCrae scored three hat-tricks before Christmas, but was one of several players to pick up frustrating injuries in the second half of the season.

He said: "I well remember the 8-0 hammering of Huddersfield, when I got a hat-trick. We were going really well at that time.

"But my favourite memory is probably the three FA Cup-ties we had against Aston Villa the previous season. We drew at Aston Villa and at Ayresome Park, but then beat them 3-0 at Leeds when I scored twice and Wilf Mannion bagged the other. They were great games.

"But it was always a pleasure to play at Ayresome Park. We got great crowds in those days and they always got behind the team."

McCrae's big pal at Ayresome was wing-half Jimmy Gordon, but he got on well with all the squad. He said: "Ugolini was always joking about. The humour was part of the life. You had to be careful what you said in the dressing-room, but that was typical all over. I enjoyed every minute of it."

DEREK McLEAN (1955-62)

DEREK McLEAN was one of the members of 'Boro's much vaunted home grown forward line of the late 1950s, which included Brian Clough.

Three of those forwards, Clough, Edwin Holliday and Alan Peacock, went on to play for England. But Derek and winger Billy Day were equally important members of one of the most exciting front fives that 'Boro have ever possessed.

Derek was around at the time of the famous Round-Robin affair, in which the majority of the players signed a statement calling for Brian Clough to be stripped of the captaincy.

McLean said: "The round robin was signed on the train coming back from an away match at Ipswich. The players did not want Brian Clough as captain."

Derek did not play in that game in East Anglia, but recalls: "I arrived at the ground on the Monday to find that a meeting had been called for the players who were on the trip. Brian and the manager, Bob Dennison, were also there. Everybody gave their views to say why they did not want him as captain.

"After the meeting the atmosphere in the dressing-room was very quiet. In fact it was like that all week. Eventually Saturday came and we were at home to Bristol Rovers. Brian was still captain, and not much was said while we were getting changed.

"The game got under way with not very much shouting on the field. However, when Brian got an early goal all the lads went up and congratulated him. The atmosphere changed immediately. Brian added another two goals and we went on to win 5-1. The supporters said later that it was one of the best performances of the season."

Derek can vividly remember another occasion when Cloughie scored four goals against Doncaster Rovers at Ayresome Park. The Doncaster goalkeeper was Harry Gregg, who played for Northern Ireland. McLean said: "Every time Clough scored, he shouted 'Pick that one out Harry'. Harry was boiling. He ran to the edge of the box every time, clenching his fist and waving his arms. He said: 'I'll kill you if I get hold of you'. Brian just grinned back. But after the match Harry came to shake Brian's hand."

'Boro beat Doncaster 5-0 that day – a scoreline they later repeated against Derby County at Ayresome Park in the third round of the FA Cup.

McLean said: "After the match the Derby manager went straight into the dressing-room and ordered three of his players to go back on to the pitch before they could get stripped. The manager stood looking at the pitch. When one of them asked him what the matter was, he replied: 'I'm looking for the big hole where you three were hiding all afternoon'."

Derek was from Brotton, and as a boy used to travel with his brother Geoff by bus to watch home games.

He said: "My mother gave us sixpence each to see the match and have a meal. The buses going to Middlesbrough were packed with supporters

Derek McLean, in action against Port Vale in 1956, was a member of 'Boro's remarkable home-grown forward line of the late 1950s.

going to see Mannion, Fenton and Hardwick.

"It was a dream come true when I signed for the 'Boro and had the chance to meet all the players I used to watch from the terraces. I signed for £3 a week and £20 signing on fee. We had a great bunch of players and staff. My one regret was that we went so close to winning promotion to the First Division every year without ever getting there."

Derek remembers the magnificent quality of the pitch. He said: "Wilf Atkinson, the groundsman, treasured the turf. He watched every home game from the players' entrance, and any player who made a sliding tackle and churned up the turf got a blast from Wilf's tongue. And in training, if anybody cut the corner and went on to the pitch when running around the track, you could hear Wilf's voice from the back of the stand yelling at them to get off the pitch.

"But it was with good reason. All the players from the visiting teams used to comment on the quality of the pitch. Wilf was a first-class groundsman."

Derek also recalls Astor, the black comedian who was 'Boro's best-known fan in the 1950s. He said: "Astor used to go round the clubs and you could hear his voice all around the ground on match days. He had the players and the crowd in stitches with his comments.

"He used to say to players 'Come on, I've got you in the sweep'. On a really hot day he would shout 'No matter how much the sun shines, you'll never be like me'. Lindy Delapenha was 'Boro's first black player and Astor used to shout 'Come on Our Kid'. To the visiting players he would say 'You'll have to watch Cloughie today, he got three goals last week.'

"Overall our supporters were some of the best in the country. They knew their football and really got behind us."

ERIC McMORDIE (1965-74)

ERIC McMORDIE was a gritty and often fiery Irishman who was the platform for many of 'Boro's attacks during the Stan Anderson years.

He was a tough tackling and ball playing midfielder who grafted around in front of the 'Boro defence and helped to make the team tick.

His ability was recognised with the award of 21 Northern Ireland caps, which makes him Ayresome Park's third most capped player of all time in official internationals.

McMordie made his 'Boro debut as a 19-year-old and was still only 28 when transferred to York City by Jack Charlton, having played 273 games for 'Boro and scored 25 goals.

In the beginning he might have been a Manchester United player along with George Best, when both lads travelled from Belfast for a trial at Old Trafford.

McMordie said: "We had just left school, and we lasted two days. We were both very, very homesick. George eventually went back to Manchester but I couldn't, so that was the end of it.

"I even stopped playing for a while, but later I started playing for a local club called Dundella, and that's where 'Boro's Irish scout Mat Willis spotted me.

"He sent me to Ayresome Park, and I liked the place straight away. I still felt homesick, but when I rang my brothers to tell them, they told me that I was staying at Middlesbrough. So that was that. I stayed and I'm glad I did.

"Raich Carter was excellent to me. I scored a couple of goals in the intermediates and he signed me straight away. He looked after me. So, too, did Bobby Braithwaite. He had played for Ireland and he helped me to settle in."

McMordie played a few games in 'Boro's relegation season in 1965-66, and it was towards the end of the following season that he finally established himself in new boss Stan Anderson's promotion team.

He said: "Stan was very good with the players. He was respected for that, and also because he was a wonderful, wonderful player.

"When I first came to Middlesbrough, Stan was still a player and he was my roommate. He was an ex-Army man and he believed in turning the lights out and going to bed. I didn't always agree with that because I couldn't sleep.

"But I had to be careful what I said to him when he was appointed manager. It changed things a bit. But I thought the world of him. He did very, very well for the football club."

Eric McMordie, was an aggressive and ball-playing midfield player who won 21 Northern Ireland caps and made 273 appearances for 'Boro.

Promotion was clinched on that emotional night when 'Boro beat Oxford United 4-1 at Ayresome Park in the last game of the season.

Eric said: "We didn't realise how big the game was until we left the Marton Country Club at five o'clock. The cars were bumper to bumper at that stage. We realised then that it was going to be a really big night for everybody.

"That's how it turned out. It was the finest night I've ever known at Ayresome Park. I don't think there has been a crowd like it since then."

Once back in the Second Division, 'Boro spent season after season just missing out on promotion to the top flight.

McMordie said: "We lost at home only occasionally, but when we went away we were poor. The players felt that money should have been spent to strengthen the side, but it didn't happen.

"Certain players wanted to play at home but didn't want to play away from home in the same way. We were so close, and couldn't bridge the gap.

"Stan was very frustrated. He wanted to do better. People said that Newcastle and Sunderland were bigger than us, but if we had bought the players we could have been bigger than them."

McMordie is still pleased to have played with so many top-quality players during his time at Ayresome Park.

He said: "Hughie McIlmoyle was out of this world. His heading ability was as good as anybody's, and he was pretty good with his feet as well. He was a cunning player. He used to jump before the centre-half, and he had a knack of climbing and staying there. The centre-half would jump as well, but he was on his way down when Hughie headed the ball.

"Don Masson was also a wonderful player. He had two marvellous feet and could knock balls all over the park. His temperament sometimes let him down because he got very excited, but it was a shame when he moved on to Notts County.

"Gordon Jones was also a quality player. You just have to look at the number of games he played. He was very, very consistent. If he had moved when he was younger, I'm sure he would have played at the highest level."

He added: "We had the characters as well. Taffy Orritt was a wonderful competitor. He wasn't the greatest player, but he was very hard, and every game was like a Cup Final to him. He never feared anybody. He just got on with his job and did it well."

McMordie was also a bit of a character himself. He could be a joker off the field, and a fireball at times on it. He said: "I knew that I could play football, but I was a bad tempered lad and I got myself into trouble with referees at times.

"I'm not proud of some of my tackles, but it was a very physical game in those days and you couldn't just walk away from it. My brothers taught me to look after myself. But I want to be remembered for the way in which I played the game. I played to win."

Eric and his mate Gordon Jones also got into trouble with the Press in one of the most talked about incidents from the 1960s.

He said: "Cliff Mitchell was the *Evening Gazette* reporter at the time and the players thought a lot about him.

"We were returning by train from a game in London, and Cliff had just bought a new trilby. He was having a meal in the restaurant at the time, and Gordon and I were in the compartment.

"Railway carriages had a little window at the time and I bet Gordon a fiver that I could throw the hat through the window. Of course it looked impossible, because the window was very small, even when it was fully opened.

"I threw it and it bounced off the window. Jonesy then picked up the hat and it sailed straight out. We were dumbfounded. We couldn't speak for ages. Then we did a disappearing act. Cliff spent ages looking for his hat. He couldn't understand it."

McMordie's love affair with 'Boro ended after the arrival of Jack Charlton. He said: "I didn't get on with him and he didn't get on with me. It happens in football. I've no regrets. Jack brought in Bobby Murdoch and he was 100 per cent right to do so. The team went from strength to strength and I was delighted for them.

"Souness, Armstrong and Murdoch was a great midfield. You have to keep progressing in football."

WILLIE MADDREN (1969-77)

WILLIE MADDREN witnessed both sides of the coin at Ayresome Park. He played his part in one of 'Boro's most successful periods of the last 50 years when, as a cultured central defender in Jack Charlton's team, he earned the tag as one of the best 'Boro players never to win a full England cap.

Later, he returned to the club as manager, and throughout his 18 months in charge watched helplessly as the club hurtled towards liquidation.

As a player, Willie had few peers, and could have played in virtually any position. In fact he did play as a striker, which is where manager Stan Anderson wanted him to play, in midfield and at full-back in addition to centre-back.

It was Anderson who initially brought Maddren into the team. Willie said: "I was 18, and I picked up the paper to read that I was in the squad for a game at Oxford.

"Nobody at the club had said a word to me. I wasn't sure what to do. But Stan Anderson lived in Billingham, like me, so I ran all the way down Sandy Lane and knocked on his door. I said: 'Excuse me Mr Anderson, it says in the paper that I'm in the squad for Oxford. Is it true?' He said: 'Of course it's bloody true' and closed the door. If he hadn't lived in Billingham I don't know what I would have done because if I had reported to the club at my normal time, I would have missed the coach."

It was that first away trip which made Maddren more determined than ever to make the grade as a professional. He said: "I was taken aback by the lifestyle, staying in top hotels, with lovely food, and being waited on hand and foot. I wanted a slice of that."

Maddren had to wait until the end of the season for his full debut, when he played as a striker at home to Bury. He said: "Stan left John Hickton out, which was a controversial decision.

"There was still a mathematical chance of us going up, but Stan wanted to test the kids. At first I found the pace very quick and I was overawed in the first 20 minutes.

"But I started to settle in, only to break my nose when I went up for a header at the far post and their centre-half back headed me.

"They patched me up and I went back on. The next time a cross came over, I jumped behind the back of the same defender again. This time the ball hit the far post and went in.

"It was hard to take in at the time. The funny thing was that the ball left a print on the post. I went in during the summer to do some jobs around the ground, and this ball print was on the post all the time. I used to stand and gaze at it."

The best goal of Willie's career came two seasons later, in a 3-0 win against Swindon at Ayresome Park. He said: "I got the ball from a throw-in just inside their half, advanced five yards, and then hit it. I knew straight away that it was going in. It was the sort of goal you would never score if you were a 28-year-old because you wouldn't take the chance. But it was just youthful exuberance."

Anderson continued to see Maddren as a striker, but the Billingham lad insisted he wanted to play at the back. He got his chance again when Bill Gates broke his jaw at Old Trafford. Willie said: "I came in and played in a 1-1 draw at home to Preston, and then we won 2-0 at Charlton. I felt so comfortable there. That's when I knew that I had arrived, and that my best position was at the back."

Maddren gradually settled in at the back, and Anderson began to put

Willie Maddren, one of 'Boro's most skilful and cultured defenders of all time, who later became a great talent spotter. He managed 'Boro during difficult times before liquidation.

together a new-look side with plenty of home-grown players in the team. But despite several near misses, 'Boro could not win promotion. Willie said: "Ayresome Park was a fortress, but we could not win away. We couldn't put our finger on the problem. But then winning is a mental thing, and so is losing. When you are in a sequence, you almost expect it to continue."

Anderson resigned in frustration after an FA Cup third-round defeat at Plymouth in January 1973. Maddren said: "Stan went at the wrong time. If he had hung on, and kept Stuart Boam and me at the back, then we would have got promoted the following season. We wouldn't have gone up as easily as we did under Jack Charlton, but we would still have gone up."

The arrival of Charlton turned a good side into a brilliant one. Maddren said: "Jack did it with sheer organisation. He kept working us on the training ground until he got it right. He had an aura about him. He commanded respect. He made the game very, very simple.

"People used to say we were a defensive side, but that was just because we were so good at the back. In training, everything was geared towards scoring goals. We used to practice knocking the ball into space and getting players into the right positions.

"It was brilliant at first. There's nothing better than to work hard on something on the training ground and then see it come off on the pitch. It must have given Jack great satisfaction as well.

"But towards the end it began to become a bit stale. We were just as solid at the back, but the goals started to dry up. We felt we were carrying the team at times, because we didn't have the luxury of a really good goalscorer.

"I'm sure the club could have afforded a big signing at the time. I've always felt that Malcolm Macdonald would have come here if we had tried for him. He would have been the last piece in the jigsaw. There was talk that we could have had David Cross, but our valuation was £10,000 less than Coventry's. Five years later Cross was top scorer in the First Division with West Ham.

"I think it was a missed opportunity. I don't think Jack realised at the time how good the players were, though I'm sure he knows it now. We could have gone all the way with a goalscorer."

Unfortunately, towards the end of his career, Maddren was having increasing trouble with a knee problem. The removal of a cartilage at the age of 16 paved the way for problems in later life. Today, his bucket-handle tear might have been stitched, but at that time cartilage removal was considered the only answer. The result was that Maddren had to quit the game at the age of 26 in 1977, after almost 350 League and Cup games for the 'Boro.

It did not take Maddren long to realise other talents. He became a coach at Hartlepool, and gradually began to bring in top quality youngsters. He worked hard on the youth policy with former 'Boro player Billy Horner, and Hartlepool went on to win the Northern Intermediate League. It was unprecedented by a Fourth Division club. Young stars at the club included Peter Beagrie, the Linighan brothers and Paul Dobson.

However, Maddren fell out with chairman Vince Barker and quit in frustration. Eventually the chance came to return to Ayresome Park. He heard that 'Boro were looking for a physiotherapist and was given the job by Malcolm Allison. He soon switched to the coaching staff, and became manager when Allison was sacked.

Maddren found the club just a pale shadow of the great club of the 1970s. He said: "You couldn't believe how far things had slipped. It was heartbreaking. And of course the job was impossible. But I was naïve. I should never have taken it because it turned out to be the hardest 18 months of my life.

"One of the first things I had to do was to sell my two best players, Darren Wood and Mick Kennedy. I didn't want to do it. Kennedy was infectious on the pitch. But I had to raise £150,000 or the bank was going to pull the plug.

"I knew that we needed new players, but there was no money at first, and when it came available, I had to spend it very carefully. At first there was only me and the physio, Steve Smelt, to do everything. Then we got John Coddington part-time, and David Mills helped a lot.

"David Mills banged in a few valuable goals as well, but we were struggling in the League. I picked up Brian Laws for £30,000 and Archie Stephens for £20,000 and we stayed up after winning that last match at Shrewsbury.

"There was money to spend next season. I rang Ron Atkinson at a bar in Marbella to agree a deal for Steve Pears.

"I always felt that Steve was the best signing I made. He was a very good goalkeeper over several years for the club." Maddren proved his remarkable talent-spotting abilities yet again when signing Bernie Slaven from Albion Rovers for just £25,000. Another six months and Willie might have started to turn the corner. But time was not on his side. 'Boro continued to struggle and the parting of the ways came following a 3-1 home defeat by Charlton Athletic in January 1986. He said: "It was almost a relief when I was asked to leave. I was always conscious of the threat of liquidation, and in these situations it's so easy to blame yourself."

Willie was still owed £4,500 in severance pay when 'Boro went into liquidation. He did not get the money until the Football League called in the bond which 'Boro's new directors had agreed to as a condition of the club's survival. It seemed an unkind wait for a man whose signings were to bring 'Boro £5 million in transfer fees.

WILF MANNION (1937-54)

WILF MANNION is widely acknowledged as the greatest footballer ever to play for Middlesbrough.

In an age of ball-playing maestros, Wilf was one of the best. Fans paid money simply to see his ball skills; his feints and his body swerves which could take three opponents out of the game in a split second, his terrific dribbling ability; and his defence-splitting passes.

The South Bank lad also possessed an eye for goal and, in addition to creating hundreds of chances which led to goals, he scored 110 himself in 368 League and Cup appearances.

His greatness earned him 26 full England caps, which remains a 'Boro record, and he also scored 11 international goals, including a hat-trick on his debut against Northern Ireland.

Mannion was originally spotted playing for junior side South Bank St Peter's, and several 'Boro directors made visits to his home before he eventually signed for the club as a 17-year-old in 1936.

Wilf recalls: "Several big clubs wanted to sign me at the time and I fancied going to Arsenal. They were a great club with some great players at the time.

"But I was too young to sign. It was all left to your mother and father at that time. The directors told me that I would be better off joining Middlesbrough because I could stay at home. So that's what I ended up doing.

"When I signed, I went upstairs and my brother Tommy told me that I had signed my death warrant. Later on I discovered what he meant, because they would never agree to release me when I wanted to get away after the war."

However, there was an excellent team spirit when Mannion first arrived at Ayresome Park in the 1930s and he settled in well.

Wilf Mannion, generally regarded as the greatest 'Boro player of all time. He possessed uncanny skills and also had an excellent goalscoring record for an inside-forward. Wilf is 'Boro's most-capped player of all time.

Wilf said: "We had a great atmosphere in the dressing-room. There were so many comedians. We also had a nice blend of players; and a lot of quality players. When people say that we would have gone on to win the League if it hadn't been for the outbreak of the war, they were absolutely right.

"We had the right men in the right positions. Bobby Baxter was a magnificent centre-half. His heading was sheer perfection. He would always head it to your feet. But he liked to show the opposition that he could play a bit as well, and you often used to see him taking people on and beating them in his own penalty area. Dave Cumming, in goal, used to tear his hair out and scream for Bobby to just get rid of the ball upfield.

"We had ability and we had strength. Billy Forrest was a good wing-half, and Benny Yorston was a very hard man. Ralph Birkett was an England winger, and Jack Milne was a brilliant wing man. And we had Micky Fenton knocking all the goals in. He was like lightning off the mark.

"We took Blackpool for nine at Ayresome Park, and Portsmouth for eight just before they appeared in the Cup Final. When we played well we could tear good sides apart."

It was the battle between the wing-halves and the inside-forward which often decided the outcomes of games, because they provided the ammunition for the wingers and centre-forwards.

Mannion said: "There were so many skilful players around before the war that it was unbelievable. Whoever you played, they all had their ball players. They were all footballers."

During the war, Mannion saw active service all over Europe and the Middle East. He was at Dunkirk, from where he escaped on a cargo boat. He was alongside Hedley Verity when he was shot beneath Mount Etna. He caught malaria in Palestine.

But Wilf also played plenty of football. He said: "We had the Army side, which was playing all the time, and when we were in England we played for whichever club was nearest.

"I played for Spurs early in the war and they paid £10. That was very good money at the time. Middlesbrough only paid the going rate.

"They had a secretary, Herbert Glasper, who was very tight. You struggled to get your expenses. Hartlepool had a better team during the war because they paid more. All the lads used to go over there."

Mannion was 26 at the end of the war, but went on to give 'Boro another eight years of service. He reached his peak during the first part of this period and as a result was a regular in the England side. But he was no longer surrounded by quality players at Ayresome Park, and tried to get away, unsuccessfully on several occasions.

"He said: "It just wasn't the same after the war. Most of the good players were too old. We didn't have the same quality. We had a couple of good seasons, but most of the time we struggled.

"I wanted to be away almost immediately. But things were different in those days. When you signed a contract with a club it was a contract for life. You could only leave if they wanted to let you go. I kept putting in transfer requests but they were turned down.

"The maximum wage was still in force but you could earn money in other ways at other clubs. In any case I wanted to play for one of the better teams. But the 'Boro directors wouldn't listen. I felt insulted, and my heart wasn't in the club."

Eventually, in the summer of 1948, Mannion refused to re-sign his annual contract or to play for the club. It was a defiant show of strength to try to earn a move. He was offered a job opportunity by Oldham Athletic, and in the September vacated his club house at 81 Normanby Road, and moved to Oldham.

'Boro dug in their heels, for a while, but eventually began to weaken as the big clubs started to queue up offering big money for Mannion. Arsenal and Everton were both willing a pay £25,000 for Wilf, which was huge money at the time. But Oldham could not match that fee. The best they could manage was £15,000 and Wilf didn't want to sign for anyone else.

'Boro made an inquiry about Carlisle United midfielder Stan Bowles in May 1972. He was not for sale at the time. Bowles later became one of the game's biggest names at Queen's Park Rangers.

It was an impasse. Oldham had no way of coming up with the money, and the matter came to an end on 14 January 1949, when 'Boro director Mr Thomas went to Oldham with the League registration forms and Mannion reluctantly signed. The following day Mannion was back in the 'Boro team at home to Preston North End, and an above average crowd of 37,000 turned up to see 'Boro win 1-0 with a goal from Geoff Walker.

'Boro bought Mannion a new house at 8 Highbury Avenue in Linthorpe, and he quickly settled back into the team. In season 1950-51, 'Boro lost just two games at Ayresome Park and finished sixth. However, they were unable to repeat that form and slipped back again. In 1952-53 Mannion put on his shooting boots and banged in 18 goals to finish top scorer as 'Boro finished the season strongly and ended up in 13th position.

The following season Mannion was 34, and even his uncannily-preserved ball skills could not prevent 'Boro from dropping into the Second Division for the first time for 25 years.

He said: "I felt that I had done enough. I'd played all my football for the club in the First Division and I had spent all my career with Middlesbrough. So I announced my retirement."

Still 'Boro retained Mannion's registration, and so there were potentially more problems when he decided that he wanted to return to League football, but with another club. Leeds, Grimsby, Colchester and Darlington were all keen, but Wilf eventually signed for Hull City for £4,500 in December 1954.

It was the end of an era.

DAVID MILLS (1969-85)

DAVID MILLS is the only home-grown player in the last 40 years to score more than 100 goals for 'Boro.

He achieved this feat in two separate spells, grabbing 94 in an illustrious ten-year period during which he was top scorer in two consecutive seasons, and then coming back just before liquidation to top the goals chart again with 14 goals.

In between, David played for West Brom, Sheffield Wednesday and Newcastle. He is widely reckoned to be the country's first £500,000 footballer, though the actual fee was £468,720 when he was transferred to West Brom in January 1979.

Ironically, Mills almost missed the chance to become a professional footballer, after suffering a bad back injury as a teenager.

He said: "I was running in the Stockton and District Schools sports, when I had a severe pain in my back. I reached the sprint final, but couldn't run in it.

"I was taken to see a specialist, who diagnosed twisted and fractured vertebrae in my lower back. It was a stress fracture. I had been competing in too many sports."

Mills was side-lined for a year, but Stan Anderson and Harold Shepherdson – who already had David in their sights before the injury, signed him without seeing him play again.

It was a gamble which was to prove highly successful. David said: "I was fortunate to have coaching from George Wright and Jimmy Headridge. They both knew how to get the best out of me, and they taught me what to expect in the future. As a result I signed pro forms after only six months as an apprentice."

Mills, who was always thoroughly committed in his football, broke into the 'Boro first team in 1969 at the same time

David Mills, a hard running forward whose commitment and dedication was a crucial part of 'Boro's attacks in the 1970s. He scored more than 100 goals in two spells at Ayresome Park.

as manager Stan Anderson was promoting a handful of other young players.

He said: "I had a lot of time for Stan. He was a gentleman. But he was prone to being moody. It hurt him deep down if the team didn't play well. He had such a strong desire to succeed, but he felt that the senior players often let him down.

"But what a great footballer he was. Weather permitting, he used to take us out on to Ayresome Park. I used to pray for fine weather. The pitch was the pride and joy of the groundsman Wilf Atkinson, and any hint of wetness and you weren't allowed on it.

"Stan would stand in the centre circle and zip 30 and 40 yard passes to your feet. He had terrific skills.

"He knew he needed good players around him and was always looking for the right players at the right price. John Hickton was a great player. And, at £20,000, Middlesbrough have probably never made a better buy.

"John responded to the crowd and the crowd responded to him. He grabbed 200 goals in his career. Not many players are capable of doing that.

"Stan also brought in players like John Craggs, Graeme Souness, Stuart Boam and Alan Foggon. They all had a big part to play in the club's future."

The resignation of Anderson in January 1973, left Harold Shepherdson in charge for the rest of the season. But then Big Jack Charlton arrived to bring First Division football back to Ayresome Park after an absence of 20 years.

Mills said: "Jack was shrewd. He looked at us and realised that he had a lot of good players. Then he developed a pattern of play to suit the players. It complemented the quality of the players.

"He must have marvelled at how strong we were defensively. We had Stuart Boam, who was such a solid player, and quick for a big fella. And Willie Maddren was very talented. He oozed quality.

"We had Graeme Souness, a marvellous player, who had that little bit of nastiness as well, and we had pace up front with myself, John Hickton and Alan Foggon.

"I know that Jack looked at me as a goalscorer. But that was not what I was all about. I like to look at myself as a creator as well as a taker. I was never going to be a 25 goals a season man, but I got my share.

"In any case, we had players who could score from all areas. Jack utilised that. He encouraged us to run at defences. He always said that when you stop running you are not so effective.

"Jack put the icing on the cake. It became like a machine. Our level of performances rarely fell below a certain level, home or away. We had a good balance. We could defend, we could attack.

"We walked away with the Second Division championship. And then we did very well in our first season after promotion. We caught a lot of teams by surprise because we were a little bit of an unknown quantity. But it was a lot more difficult the second season up."

'Boro never quite reached the pinnacle which the fans had hoped for. Charlton maintained a quality side throughout his four years with 'Boro, but failed to bring in the two big name men who might have transformed the team into championship potential.

Mills said: "I think that was one area where Jack didn't succeed. His judgement of when a player was just past his best. And people had realised how we utilised Alan Foggon. We were getting a big predictable.

"I think Jack could have picked it up again. But he always said that he would give himself only three or four years. He has mellowed since then and I'm sure he has regretted it. He must have wondered what he could have achieved. It was a mistake to leave when he did."

The old Charlton team gradually broke up after his departure. In 18 months Mills was on his way to West Brom, after feeling that the success he was striving for was not going to come his way at Ayresome Park.

Mills could never have imagined at that time that he would be back scoring goals on Teesside within a few years. But it happened, when Willie Maddren offered him a job as player-coach in 1984. The original plan was to score goals for the struggling first team and coach the apprentices.

David admits that he received a shock when he first walked back through the door. He said: "I just couldn't believe how much the club had changed. It had gone back so much. I don't believe the fans at the time really appreciated the full extent of the problems.

"The club was short, numerically and financially. It was summed up when our old kit man, Ken Smith, came into the dressing-room before one match and said there weren't enough tea bags to make tea at half-time as well at full-time. We had to choose.

"I felt very, very sympathetic towards Willie because of the circumstances he had to work in. He didn't have much money, but his buys were terrific.

"Willie bought Steve Pears for £80,000, and he was 'Boro's best goalkeeper during my time. He bought Bernie Slaven for £25,000, and he went on to score lots of goals for the club. And he signed Gary Pallister, who was sold for more than £2 million."

He added: "It was very hard work. Willie and I went all over. We trained in the morning and set off to watch games on the afternoon. I worked with the kids and played on a Saturday. But Hutton Road was a shambles. There was nowhere decent for the intermediates to play.

"It was just a struggle for everybody to get by. There was only Willie, me, and the physio Steve Smelt. We had no other coaches.

"But we were all very committed. I felt that I was a better player then, than I was earlier in my career. I had more knowledge. I scored 14 goals by February, but then I picked up an Achilles injury and was out for a long time. I was just about to start training again when I broke my arm.

"That was the finish as far as my playing career with Middlesbrough was concerned. But I didn't want to finish through injury. I wanted to finish as a player. So I went back to a rehabilitation centre, joined Darlington and had an enjoyable spell there."

The Watch Tower Bible and Tract Society of Pennsylvania paid £200 to hire Ayresome Park for a religious convention from 23-26 July 1959. They were allowed use of the stands, but not the pitch.

TONY MOWBRAY (1982-91)

TONY MOWBRAY was the epitome of what every 'Boro supporter was looking for in a player at the club.

A hard-working defender who courageously attacked the ball, Tony was totally committed to the club and his teammates and never gave any less than 100 per cent.

His wholehearted determination was an inspiration to the players around him, and he was a dream player to have around as captain in manager Bruce Rioch's young side in the years immediately following liquidation in 1986.

Hence Rioch's immortal statement: "If you were in a rocket ship going to the moon, the man you would want sitting next to you would be Tony Mowbray."

Mogga, as he has always been known to friends and fans alike, went on to join an exclusive club by playing more than 400 League and Cup games for 'Boro.

He had been spotted at the age of 11 playing football for Lakes Primary School in Redcar by 'Boro's erstwhile scout Ray Grant, and stayed with the 'Boro for 17 years.

Tony said: "It was always 'Boro for me. My father made me go to Aston Villa for a couple of weeks just so that I knew what it was like at another club, but there was never any danger that I wouldn't sign for 'Boro."

He was one of three apprentices taken

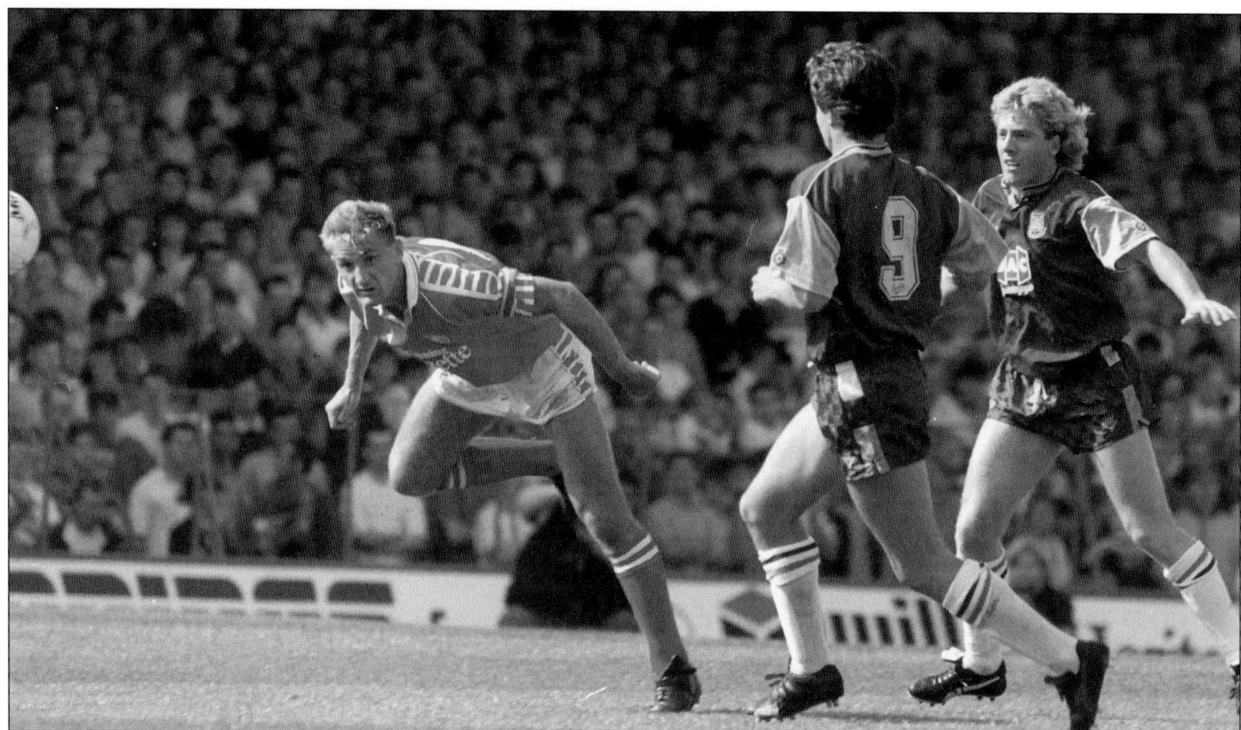

Tony Mowbray, in action against West Ham in 1990. Mowbray was the inspirational captain who helped guide 'Boro to two consecutive promotions under Bruce Rioch, and became a big crowd favourite. He played more than 400 games for the club.

on that year, along with Darren Wood and Steve Tupling, all of them going on to play first-team football at Ayresome Park.

Tony said: "I had a lot of cleaning to do, and I had seven professionals to look after. You had to clean their boots and get all their kit ready. David Hodgson was one of my pros. One of the things I had to do was always make sure he had white socks. All the players had fussy little things like that."

Another thing that Tony had to go through was the apprentices' initiation ceremony. He said: "The second year lads always initiated the first years. You were stripped naked, and covered with boot polish and olive oil. You were totally blackened. Your hair was matted for weeks. Then you were rolled in cut grass.

"It wasn't too pleasant to go through, but it was great when you became a second year yourself and did it to the new intake. They knew it was coming, so half the fun was catching them when they least expected it."

Tony made his senior debut in a 1-1 draw against Newcastle United at St James' Park in September 1982, when he was called up by Bobby Murdoch along with Paul Ward.

He went on to establish himself in the side, and was a permanent fixture throughout the Malcolm Allison and Willie Maddren eras. But they were difficult times.

Tony said: "It was a very hard upbringing in football. I learned a lot through those times, because I discovered that football was a tough business. If we got a result we were on a high. It didn't happen too often."

It was one relegation battle after another, which eventually ended with 'Boro sliding into the Third Division in 1986, quickly followed by the news that the club had gone into liquidation.

Fortunately the club was saved, and Mowbray became one of the mainstays in the side as Rioch pitched in the kids and went on to win consecutive promotions in reaching the First Division.

Tony said: "Bruce just fell upon the situation. He had to get rid of some of the older players, and at the same time he was forced to pitch in the kids.

"But Bruce was the perfect man for the job. He created a special feeling within the club. He was such a strong personality, but we needed someone like that. He had so much knowledge and tactical awareness, that he got the best out of everybody.

"I was proud to be captain, and I found that I thrived on the responsibility. When the 'Fly Me To The Moon' comment came, obviously I was slightly embarrassed, especially as it was highlighted everywhere. At the same time, I knew my contribution was appreciated and it kept my confidence high."

One of the great things about the Rioch era was the togetherness, a tight-knit family style atmosphere created in the dressing-room.

Tony said: "I'm sure that this period will become one of the great moments in 'Boro's history. Everybody got on so well together, and we still do. I think Colin Henderson summed it up when he said that 'Out of adversity comes a special togetherness'. That's how it was. We became a winning team, and when we won promotion it was like winning the FA Cup."

One of the features of the team at the time was that they all had dyed blond hair. Tony said: "Everywhere we went people took the stick out of us, but we were all young lads, and it was a fashion thing. In a way, it was another part of the togetherness."

The promotion season to the First Division was a terrific time, full of great games and memories. Tony said: "Probably the one I remember most is the home game against Everton in the FA Cup. I got the equaliser in injury time, and then Alan Kernaghan put us ahead in extra-time.

"It was very exciting. We were winning 2-1 with only minutes to go against the League champions. Then Trevor Steven and Colin Cooper went up for a header together and the ball bent agonisingly into the corner of the net.

"When we went back to Everton for the second replay, I put through my own goal. I got so many letters from fans telling me not to worry about it.

"Then, at the end of the week, I scored that diving header against Aston Villa which got me so much national publicity, because the match was live on

John O'Rourke, pictured centre, achieved cult status in his 18 months at Ayresome Park, scoring 30 goals in 'Boro's promotion from the Third Division in 1966-67. He is pictured with John Hickton (left) and Johnny Crossan.

A collection for the Munich Air Disaster Appeal Fund was held at Ayresome Park during a match against Blackburn Rovers on 12 April 1958. The collection raised £75 12s 8d, which was made up to £100 by the club.

TV. It put me on the map. I got another load of letters for that one."

Despite that goal, the one which Tony remembers most came at the start of the next season in the First Division, when 'Boro entertained Norwich City in their first home game.

He said: "I scored a cracker. Mark Brennan rolled the ball across for me and I just whacked it. It flew into the net. You don't get many like that. It was definitely my most memorable goal."

That season in the top flight was the last full season of Mogga's tremendous defensive partnership with Gary Pallister, who was to move to Manchester United the following August.

Tony said: "Pally was a very accomplished footballer. He needed bullying a bit at times, but he responded and he developed into a quality player. We got on well on and off the pitch. I think we complemented each other so well."

Two years later, Mowbray eventually left 'Boro to join up with Scottish giants Celtic. He admitted: "I had seen Pally move on, and ultimately I became a bit stale. The club was not progressing so well after relegation and sometimes you have to move on for everybody's benefit. Obviously it was sad to leave. The club will always mean a great deal to me."

MEL NURSE (1962-65)

MEL NURSE was a big, solid Welsh international who held the 'Boro defence together through difficult times. He was a commanding figure who won seven Welsh caps while with 'Boro.

Signed from Swansea Town for £25,000 in September 1962, Mel captained 'Boro until returning to the south-west with Swindon three years later.

Mel Nurse, the Welsh international centre-half was a key defender throughout part of the early 1960s.

His memories of his stay at Ayresome Park are all of the friendliness of the people.

Nurse said: "As far as my wife and I are concerned, the four years we lived in Middlesbrough were very exciting and enjoyable. Since moving back down south we have never been on holiday – but if ever we decide to take one, our first option will be Middlesbrough!

"We lived in Acklam and the locals were wonderful people. Unfortunately we have lost touch since moving away, but I was very upset to hear of the death of Bill Harris. He was a great friend and football player."

JOHN O'ROURKE (1966-68)

JOHN O'ROURKE may have spent 18 short months at Ayresome Park, but he is a folk hero to the fans who remember him.

He was the 30-goal top scorer who helped fire 'Boro back into the Second Division in their first-ever season in

Division Three. John scored three hat-tricks that season, including one in the final game when 'Boro clinched promotion by crushing Oxford United 4-1 in front of a packed house at Ayresome Park.

The following season O'Rourke scored 12 goals in 28 games before moving on to Ipswich Town, much to the disappointment of the Ayresome Angels.

John said: "Of all the clubs I played for, Middlesbrough was my favourite. It was the best time of my career.

"I knew as soon as I arrived that we were not a Third Division team. We had a big ground and a magnificent playing pitch, and Stan Anderson brought in vital signings like David Chadwick and John Hickton to build a promotion team.

"However, we didn't start off very well. I think we were second bottom after half a dozen games. So Stan called us in for a crisis meeting and we discussed what we needed to do to turn things around.

"After that we went from strength to strength. That night against Oxford was fantastic. We knew we were going to win. And for me it couldn't have been better, scoring a hat-trick.

"That hat-trick earned me an extra fiver, because I had earlier bet Bill Gates that I would score 30 goals in the season. I had to score three to win the bet."

O'Rourke remembers the wing play of Chadwick and Derrick Downing as crucial to the team's performances. He said: "Both players were very underrated. They were excellent at getting the ball across and created a lot of goals for John Hickton, Arthur Horsfield and myself."

He added: "We had a great team spirit and a great atmosphere in the dressing-room. I was the only Londoner there, but I got on well with everybody. I remember Eric McMordie used to call me the Guvnor."

One of John's best friends outside of football was the comedian Jimmy Tarbuck. He said: "Jimmy was appearing at the Fiesta in Stockton one week, so I spent a lot of time with him. He was getting £4,000 for that one week, compared to my £35 a week!

"Jimmy loved his golf and, so too, did Stan Anderson. I had arranged to play a round with Stan, so I asked him if I could bring a friend along.

"Stan asked me who it was, and I said it was Jimmy Tarbuck. He laughed, and clearly didn't believe me. So his face was an absolute picture when we turned up together for the round of golf."

In his second season with 'Boro, O'Rourke was on target for at least another 20 goals. He said: "It was going all right, but I felt that I wasn't playing to my capabilities. You set yourself standards and you know when you are not achieving them.

"When the chance came to join Ipswich I was happy to take it because they looked like winning promotion. It was my big ambition to play in the First Division, and I was absolutely determined to prove Tommy Docherty wrong, because he gave me a free when I was a youngster with Chelsea. I had a bee in my bonnet over it.

"But I've never forgotten Middlesbrough, and wondered what I might have achieved if I had stayed."

John later returned to Ayresome Park to play in Gordon Jones's testimonial game. O'Rourke said: "I changed next to Brian Clough, which was marvellous. Just before the game, Gordon Jones came in and said: 'Enjoy the game and let's have a few goals'. Brian replied 'If you think we have come here to mess around you are wrong'.

"The first half was like a Cup Final. You couldn't stop for breath. That's when I fully appreciated why Cloughie scored 40 goals a season. He went up for a header on the edge of the 18-yard box and headed it like a rocket, as hard as I could kick it.

"Then, at half-time, Clough picked on Cyril Knowles and gave him a right rollocking. In a testimonial! He wasn't happy with something Cyril had done. Cyril was a great bloke, and he just took it. I was left in no doubt why Clough was so successful throughout his career, because his standards were so high."

HEINE OTTO (1981-85)

DUTCH international Heine Otto was a popular player at Ayresome Park, but never had the opportunity to use his ball playing talents in a winning side.

The midfielder, who also played up front, tasted relegation in his first season and then endured three successful battles to stay in the Second Division before returning to Holland.

Heine said: "I had four smashing years with Middlesbrough, but it was hard because the club was always near the bottom of the League.

"The club always seemed to be struggling for money. Craig Johnston and David Armstrong had just been sold when I arrived, and things seemed to go from bad to worse.

"But there was always humour in the dressing-room. There was a good set of players."

Heine well remembers his League debut, when he scored against Spurs at Ayresome Park in front of more than 20,000 fans.

He said: "I scored the opener, but we lost 3-1. It was always a struggle after that."

Otto also has fond memories of the 1-1 draw at home to Arsenal the following season in the fifth round of the FA Cup, when he scored a last-gasp equaliser before another 20,000 crowd.

He said: "We didn't play as well as we could, but the crowd was right behind us. There was a terrific atmosphere at Ayresome Park. After I had scored, we might have won it, but we couldn't get the ball in the net again.

"The crowd gave us a big send off at the end of the game. It meant a lot to the players to see the fans happy on the terraces.

"One of my biggest regrets when I left Middlesbrough was that I never had the opportunity to thank the fans for the way they supported me. I would like to do that now."

Heine Otto, seen here powering a header just wide of the Brighton goal in 1983, was top scorer with just five goals when 'Boro dropped into the Second Division the previous year.

Gary Pallister leaps above two Newcastle United defenders during a derby clash in 1989. Pallister, whose wages were paid by 'Boro director Richard Corden when he first arrived at Ayresome Park, was in the England squad three years later.

GARY PALLISTER (1985-89) & (1998-2001)

GARY PALLISTER'S early story at Middlesbrough is a remarkable tale of initial rejection, followed by a second chance at a time when the 'Boro could not afford to pay his wages.

He was originally given a trial by Malcolm Allison, but was turned down. Willie Maddren later brought Gary back to Ayresome Park, but there was no cash to pay his wages so director Richard Corden footed the bill.

The rags to riches rise which followed was almost without parallel. Pallister quickly established himself in the 'Boro first team, and by March 1988, he was an England international.

Gary played his part in two consecutive promotions under Bruce Rioch, but when life in the First Division turned sour, he became unsettled and was sold to Manchester United for a record £2,300,000, going on to win European Cup-winners' Cup and League championship medals.

His success was a far cry from the dark days when Pallister joined the 'Boro. He said: "They were depressing times. We were playing in front of 4,000 crowds and struggling near the bottom of the Second Division.

"In those days you could hear all the comments from the crowd. The worst bit was the Chicken Run on the South Terrace. There always seemed to be one voice criticising you, louder than all the other voices. You had to try to put the comments out of your mind, but it wasn't easy.

"At the end of my first season in the team, we were relegated to the Third Division. It was a difficult time. But I probably didn't feel it as hard as some of the senior players. It was still an experience for me just to be playing in the Football League.

"But it started to hit a lot harder when the club went into liquidation. I knew that the club was in dire trouble when Dick Corden paid my wages for six months. But you never expected Ayresome Park to shut. It was very bleak."

For a long time it looked as though it might be the end of the road for the club. When the Football Club gave the 'Boro players permission to talk to other clubs, Gary talked to Crystal Palace boss Steve Coppell. He said: "They offered me a deal, but it wasn't very good. If it had been better, I would probably have left."

'Boro did survive, in that summer of 1986, but with few experienced players left, the future for the team still looked uncertain.

Pallister said: "We were left with a lot of kids. Lads like Gary Parkinson, Colin Cooper and Stuart Ripley were virtually untried. But there was no alternative, because 'Boro weren't allowed to enter the transfer market at the time. Luckily for the club, the kids were all good players. It made all the difference."

He added: "We were all thrown into the pot. It was a case of sink or swim. But a lot of the lads were local, and so they had pride in the club. And there was plenty of support from the terraces.

"The spirit in the dressing-room was brilliant. There were no cliques – except for the chocolate bar clique that Bernie Slaven and I had on Friday nights before away games. We used to lock our hotel room door, eat our chocolate bars and try to keep out the rest of the players.

"Basically we all got on so well. We took it on to the pitch. The Third Division was notoriously tough at the time. There was a lot of physical stuff. It's hard to believe we won promotion, but we did."

'Boro finished second behind Bournemouth, and then maintained their remarkable form in the Second Division. By the end of that second season, they needed only to beat Leicester City at home in the last game to make sure of a place in the First Division.

Gary said: "The vibes were all wrong. It was a party atmosphere. There were smiling faces everywhere. People thought Leicester were going to lie down and die for us.

"I went into the dressing-room and there was a cut glass memento of the day for every player. It was all wrong. It was one big party, without any preparation for the game. The players were not in the right frame of mind, and it was really no surprise that we lost it 2-1."

'Boro finally made it to the First Division through the Play-offs, and Gary remembers the Bradford City game at Ayresome Park as one of the most memorable he played in. He said: "The atmosphere was incredible. Both teams wanted to win really badly. They took us to extra-time, and then Gary Hamilton grabbed the winner. We deserved to win it, but I think that Bradford were a bit aggrieved, because they had already beaten us three times that season."

After playing alongside Tony Mowbray for two years, the pair had developed a terrific playing partnership at the time of 'Boro's second promotion. Pallister said: "We seemed to complement each other. I knew his faults and he knew mine. We always seemed to know what the other was going to do, and reacted accordingly."

Pallister had also cemented his strong friendship with goal ace Bernie Slaven. He said: "Bernie was a complete prankster. He was always messing about and winding people up. We had a water fight one night in a hotel which made the papers.

"He had a temper as well. Bernie was never afraid to tell managers what he felt. But as a footballer, he was a top-class finisher. Give him half a chance and he would put the ball away. He thrived on scoring goals.

"In fact Bernie was the only player who did himself justice in the First Division. He proved that he could score at any level. But the rest of us found it hard. The gulf was too great. We didn't perform at all."

While Gary has few happy memories from that season in the top flight, he does remember the best goal of his career. He said: "We were at home to West Ham, and I'd just had my first international cap presented to me by the chairman, Colin Henderson, before the game.

"Then I went on to have a nightmare. I couldn't kick the ball, I couldn't pass it, and I could sense that the crowd were on my back. Then, five minutes into the second half I got the ball, beat two men, played it out to Bernie, took the return pass and blasted it into the net for the greatest goal of my career.

"I was a hero for a couple of minutes. Then I went back to having a complete nightmare again!"

The season turned out to be a nightmare for 'Boro, and they were relegated on the last day of the season after losing at Sheffield Wednesday. It was virtually the end of Pallister's first spell with 'Boro, because he was to play only three more games for the club at the start of the following season, before his move to Old Trafford.

He said: "The club wasn't the same. The lads had grown up and were no longer prepared to do whatever they were told. There was a lot of bitchiness and bad feeling creeping in.

"I just decided during the summer that it was the right time for me to go. In any case I had to look at the direction where my career was going. I had been in the England set-up and left out again.

"I couldn't believe the fee, but it was a good one for the club. Even so, it was still disappointing to see them struggle. I was very relieved when they beat Newcastle to stay up at the end of the season."

ALAN PEACOCK (1955-64)

ALAN PEACOCK won four England caps as a 'Boro striker in 1962.

The North Ormesby lad emerged in the mid-1950s, at the same time as a lot of other talented young locals.

The major problem was that they were all forwards. Brian Clough, Derek McLean, Billy Day, Edwin Holliday and Peacock used to knock them in at one end, but the defence kept very few clean sheets at the other end.

Peacock was a great taker of chances, and was particularly good in the air, but he was also a provider and, as a young inside-forward, set up many goals for Clough. Peacock said: "The forward line was phenomenal. We linked up so well together. But Middlesbrough never ever bought to strengthen the defence. What would Cloughie have done as a manger if he had had a forward line like that?

"But we always promised a lot and never did anything. I always regarded us a Second Division team. To get into the First Division you had to have a First Division team. I always felt we were playing at the right level."

Like most of 'Boro's youngsters, Peacock learned his trade in the old North-Eastern League. Most of the teams in the League were colliery sides, packed full of tough miners and wily old pros.

Peacock said: "I can remember playing one of my first games against one of the Shield sides. Frank Brennan, who had been a great player with Newcastle, was their centre-half.

"We won a corner, and I lined up against Brennan, waiting for the ball to come across. All of sudden, Frank stamped very hard on my foot, and I was jumping about holding my foot, while he headed it clear.

"You had steel toe caps in those days and the steel was pressing on to my toe. Micky Fenton had to hammer the steel back into shape on the touch-line.

"Then Micky told me to get back on there and hit Brennan in the ribs as hard as I could. I did. But it had no effect. I knew I was in for it then. The next time I went for the ball something hit me. I thought I had broken my jaw. There was blood and teeth everywhere.

"But it was a great upbringing in that League. You learned to take care of yourself. It was the making of a lot of players."

Peacock was eventually ready for his first-team debut, and was pitched into the fray at Bristol Rovers by manager Bob Dennison. 'Boro lost 7-2.

It was the first time the teenager had been away from home, and everything about the trip was strange.

Peacock recalled: "Lads from North Ormesby never had the chance to go anywhere in those days. I didn't even have any pyjamas. My mother had to borrow a pair from Mr Cook next door.

"I packed them away in my case, and left it in the dressing-room while I did a couple of laps before we left for Bristol.

"When we got to the hotel in Bristol, Derek McLean discovered that somebody had sprayed wintergreen all over the contents of his case. I checked mine straight away. But, fortunately, the pyjamas were still in there.

"We went to the pictures, and when we got back I started to get ready for bed. I pulled on my pyjama bottoms only to discover that I had only one leg. They had cut a leg off the pyjamas. All I could think of, was what I was going to say to Mr Cook!"

Alan Peacock, was Brian Clough's striking partner for several years, before taking over the leading role when Clough moved to Sunderland. He quickly established himself at centre-forward and played for England in the World Cup in Chile.

Practical jokes have always been regular occurrences in the 'Boro dressing-room. Peacock recalled: "We had a full-back called Tom Brown who always wore long johns. One day he came back from training to find them nailed to the dressing-room ceiling.

"I often used to come in for training in my working gear. I worked in the steelworks at Cargo Fleet for 29s 11d a week. I got another £3 as an apprentice professional at Ayresome Park. It was good money.

"Depending on what shift I was on, I trained either in the morning or the afternoon. I used to leave my work boots on the floor. Once I came back to find that I couldn't lift them up. They had been nailed to the floor.

"There were plenty of jokers about. Micky Fenton was one of them. He did all sorts of things. It kept everybody on their toes."

Alan soon established himself in the side, and still managed to play regularly when called for his national service.

He was stationed in the Army at Catterick, but was never expected to live the normal life of a squaddie. Most weekends he was available to join up with the 'Boro.

Peacock said: "I was made a PT instructor. In fact I even had my own batman. He was the brother of Grenville Hair, who played for Leeds United."

Many people reckon that Peacock really started to blossom when Clough was transferred to Sunderland. But Peacock says: "All that happened was that I was moved into his position at centre-forward.

"There's a lot of talk that Cloughie and I didn't get on, but that's not true. I played with him for many years, from the North-Eastern League days, and always got on with him very well."

Alan never managed to emulate Clough's remarkable scoring prowess, but still grabbed a very healthy 141 goals in 238 appearances. It earned him twice as many caps as Clough during their 'Boro days and, like Clough, also produced a big money transfer.

He was sold to Leeds United for £55,000 in February 1964, and went on to win a Second Division championship medal.

Peacock won a further two caps with Leeds, before his career was ended by a knee injury picked up in a friendly match in East Germany.

He thought those six England shirts were safe at home at his mother's, until he received a phone call one day. It was from a local man who was putting together a five-a-side team and had bought the shirts for 7s 6d each off North Ormesby market.

Alan said: "I went to my mum's and she said that she must have given them to the Salvation Army. Naturally the lad who had bought them at the market realised their value, and handed them back to me. But I had to buy him a new kit in exchange – a full kit. It cost me a fortune!"

Charlie Cole, George Camsell, Micky Fenton and Harold Shepherdson all gave more than 30 years loyal service to 'Boro in a variety of capacities.

STEVE PEARS (1983-95)

STEVE PEARS was one of those irreplaceable assets that every club yearns for – a solid and dependable 'keeper, who prevents dozens of goals every season and gives the rest of the side confidence.

In ten seasons at Ayresome Park, in addition to two earlier loan spells, Steve was a tower of strength.

He was a key man in Bruce Rioch's post-liquidation side, compiling 30 clean sheets in the Third Division promotion season, which is a club record.

National recognition was delayed until 1992 when Pears was called up by England for a trip to Czechoslovakia, but a fractured cheekbone prevented him taking part and the chance never came again. The same season he was Hennessy North-East Player of the Year.

The Brandon-born player joined Manchester United from school, but came to Ayresome Park on a month's loan in 1983, making his debut against Cardiff City on Guy Fawkes' Day.

Steve said: "That match will always be one of my best memories from Ayresome Park. Cardiff had a lot of the play and I was kept busy all the way through the game. I made some good saves and we won the game 2-0. It was the perfect start."

Steve Pears, one of 'Boro's goalkeeping greats, he kept a record 30 clean sheets in the Third Division promotion campaign of 1986-87. His deserved testimonial in the summer of 1995 was the last scheduled match at Ayresome Park.

The performance also won over the fans, and Steve was given terrific backing from the terraces throughout his career.

Steve later had a second month on loan at Ayresome, but it was not until the summer of 1985 that he became a permanent 'Boro player when Willie Maddren paid £80,000 for his signature.

He said: "We struggled throughout most of that first season. I felt that I had done well, and Willie gave me a lot of confidence. But we were relegated and I wondered if I had done the right thing leaving Old Trafford."

Liquidation followed relegation, but Steve stayed put. He said: "I could have gone to Leeds or Fulham that summer, but I wanted Middlesbrough to survive and stuck it out. What followed was brilliant, because we had two tremendous years on the trot and put the club back on its feet.

"We had a great young side under Bruce Rioch. We didn't know it at the time, but we had six or seven million-pound players. I think Bruce had something to do with that. He made them better players. He gave them the chance early on and they benefited.

"Tony Mowbray and Gary Pallister worked very well together, and players like Colin Cooper, Gary Hamilton, Stuart Ripley and Bernie Slaven were tremendous. We all got on so well together, and still do when we meet up.

"Bruce kept it all going. I had a lot of time for him and Colin Todd. Bruce always came across as a hard man, but he made people play. He had a great knowledge of football, and had a good team plan. Everybody benefited.

"Naturally Bruce inherited a lot of those players from Willie. He was fortunate in that respect, but he also brought them on. It's still a shame that Willie was lost to football. He was a great talent spotter."

In many respects 'Boro were promoted too quickly, and the small squad struggled in the First Division when injuries struck. Relegation followed with Pears already side-lined with a stomach hernia, which needed an operation and kept him out until the following December.

Steve said: "I'll never forget my comeback. It had taken me a while to get back. I had lost three stones through the illness.

"Then Bruce phoned me on the Friday night and asked me if I fancied playing at home to Leicester the next day. I didn't know how I would be, and it turned out to be a bombardment. Leicester had Kevin Campbell on loan from Arsenal and I seemed to be saving shots every few seconds. In the event we hit back and beat them 4-1. It was just the comeback I needed because my confidence was fully restored in that 90 minutes."

Rioch left Ayresome the following March and was replaced by his assistant Colin Todd. Pears said: "It's a shame that Bruce didn't lead us out at Wembley in the Zenith Data Systems Cup Final. But that's football. Good managers have to move on because of a few results.

"But Colin did well. He brought in some good players like Jimmy Phillips, Robbie Mustoe and John Hendrie and got us into the Play-offs."

Steve missed half of that season with a fractured little finger picked up in training, but was back the following season when Lennie Lawrence arrived and brought new impetus.

Pears had a magnificent season as Lawrence led 'Boro to promotion, and remembers the highlight as the two games against Manchester United in the Rumbelows Cup semi-finals.

He said: "They were both really exciting games to play in. I always enjoyed going back to Old Trafford, but the second leg was really special. We lost the game, but it could have gone either way. We were so close to reaching Wembley again."

England selection came at the same time, and Pears' career had reached its high spot. But disaster followed, when Steve was caught by Dion Dublin's elbow in a night match at Cambridge United and he suffered a fractured cheekbone.

He said: "Obviously it was very frustrating. I had a good idea that it was fractured. I had the operation a couple of days later."

Ironically, Pears never missed a 'Boro match as a result, but he added: "I had to drop out of the England squad. I had no choice. I hoped that the chance would come again, but it never did. It was just one of those things. Nigel Martyn was not involved in the squad for Czechoslovakia, but later went on to the European Championships. So you never know what might have happened if I had played."

Pears had to contend with one or two injuries in 'Boro's following season in the Premier League, but bounced back with one of his most consistent seasons in 1993-94 as 'Boro failed in a late bid to reach the Play-offs.

He added: "I'm very fortunate to have enjoyed a good career at Ayresome Park. I enjoyed playing for every manager, and I made a lot of friends, so you can't ask for anything more."

Jim Platt, pictured with a Mecca loyalty award after playing his 300th League game. Platt, a thoroughly consistent 'keeper, played 468 games for 'Boro, a post-war goalkeeping record.

JIM PLATT (1971-83)

JIM PLATT was one of the key men in 'Boro's dynamic side of the 1970s which included players like Graeme Souness, Willie Maddren and David Armstrong.

As a last line of defence, Platt had a good command of his area, was an agile shot stopper and above all, was very consistent.

This was borne out by the fact that he played 468 games for the 'Boro, which puts him fifth in the all-time list.

Jim was spotted playing for Ballymena by 'Boro's Irish scout, Bobby McAuley, and signed for the 'Boro in a £10,000 deal after Harold Shepherdson flew out to run the rule over him.

Platt admitted: "The first year was very difficult. I was very homesick. I started off in the hostel, but then moved into digs. It was very hard to adapt, but I was determined to stick at it because I wanted to be a professional footballer.

"I really started to settle in during the second year, especially as I broke into the first team. Willie Whigham was having a bad spell, and Stan Anderson was forced to play me, even though I was a bit of an unknown quantity.

"But I did well as soon as I came in, and I stayed in. It's easier for a goalkeeper to become a regular because if you are playing well then there's no way you can be left out."

Jim did so well that he was 'Boro's Player of the Year in his first season. It was to be the first of several club awards, while he went on to become North-East Footballer of the Year towards the end of his 'Boro career in 1981.

'Boro really took off when Jack Charlton arrived in the summer of 1973. Platt said: "Stan was a very good manager, but sometimes you have to have a change at the top, and when Jack arrived he provided a new impetus.

"Stan had bought Graeme Souness the previous season but he didn't really do it at first. He came through under Jack, while Bobby Murdoch gave us balance. He could read a game well and was a superb passer of the ball.

"In Jack's first match in charge we went to Portsmouth. They had bought big and were pre-season favourites to go up. They bought Peter Marinello, Paul Went and Ron Davies for a total of around £500,000, which was a lot of money at the time. But we beat them 1-0.

"Our next game was at home to Fulham, and we lost 2-0. Jack was absolutely furious afterwards. We used to have a crate of Lowcocks lemonade brought into the dressing-room after games and Jack picked it up and rammed it against the floor.

"When we came in on the Monday, Jack said he was sorry for losing his temper. He said he should have left it for the Monday. But when we started to discuss the game again, he lost his temper again!

"But Jack knew what he was talking about. We went another 24 games unbeaten after that and never looked back."

'Boro waltzed to promotion before the end of March, when they beat Oxford United 1-0 at Ayresome Park.

Jim said: "We were promoted that day because the other results went our way. But at first it was unconfirmed and all we had to go on was the celebrations of the fans because they heard it on their radios.

"However, Jack wouldn't let us go out and do a lap of honour until he had seen it for himself. It must have been the longest delayed lap of honour of all time."

'Boro carried on the momentum in the First Division and were a good side both under Charlton and John Neal.

Platt said: "We were a good side. Nobody enjoyed playing us. We were top for a while when we first went up, and we eventually finished seventh.

"Jack's only problem was that he didn't strengthen the side. Bobby Murdoch and John Hickton were coming to the end of their careers and needed replacing, but Jack didn't do it.

"John Neal did change things around and he brought in lads like Craig Johnston, David Hodgson and Mark Proctor. They did well for us. We still had a side that nobody enjoyed playing.

"The only regret I have from these periods is that we never got to Wembley. We had our chances. We should have done better against Manchester City in the League Cup semi-finals, and we should never have lost to Orient in the quarter-finals of the FA Cup. I played at

Wembley for Northern Ireland, but it would have been marvellous to go there with Middlesbrough."

Platt went on to win 20 international caps for Northern Ireland, playing twice at Wembley. But the peak was his appearance in the World Cup Finals in Spain against Austria.

That World Cup jersey will be a prized memento. Not that Jim has many from his 'Boro days. He said: "In my last few seasons at Middlesbrough, I used to throw my jersey into the crowd after the last game of the season. I can remember Jimmy Headridge telling me not to do it, but I always got on well with the fans and I think they enjoyed it."

Remarkably, in his long career, Platt saved just one penalty at Ayresome Park. He said: "I saved a few away from home, but the only one at Ayresome was in the first few minutes of a derby against Newcastle. Tommy Craig took it and I dived low to my left and saved it. We went on to win it 2-0!

Jim was awarded a testimonial match in September 1981, against Sunderland. He came out of goal in the second half to play at centre-forward, much to the surprise and appreciation of the crowd. But it was nothing new to Platt – he had scored a hat-trick for 'Boro reserves at Lincoln early in his career.

Platt's testimonial was notable for the appearance of the great George Best. Jim said: "It was great of George to come, and he had a good game. I can remember saying to Bobby Murdoch afterwards that he could do worse than to think about Besty. We weren't a very good team then, and he might have provided a spark. Bobby followed it through, but nothing came of it."

'Boro were starting to slide when Murdoch took over from John Neal, and the club hurtled towards the Second Division. Jim said: "We had a nightmare season. We were down virtually from the word go. I felt very sorry for Bobby. He was a great guy. But looking back, it was probably the wrong appointment."

Jim was appointed club captain in 1982-83, but still things didn't go well and Murdoch was sacked and replaced by Malcolm Allison. Platt said: "I don't think Malcolm did anything for Middlesbrough. He just wanted young players in the club. We had a lot of experience in the reserve team that season.

"His first match was at Rotherham and we all had to stand in a circle, holding hands in the dressing-room. Then we had to shout 'We are going to win'. Malcolm was a very good coach, but his team talks were terrible.

"Obviously I didn't see eye to eye with him. It's probably why I left the club when I did. But that's my one regret in football. I was only 31. I should have stayed longer because I still had a lot to offer at that level."

MARK PROCTOR (1978-93)

MARK PROCTOR spent two separate stints at Ayresome Park, at both ends of his professional career.

As a teenager, he was drafted into the First Division line-up at the same time as fellow youngsters Craig Johnston and David Hodgson. The trio brought a vibrancy to the side which sparked the senior professionals and helped 'Boro to make a continuing impact amongst the country's élite.

Mark was sold to Nottingham Forest as a 20-year-old, a few months after the 1981 FA Cup defeat by Wolves, and saw service with Sunderland and Sheffield Wednesday before returning home in 1989.

His return, ten games before the end of the season, came too late to prevent 'Boro from being relegated to the Second Division, but he had the honour of captaining the club in their first-ever appearance at Wembley the following year.

It was as a young professional that Proctor enjoyed his most successful days at Ayresome Park.

He said: "I came into the side in a transitional period. John Neal had inherited Jack Charlton's team, and was starting to bring in new faces and stamp his own personal type of management on the club.

"John was great with the kids, and to be fair to him, it paid off. Craig Johnston came through six months before me, and David Hodgson followed me into the team.

"We were the mainstays. But there were lots of other lads who got their chance at that time like Billy Askew, Peter Johnson, Jeff Peters, David Shearer, Charlie Bell and Mickey Angus.

"All the lads had that will to win. They were full of endeavour and they helped change things around."

Proctor made his first-team debut as a 17-year-old in a 3-1 win at Birmingham City in August 1978, and quickly became a permanent fixture in the side.

He said: "We had a good dressing-room. We had the experienced players that John Neal had inherited like Jim Platt, Stuart Boam, Tony McAndrew, John Craggs and David Armstrong, and we had the players he had bought like Billy Ashcroft, Terry Cochrane and John Mahoney.

"We finished 12th that season. It was a decent side. It was a wonder season for me. I was 17 and just out of school. I got nine goals in 33 appearances, and it was all down to sheer enthusiasm.

"But then I had stood on the terraces. It meant so much to me because it was a dream come true. I felt so proud just to be a part of it."

John Neal had a hard act to follow when he replaced Jack Charlton, but his side never struggled in the First Division.

Proctor said: "John was a mild mannered man. He wasn't a raver.

Mark Proctor, seen scoring against Nottingham Forest in February, 1979, played more than 250 games for 'Boro in two separate stints at Ayresome Park.

Sometimes, when he was talking, you couldn't see him for the smoke from his cigarettes, but he knew his job and was very thorough.

"Basically he was a cajoler. He used to get the best out of me by encouraging me. Really he was just the job for the kids, because he helped us a lot, and that got us started."

The end for Neal and eventually Proctor, was the Wolves cup defeat. Proctor said: "That Cup-tie led to the break up of the side. The senior professionals were disillusioned. The Cup run had been brilliant, and if we had reached the semi-finals things might have been different.

"But the spark went out of our game. Craig Johnston left after the Wolves game, and suddenly everybody wanted to follow him. My contract was up that summer, and when Brian Clough and Peter Taylor came in I thought it was a good move. I had played for them when they ran the England youth team.

"I had 100 League games under my belt and thought that I knew it all. But I didn't. I don't regret joining Forest, but I was only 20 and it came a bit early in my career. But I knew that things were bad at Ayresome Park, and it was a move I couldn't afford to miss."

It was almost eight years before Proctor became a 'Boro player once more, when Bruce Rioch signed him from Sheffield Wednesday to try to help keep the young 'Boro side in the First Division.

Proctor said: "Both Wednesday and 'Boro were struggling to stay up, so it was a move out of the frying pan into the fire.

"I didn't realise that the 'Boro team was so young. I think I was the only player with children. And everybody seemed to have blond hair. I thought I might have to dye my hair in order to qualify for my place in the team.

"We had some good players, but there was not enough experience. It's a tough, tough League, and we just weren't strong enough or experienced enough. It might have been different if we had just stayed up, because I think we could have gone from strength to strength.

"But it threatened to fall apart when we were relegated. Everybody thought we were favourites to go straight back up again. But Gary Pallister was transferred to Manchester United and the season turned into a nightmare.

"There was a lot of tension in the dressing-room and players kept getting on each other's nerves. We still had terrific support, but I don't think we got out of the bottom six. Bruce had problems with a few players, and it wasn't a surprise when he eventually left the club.

"Obviously it was an honour to lead the team at Wembley. As a Middlesbrough lad, it gave me a great sense of pride. But I was probably more happy when we beat Newcastle on the last day of the season to stay up."

He added: "We turned it around under Colin Todd the next season and reached the Play-offs. But we were well beaten by Notts County in the end. It was followed by the summer of ten or 11 for sale, but it was Toddy who went instead. I always felt that he was a terrific coach, but I'm not sure if he was cut out for management."

The following season Lennie Lawrence arrived and Proctor played his part in a successful promotion campaign.

Mark said: "Lennie made two great signings in Paul Wilkinson and Willie Falconer and it turned us into a good side.

"Even so, when we went to Wolves for that final game of the season I think that even the fans believed that we wouldn't do it. But Lennie said that he was a great believer in fate, and he always felt we were going to do it.

"It might have looked unlikely when we were 1-0 down with 15 minutes to go, and Nicky Mohan was sent off, but goals from Jon Gittens and Paul Wilkinson settled it.

"I always felt that season was my great achievement in football, even though I missed the last game at Wolves. I can remember sitting on the bench, wearing one of those big chunky track suits, and I took it off and threw it to the crowd. And all I had left was a pair of boxers shorts. But I've never had a better feeling in football."

Proctor failed to secure a regular place again with 'Boro, and was particularly disappointed to miss out on regular Premier League football. He said: "At 31, I felt I could still do it at top level, and I was frustrated to miss out. But that's football. I eventually went on loan to Tranmere and then the move became permanent."

DICKIE ROBINSON (1946-59)

DICKIE ROBINSON was a great 'Boro club servant, coming straight into the side immediately after the war and going on to make 416 appearances for the club.

Whitburn-born, he was brought to Ayresome Park during the war by manager David Jack and was initially tried as a left winger. However, it was at right-back where he quickly settled into the side, and went on to become one of the most respected defenders in the First Division. Dickie represented the Football League on five occasions between (1947 and 1951) and, although he was said to be on the verge of England honours, a full cap unfortunately never came his way.

He went on to taste good and bad times at Ayresome Park, playing through the relegation season in 1953-54 and the early days back in the Second Division as an emergency centre-half.

One of Dickie's first games for 'Boro came in a wartime derby at home to Sunderland on 1 January 1946. He said: "I played at outside-left and I scored the winning goal. It hit the underside of the bar and dropped over the line.

"I can remember getting a lift home on the Sunderland coach and their manager, Bill Murray, said that it was a silly goal. I said that it might have been a silly goal, but it was still worth £22 in win bonuses to our team."

Dickie was quickly switched to full-back, and was at left-back for all the games in 'Boro's terrific FA Cup run in 1946 when they reached the fifth round. George Hardwick played centre-half in those games.

Robinson said: "We played three games against Blackpool in the fourth round and they were marvellous games. They beat us by one goal over there, we beat them by the same at Ayresome Park, and then we had the marvellous decider at Elland Road.

"Before the game we stayed at a hotel, and I can remember Charlie Cole, our trainer, had me sprinting up and down the corridor in the hotel to keep me on my toes. He was a great fella, Charlie, and always looked after me.

"The Leeds game was still undecided after 90 minutes, and after extra-time, but then George Hardwick scored the winner from the penalty-spot in sudden death.

"We lost to Bolton in the next round, but the biggest disappointment came the following season when Burnley beat us in the sixth round on a disputed goal."

Robinson played in all the big games after the war, and had a good rapport with the fans. He said: "We played in front of big crowds at Ayresome Park all the time. You just accepted it. We had the record crowd against Newcastle in 1949. They were great days.

"The fans were always very supportive. In all the time I was there I never had a bad word said against me by a fan. I always got on with them very well."

Dickie played right through two different eras at Ayresome Park, and was a member of the side which included Brian Clough and Alan Peacock.

He said: "I can remember Brian Clough sitting next to me on the coach as we were leaving Ayresome Park for an

Dickie Robinson, a great club servant throughout the 1940s and 1950s, playing at full-back and centre-half and making more than 400 'Boro appearances.

In October 1967, 'Boro had two players, Des McPartland and Eric McMordie, sent off in a match. Fortunately it was only during a practice game and manager Stan Anderson described the incident as 'just a bit of a punch-up'.

away game, and he waved to Joe Clough who worked at Garnett's sweet factory which was over the road from the ground.

"The players regularly went into the factory to get boxes of sweets and I knew Joe very well.

"I said to Brian, I didn't know you knew Joe Clough, and he said: 'Yes, he's my father'. All those years and they had never let on that they were related."

HAROLD SHEPHERDSON (1937-46)

HAROLD SHEPHERDSON was a terrific all-round sportsman. He captained 'Boro Boys at both football and cricket.

So it was perfectly natural that he should eventually take the eye of the 'Boro directors. The Middlesbrough-born lad was big and strong for his age, and a commanding centre-half. In fact he was one of several promising local players to join the club in the mid to late 1930s.

Harold said: "The very thought of walking into Ayresome Park at that time was like a Catholic walking into the Vatican. It was a great experience for any young lad because the football club was the focal point of the community.

"George Camsell was my hero. I had to pinch myself to think that I was changing in the same room as him. He was a great player and a great scorer of goals.

"Bobby Baxter was another marvellous player. He was the Scottish international centre-half and I was his understudy at Ayresome Park. He was great to me. Always helpful.

"But then all the senior players were wonderful. There was a great camaraderie about Ayresome Park. There were so many jokers, so many witty players."

Harold was working as an office boy with Richard Hill and Company, earning £3 a week, when he joined 'Boro. He immediately doubled his wages to £6 a week. But it was not easy trying to break into the first team when Bobby Baxter was ahead of you, and Shep's senior appearances were strictly limited.

However, he did have the distinction of playing against the great Everton centre-forward Dixie Dean. Shep said: "I had a good game that day, and we won. After the match Dixie put his arm around me and said: "Where have they dug you up from son?" When I saw him again in later years he said: "I have never forgotten you. You used me as the ball that day!"

Shep went on to become the 'Boro trainer in a strong and loyal association with the club which lasted more than 50 years. He also brought many honours to 'Boro by becoming England's trainer, a role he held with distinction during the successful 1966 World Cup campaign. But Harold learned little from his days training at Ayresome Park.

He said: "We had a trainer at Middlesbrough called Charlie Cole. A lovely fella. But for him training involved running round and round the pitch. It was so monotonous. You ended

Harold Shepherdson, dedicated 'Boro servant who spent 51 years at the club as player, trainer and caretaker manager. He was also England trainer from the late 1950s until the 1970s, covering four World Cup campaigns.

up chatting to the next guy as you were running to try to get some mental stimulation.

"I knew that there had to be something better than this. I wanted to take part in team practice games. But Charlie wouldn't give us a ball. He used to say 'I give you a ball on a Saturday and you don't know what to do with it, so I'm not giving you one today'. Basically Charlie was frightened that somebody would get injured. He was answerable to the board. They didn't want to pick up any injuries in training."

While Shep was finding it difficult to break into the 'Boro first team on a permanent basis, his career really took off as a result of World War Two. He became a PT instructor in the Army, and learned physiology and anatomy. As a result Shep was one of a wave of new trainers with modern ideas to sweep through the English game after the war.

After a short spell at Southend, Shep returned to Ayresome Park and became head trainer very quickly following the retirement of Charlie Cole and Tom Mayson. He was able to introduce his own ideas and make training interesting. Within a few years he had graduated to become England trainer as well.

It was in the early 1950s that Shep first met Brian Clough. Shep said: "We often popped over to Garnett's sweet factory, which was just over the road from the ground. Brian was often hanging about outside. He used to say 'I'm going to play for the 'Boro'. How true his words turned out to be.

"He was a great finisher, and a very dedicated footballer. He deserved more caps, but then people couldn't always come to terms with his manner. He always let people know what he thought.

"Cloughie was part of a great Middlesbrough forward line, all of whom were local boys. We had Day, McLean, Clough, Peacock and Holliday. The last three all played for England. Peacock was the perfect foil for Clough, while McLean was the grafter. And we had two very good wingers. Unfortunately the defence at that time wasn't half as good as the forward line."

Shep became assistant manager at Ayresome under Stan Anderson, and it was a role he enjoyed virtually until the early 1980s, when he became chief executive of the football side of the club.

He had the honour of working closely with Jack Charlton, who transformed the club in the 1970s. Shep said: "Jack knew exactly what he wanted and how he was going to do it. He got the best out of players and blended them into a team.

"I remember when he arrived, one of the things he insisted on was that the team trained on the pitch. He never asked the groundsman. He just took the players on there. They started training, and then the groundsman started cutting the grass. Jack stopped training and told him to get off. It was a marvellous pitch in those days. One of the best in the world. And Jack insisted that the players had to train on it so that they knew every blade of grass."

BERNIE SLAVEN (1985-93)

BERNIE SLAVEN was 'Boro's most prolific goalscorer of modern times. Playing his football in an era where football defending had become an art, Bernie's clinical finishing made him a great asset to the club in the difficult days following liquidation.

His final tally of 134 goals made him the club's seventh-highest goalscorer of all time. But for his relatively late arrival at Ayresome Park, when he was almost 25, and for his untimely departure, when he fell out of favour, Bernie could have had a goalscoring record to match the old-time greats.

It was his record with Albion Rovers, when his 31 goals made him the top scorer in all Scotland, which won him a trial at Ayresome Park, and it was in his second season – as remarkably one of the elder statesmen in Bruce Rioch's young side – that his career really took off.

Slaven said: "I knew a lot about Bruce from my time in Glasgow. He was a former Scotland captain. I knew him as a tough nut, and I thought that I would be on my way when he took over because that was not a side of my game.

"But then when I realised that he wanted footballers I knew that I would be all right. He brought all the young lads in and encouraged them to play football and knock the ball around. That suited me down to the ground.

"And I don't think I would have been as good a player if it was not for Bruce. He was a motivator, and I responded to him. He helped me to establish myself in England.

"He used to set everybody targets, and I always tried to achieve mine. He used to give great talks, and make you feel as though you were Real Madrid when you went on to the pitch.

"I can remember when the team sheet was pinned up once. The number seven was left vacant. That was my position. Bruce pointed out that the number seven didn't perform last week. He said that if he wanted his name in the vacant space this week, he had to perform. That was all the motivation I needed. I went out and played well.

"So I had a lot of respect for Bruce. I think some of the young lads were scared of him at first. But he was great at winding us up. He did a lot for all of us."

In the early days, Slaven's partner up front was Archie Stephens. Between them, the pair grabbed the goals which helped 'Boro win promotion from the Third Division in Rioch's first full season.

Slaven said: "Archie did a great job. He was smaller than me, but he leapt really well. He used to take all the kicks, but he was always knocking balls down for me to score.

"But it was a team thing. We got the blend right. Tony Mowbray was a great leader on the pitch as well. In our own ways we all had so much to prove. I had

'Boro's Scottish international forward Andy Wilson represented England at bowls in 1948.

Bernie Slaven, the last man to score more than 100 goals for 'Boro, was a prolific marksman in the years following liquidation. He made 370 appearances for 'Boro and won Irish international honours.

The most League defeats suffered by 'Boro in one season at Ayresome Park was 11 in 1923-24.

seen the other side of the fence. I had been a part-time footballer on the dole. This was my big chance."

Slaven kept slamming in the goals and 'Boro stormed right through to the First Division in consecutive seasons. However, they had a nervous moment when they lost at home to Leicester in their final game, and had to reach the top flight through the Play-offs.

He said: "We had gone to Barnsley and I scored twice in a 3-0 win. We knew as we were driving home that we were in the First Division if we beat Leicester the following Saturday.

"There was a full house and it was on TV. There were balloons everywhere. It was a carnival atmosphere. But it didn't happen for us. Leicester outplayed us.

"Leicester's two Scots, Peter Weir and Gary McAllister, grabbed their goals. I had a chat with Mac afterwards, and he said that he hoped that we still made it. He said that it was easier to play your football in the First Division than in the Second.

"We did eventually make it through the Play-offs. I kept on remembering what Mac had said, and I didn't find it any more difficult in the First Division. I knew that I would score goals at any level if I got the service. In the end I got 18.

"The team played well for a long time. But we didn't get enough goals from elsewhere. When we lost possession, we were usually punished. All the other teams had quality players. It was hard on the players to try so much, and get punished for mistakes."

'Boro struggled again the following season, yet Slaven scored a remarkable total of 32 goals. It was perhaps his greatest season. 'Boro's only achievement was in reaching Wembley for the first time in the Zenith Data Systems Cup, but they narrowly avoided relegation. Rioch was sacked shortly before the Wembley Final, with his long-time assistant Colin Todd taking over the hot seat.

Slaven said: "I thought that we would bounce straight back up again. We got a great start, but it didn't happen for us. The lads were older and they didn't respond the same way.

"I think that Bruce had gone as far as he could go. He had done a great job and couldn't do any more. But I was disappointed that he didn't lead the team out at Wembley. It was the first time in the club's history we had got there, and he would have been right for it."

Slaven's great pal at Ayresome was always Gary Pallister. Slaven said: "I didn't like him at first. But he went to Darlington on loan, and when he came back, we were great mates.

"We still see a lot of each other. I was gutted at first when he moved, but he did the right thing for his career. He was always a good player, always comfortable, and never flustered."

Ironically, both Slaven and Pallister went on to become internationals. Though Slaven's choice of the Republic of Ireland may have come as something of a surprise, considering that he was born in Scotland.

He said: "I always thought it was right for play for the Republic. My grandparents were Irish, and so I knew my father wouldn't mind. In any case I was a big Celtic fan, and there was an affinity between Celtic fans and Ireland.

"I did talk to the Scottish manager, Andy Roxburgh, but Jack Charlton promised that he would play me against Wales and so that was good enough for me. I never regretted it. I went to the World Cup Finals after only two and a half games for Ireland. It was a great experience."

Bernie kept banging in the goals for 'Boro, but never really fitted in under manager Lennie Lawrence. The pair didn't always see eye to eye, and the writing was on the all for Slaven when he had a public slanging match with Lawrence after being dropped for a night match at Bristol City on 7 April 1992. Ironically Slaven still went on to be top scorer in the League in that promotion campaign.

He said: "Lennie had his own ideas and his own players, but I ended up top scorer despite missing quite a few games.

"In the end Lennie thought it was in everybody's best interests that I left. He gave me a free transfer to acknowledge my loyalty to the club. But I was gutted to leave. I still felt that I had a lot to offer.

"Port Vale were good to me and I made two further Wembley appearances with them. But Middlesbrough will always be my club."

FRANK SPRAGGON (1964-76)

FRANK SPRAGGON was a hard-working defender who gave 'Boro great service during a series of different eras in the club's history.

He arrived at Ayresome Park as an

Frank Spraggon, a good club servant and alert defender who made 322 League and Cup appearances for the 'Boro.

apprentice when Brian Clough was still with the club, and played under four managers before winning a Second Division championship medal as part of Jack Charlton's all-conquering side.

Frank was initially a traditional wing-half, but developed into a solid central defender and later a left-back, going on to play 322 League and Cup games for the club.

Born at Marley Hill near Stanley, Spraggon was spotted playing for his district schools side playing against Middlesbrough at the Dorman Long ground. The man who spotted him was 'Boro coach Harold Shepherdson – later to become his father-in-law.

Frank said: "I was all prepared to go to Preston, but I'd never left home before and when Middlesbrough offered me the chance to become an apprentice professional I decided to come here instead.

"In those days apprentices were either on the outside ground staff or the inside ground staff. I was outside, so I didn't clean boots. I worked with the groundsman and cleaned the stands and the toilets, and the away dressing-room.

"It's a fact that we had to scrub the toilets out. We had to whitewash them in the close season as well. I was once whitewashing the toilets, standing up a ladder, when Bob Dennison came in. I didn't see him, and dripped whitewash all over him!"

The apprentices got up to tricks in those days, just like the players. Spraggon said: "There used to be a scoreboard at the back of the East End, and we went in and put up the sign 'Come and play Bingo on a Saturday afternoon, instead of watching football'. We made the mistake of leaving it there. People started ringing up and the *Evening Gazette*, who sponsored the scoreboard, were very upset. We all ended up on the carpet."

One apprentice ended up shot. Frank recalls: "The groundsman, Wilf Atkinson, was having a problem with pigeons on the pitch. So Bob Appleby, our goalkeeper, said he would bring in his gun and shoot them.

"Bob was a lovely fella, but as mad as a hatter. He did turn up with his gun. When he fired his first shot there was a yell. Arthur Proctor, one of the apprentices, had been sweeping the stand and was shot. He fell out of the stand and into the terracing. One of the pellets, or whatever, had hit him. There was a panic at the time, but fortunately he was all right later, and then we could laugh about it."

Ironically Spraggon made his first-team debut without ever having played for the reserves. He said: "I went straight from the juniors and played in a League Cup-tie at home to Bradford when I was still only 17."

Frank went on to play a lot of reserve-team football as he battled to break through on a permanent basis. He said: "Micky Fenton used to take the reserves and he always had to be on the winning side. We used to play on until his side had won. It might be 33-30 or something, and Micky had to score the winner. But it was always good fun."

As a 19-year-old Spraggon played at left-back in 'Boro's 5-3 defeat at Cardiff City in 1966 which took 'Boro into the Third Division for the first time.

He said: "It was my biggest disappointment in football. Whoever won stayed up. We felt that we could win, but it would never have happened. There was a feeling the game had been bought."

Spraggon finally established himself in the 'Boro team in the first season back in Division Two, and became one of the mainstays of Stan Anderson's team which went so close to promotion on so many occasions.

Frank said: "We had a lot of good players, like Gordon Jones, Willie Whigham, Eric McMordie, Bill Gates, John Hickton and Derrick Downing. We were virtually guaranteed to win at home, but we could never win enough games away from home.

"Hughie McIlmoyle came in and scored a lot of goals with John Hickton, but somehow we couldn't score with the same frequency away. As soon as we went a goal down we knew that we were going to struggle to get anything out of the game."

In 1971, Spraggon needed a cartilage operation. Ironically, the operation left him with blurred vision, something he discovered later was the result of having had too much anaesthetic, which affected his optic nerve.

He said: "At first I couldn't adjust. The ball kept hitting me all over, and Stan knew I wasn't right. However, I worked hard at it and finally adjusted."

The reward was a regular place back in the side, and the opportunity to be part of Jack Charlton's illustrious team.

Frank said: "Jack had us playing to our strengths, and when we did that we were a very good side. It's only when you look back that you realise how good we were. We were promoted well before Easter.

"The main thing was that we set out not to give anything away. That suited my style. I was purely a defender. I just liked to defend. I very rarely came forward."

Spraggon's defensive colleague was Willie Maddren. Frank said: "Willie was very quick. He used to nip things in the bud. He was unfortunate to have Norman Hunter and Bobby Moore ahead of him or he would definitely have played for England.

"Then he developed his bad knee. I had one as well. We used to compare knees on the pitch."

As a result of his defensive duties, Spraggon rarely came forward and joined attacks. However, he did score three goals for the club, all of them at Ayresome Park.

He said: "The first came in a 4-2 win against Birmingham. It was a flashing header from a Derrick Downing corner. I got another header against Norwich, and then I scored with my feet when I had a tap-in against Millwall in the promotion season."

While Spraggon scored against Birmingham, the Midlands club provided another of his disappointments.

He said: "In the year after we were promoted, we were sure that our name was on the Cup because we felt we were the best side left in it.

"We had beaten Birmingham twice in the League. But we didn't perform in the Cup. I felt sorry for all the fans who went down there.

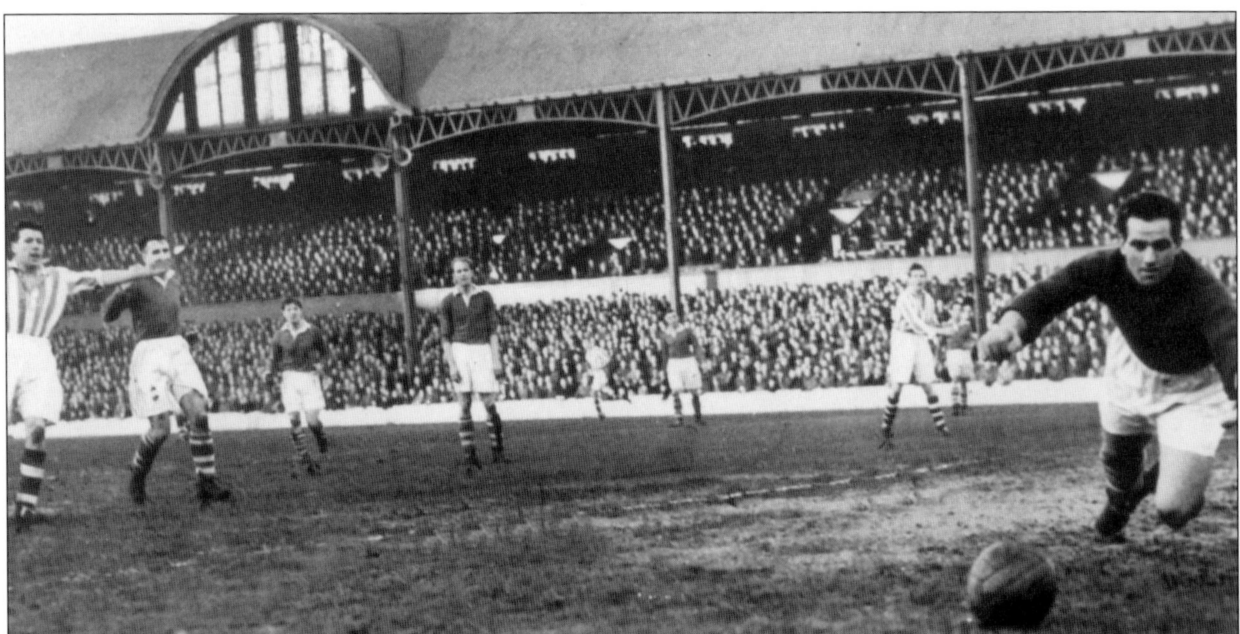

Rolando Ugolini, pictured in action in a 3-0 win at home to Stoke City on Boxing Day, 1951, was a solid and acrobatic goalkeeper who was a regular in the side for eight years.

The most League wins in a season by 'Boro at Ayresome Park was 18 in 1926-27.

"I can remember we went to Birmingham in our opening First Division game and won 3-0. People couldn't believe it. Neither could we at the time. But we carried it on from there and started to believe in ourselves.

"We went to Liverpool and were turned over. But then we went back to Anfield in the League Cup and won 1-0 when Willie Maddren scored. It showed that we were quick learners and had adapted to playing the top sides. It was a great time to be at the club."

Frank later lost his place to England international Terry Cooper, before trying his luck in the United States, where he played for Minnesota Kicks against some of the biggest football names in the world.

JOHN SPUHLER (1946-54)

JOHNNY SPUHLER was a committed forward who could play at centre-forward or on the wing. He was one of the mainstays of the 'Boro side in the difficult days after the war, having joined the club for £1,750 from neighbours Sunderland.

His final tally of 81 goals at an average of a goal every three games was respectable by any standards.

One of Johnny's best performances, and most vivid memories, comes from the FA Cup fourth-round tie at home to Chesterfield on 25 February 1947.

He said: "The match was played in front of 42,000 people with a great atmosphere. Our team was Cumming; Stuart, Robinson, Bell, Hardwick, McCabe, Spuhler, Gordon, Fenton, Mannion, Walker. Chesterfield scored after only four minutes, but I scored the equaliser three minutes later.

"In an end to end second half, Geoff Walker dribbled to the bye-line and from a perfect centre I made the game safe for 'Boro. It was one of many happy days at Ayresome Park. It's a great club with great supporters always."

Spuhler, whose whole career with 'Boro was spent in the First Division, also recalls the terrific wit within the team camp. He said: "We were playing at Liverpool on one occasion and the ref was new and green. Play was rough in the centre circle, with players everywhere. The ref stopped the game and began asking names. Mannion suggested the ref should leave the field and buy a programme!"

Johnny Spuhler, a useful post-war signing, the powerful striker was a key man in the side, playing on the wing or at centre-forward and scoring 81 goals in 241 appearances.

ROLANDO UGOLINI (1948-56)

ROLANDO UGOLINI was a top-quality goalkeeper who served 'Boro with great distinction during their First Division days after the war.

Signed from Celtic for £7,000 in 1948, he went on to play 335 League and Cup games for the 'Boro.

Rolando was born of Italian parents who moved to Armadale in Scotland in the 1920s and took up a fish and chip business. He became a naturalised Scotsman, and took out British citizenship shortly after joining the 'Boro.

However, Ugolini has unhappy memories of his first game for the 'Boro. He said: "It was the pre-season practice match at Ayresome Park. 'Boro had just signed Andrew Donaldson from Newcastle for £17,500 as well. He was the understudy to Wor Jackie.

"During the match the ball was played in from the wing and I dived in to punch it away. Andrew came in as well, and broke a bone in his foot in the collision. It was an accident, but it was very upsetting."

Rolando quickly settled in, and remembers his days at Ayresome Park with great affection. He said: "We had a very good side, with some great players like Wilf Mannion and George Hardwick.

"We had a marvellous team spirit. We also had a lot of laughs. We had all the usual horseplay, like pinning players' shirts to the dressing-room walls, and throwing gear into the baths.

"The one thing which really sticks out was the day that Micky Fenton got a brand new Jaguar. He was really proud of it. But we thought 'We'll fix him'. So the groundsman, Wilf Atkinson and I got a pail of whitewash and painted it all over Micky's new car. It was absolutely hilarious. But naturally Micky wasn't too pleased!"

Ugolini was not a player who accepted nonsense from anybody when he was on the pitch. He said: "One of the things which started to come in at that time was centre-forwards backing into goalkeepers. It made things difficult, so you had to find a way of stopping it.

"I can remember Don Revie doing it, so the next time we went up together I squeezed the loose part of his hip as hard as I could. He was shouting to the ref. But he didn't come back near me again.

"You had to react that way against centre-forwards, but you could get away with it then. There were no action replays in those days to have trials by television.

"In fact things were often bubbling over. Lindy Delapenha was my pal at that time. We used to room together. He could be a bit naughty on the pitch at times, but then players were often picking on him. There's many the guy I've punched in the back of the head in the tunnel coming off the pitch. You could get away with it."

Ugolini played in front of 'Boro's record attendance, when 53,802 fans watched the derby game against Newcastle on 27 December 1949. He said: "The fans were great, especially at derby games. There was never any trouble. They came to see the great players. You had the likes of Shackleton at Sunderland and Scoular, Mitchell, Wor Jackie and the Robledo brothers at Newcastle.

"They were always very hard games, and very physical. The referees used to let the games flow, and you could speak to the referee. You can't do that now."

One of the most disappointing moments in the early part of Rolando's career at Ayresome Park came in the FA Cup – when 'Boro lost 3-2 in the fourth round away to Third Division Chesterfield in 1950.

He said: "We had beaten Aston Villa after three great games in the third round, including a goalless draw after extra-time at Ayresome Park. Then we went to Chesterfield and suffered a terrible defeat. George Hardwick and I were dropped after that game, but it was very unfair because it was a one-off."

While Ugolini was rated as one of the best 'keepers in the country, the 'Boro directors at one time expressed doubts about his eyesight. Rolando said: "It was ridiculous. It was all blown up out of nothing. Peter McKennan started it; he started saying that I was eating a lot of carrots and eventually it reached the directors.

"It was silly. My eyesight is as good now as it was then. I still play off seven handicap at golf."

Rolando was in fact a fitness fanatic during his time with 'Boro. He said: "I was so fit it was not true. I did the power training in the gym as well as lapping, and I could sprint as fast as the best of them. In fact I could walk across Ayresome Park on my hands."

The end of Ugolini's career on Teesside came after 'Boro were relegated to the Second Division in 1954 after 25 years in the top flight.

He said: "Relegation was a bitter pill to swallow. We desperately wanted to stay up. We signed some good players, but they didn't fit in and the team didn't play as well together."

Rolando still played for 'Boro for another two full seasons before eventually moving on to Wrexham. He said: "I used to impersonate the manager Bob Dennison, and one day he turned around and caught me. I think the writing was on the wall after that.

"He signed Peter Taylor and brought him in when I dislocated my shoulder. I couldn't get back in, and eventually moved on.

"But I've no regrets. I always look back at my time at Ayresome Park as the happiest of my life. They were great times to be a professional footballer."

GEOFF WALKER (1946-54)

GEOFF WALKER was an astute signing by 'Boro manager David Jack at the end of the war. Jack paid Bradford £8,000 for Walker's signature, which was a huge fee to pay for a 19-year-old at the time.

But Geoff went on to repay that fee several times over. An orthodox left winger, he won a First Division place immediately and went on to become one of the most feared flank players in the game.

Like many wingers, Geoff was a creator of goals, but he also scored his fair share as well, ending with 53 goals from 259 senior appearances for 'Boro.

However, while Geoff made his mark on Teesside, he had an inauspicious arrival. He said: "David Jack signed me, and when I arrived at Ayresome Park from Bradford, I went straight to his office. Eventually he looked up and said: 'Yes, what can I do for you?' He didn't recognise me for a couple of minutes. David Jack was a nice man, who liked a drink, but he hadn't been drinking on that occasion!"

Geoff came to 'Boro's attention as a raw 17-year-old, when he first came to Ayresome Park with Bradford for a wartime game and scored a hat-trick in an 8-1 win for the Park Avenue club.

He was thrilled to return to Ayresome Park as a player to join the likes of returning senior professionals Wilf Mannion and George Hardwick as the serious business of League football started up again in 1946.

Geoff Walker was a busy and skilful winger who created lots of goals in the First Division days following World War Two.

Brian Clough is the only post-war player to score five goals for 'Boro in a League game at Ayresome Park when achieving the feat against Brighton in 1958. Andy Wilson was first to do it, against Nottingham Forest in 1923.

Walker said: "I looked at players like Mannion and Hardwick and couldn't believe I was playing in the same team. They were like gods.

"They were both great players, but they were also nice people. I used to play on the left wing, in front of George, and he was always very supportive. He didn't scream at you. A clap of the hands was enough.

"We had a lot of good players. Alex McCrae was a very good inside-forward, and we had men like Johnny Spuhler, Jimmy Gordon and Dickie Robinson, who was very unlucky not to win international honours of some kind.

"In fact we had a good, big staff. You had to prove yourself and keep doing it, because there was always somebody trying to get your place."

Ironically, Geoff did not move to Middlesbrough until the closing years of his eight years with 'Boro. He continued to train with Bradford, with the permission of both clubs, and did not meet up with his 'Boro teammates until the eve of matches.

Geoff said: "I trained at Bradford for five or six years. It was an arrangement I had. I suppose it looks unusual today, but it worked very well. I always kept myself fit at Bradford, and Middlesbrough must have been satisfied because I stayed in the team."

Walker had a marvellous rapport with the 'Boro fans. He said: "I always received a lot of backing from the supporters. They were very good to me."

However, Geoff remembers that it wasn't always the same for every 'Boro player. He said: "Some of the centre-forwards were given a hard time. The fans had been brought up on Camsell and Fenton, and if they weren't happy with the centre-forwards, they let them know it.

"We had some good players like Neil Mochan, Andy Donaldson, Alec Linwood and Ken McPherson. But they all took a bit of stick from the terraces. Mochan was a great player, but he never really managed to do it at Middlesbrough. When he went back to Scotland, he went on to play for his country."

One of Geoff's early games at Ayresome Park was at home to Huddersfield. In fact the Yorkshire side gave him a lift up to Teesside to play for 'Boro in the game. He said: "We beat Huddersfield 4-1 and I scored two goals. I was lucky to get a lift home to Bradford afterwards. David Steele, the Huddersfield manager, said: 'I've a good mind to make you walk home'."

WILLIE WHIGHAM (1966-71)

WILLIE WHIGHAM was a crucial part of Stan Anderson's defence, providing a solid last line of resistance which gave the rest of the team confidence.

A bargain £10,000 buy from Falkirk, Willie joined the fray shortly after the start of the 1966-67 season and played a crucial part in promotion to the Second Division.

He went on to make 210 appearances in goal for 'Boro and was a virtual ever-present in the first four seasons back in Division Two when 'Boro went so close to reaching the top flight.

Willie was left with a strong love of Teesside, though he admits he found it hard at first.

He said: "When I first arrived I stayed in the Corporation Hotel. When I went outside and looked around, I wondered what I had let myself in for. It didn't look too impressive.

"But I didn't have any problems settling in. The fans in Falkirk gave me a fine send off. Five bus loads came down from Falkirk to see me make my home debut for 'Boro and gave me a lot of support.

Willie Whigham, a crucial signing in the 1966-67 Third Division promotion season, he was a brave and commanding goalkeeper.

"Boro were second bottom when I arrived and that was another reason why I thought I might have made a mistake. But then we started to put together an unbeaten run and we gave ourselves a chance."

Three wins in a row in April put 'Boro right into the reckoning and they went to Brighton for their third last game. Willie said: "The Ayresome Angels were going strong then. Some of them left on the Wednesday to go down to Brighton. They were brilliant. Devoted to the team. I met up with a couple who didn't have a penny between them. I gave them a couple of bob to keep them going.

"We drew at Brighton, but that left us with two home games and nobody was going to beat us at Ayresome Park. We pulled in 32,000 fans against Peterborough and beat them.

"It was all over then. We knew we would beat Oxford in the last match. It was party time. The atmosphere that night was unbelievable. I've never known another night like that.

"There were 40,000 there and they invaded the pitch every time we scored. John O'Rourke knocked the goals in. He was some boy. And we had John Hickton, and Arthur Horsfield. We had three goalscorers and sides struggled to stop them."

Willie well remembers the great atmosphere in the side at the time. He said: "Jones, Horner and McMordie. They were crazy. Particularly McMordie, he never stopped. But they were good players as well. Jones was a great player. He had the best left peg I have seen, and he could drop the ball on a sixpence.

"He could drop the ball right on Hughie Mclmoyle's head. He was the best header of a ball I have ever seen. I can remember the match against Queen's Park Rangers when we were 2-0 down after five minutes.

"Jonesy started knocking them in and McIlmoyle had a field day. They couldn't cope with him. He was unbelievable that day. He could have been a world-class player."

Willie's best memories come from two FA Cup clashes with Manchester United in the early 1970s, both of which went to replays.

In the first meeting, 'Boro drew 1-1 at home in the fifth round on 21 February 1970, but lost the replay by 2-1 at Old Trafford.

He said: "Hickton scored a cracker in the first game, but it ended 1-1, and we went to Old Trafford and it was 1-1 again. Then United got a penalty. Joe Laidlaw came up to me and told me to go to my left. I was going to, but then I went right. Willie Morgan scored. If I had gone left I'm sure I would have saved it, and then anything could have happened. You never forget something like that.

"But we beat them the next year. We drew at Old Trafford and we beat them in the replay at Ayresome. We won 2-1 in front of another full house."

Willie continued to be one of the mainstays of the side, but his reign at 'Boro was to end quite suddenly. It happened after a 4-1 defeat at Sunderland on a Wednesday night in September 1971. Willie was dropped, young Jim Platt came in and did well, and the Northern Irish lad stayed in the side.

Whigham said: "I had a nightmare at Sunderland. It's funny, I had a feeling about the game beforehand. I asked to be left out, but I was picked. I made a couple of great saves early on, but then Sunderland won a corner. Bobby Kerr hit a screamer. I should have saved it, but it jammed between my legs and rolled over the line. After that I went to bits.

"But it happens in football. I still look back at Middlesbrough as the best time of my career. I wouldn't swap it."

BILL WHITAKER (1947-54)

BILL WHITAKER'S defensive play was crucial to 'Boro's stability in the early years after the war, signed from Chesterfield for £9,500, he went on to play 184 games before his career was

Bill Whitaker, pictured with George Hardwick before his 'Boro debut against Manchester United in 1947, was a strong centre-back who made 184 appearances before injury ended his career.

ended by injury. This is how Bill remembers his 'Boro debut at home to Manchester United in August 1947:

"The alarm clock woke me and I dashed downstairs after putting on my Sunday best suit, minus the waistcoat, because England was in the middle of a heat wave.

"As I gobbled my spam sandwich I contemplated the task in front of me. I had to be in Middlesbrough for 2pm and ready to play at 3pm. I had tried to get the mine manager to give me Friday off work, but he considered that letting me off on Saturday was enough. At that time mineworkers had to complete six shifts in the week in accordance with wartime restrictions or they could be sent to gaol.

"I walked to the station at Chesterfield to catch the 7am to Sheffield. The sweat was pouring off me. The sun shone down remorselessly and I was pleased to get in the train and head for York. At York I caught a train to Darlington and then caught the coastal train to the 'Boro. I had a piece of toast in the buffet on the station and proceeded by way of the town hall to Ayresome Park.

"The land next to the town hall looked like the Gobi Desert with a broken down bandstand in the middle.

"I eventually reached Ayresome Park and presented my boots to Charlie Cole, the trainer, and he told me to 'Get under that bloody shower and cool off'.

"Afterwards I presented myself to David Jack, a very understanding manager. As we stripped for action I felt absolutely shattered, but the show had to go on. Both sides ran out and got into position on the iron-hard pitch.

"We kicked off and in Manchester United's first attack there was something different about the way they played. They were the first English club to employ their wingers all of the time.

"What a forward line it was. Jimmy Delaney, Johnny Morris, Jack Rowley, Alf Pearson and Charlie Mitten. These boys were interchanging and our defence didn't know which players to mark.

"They ran us silly in the first half with Rowley grabbing two goals. We picked up a bit in the second half and Mick Fenton scored twice to give us a share of the spoils. But what a football lesson we got.

"I firmly believe that Manchester United side was the best ever and that they shaped the way for English football. Before then, football in this country was stereotyped. Wingers were marked by full-backs, centre-forwards by centre-halves, and it meant that wingers and centre-forwards weren't employed half of the time.

"This method of English football was born at Ayresome Park in August 1947, by Manchester United."

RAY YEOMAN (1958-64)

RAY YEOMAN was a bargain £3,500 buy from Northampton Town but was one the hardest working and committed players of his era. A strong tackling wing-half, Yeoman became a crowd favourite and went on to play more than 200 games for the club.

He said: "I played in some good teams. The player who helped me most at 'Boro was Willie Fernie. I remember my first game at Sheffield Wednesday. Willie said to me: 'If you are ever in any trouble, just give me the ball'. That boosted my confidence right away.

"I thoroughly enjoyed every bit of my time at Ayresome Park. It was the icing on the cake of my football career. I was a first-team regular for most of my time, and played only 30 reserve games in my whole playing career.

Ray Yeoman, an aggressive wing-half and ball winner who made more than 200 consecutive appearances for 'Boro.

'Boro reached the fifth round of the FA Cup in 1930 after wins against Chesterfield and Charlton. They were asked by the FA if they would take up their full quota of 7,500 tickets if they went all the way to the Final. They said they would. It hardly mattered because they went down 2-0 at home to Arsenal three days later.

"I was always very honest in my approach to the game. So what I lacked in skill I made up for in effort. I always had the crowd on my side and that was a big help. The supporters were great to me."

Yeoman's tireless work was a feature of 'Boro's play in the closing years of Bob Dennison's reign, but the writing was on the wall when Raich Carter took over as manager in 1963.

Ray said: "The saddest day of my career was when Raich Carter dropped me for the first time after playing 209 games for the club.

"It was the first game of the 1963-64 season at home to Plymouth Argyle. He told me that he didn't feel I was suited to the conditions. I still managed to play half the season, but I moved on to Darlington at the end of the season."

"The real voice of football does not come from the boardroom or the manager's office. The real voice is that of the fans. It is a noisy, rumbustious, yet knowledgeable voice and anyone who underestimates its power or intent does so at their peril. The real voice knows what it is saying."

So said Peter Thomas, the late *Daily Express* football columnist, relative of former Middlesbrough directors and lifelong supporter of his 'Bonnie 'Boro'.

Supporters' Memories

Considering that Middlesbrough Football Club had to wait 128 years to win a major trophy, the deep-seated level of support the team has enjoyed over the years has been quite astonishing. Apart from the middle 1980's when the club was on the brink of extinction the undying optimism displayed by the followers of the 'Boro borders on the masochistic. Never has a major football club's supporters had to endure so much promise, only to have it extinguished by constant heartbreak.

The supporters contributions in the following chapter vividly highlight how much Middlesbrough Football Club means to the people of the town. It enters into and permeates the very fibre of their lives. Their descriptions of specific matches, favourite individuals and general memories constitute the generations of euphoria and anguish played out at Ayresome Park. They reveal an interesting and often highly personal insight into the psyche of a typical 'Boro supporter but above all, they are written from the heart.

Philip Griffin
Castleton, near Whitby

'Boro robbed by linesman's flag

'Boro's players received a bonus of £165, to be spread among them, for finishing third in the Football League in 1913-14.

"It was 6 March 1947, and the 'Boro were playing Burnley in the sixth round of the FA Cup. The ground was packed with 53,025 people. To get a better view I managed to climb on to a bent tin sheet at the back of the Boys End. All I could see of the pitch was the goal at the Bob End.

"The atmosphere was indescribable and the roars of the crowd were deafening. So bad was the crush at our end of the ground that all through the match I could see spectators being carried out of the stadium. Fans were packed in like sardines and there were still thousands outside when the game kicked-off.

"No sooner was the match under way when the large double gates, which are still at the back of the Bob End, were kicked in and hundreds if not thousands of people poured into the ground without paying.

"On the pitch the 'Boro had taken the lead through Walker and I was clinging on to my tin sheet for grim death. Even though I had a lousy view I was pleased not to be actually standing on the ground. With the 'Boro in the lead the roars of the crowd reached a crescendo and the whole ground seemed to be pulsating with noise. People were still being carried out of the Bob End, some in a very distressed condition.

"In the second half the 'Boro kept up the pressure and were awarded a free-kick near the penalty area. Micky Fenton struck one of his specials and scored. For a few seconds the crowd went wild, only to find that the goal had been disallowed for offside against Johnny Spuhler, who was nowhere near the ball. Almost immediately Burnley equalised and the game ended 1-1.

"The 'Boro had to replay at Turf Moor in midweek. That game, which should never have been played because of an icy pitch, went into extra-time.

Micky Fenton, whose disallowed free-kick 'goal' against Burnley in 1947 caused so much FA Cup controversy.

"The 'Boro were robbed by Harry Potts, who handled the ball into the net."

A.J.Cooper
Redcar

A brave new world

"My outstanding memory of Ayresome Park coincided with my 13th birthday and was the first Division One game to be played there after World War Two against Stoke City. It certainly was a 'Brave New World' with the biggest war in history over and big time football back.

"'Boro had opened the season well with two great away wins at Aston Villa and Liverpool when Stoke City arrived on that glorious late summer's day. There was an early disappointment for the enormous crowd of over 43,000 when it was announced that Stanley Matthews, who was without doubt the single biggest attraction in the game during that era, was not playing. Legend had it that he didn't like playing against 'Boro captain George Hardwick.

"I watched the match from the Bob End and what a nerve-tingling game it was with the 'Boro finally winning 5-4, Micky Fenton scoring four and Wilf Mannion the other. For Stoke, Freddie Steele scored a hat-trick.

"What a start to a new era."

Stan Coates
Guisborough

'Boro 'keeper floors Arsenal centre-half

"I was present at the Arsenal game on 7 December 1946, among a crowd of over 30,000. Following an Arsenal corner at the Holgate End there was a mêlée in the 'Boro goalmouth. I shall never forget watching in amazement as the 'Boro 'keeper Dave Cumming marched out purposefully to the towering 6ft 4in Arsenal centre-half Leslie Compton, who had clearly been kicking him as he lay on the goal line, and flattened him with a world-class right hook.

"The disparity in the respective builds was such that Dave almost had to leap in the air to land the fateful blow on Compton's jaw, but he succeeded wonderfully. Then without waiting for the intervention of the referee he took off his jersey and strolled off the pitch.

Dave Cumming (left) whose punching power against Arsenal's Leslie Compton brought him an early bath in 1946. Cumming is pictured with Micky Fenton as the international duo survey the morning papers before an away match.

"Johnny Spuhler, who had scored one of the 'Boro's goals, took over in goal and managed to keep a clean sheet until the final whistle. The 'Boro won 2-0. Interestingly enough as far as I can recall Dave Cumming was neither reprimanded nor suspended for his incursion into the realm of fisticuffs, apparently because of his hitherto unblemished record on the soccer field."

Janet Thomas
Marske

True love blossoms at the Wilf Mannion-George Hardwick Testimonial Match

"My favourite memory of watching football at Ayresome Park is of the Wilf Mannion – George Hardwick Testimonial match in May 1983. It has a very special significance for both my husband and I as it was the venue of our first date and it ultimately proved to be the night that changed our lives.

"I had never been to a football match before even though, like most of the locals, I had grown up the 'Boro. It was while I was on a night out with a friend that I met a nice young man who, at the end of the evening asked me if I'd like to go with him to the Wilf Mannion-George Hardwick Testimonial Match. He admitted to me soon after that he didn't think I would go, which explained why he looked so dumbstruck when I said yes! The following night we went to the match with his father and brother. I had a terrific time and I even enjoyed the half-time Oxo.

"Seven weeks later my football date and I were married. Through all our ups and downs we always remember Ayresome Park as somewhere very special to us and our four children think it's a 'hoot' that their Mum and Dad's first date was at Middlesbrough Football Club."

Anthony Solan
Marton

Maddren scores a screamer

"One of my most treasured memories of Ayresome Park was when Willie Maddren scored with a 35-yard shot into the top corner of the Holgate End goal against Swindon in March 1971. I think the 'Boro won 3-0 that day.

"I was playing for 'Boro boys at the time and was a ball boy on the right-hand side of the Holgate End goal and as Willie's shot hit the back of the net I jumped six feet in the air. The funny thing was that my celebrations were shown every Sunday lunchtime on the opening credits to the Tyne-Tees TV football programme *Shoot!* There I was week after week on the telly. I would

Thank you for coming! Wilf Mannion and George Hardwick shake the hands of the England team before their joint testimonial match at Ayresome Park in May, 1983.

Willie Maddren, whose long-range goal against Swindon in March 1972, was a bit special.

When 'Boro won promotion back to the First Division in 1929, the directors bought 13, 18ct gold watches at £17 2s 6d, plus extra for the inscription and monogram, for the players.

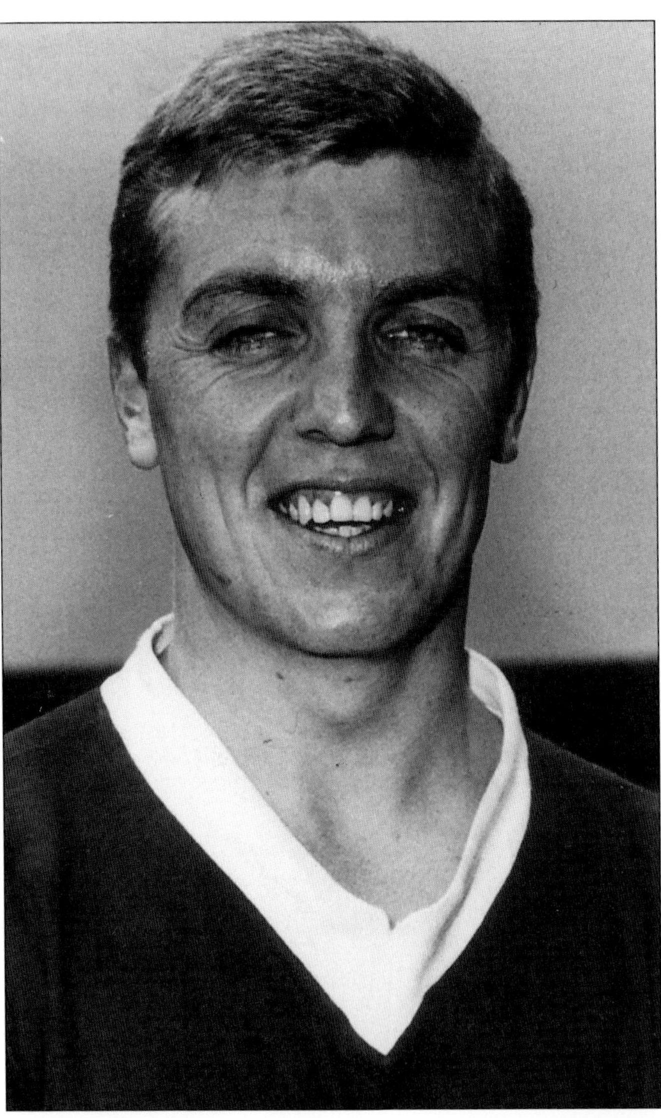

Bryan 'Taffy' Orritt, who was a popular 'Boro player in the 1960s and could play anywhere.

be overjoyed to obtain a video of my antics to show my own kids, who are 'Boro daft."

F.McIlheron
Acklam

Memories of Bryan 'Taffy' Orritt

"Although only a school kid in the early 1960's my mind goes back to remember one 'Boro player in particular, Bryan 'Taffy' Orritt. Bought for a nominal fee from Birmingham City, he was a fiercely patriotic Welshman who soon won over the Teesside fans with his never-say-die attitude and the smile on his face. He was also Mr Versatile, playing in many different positions for the 'Boro.

"There are two matches that stick in my mind concerning Taffy. Firstly we were playing Charlton Athletic and trailing 2-0 when our goalkeeper Bob Appleby was injured and couldn't continue. To a tremendous backing from the crowd, up stepped an undaunted Taffy to take over the goalkeeping jersey. The 'Boro staged a great fight-back to draw 2-2 and Taffy was able to claim a clean sheet.

"The second game I recall was against high flying Sunderland which I watched from the back fence of the Holgate End. Taffy had been chosen to play centre-forward and found himself up against the highly-rated Sunderland centre-half and idol Charlie Hurley, but that didn't seem to worry him as he scored both the 'Boro's goals in a 2-0 victory. The first one was the result of beating the Sunderland offside trap, running half the length of the pitch and coolly firing the ball home. The second was a spectacular diving header.

"Taffy married a local girl and when he moved from 'Boro he went to play football in South Africa."

Barry McQuade
Middlesbrough

The day I missed eight goals at Ayresome

"A memory that will always stay with me is of the match played at Ayresome

Hugh McIlmoyle, who could destroy teams when he was on top form, scored twice in 'Boro's fine recovery against Queen's Park Rangers in 1970.

Park on 26 September 1970, between the 'Boro and Queen's Park Rangers.

"I was getting married on the

It's a TV spectacular from Tony Mowbray, as he heads home a golden goal against Aston Villa in 'Boro's first ever live appearance on television. Mowbray remains one of the 'Boro fans' all-time favourites.

In October 1930, the 'Boro directors gave manager Peter McWilliam permission to buy a gramophone for up to £5 and one dozen records to entertain the players on away trips.

following Monday at the Registry Office and still had a lot of arrangements to make. In a panic I arrived at the game late, only to be told that Queen's Park Rangers had taken a two-goal lead in the first five minutes. Disaster! I suddenly remembered I had forgotten to order the flowers for the wedding, so I had to leave the ground immediately in a hurry.

"A blessing in disguise I thought, two down. I didn't really want to watch my heroes slaughtered.

"Imagine my shock and delight when I found out the final score was 6-2 to the 'Boro. Looking back however, I'd paid my entrance fee to the Holgate, left after a few minutes and never seen any of the goals. To make matters worse my idol, big John Hickton, scored a hat-trick along with McIlmoyle two and Downing one.

"I must be the unluckiest 'Boro fan ever!"

Paul Mundy
Redcar

Memories of Tony Mowbray

"My favourite 'Boro player of all time would have to be Tony Mowbray. He was a real 'Man of Iron', Middlesbrough through and through and in my opinion one of the best players to pull on a red shirt since the war.

"Tony, or Mogga as he affectionately became known, not only commanded his defence and the team, but in the post-liquidation era he became the heart and soul of the club helping to pick it up when it was most needed.

"One of the incidents I will always remember was during the live TV match against Aston Villa in February 1988, when he strode out of the defence to send an unstoppable diving header into the back of the net to win the game for the 'Boro.

"Another game that sticks in the memory was the way Mogga led his team brilliantly in the hostile atmosphere of the Play-off Final at Stamford Bridge against Chelsea. This was a backs-to-the-wall rearguard action for nearly the full game and his attitude and determination on that day will live with me forever.

"My greatest disappointment was when the 'Boro finally got to Wembley and Mogga was injured and couldn't play. Even though he led the team out it wasn't enough to lift the lads to win the Zenith Cup.

"In conclusion I for one have to agree with former 'Boro manager Bruce Rioch that if I was going to fly to the moon I would want Tony Mowbray alongside me."

S.Smith
Linthorpe

Goodbye 'Mogga'

"Tony Mowbray's testimonial game against Celtic must rank as one of the most poignant matches played at Ayresome Park.

"Mr Middlesbrough had led us through our darkest days on to the magical double promotion and he deserved every last one of those resounding cheers afforded him that afternoon.

"Celtic and their travelling hordes gave it everything and even the weather was glorious. There was hardly a dry eye in the house as Tony bade farewell to his adoring Teesside public. Never have so many owed so much to one man and we let him know it.

"This was a testimonial in the truest sense of the word."

Tony Russell
Linthorpe

Give us a goal John O'Rourke, John O'Rourke

"I was only 13½ when my hero worship began. It was 1966, the year of England's World Cup victory and my devotion to The Beatles began to be challenged by the arrival at Ayresome Park of my all-time hero. He only stayed 18 months but in that time he made 71 appearances and scored 41 goals and his name was John O'Rourke.

"Photographs from the *Gazette* plastered my bedroom wall alongside those of the 'Fab Four' but the big difference between O'Rourke and John, Paul, George and Ringo was that I could visit Ayresome Park every other week and see John O'Rourke in the flesh. I can still remember the sheer joy of waiting in Warwick Street to get his autograph.

The man who gave the fans the goals. John O'Rourke attained cult status during his 18 months at Ayresome Park.

"In fact I wanted to be John O'Rourke. Not only did he score goals with great panache (I remember that his heading action was very similar to that of Denis Law – hanging in the air and jack-knifing to flick maximum power on to the header) but he was handsome enough to have been a male model.

"He had his own song from the Holgate End to the tune of The Troggs *Give it to me* – 'Give us a go-o-al, give us a go-o-al John O'Rourke, John O'Rourke.'

My enduring memory of that time has to be Davy Chadwick jinking down the right wing towards the Holgate End beating the full-back and delivering a superb cross for O'Rourke to bullet a header into the back of the net. I wonder how many goals were scored in that way?

"Many players have achieved a lot more for the 'Boro but then hero worship is not as simple as that, is it? Perhaps it was the fact that he didn't stay long at Ayresome Park that has kept him as my personal hero but I don't think so. I think it's because your first hero is always the biggest. I cried the day John O'Rourke was transferred to Ipswich Town."

Tony Coleman
Ormesby

North-East derby decides relegation and promotion

"I've been following the 'Boro since my dad first took me in 1968 and my lasting Ayresome Park memory is of a warm spring May afternoon in 1990 when the opposition was Newcastle United. Both teams needed to win for different reasons, the Geordies for promotion to the old First Division and the 'Boro to avoid relegation to the third. It was an amazing match, with so much at stake for the final Saturday of the season and arguably it was one of the most dramatic Tyne-Tees derbies ever played.

"I'll never forget the tension going to Ayresome Park that day, it was a mixture of passion and fear. Nobody dared imagine the unthinkable, being relegated again. Yet we wondered how the 'Boro could beat the high-flying Magpies with their strikeforce of Micky Quinn and Mark McGhee, who had scored over 50 goals between them that season.

"Despite superb backing and a wall of noise from the 'Boro faithful, the first half drew a blank, with Newcastle having the edge. It was obvious that both sides didn't want to make a fateful mistake.

"Then mid-way through the second half Ayresome Park exploded when Bernie Slaven gave 'Boro the lead with a shot that trickled in off a post. It didn't matter how it went in, we were in front. Soon after, an error in the Magpies defence handed Ian Baird our second and the noise in the ground was unbelievable. The 'Boro were on a roll.

"Despite an own-goal by Owen McGee that gave us all the jitters, Ian Baird scored one of the greatest goals I've seen at Ayresome Park when he hit the ball on the run with such power that it nearly broke the net.

"Near the end, to everyone's sheer delight, Bernie added a fourth and as the final whistle blew, amongst the cheers and the singing was the news that Leeds had beaten Bournemouth – our nearest rivals – so we were safe.

"The emotion and passion of that day will live in my memory forever. It's always great to beat Newcastle but to crush them 4-1 in such circumstances was beyond my wildest dreams."

Adrian Bevington
Acklam

The goal that never was!

"As a true 'Boro fan the 1984-85 season provided me with a real treat when I spent the whole campaign as a ball boy. What more could a 13-year-old lad ask for, free entry into your own theatre of dreams, permission to actually run out of the tunnel on to the centre circle, acknowledge the crowd and then sit on the touch-line once play had commenced.

"Despite a season of poor performances, my outstanding memory occurred during a rare victory against Brighton.

"It was a hot spring afternoon when mid-way through the first half Heine Otto picked up the ball in the centre circle, he progressed a few yards and unleashed a very hopeful shot. As the ball carried towards the Holgate End – where I was seated next to the goal – the

Ian Baird, pictured in action against Oxford United. Baird's goals against Newcastle United in 1990 ensured 'Boro's survival in the Second Division.

Heine Otto, whose goal against Brighton in 1985 caused a furore, is pictured third from the left on the back row of this 1984-85 'Boro line-up. Back row (left to right): David Mills, David Currie, Heine Otto, Tony Mowbray, Kelham O'Hanlon, Paul Ward, Gary Gill, Geoff Scott, Darren Wood. Front row: Paul Sugrue, Stephen Bell, Gary Hamilton, Steve Smelt (physiotherapist), Willie Maddren (manager), Irving Nattrass, Mick Buckley, Alan Roberts.

Brighton goalkeeper Graham Moseley decided against coming to claim the ball and stepped backwards to catch it. As he did so my instant reaction was to jump in the air and wave my arms vigorously in celebration of a goal.

"Moseley, I believed, had stepped over the line with the ball in his hands. On my reaction the linesman immediately began flagging furiously to attract the referee's attention. After an animated consultation a goal was awarded causing mayhem to break out.

"Brighton manager Chris Cattlin stormed out of his dug-out to join his players in protest against the decision while Moseley raced towards the mêlée to voice his opinion.

"Cattlin was duly banished to the North Stand (a story which was well documented in the following day's tabloids) and Moseley, who was cautioned for his protestations, turned angrily and charged towards the goal – or so I thought! He made straight for me and yelled 'Well was it in then?'

"To which I, quaking in my boots, whispered sheepishly 'Probably'.

"For the rest of the game I made a conscious effort to avoid eye contact with Mr Moseley while turning to a group of friends in the crowd I tried to keep a smile off my face, convinced I had helped the 'Boro on to victory."

Anne Rowntree
Hartburn

The *Evening Gazette* made my day

"My favourite memory was when the *Evening Gazette* had a competition to name the Man of the Match for each home game. One particular Saturday having voted for John Hendrie I sent my competition entry off and thought no more about it.

"I was at work a few days later when I received a phone call from the *Evening Gazette* informing me that I had won the competition which was to meet John Hendrie on the pitch before the next home game.

"When the great day arrived I was shaking like a leaf, I was so excited. At Ayresome Park I was met by an officer of the club and taken to the executive suite. I felt like a queen. I was wined and dined and made to feel very important indeed.

The 'Boro board wrote to the United Bus Company in September 1932, to complain that Grangetown and South Bank supporters could not get buses to matches because they were already full on their arrival from Redcar.

John Hendrie, whose skill and commitment has made him one of the 'Boro heroes of the 1990s.

"At about half-past two I was taken on to the pitch in front of a packed crowd to have my photograph taken with John Hendrie. I don't remember much about the match as I was still on cloud nine.

"After the match we went back to the executive suite for more food and drinks and I met some of the players. Everybody was so kind, they really went out of their way to make me feel so important.

"It is a day that I will cherish forever."

F.N.Mallon
Thornaby

George Camsell and the penalties

"Towards the end of World War Two, Billy Birrell, that much-respected Middlesbrough forward of the 1920s and then manager of Chelsea, gave a talk and held a quiz on football at the aerodrome where I was stationed.

"Speaking to Billy afterwards I told him that as a schoolboy my pals and I ran from Middlesbrough High School on the Wednesday afternoon of a match – no floodlights in those days – to get in as the gates were being opened to let the crowd out. We hoped that in the last few minutes we would see our hero George Camsell score a goal.

"When Mr Birrell heard that our idol had been George Camsell he recalled a story concerning that famous season in 1926-27 when the 'Boro won the Division Two championship and Camsell broke the individual goalscoring record with 59 goals.

"Apparently during that season Camsell had been taking all the penalties but one afternoon he failed to score with one attempt and had his leg pulled so much in the dressing-room afterwards, that he didn't take another penalty that season (of which there were at least three) and finished with a record total of 59 goals. The following season 'Dixie' Dean of Everton beat Camsell's record when he scored 60.

"It makes you wonder that if Billy Birrell's story is true and I have no reason to doubt it, and Camsell had not vacated the roll of club penalty taker, whether he would still be the all-time leading goalscorer and not just the Division Two top marksman."

The great Billy Birrell, who was as an important part of 'Boro's free-scoring forward line of the 1920s.

In 1932, 'Boro turned down a request from a Mr Voss of Liverpool to rent Ayresome Park for greyhound racing.

Neil Wheldon
Coulby Newham

We all agree, Horsfield is better than Pelé

"My first visit to Ayresome Park was in the early 1960s. I stood in the top corner of the ground next to the North Stand known as the Boys End. Large notices were painted on the walls warning boys not to climb out of the enclosure. The notice had little effect because by half-time it was deserted, the lads dispersing to better vantage points all over the ground.

"I once got the autograph of the world's greatest footballer Arthur Horsfield, regarded by many 'Boro fans to be better than Pelé. The second greatest player was Eric McMordie, who was better than Eusébio, and 'keeper Willie Whigham, who was better than Yashin. 'We all agree Horsfield is better than Pelé' was sung to the tune of *You Me and Us* by Alma Cogan.

"Horsfield was also the greatest player to travel on the N bus from the Town Centre to Park End along with Pat Cuff, a former 'Boro goalkeeper, Steve Gibson present 'Boro chairman and Paul Rodgers writer of the Free song *All Right Now*.

"Some memorable moments have been the many promotions accompanied by the club records that have sold in their thousands all over the world! Who could forget lyrics like 'Middlesbrough Football Club they are a good club, they are a great club,' with Alan Foggon on lead vocals and 'Oh the 'Boro's going up, the 'Boro's going up to stay-ay' and 'We are men of iron,' with Bernie Slaven and Tony Mowbray on harmonies.

"I can also recall vividly the night the floodlights failed against Leicester City when thousands of Woodbines lit up the dark sky. The loudspeaker crackling into life and Bernard Gent asking for any electricians to report to the players' tunnel.

"Then there was our first £100,000

Billy Ashcroft, he of the golden boot and golden locks to match.

signing, the legendary Billy Ashcroft, the first player to be televised sporting a ginger perm, and the collective sigh of relief when Bobby Murdoch's £1 million bid for Justin Fashanu was turned down.

"Finally the visit to Wembley and the sight of the 'Boro's name on the scoreboard. I could not believe it, here I was in the ground where some of London's best greyhounds had once raced and seeing a Newbould's pie advert on the hoardings around the hallowed turf!"

Willie Armstrong
Billingham

Memories from the mists of time

"My first visit to Ayresome Park was when as a young boy I watched the great George Elliott play when the 'Boro beat Sunderland 2-0 on 18 April 1923. This was a marvellous era of 'Boro football with Jackie Carr a star player.

"The attitude of the crowds was vastly different to that of today. There was no segregation and rival supporters mingled freely with the 'Boro fans. Police attendance at matches was limited to four and perhaps one at the entrance. There was no chanting or abuse hurled at the referee and linesmen except of the odd shout of 'Go to Silbeck's!' (the local optician). There was much banter but no obscenity.

"Strident canned music was unheard of in those days. The entertainment was often provided by the local works brass band who used to play an old ragtime number called *Old Charlie take it away*. The tune became very popular with fans, many believing that the 'Boro never lost when it was played.

"'Boro were lifted out of the doldrums in the mid-1920s by the emergence of George Camsell, who was from the Durham mining district. His arrival started years of success for the 'Boro, with the feared and famous forward line of Pease, Birrell, Camsell, Carr and Williams. Camsell broke all club scoring records (which still stand to this day) and was a great crowd favourite.

"The bleak depression years did not deter the often hard up 'Boro supporters. Prior to the opening of the Newport Bridge, many fervent Stockton fans would walk the long, dreary stretch of road named 'The Wilderness' between Thornaby and Middlesbrough. Bad weather did not deter them as they faced the long trek home after the match.

Wily winger Owen Williams was a quick raider who supplied much of the ammunition for 'Boro's prolific scoring machine, George Camsell.

"Some North Bank supporters would go via the transporter. Many had a spartan budget consisting of a penny each way across the bridge, a shilling into the match and eight pence for a pint in the Shakespeare after it. If you didn't buy a key card (early type of programme) for two pence, then you could have a delicious gravy drowned Newbould's pie. Total for the day out two shillings (10p).

"Wilf Mannion was easily the most talented and admired player the 'Boro ever had. A local South Bank lad, he signed for the 'Boro in his teens. He was very unlucky to have his career halted by war service from 1939-45 and was reputed to have been with the famous Yorkshire cricketer Hedley Verity when he was killed in action in Italy.

"Probably the best 'Boro side ever was just prior to the outbreak of World War Two in 1938-39 when they were challenging for the First Division title. The team was a mixture of youth and experience, studded with internationals such as Cumming, Fenton, Yorston, Forrest, Milne, Baxter and Mannion.

"For much of the time I was a 'Boro fan, 'Old Bird' was the sportswriter on the local paper and some of his match reports were very odd. One in particular stands out when the 'Boro beat Sheffield United 10-3 in 1933. He wrote: 'Camsell scored four goals but did little else.'

"Faraway happy memories indeed."

Don O'Neil
Linthorpe

The Mannion Match

"All football fans have their special period of reminiscence. For me, the best time was the four or five years after World War Two and in particular Middlesbrough's home match against Blackpool in November 1947, known to all who witnessed it, as 'Mannion's Match'.

"Wilf Mannion was the best inside-forward of his era, a player who generalled the play. He had a highly developed capacity for controlling a game, for tidying up scrappy play, for slowing the game down or speeding it up as necessary and for always being in the right place to link defence and attack. His gifts with the ball were prodigious. He would demoralise defenders with his dummies, feints, dribbles and the excellence of his passing.

"And so to the match of matches. There were nearly 39,000 of us at Ayresome Park on that fine autumn afternoon. The Bob End gossip was that Wilf had got engaged that week and that his fiancée was in the stand. Whatever it was, you could feel a special buzz in the air.

"In the first half Wilf was at his classical best. There were no frills, he played like the brilliant international he was, fast and direct, and by occasionally using his little sway he began to unnerve the Blackpool defence.

"His passing was remarkable, perfectly weighted whatever the distance, sometimes finding extraordinary angles to baffle the opposition and always finding his man. He scuttled about the pitch, blond mop bobbing up and down, perfectly

The Golden Boy himself. Wilf Mannion was a great crowd pleaser, and produced the performance of his illustrious career at home to Blackpool in 1947.

balanced as always, palms down and fingers pointing. Wilf was deceptively athletic, he seemed to lope rather than sprint, but he was fast and I can never remember him being outrun.

"He was always in the game, never seeming to tire or to need a breather. Nobody in the Blackpool defence could get anywhere near him. At half-time it was 2-0 and the game was to all intents and purposes won.

"The rest of the 'Boro team had risen to the occasion but we had no idea of what was to come in the second half. Wilf turned the game into his own scintillating showpiece. He opened up his box of tricks for all of us to see. You would swear the ball was bewitched. He

Second Division here we come! 'Boro celebrate promotion after beating Oxford United 4-1 in 1967. Back row (left to right): Don Masson, John Hickton, Gordon Jones, David Chadwick, Geoff Butler. Front row: Derrick Downing, hat-trick hero John O'Rourke and Eric McMordie.

did things with that ball I've never seen done before or since.

"The Blackpool defence was mesmerised, he dribbled round them, through them and if his passing in the first half was textbook, it was now sheer magic. Passes like rifle shots were mixed with gorgeous lobs and chips. Sometimes he worked his hypnosis without touching the ball.

"I can see him now man to man with Harry Johnston, the Blackpool half-back, swaying behind the ball. Then with a drop of the left shoulder Johnston appears to voluntarily throw himself on his back as Wilf glided past him with the ball. Poor Johnston, he got up wearily and looked high up into the stand for his manager and threw up his arms in total bewilderment.

"The atmosphere in the second half was electric. The crowd roars were like a bullfight sounds when the matador is tormenting the bull. We had witnessed a display of football genius by our favourite, Wilf Mannion of South Bank. It was a once in a lifetime show.

"The final score was 4-0 with McCormack 2, Fenton and Spuhler scoring the goals and to this day you can bet your season ticket that when a few of us golden oldie 'Boro fans get together, after a couple of pints someone will say 'Do you remember the Blackpool match…?' Will we ever forget!"

Andy Smith
London

Tick, Tick, Tick Mansfield Town 4… Pause… Middlesbrough 5! Tick, Tick

"We went through the open gates and we climbed the steps. The floodlights illuminated the vast green pitch with various figures moving through a haze. We stood on the terrace and tried to take it in. This was Ayresome Park. It was 10 December 1966. I was nearly eight years old and my brother, ten years older and already worldly wise in 'Boro supporting, had taken us along for the last 20 minutes when the gates opened.

"It was some months later before I experienced the joys of a full match. The Power Game theme, the hot but weak Bovril and the dulcet tones of Bernard Gent mispronouncing the names of the players over the Tannoy, 'and your substitute is Alan Murraaaaay.' Then there was the shock of grown men using the same swear words we used in playground, the Holgate songs and the heroes on the pitch.

"The 1966-67 season saw the 'Boro in the Third Division for the first time. They made a poor start, beaten at places like Scunthorpe, Watford and Gillingham. The turning point came one Saturday afternoon when Frank Bough read out the football results on Grandstand from the stuttering, clattering teleprinter.

" 'Division Three, Mansfield Town 4…' he said as the teleprinter then seemed to nod off to sleep for a while. Oh dear here we go again, I thought during the pause. Then the teleprinter woke up, 'Middlesbrough 5!'

"They were on their way and I was bitten by the bug that affects thousands of kids of every generation. A life of following one of the great mediocre clubs of English football.

"The season was to end in promotion on a wondrous night when 39,683 people packed into Ayresome Park. We sat in the seats opposite the Holgate End. There were so many glory-hungry fans in those far-off days before all-ticket matches, that they had to let people sit on the cinder track. Oxford, with Ron Atkinson as their skipper, never knew what hit them and 'Boro won 4-1.

"After the pitch invasion, the players threw their kit to the crowd and my brother Pete buried a red and white painted frying pan in the centre circle. Rumours abounded at school days later that a relation of Eddie Smith's had sat on a bus next to someone whose next door neighbour had a piece of Derrick Downing's shirt collar.

"The *Evening Gazette* now entered my life for the first time, teaching me how to read newspapers properly – from the back page. Cliff Mitchell became my

Stanley Anderson's Red and White Army! The marvellous Ayresome Angels are in full voice in the Holgate End in 1967.

favourite uncle as he wrote to me every evening and I started to cut out the grey pictures of my new heroes.

"The 'Ayresome Angels' were created, an unofficial supporters' club which held sojourns to the far corners of Division Three with thousands in tow, many bedecked in red and white painted warehouse coats, safety helmets and ...frying pans. The good people of Workington, Mansfield and Doncaster had never seen anything like it and in that period before away days became aggro days, the Angels became my adopted cousins.

Season tickets were issued for the first time for the West End of the ground in 1933, price 26s.

"At this time someone somewhere changed the latest 1960s pop songs into homages to our heroes. I really thought the Beatles sang *All you need is Lugg* and Manfred Mann's *Mighty Quinn* became *Mighty Jim* after big Jim Irvine. I have never since been able to listen to the Who's *Happy Jack* without singing the 'real' lyrics. 'John O'Rourke's not so tall but he gets the goals dum dum dum dum, and that's why the net is so full of holes, dum dum dum dum.'

"John O'Rourke was our hero. He was young, good looking and possibly the first folk hero at Ayresome Park since Wilf Mannion or Gorgeous George Hardwick. Our Uncle Tom always called him 'O'Rook'.

"Uncle Tom lived close to Ayresome Park just off Parliament Road. Many an evening was to be spent with him sipping Auntie Joyce's tea as we analysed the latest disappointment. 'Crossan? Crossan? I wouldn't pay him in washers!' was a common declaration.

"Another voice of reason, Uncle Stan, was not a relative but a friend of the family. He was another 'Boro fan of the 'washers' variety but both Tom and Stan were there week in week out, shifts permitting. I never really understood their criticism. I was only nine. I did not know that Uncle Tom was right. 'Boro never won anything. They always promised a lot and delivered nothing. Even promotion from Division Three was all another faint glimmer of hope soon to be dashed, as John O'Rourke was sold to Ipswich Town.

"*The Power Game* was probably the first piece of music that made my hair stand on end. If I ever get on Desert Island Discs I can hear Sue Lawley say 'that was *School's Out* by Alice Cooper. Now your next choice is a rather odd one...' but thousands of other people will know.

"For several years 'Boro were there or thereabouts at the top of the Second Division without having the necessary killer touch to get promotion. For this young fan time began to run out. The humdrum Second Division opposition and the realisation that getting autographs of the same players over and over again was not over exciting, cooled the hero worship.

"Whinney Banks fifth formers invariably supported the big clubs and this young first year copied the big lads. Jacko had a brilliantly painted haversack with the Arsenal badge on it and I became an Arsenal fan. Other treacherous first years chose Leeds, Liverpool, Chelsea or even Newcastle!

"Slade and T-Rex made way for Emerson Lake and Palmer, then Pink Floyd and Frank Zappa and the Mothers of Invention. Girls became interesting all of a sudden. John Peel seemed like he would always be ahead of John Hickton as the most important person in the world.

"Then in 1973, Jack Charlton walked into Ayresome Park. We went back to the Holgate End in droves. The Leeds fans at school became a sad minority. The 'Boro were unfashionable to football in general but we didn't care – they were winning every week!

With our satin scarves tied around our wrists we learned the songs the Ayresome Angels had started but with a heavy dose of menace and obscenity added that was common to football in the mid-seventies.

"Our stars were as rugged and ruthless as their names suggested: Platt, Craggs, Boam, Maddren, Murdoch, Mills, Foggon, Hickton and Armstrong. The young Graeme Souness became our hero, graceful, tough in the tackle, with a scorching shot.

"As 'Boro climbed the table, won the Second Division easily and at one stage in 1975 were perched on top of the First Division, I remember standing at the end of a game in the middle of the Holgate and marvelling. Promotion at last! International recognition for 'Boro players! At the back of my mind it seemed vaguely familiar 'Promise a lot deliver nothing' but I didn't care, here was my home of dreams."

Christopher Bartley
Normanby

My first match

"In 1972 I was eight years old and a pupil at South Eston Primary School. The girls at the school were in love with David Cassidy who was number one at the time with a forgettable piece of drivel called *How can I be sure?*, and the boys were in love with Leeds United, the crudely unimaginative FA Cup holders. On 3 October, however, I found an object of desire that still holds me transfixed over 30 years later – Middlesbrough Football club.

"This was the momentous day that my father took me to Ayresome Park for the first time. I remember being very excited all day and as none of my friends were going, it made the event seem even more important.

"The match was against the glamorous North Londoners Tottenham Hotspur in the third round of the League Cup. I knew they had stars like Martin Chivers, Pat Jennings, and Alan Gilzean but I was undaunted because we had Nobby Stiles, the toothless Mancunian legend from the 1966 World Cup winning team.

"I can still remember the night with an extraordinary degree of clarity. The pulse-quickening wait for the bus at Normanby. The nervous anticipation of the journey and the thrill of seeing the retina-blasting radiance of the floodlights in Linthorpe Village.

"After getting off the bus, my little legs walked as fast as they possibly could to the ground, only stopping once

Half a million pounds worth of magic – that's 'Boro striker David Mills, who was sold on to West Bromwich Albion.

to purchase a programme with a picture of David Mills on the front for sixpence. A programme which not surprisingly I still own.

"Upon entering Ayresome Park, I was simply awestruck. There was a crowd of over 23,000 and as we didn't get colour television until 1974, I couldn't believe the greenness of the grass, bathed in the glow of those almighty floodlights.

"The match itself lived up to all my expectations. John Hickton scored the first of many goals that I would see him score and Nobby Stiles ran and tackled just as I knew he would. Although the game ended 1-1 there was no doubt that I left Ayresome Park on that cold autumn evening the happiest eight-year-old in the county. I had just been to my first 'real' football match."

Come on you Reds! Han Bong-jin sparks a North Korean attack against Russia in the World Cup game at Ayresome Park in 1966.

Ian Johnson
Middlesbrough

The Korean Experience

"My favourite memory of Ayresome Park goes back to the World Cup of 1966. The initial choice of the teams, Chile, Russia, Italy and North Korea, was scorned by many of the fans and some of the old soldiers who had been in the Korean War refused to go to the matches. But for those who did attend they were rewarded with a real treat.

"The admission prices which were increased by 250 per cent seemed extremely high, compared to a normal League game, and I remember my dad saying 'I never thought I'd see the day when you had to pay 7s 6d to stand at a football match!'

"Against Russia, North Korea were given a football lesson and were totally outclassed by a team which, much to the disappointment of the 'Boro fans, did not include the legendary goalkeeper Lev Yashin, who was apparently injured.

"The next Korean match against Chile saw an entirely different game when centre-forward Pak Seung-zin gained a well-deserved draw with an equaliser ten minutes from time, much to the delight of the crowd. The Ayresome Park fans had now well and truly taken the North Koreans to their hearts.

"In their third match against the well-respected and experienced Italians, the Koreans fought for every ball in an attempt to unsettle their opponents. Playing in red and white, it was like watching the 'Boro, and when Pak Do Ik scored for Korea, pandemonium broke out in the Holgate End with everybody singing 'K-O-R-E-A.!' It was a night I will never forget. The Italians seemed shell-shocked and tried everything to equalise but the little Korean goalkeeper Li Chan-myung played his heart out and he and his teammates were given a well-deserved standing ovation by the Ayresome Park crowd.

"It was the first time I had seen summer football and I feel rather sorry for those people who stayed away because they missed one of the most memorable nights in world football history."

Malcolm Danby
Fairfield

My 'golden' moments

"My memories of Ayresome Park begin on Saturday 30 September 1950, when I was taken to see my first match by my grandad, who just happened to live opposite the South Stand. The opponents were Huddersfield Town and the match was to leave an indelible impression on my young mind as the 'Boro won 8-0.

"Sitting high up in the South Stand on the old wooden seats I was introduced to the skills of Mannion, the cultured play of Hardwick and an overall display of dazzling football which decimated the opposition. As my second game was a 7-3 victory over Charlton, 1950 was a momentous year in terms of football for me – I was a 'Boro addict from then on.

"The first match I went to on my own was against Stoke City on Good Friday 1951, and I had the misfortune to witness 'Boro's young full-back George Hepple break his leg. In those days it was perfectly safe to go on your own as a ten-year-old into a near 40,000 crowd and on that occasion 'Boro won 1-0 despite having only ten men for part of the game.

"It was during that season that I decided to post my autograph book to Wilf Mannion so that he would obtain the 'Boro team's autographs for me. The book was returned duly signed, but there was one signature missing – that of George Hardwick. The book has been preserved and I took the opportunity in 1994 when I met George at the ground, to ask for the missing signature. He was happy to oblige and so 42 years later I was in possession of the 'full set'. I also had the opportunity of meeting the 'Golden Boy' himself and he was amazed to see those original signatures still intact.

"The opening game of the 1951-52 season was against Spurs and it was so crowded (44,000) that my grandad and I were allowed to sit on the South Stand stairs, a situation unthinkable in these safety conscious days. Under brilliant sunshine the 'Boro won 2-1 although new signing Neil Mochan was carried off injured.

"It was during this season that I experienced the unpredictability that the 'Boro have so often been 'tagged' with. An early exit from the FA Cup at the hands of Second Division Doncaster Rovers, 4-1 at Ayresome Park, shattered my illusions for a while and I was glad that I had chosen not to miss school to see the midweek afternoon game – pre-floodlit days.

"My first experience of continental football was in May 1951, when Partizan Belgrade played a friendly match in celebration of the Festival of Britain. They won 3-2 and I can remember being amazed at the slick passing and general ball skills of that team from Yugoslavia.

"The Clough era was to provide me with many memorable moments. By that time I was a regular in the south-east corner. 'Cloughie' became a cult figure with the fans and it wasn't so much 'Are you going to see the 'Boro' as 'Are you going to see Cloughie score'.

"I remember a goal against Fulham when he was forced wide out to the left and Ian Black, Fulham's Scottish international 'keeper, moved too far out of his goal. Brian coolly curled the ball round him and into the middle of the goal. Another hapless 'keeper was Dave Hollins of Brighton, who saw Cloughie score five times in his side's 9-0 thrashing on the opening day of the season in 1958.

"When Brian was in his hey-day, floodlights were installed at Ayresome Park. Many supporters will remember the infamous penalty incident in the inaugural game against Sunderland in October 1957 when Lindy Delapenha, the 'Boro's penalty king, hit a rocket shot into the bottom left-hand corner of the net at the East End. To some people, the referee included, the ball missed.

"Stan Anderson quickly collected the ball from behind the goal for a goal-kick, much to the annoyance of Delapenha and the East End crowd, who thought a goal had been scored. It had! But the ball had gone through a hole in the net and the quick-thinking Anderson had denied 'Boro a goal. We still won 2-0, however, so it was the right result in the end.

"The structural alterations to the stadium in preparation for the 1966 World Cup matches signified a departure from the old order but can anybody who witnessed it forget the total delight of Pak Do Ik of North Korea when his goal defeated the mighty Italians to put Korea into the World Cup quarter-finals.

"The 1966-67 promotion campaign from Division Three, culminating in the well-documented finale against Oxford on 16 May 1967, kept everybody on edge wondering whether the 'Boro could make it back to the Second Division at the first attempt.

"Standing in my favourite spot in the south-east corner, I watched the crowd building up. The ground limit was around 40,000 but Ayresome Park could have been filled by half as much again, as everybody and his dog came out of the woodwork that night.

"During the second half some brave supporters actually made it on to the roof of the Holgate End and such was the pressure on the safety wall near to the players tunnel that a small section collapsed. Fortunately there were no serious injuries.

"The 1973-74 season with its newly-established records, brought about by an excellent blend of good players and effective tactics so skilfully orchestrated by supremo Jack Charlton, was in my opinion simply the best. The icing on the cake was the 8-0 home victory over Sheffield Wednesday in the last home match of the season.

Great Scot... Bobby Murdoch was an inspired midfield signing by Jack Charlton in 1973. His precise passing helped 'Boro walk away with the Second Division championship.

"Who can forget 'roly-poly' Bobby Murdoch spraying passes to the front men. Surely one of 'Boro's best buys – on a free transfer!

"Since the early 1970s as my contact with the club has grown I became acquainted with many of the personnel and a lasting memory is that of Bruce Rioch taking me on a guided tour of the re-furbished North Stand, the development of which he was immensely proud.

"In my capacity as the secretary of the Cleveland Schools' FA, I became the liaison officer between the club and the schools and had the opportunity of overseeing the organisation of several important school games at the highest level. The 'jewel in the crown' was the Under-19 England v Austria game played at Ayresome Park in April 1992, when nothing was too much trouble for the club.

The personal satisfaction that I felt when the match was over and the function concluded will last long in my memory.

"Forty-five years association with Ayresome Park is a long time by any standards and the final whistle was a sad occasion. But a part of me will always remain there."

It's another one for Brian as Cloughie produces a spectacular diving header against Ipswich on his way to 200-plus 'Boro goals.

'Boro made an audacious inquiry about Stoke City winger Stanley Matthews in 1933. They were told he was not for sale.

Norman Pinkham
Guisborough

'Boro hit nine on opening day of the season

"The date was 28 August 1958, and I was standing in the old Bob End with my late father, eagerly awaiting the start of a new 'Boro season at Ayresome Park. Brighton, who had just gained promotion from Division Three, were the opposition. It was also Brian Clough's first game as 'Boro captain and the pre-match Press speculation surrounded whether the responsibility of the captaincy would adversely affect his goalscoring flair.

"They needn't have worried because on that marvellous day, the 'Boro seemed to score every time they moved forward and my dad and I were soon hoarse from cheering goal after goal.

"By the time the score got to 9-0, recounts were beginning to take place in the crowd and despite the feast of goals there was much annoyance among the supporters when, what seemed a perfectly good goal scored by McLean was disallowed, thus robbing the 'Boro of a double-figure scoreline. Perhaps the referee wished to spare Brighton's total humiliation on their Division Two debut.

"After the match Clough commented with typical sarcasm, no doubt aimed at the Press, that he felt he should have scored more goals but that the burden of captaincy had held him back. His tally that day? Five goals! Some burden!"

Fred Gibson
Guisborough

The red-hot telephone line

"In the 1950s, during reserve matches the first team away score was always displayed on the *Evening Gazette* scoreboard at the Bob End. All regular supporters knew that when the phone rang in the box it usually meant that a goal had been scored.

"On 29 August 1959, the 'Boro were at the Baseball Ground, Derby, when those of us watching the reserves heard the phone ring. Great delight, 1-0 to the 'Boro was posted on the board. The phone rang again 2-0, then again 3-0 and again 4-0 until finally the result was a resounding 7-1 away victory for the 'Boro.

"Alan Peacock hit four that day and

Alan Peacock was a fine all-round striker who earned England recognition in the World Cup in Chile in 1962.

surprisingly in such a large scoreline Brian Clough failed to find the net, although he did rectify the situation shortly afterwards in a 6-2 home win over Plymouth with four goals of his own.

"Never had the phone been so hot in recording a 'Boro away win."

Ian Porley Middlesbrough

The sympathetic ticket tout

"Amongst all the wonderful memories I have of Ayresome Park I would have to go back to 25 February 1970, for my greatest recollection.

"'Boro had been drawn at home in the sixth round of the FA Cup and the excitement on Teesside was at an all-time high. As a 12-year-old schoolboy I gained great pleasure in seeing 'Boro dispose of Bobby Moore's West Ham United in the third round with a Derrick Downing diving header. York City were crushed 4-1 in front of 32,000 fans in the following tie and Carlisle were beaten 2-1 in the fifth round. The crowd on that occasion was 27,000 which to this day remains a record attendance for the Cumbrian club. So when Manchester United became our next opponents 'Cup fever' really hit town.

South Bank FC and South Bank St Peter's officially became 'Boro nursery clubs in 1934. South Bank were paid an initial £50, and St Peter's £15.

"For me however, there was to be one huge stumbling block because when the tickets went on sale, the Sunday morning prior to the game, to my complete and utter dismay I was confined to bed with some dreaded bug.

"When the day of the game came, I had to be part of the atmosphere, so I arrived at the ground a couple of hours before kick-off – ticketless.

"With the thought of Best and Charlton gracing the Ayresome Park turf, the crowds were already building around the stadium. As I savoured the atmosphere I noticed a small group of people gathering around a man who was obviously a United fan judging by his scarf and badges. He was furtively offering match tickets to those who could meet his inflated prices. At that time tickets for the South Terrace cost the princely sum of 7s (35p). I had saved up weeks of my pocket money 12s (60p) and naïvely offered it to the tout. He quickly dismissed my derisory offer but as I dejectedly turned away, he tugged on my arm and amazingly handed me a ticket. I could not believe that this was happening, as he did not even ask for any payment. He just told me to go and enjoy the game. I thanked him and dashed off into the crowd.

"That afternoon I watched the 'Boro take on the famous Manchester United. In a terrific game I saw Big John Hickton receive the ball on the halfway line, power down the left flank, ghost past the United full-back, then cut inside and float a brilliant shot over the advancing Stepney. Total commitment continued in this pulsating Cup-tie with United eventually scrambling a 1-1 draw.

"I felt very proud of my team that day and very fortunate to see those United stars and it was all made possible by the generosity of a Manchester ticket tout."

It's another salver for John Hickton, who was voted one of the most popular 'Boro players.

Edward Cole Middlesbrough

The mystery of the disappearing olive oil

"My father Charlie Cole was assistant trainer and trainer at Ayresome Park for over 35 years and during that time I was very privileged to become quite friendly with some of the personalities who played for Middlesbrough Football Club.

"The greatest player I ever saw in a red shirt was Jackie Carr from South Bank, who was a very skilful inside-forward. He dedicated nearly 20 years of his life to Middlesbrough and gained two England caps.

"Although I have many happy memories of helping my father at first-team training sessions, two stories in particular stick in my mind.

"In the late 1920s 'Boro signed a half-back called Joseph Peacock from Everton. My father, who also trained professional athletes, believed that stamina training was very important in becoming a successful footballer, so consequently much emphasis was given to running around the cinder track, which circled the Ayresome Park pitch.

"As the players set off this specific day, it quickly became apparent that Peacock was struggling at the back of pack. As the players finished a few circuits, my father shouted some words of encouragement to the gasping Peacock who yelled back, 'What are we training for Charlie, the ruddy Grand National.' This remark certainly made my father laugh but Peacock was still made to finish his required number of circuits.

"The second story concerns the olive oil with which my father used to massage the aching muscles of the players and was kept in an unlocked medical cabinet in the 'Boro's dressing-room.

"One day he remarked how quickly the contents of the jar seemed to be disappearing, so without hesitation he filled it. A short time later however, when examining the jar he discovered that the oil had again vanished, so he secretly marked the jar and waited.

"When the ground was quiet, the dressing-room door creaked open and a leather gloved hand removed the olive oil from the cabinet. The culprit took the jar outside and proceeded to lubricate his motorbike with the contents. When my father confronted the miscreant he found it was very well-known member of the first team squad who was full of embarrassed apologies.

"From that day on, my father fitted a large lock on the medical cabinet door and kept a very close watch on his medical supplies.

An early picture of Charlie Cole, who spent more than 35 years as trainer at Ayresome Park.

"The game that I remember most vividly at Ayresome Park took place on Boxing Day 1926 when 'Boro played Manchester City. The previous day, Christmas Day, Middlesbrough had won 5-3 at Maine Road with George Camsell scoring all five goals, so consequently there was a great deal of interest in the return fixture.

"In those days there were no all-ticket games and I remember watching as the crowd got larger and larger until they had to close the gates. Unfortunately the thousands of people locked out were determined to get in and the gates were broken down. As the throng surged forward the wooden barriers behind the goals began to collapse and people took refuge by standing on the cinder track. We were eventually so close to the action near the goalmouth that before a player could take a corner we had to move back from the goal-line.

"The 'Boro eventually won the match 2-1 with Camsell scoring both goals. The attendance was given at over 43,000, which was a new ground record, but I believe there were a great many more supporters inside Ayresome Park that day.

"As a result of this match the flimsy wooden barriers behind the goals were replaced by solid concrete ones and I will certainly never forget that Boxing Day experience."

E.Davies
Billingham

A tragedy at Ayresome Park

"My most vivid memory of Ayresome Park was when Mr and Mrs Roxby of Eaglescliffe were killed outside the East End of the ground on 12 January 1980.

"I was one of the few 'Boro supporters in the Manchester United enclosure that fateful day and at the end of the game I made my way to the exit. Unfortunately the officials in their misguided wisdom had kept the gates closed, to allow the 'Boro supporters to clear the stadium first. The area behind the gates quickly filled up with restless away fans who soon began to surge forward. The wooden double gates and brick pillars kept moving under the pressure of the pushing bodies. I heard a voice shout out 'One more shove and the gates will open!'

"I was right at the front of the crowd when the gates and the pillars collapsed and I ended up on top of the gates lying on my side. The next thing I remember was the police with their dogs rushing towards us. One of the dogs bit my arm and ripped my coat. I then heard a policeman say that there were some people buried under the rubble of the pillars. I started to help move the bricks and found somebody's arm. When this happened I began to shake all over. I went to my car to go home but I was in such a state of shock I couldn't drive and had to go to my brother's house in town until I settled down and was well enough to go home.

"The memory of what happened that day will remain with me forever."

Mike Millett
Billingham

Headteacher encourages truancy

"Nearly 40,000 people attended the FA

Surveying the damage. This is the collapsed wall at the East End of Ayresome Park which tragically claimed the lives of Norman and Irene Roxby following a match against Manchester United in January, 1980.

These are the 'Boro boys in 1934-35. Back row (left to right): Billy Forrest, Billy Brown, Jack Jennings, Joe Hillier, Bobby Baxter, George Camsell, Charlie Cole (trainer). Front row: Fred Warren, Joe Williams, Tom Griffiths, Bobby Stuart, Micky Fenton, Tim Coleman.

'Boro's biggest crowd of all time – 53,802 for the home derby against Newcastle United on 27 December 1949 – had two reasons for getting in a sweat. In addition to the crush in the crowd, it was the hottest Christmas for many years.

Cup replay against Manchester United in 1972 which was played on a Tuesday afternoon because of the miners' strike power-cut threats.

"Although we should normally have been at our school desks that afternoon, Manchester United, despite being past their best still had Bobby Charlton in their team, so we all queued for our tickets anyway. On the Monday morning before the match the headmaster ordered all pupils who had tickets for the game to stay behind after assembly. There were quite a few of us. The headmaster proceeded to launch into a vitriolic condemnation of us for daring to even contemplate truancy just to watch a football match. He angrily denounced us and threatened us with all manner of punishments should we ever be so presumptuous again.

"He then informed us that the school had organised a coach to take us and the teachers who had bought tickets, to Ayresome Park. Apparently many of the pupils who remained listened to the game on the radio.

"In total contrast, I have never experienced such a mood of anticlimax and gloom as after our last match of the season in 1988 against Leicester City. The 'Boro needed to win to ensure automatic promotion and nothing but a victory was contemplated. Parties were planned for after the game. The ground was full at ten

It's a mixture of agony, disbelief and despair for these young fans after 'Boro failed to beat Leicester City at Ayresome Park in May 1988, and thus missed the chance of gaining automatic promotion to the First Division.

past two and there was a carnival air of celebration about the place.

"Unfortunately, Leicester forgot they were supposed to roll over and play dead. The 'Boro were well beaten 2-1 and even their consolation goal was one of the most blatant Bernie Slaven offsides I ever saw. The awful realisation that 'Boro had missed promotion and were condemned to the Play-offs hung like a depressing cloud as I trudged wearily out of the ground."

Ken Cook
Chop Gate

The milkmaid supporter

"In the 1930s my father was a farmer. He and my mother used to travel quite often to Ayresome Park to watch Middlesbrough who were an established First Division team at that time.

"My mother, who was only five feet tall, used to take along to the match a three-legged milking stool to stand on in order to see the players. At one local derby they attended against Sunderland there were nearly 50,000 supporters in the ground and there was mother perched precariously on her stool and as far as I am aware, despite all the swaying and shoving, my mother never came to grief."

The team of all the talents. 'Boro in 1938-39. Back row (left to right): Henry Fowler, Duncan McKenzie, Jackie Milne, Dave Cumming, Billy Forrest, Bobby Stuart. Front row: Micky Fenton, Benny Yorston, Bobby Baxter, Wilf Mannion, Cliff Chadwick.

F.R.Bingham
Stainton,
Middlesbrough

Match abandoned as player refuses to leave the field

"I was taken to Ayresome Park by my father for the first time in 1912 when I was five years old.

"I had the pleasure of watching many famous 'Boro centre-forwards over the years. George Elliott, Andrew Wilson, Jimmy McClelland and George Camsell, Micky Fenton, Charlie Wayman, Brian Clough, Alan Peacock and John O'Rourke to mention a few.

Andy Wilson, 'Boro's famous Scottish international centre-forward who played for the club before and after World War One.

"The most bizarre incident I saw at a match was when at the age of eight in 1915, Middlesbrough were playing Oldham Athletic in a Division One game. After about an hour's play the Oldham full-back Billy Cook was given his marching orders for dirty play, but he refused to leave the field. In spite of the efforts of all the officials he still refused to go off and the referee had no option but to abandon the match. The points were subsequently awarded to Middlesbrough, who were leading 4-1 at the time. Incidentally this was the last season of League football until after World War One.

"In conclusion just to emphasise my support for the 'Boro, my wedding day was organised for Monday, 2 September 1935, because the 'Boro had a home game against Aston Villa on the Saturday. My daughter also delayed the departure of her honeymoon until after a match and had to be taken hurriedly to the station to catch the train."

Burglars who broke into the Ayresome Park office in January 1935, took the back off the safe and emptied the cash boxes. They escaped with £73 9s 11d of petty cash, consisting of change for the turnstiles and Cup-tie bookings. As a result, the directors decided to take out insurance against burglary for £100.

The maestro. Bobby Baxter, the Scottish international who is reckoned by many to be the best centre-back ever to play for 'Boro.

G.M.Jones
Middlesbrough

Remembering the era of the great Bobby Baxter

"In the 1930s my father took me to Ayresome Park for the very first time. It was New Year's Day and I saw Middlesbrough beat Grimsby 2-1 with goals from Jennings and Camsell.

"Over the years I saw some great players and great teams in 'Boro shirts. Early favourites were Mathieson, Jennings, Warren, McKay, MacFarlane and the legendary partnership of

Pease and Camsell. A little later came Yorston, Bruce, Forrest, Brown and Martin in fact so much talent that we sold Bert Watson, Jack Holliday, Billy Scott, Ernie Muttitt and later Jim Mathieson to Third Division Brentford, who later ended up playing in Division One.

"Then there was probably the best 'Boro team of all time between 1937-39 with the likes of Scottish international Bobby Baxter, who played in every position including goalkeeper, before he settled at centre-half. He was undoubtedly one of the most skilful players ever to grace the Ayresome Park turf. He was partnered by Cumming, Laking, Stuart, Milne, Fenton, Birkett, Hardwick and Mannion. Most of them were, or became full internationals, and I am sure that this team would have won major honours had it not been destroyed by the onset of World War Two.

"In conclusion I must mention two Ayresome occasions which were not connected with football but stick in my memory. The first was to commemorate the centenary of Middlesbrough as a town when a great many of the local schoolchildren, me included, lined up on the pitch, boys wearing white shirts and the girls navy gymslips and on a given signal we all had to bend over to form a huge coat of arms. The second occasion was when, again as schoolchildren, we were taken to Ayresome Park for a royal visit and the Prince of Wales (later Edward VIII) drove round the running track waving to us from his Rolls-Royce."

Peter McClone
Stockton

The day I think I met John Hickton's mother-in-law

"As a young lad in 1968, a season ticket holder friend of my father's asked me to join him in the North Stand because his mate was ill and there was a spare seat. I normally stood in the boys' end.

"The game was 'Boro v Derby. Cloughie was their manager and Dave Mackay the captain. During the course of the game Mackay never let John Hickton have a kick. By the second half I was starting to get frustrated so I shouted out 'Hickton get your finger out'. No sooner had I got the words out of my mouth when I was hit across the back of the head with a handbag. I hadn't realised that I was sitting four seats away from John Hickton's wife and mother-in-law. Needless to say I was never invited again.

"I have been a 'Boro supporter for over 40 years and by far the best players

Paul Kerr, pictured in action against Tranmere Rovers, scored the goal which ensured that 'Boro were on their way to Wembley in the Zenith Data Systems Cup Final.

I have seen in red shirts were Graeme Souness, easily the most skilful player, John Hickton, his left-wing runs could leave you breathless and they regularly ended up in goal, and John Hendrie. Why this lad never represented his country was an absolute mystery to me.

"My most memorable match at Ayresome Park would have to be the ZDS Cup semi-final against Aston Villa when the 'Boro made history by winning through to a Wembley Final. Paul Kerr and Bernie Slaven were magnificent that night.

Bruce Rioch, whose remarkable contribution to the revival of the 'Boro after 1986 will never be forgotten by the club's supporters.

Jimmy Gordon, front row second left, was said to be the fittest man at Ayresome Park after World War Two. The 'Boro team, with manager David Jack at the back, are pictured at the start of a golfing trip.

In 1935 the tops of the trees at the back of the East End were cut down because they were interfering with the view of the scoreboard at Ayresome Park.

"Jack Charlton gets my vote as the best manager. Had he stayed we would definitely have won the championship and probably a cup.

"The saddest moment I have ever witnessed at Ayresome Park was going to a reserve match to see Willie Maddren attempt a comeback only to watch him break down and break his heart. He was a great, great player and a tremendous loss to the club. How I wish he could have made a success of the manager's job.

"Finally we all owe a deep debt of gratitude to Bruce Rioch whose contribution in saving Middlesbrough Football Club from extinction in 1986 should never be forgotten."

J.Thompson
Coulby Newham

'Blenky'

"I was a member of St Philomena's Boys' Club Cadet Force and we used to train behind the Ayresome Park stands so, I became very familiar with the layout of the ground towards the end of World War Two. Oh those post-war games memories of 'Wilfie' with a little shake of his body to send not one but three and four defenders the wrong way. The Brazilians and Italians were not in the same League.

"The pre-season matches, first team versus the reserves were always interesting. There was Gorgeous George Hardwick with his big thighs and spare-tyre middle struggling in the early games, but his uncanny positional sense always seemed to pull him through. I remember his wife in a butcher's shop demanding best steak for George regardless of rationing. That caused more than a few mutters from the local ladies I can tell you.

Tom Blenkinsopp, one of the characters of Ayresome Park in the post-war years.

"One 'Boro player of whom there were numerous folklore stories retold in Testers barber's shop near the ground was Tommy Blenkinsopp. He was one of the great characters.

"On a Saturday night my friends and I used to frequent the Assembly Rooms in Linthorpe Road and more often than not the younger 'Boro players were there. Blenky could always be relied upon to entertain us particularly with his party piece of dancing alone with a pillar in time to the music under the grinning faces of his teammates.

"In the 1950s professional footballers were not on the extravagant salaries of today so it was quite commonplace to see the likes of Lindy 'Our Kid' Delapenha and Dickie Robinson travelling around Middlesbrough on the bus. Talking of buses I recall Jimmy Gordon running after a bus on Linthorpe Road. He overtook two cars, three bikes and then jumped on. Definitely my candidate for the fittest 'Boro player ever. The 20 years after World War Two was a period of lost opportunity for Middlesbrough. Potentially brilliant teams were ruined by the weak management of David Jack and Bob Dennison and lack of leadership from the board. The team of 1959-61 with Clough scoring from all angles, backed up by Peacock with two brilliant wingers in Day and Holliday was so nearly the best I've ever seen, but everything was lost through the club's indecision. But that is what being a 'Boro supporter is all about. We have seen opportunities lost before and no doubt we'll see them again."

Colin Lillie
Acklam

Living near the ground

"I was born and lived for over 20 years in Addison Road at the bottom of Clive Road next to Ayresome Park. I can remember being able to see the Bob End goal from our back bedroom window before the new South Stand was built.

"On match days my friend and I used to mind bicycles whilst their owners were at the match. Usually we looked after at least 100 for 1d or 2d each.

"In the old days the queues to get into the ground regularly stretched along Addison Road and down St Barnabas Road to Linthorpe Cemetery and I used to watch from our front bedroom window as they began to form.

Real Madrid wanted to play at Ayresome Park in September 1967. But the Spaniards asked for £6,500 in cash guarantees with insurance on top, so 'Boro said 'No'.

"Behind the Holgate End of the ground, before they built Middlesbrough General Hospital, there used to be a workhouse and I can remember many a time climbing over the workhouse wall, which was about two foot wide, and getting into the ground for free.

"I have spent many hours watching 'Boro players like George Hardwick training by kicking balls against the walls that backed on to Shaw's Club and looked on as George Camsell put Johnny Spuhler through his shooting practice against the door of the old stand.

"Several of the famous 'Boro players lived in and around Addison Road, including Bobby Baxter. I remember George Camsell walking through St Barnabas Park to his house in Chipchase Road and Jimmy Gordon striding out very briskly to and from the ground. His walk would have been a trot to most people."

Susan Thomas
Stockton

Eating Pallister's Just Desserts

"The season I most enjoyed was 1973-74 when we had a great team that played with style. At the end of that season the club held an open day and thousands of supporters took the opportunity to visit the ground. On that day I met some of

Stuart Ripley, a pacey winger and a good crosser of the ball, who was sold to Blackburn Rovers for £1.3 million in 1992.

the most talented players the 'Boro have ever had like Graeme Souness, Willie Maddren and Bobby Murdoch.

"In later years I thought how sad it was that the club's most talented players were sold, resulting in the Ayresome Park gates being padlocked when it looked as though we were folding. That period definitely provides me with my worst memory.

"One of my more recent memories was during the season 1988-89 when after a match against Derby County I nominated Stuart Ripley as my man of the match and was very surprised to learn that I had won the competition. I was presented with my plaque and found Stuart to be one of the nicest lads in the team.

"Towards the end of the same season I received an invitation to attend the 100 Club room where, with a friend, I not only had dinner but met all the players and had my photograph taken with the then manager Bruce Rioch. The menu card for the meal was made up of the players' names for example Roast Beef Davenport and Pallister's Just Desserts, I managed to get it autographed."

William C.Mills
Middlesbrough

The return of the transferred players

"I attended the match against Brentford on 14 November 1936, when five former 'Boro players, Mathieson, Brown, Scott, Holliday and Muttitt, all returned to Ayresome Park. There had been a good deal of controversy about their initial sale to Brentford who, with the help of these talented 'Boro exiles, had won promotion into the top flight all the way from the Third Division. The atmosphere in the ground and on the pitch that day was quite hostile.

"When the 'Boro were leading 2-0 they were awarded a corner and as it was being taken the 'Boro centre-forward George Camsell was seen lying injured on the ground. This enraged the crowd and several supporters rushed on to the pitch to grapple with the alleged culprit, the Brentford centre-half James. Pitch invasions were unheard of in those days and the result was that one man was arrested."

Norman Miller
Stokesley

Gone for a Burton!

"The first match I went to at Ayresome Park was on New Year's Day 1924, when Middlesbrough played Cardiff City. I was taken to the ground by George Burton, who had played for

George Burton, a former 'Boro forward from 1910 who took Norman Miller to his first game at Ayresome Park.

Cardiff some years previously and had also had a spell with the 'Boro from 1909-10 but was kept out of the side by the great George Elliott.

Before the game started George went into the Cardiff dressing-room to see his old teammates such as Hardy and Keenor, who had played for Cardiff for many years. When he came back into the North Stand he confided to me, 'The 'Boro should win easily today as five of the Cardiff team are unfit to play.'

"The result was a 1-0 win for Cardiff. Sounds familiar!"

Graham Dresser
Blackpool

Peaches and team

"I started going to Ayresome Park in 1955. My hero was Brian Clough. I can't remember any outstanding pieces of skill he displayed, just the numerous goals he scored from all parts of the pitch.

"Even as a small boy at that time I knew I was watching an exciting forward line. Two wingers of quality in Billy Day

Bill Harris, one of the great 'Boro ball-players of all time who played more than 350 games for the club.

and England international Eddie Holliday, Brian Clough, Alan Peacock an outstanding header of the ball and the little Scottish inside-forward Willie Fernie.

"There were other characters in the team too. Goalkeeper Peter Taylor who could throw a ball as far as he could kick it. Ray Yeoman, not a hair on top of his head, but one of the hardest men I've ever seen and Ray Bilcliff, another balding hard man. Bill Harris, the cultured Welsh international half-back who lacked pace but had a delightful left foot and a strong shot.

"I was really upset when Brian Clough left but I remember vividly Alan Peacock's first game wearing the number-nine shirt that he had always wanted. The match was against Rotherham United, who threatened to spoil the occasion by scoring straight from the kick-off. However, it was always going to be Peaches' night and he scored four in an easy 5-1 victory. Peacock was such a success at centre-forward that he eventually signed for Leeds United and went with England to the World Cup finals in Chile in 1962.

"One of my worst memories of Ayresome Park was the time when John Hickton missed his first penalty for Middlesbrough. I was dumbstruck, it just never happened, Big John always scored. It was against Hull City in 1968 in a 1-1 draw and it was saved by the Tigers' fine goalkeeper Ian McKechnie."

George Glasper
Middlesbrough

Hotshot Lindy

"Although George Camsell, Brian Clough and Micky Fenton were prolific

Power shooting was one of Lindy Delapenha's strengths. The busy striker had one of the hardest shots in football during the 1950s.

scorers for Middlesbrough, undoubtedly the most spectacular goalscorer was Lindy Delapenha, who never scored a bad goal. They always seemed to fly into the net like rockets. To be fair however, the shots that missed the net usually ended up in either Linthorpe Road or Linthorpe Cemetery, depending which way the 'Boro were attacking.

"Another player of the same era who was much loved was goalkeeper Rolando Ugolini. He always kept the crowd entertained with his antics.

"In the 1950s reserve-team games were played on a Saturday in front of quite respectable crowds. There were always good players on view and plenty of incident. I can recall a 'keeper bringing down 'Boro winger Geoff Walker and a very, very angry Walker getting up and putting the ball on the spot. He then stormed out of the penalty area to take this long run at the ball only to find the goalkeeper refusing to stand on the goal-line. After a lengthy discussion with the referee he went back in goal but before Walker struck the ball the 'keeper had gone again."

Wilf Mannion scored an own-goal at the City Ground to give Nottingham Forest an equaliser in a 2-2 draw in the FA Cup fifth round in 1947. He made amends by scoring a hat-trick as 'Boro beat Forest 5-2 in the replay at Ayresome Park.

David Noble
Stockton

My son's first match

"One of the fondest memories of Ayresome Park I can recall was taking my seven-year-old son to his first ever big game. Middlesbrough were playing Liverpool, who were champions elect, and the 'Boro were doomed to relegation from Division One. It was 1982.

"My son was in awe of the occasion, with the size of the crowd and the names playing on the hallowed turf. He asked me if he could whistle, which I said he could do. Using two fingers, I have never heard such a shrill sound come out of a such a small mouth. The look on his face when he'd done it was a treat. He felt so important being part of the crowd and needless to say he became hooked on the 'Boro."

A W Kent
Guisborough

Jackie Carr points the way

"My first visit to Ayresome Park was when I was seven years old in 1925 and my father used to sit me on his shoulders.

"One funny incident I remember in particular happened during one match when the 'Boro were awarded a penalty. Jackie Carr picked up the ball, walked

The remarkable Jackie Carr, who played at Ayresome Park for more than 19 seasons from 1910 to 1930 and was one of the most skilful inside-forwards of his generation.

The 'Boro directors made a special request to the police in 1935 to place four plain-clothed officers at the East End for three home matches to try to stop barracking and insulting remarks to the players. The chief constable came to see the board, and the matter was left in his hands.

towards the spot and pointed to the goalkeeper's right, playfully informing him where he was going to place the ball. He then put the ball down, stood up and kicked the ball exactly where he had predicted. The goalkeeper however, dived to his left and Jackie went up to him and shook his hand while the crowd cheered."

George Crawford
Redcar

A recollection of Astor

"During the 1950s while I was watching a match at Ayresome Park an announcement came over the loudspeakers that the next game on the ground would be on the following Wednesday when England and Germany would play a youth international. I was standing next to Astor, the local night-club comedian and friend of 'Boro player Lindy Delapenha, when he shouted up to the directors box, 'Don't you remember what happened between England and Germany between 1939 and 1945?' Everybody laughed."

Don Chesney
Eston

In praise of Swifts Liquorice Toffee Rolls

"My father first took me to Middlesbrough FC when I was eight years old in 1962. Those were the days when teams had decent V-necked shirts and the players had either manly crew cuts or wore lashings of Brylcreem.

Our match day routine went like this: My dad, who was a football nut, would take me to the sweet shop on Eston Square, at 1.40pm on the dot. He always bought a quarter of Swifts Liquorice Toffee Rolls, the ones in the black blue and silver wrapper, for himself and a packet of fruit gums for me. We then boarded the 1.55pm 63 bus and joined the crowd heading for Ayresome Park. On arrival at the ground my dad would ask for a 'squeeze'. If he was unsuccessful I would stand in the Boys' End and my dad would stand in the Bob End terracing in front of me.

"Those were the days, but time marches on and soon standing at football matches was a thing of the past... just like Ayresome Park."

Michael Wright
Linthorpe

Gasman signs for 'Boro!

"During the school holidays in the 1960s my mates and I used to hang around Ayresome Park hoping to collect autographs from the players as they returned from training. At this particular time it was rumoured that the 'Boro were interested in signing Celtic's reserve centre-half John Cushley.

"One afternoon we were not having much luck on the autograph front when this big fella emerged from the players exit. To echoes of 'Who are you mister?' he replied that he was John Cushley and he had just come down from Scotland to sign for the 'Boro.

"He duly signed all our autograph books and my mates and I were 'over the moon'. We had a scoop, not an *Evening Gazette* reporter in sight. Our euphoria was short lived however, as 'John Cushley' got into this gas van and drove off down Warwick Street waving with big grin on his face.

"The real John Cushley never did sign for Middlesbrough. He went to West Ham United instead and as for the gasman I don't think he went on to play for anybody."

Marie Bushley
North Ormesby

A crackpot wheelchair marathon

"In the 1960s my friend Brenda and I were 'Boro fanatics. We went to every home game at Ayresome Park and if the first team were away we would go and watch the reserves or the youth team.

"My memory starts a couple of days before an evening match when Brenda and I were playing football with the lads on the local field. That was in the days when it was considered strange for girls to play football. Unfortunately during the course of the kickabout Brenda broke her ankle and had to have her leg put in a plaster cast.

"When I went round on a visit her mother said 'There is no way that she's going to the match.' 'That's fine', I replied, 'I was only going to push her wheelchair to the park.' So her mum let her go. Little did she know that the park in question was Ayresome Park and that we had arranged to leave the wheelchair at a friend's house who lived near the ground.

"I pushed Brenda in the chair all the way from Brambles Farm along the Longlands Road, over the bridge past Clairville Common and into my friend's house. From there Brenda had to hop to the ground because the plaster was still wet and hadn't set properly. To make matters worse it began to rain heavily and we got soaking wet. Brenda hopped towards the main entrance but she slipped on the cobblestones outside the ground and broke the pot.

"We eventually got into the ground late and would you believe it after all that effort the 'Boro lost 2-0. Disconsolately I pushed the chair slowly home trying to work out what I was going to say to Brenda's mum, but as far as I recall she didn't say that much because she could see how miserable we were.

"Brenda became a steward at the ground and I will certainly remember that wheelchair marathon."

Martin Connelly
Stockton

Risking the cane to watch 'Boro train.

"In 1956 I played in a Youth Cup Final for St Philomena's Boys' Club at Ayresome Park. Although I scored all my team's five goals I still ended up on the losing side as we went down 6-5.

"Being a 'Boro Schools and Yorkshire youth player I naturally signed for Middlesbrough. During my time with the 'Boro I had the pleasure of playing with Eddie Holliday, Mick McNeil, Bob Appleby and many others before having to finish with cartilage problems.

"When I attended St Philomena's School, which is next door to Ayresome Park, it was my job to return the footballs to the ground that had come over the school fence during the 'Boro players' training sessions. What should have been a two minute job often got me into trouble, but what young boy wouldn't have risked a caning to watch the likes of Wilf Mannion and George Hardwick practising?"

Kenneth Yale
Acklam

Memories of a turnstile operator.

"I started working at Ayresome Park in 1968-69 as a steward and by 1972-73 I had progressed to be a turnstile operator.

"When working at the Holgate End of the ground you became aware of the same few youths who tried to gain entry for nothing, usually by stepping over the turnstile barrier and then running on to the terraces. To counteract this method I used to wait until a youth started his approach, as he stepped over the barrier I would close the inner sliding door thus denying him access to the ground.

"Word soon spread about the tactic being adopted by the operators so the ever-determined youths then took to hurdling cleanly over the barriers before you could close the sliding door. There was little that you could do to stop this practice.

"However, one particularly lanky lad who had obviously never hurdled a barrier before came running flat out towards the turnstile but unfortunately because he was so tall struck his head in the concrete beam above the sliding door and knocked himself out. I couldn't stop laughing. As he staggered to his feet I told him because his efforts had been so funny if he promised to repeat the same performance each week he could get in for free.

"To highlight the extremes of the 'Boro's fortunes during my time as a turnstile operator these two incidents remain in my memory.

"In the mid-eighties when the 'Boro were going through a really bad time and crowds were below 6,000, this tough looking man about 30 years of age nonchalantly stepped over the barrier and walked into the ground. I closed my turnstile and told a policeman what had happened. We went on to the terraces and quickly located the non-paying supporter among the sparse crowd and gave him the option of being arrested or paying his entrance money. He was certainly not happy about the situation but he reluctantly paid up, then had the audacity to insist that the turnstile be clicked round to record his entry!

"From those quiet days to the other extreme. I was working at the visitors' end when we played Newcastle United. The cost of entry was £1 and because of problems at a previous Newcastle game there were extra police on duty at the turnstiles. Just before the kick-off I had taken over £2,000 but as the referee blew the whistle the police went to watch the match and I had to fend for myself. I somehow managed to keep taking money, protect my takings from the thieving hands trying to reach through the grill but I was unable to stop anybody from not paying. After about 30 minutes I'd had enough and managed to get my turnstile sliding doors shut and began the task of counting the cash.

"It took me until almost full-time to sort the money out into the correct denominations and deliver it to the office. I had worked from 1.30pm to 4.45pm and had been threatened and abused but I still managed to collect £3,430 for which I was paid the princely sum of five pounds.

"In conclusion if I mention the word 'squeeze' I am sure it will rekindle the memories of many a 'Boro supporter who first entered Ayresome Park by this method."

David Sinclair
Darlington

The birthday present that changed my life

"It was September 1993 and another birthday present problem for my son Jamie approached. He requested a visit with his friend Daniel, to Ayresome Park. 'They are playing your team dad, Sunderland,' he informed me to add spice to his request.

"I couldn't remember the last time I had been to a football match, but it must have been at Roker Park. So the visit was duly set up and on a sunny afternoon we stood on the north-east corner of Ayresome Park waiting for the Tees-Wear derby to start.

"As I looked around Ayresome Park the memories came flooding back. The ghosts of Ugolini, Delapenha, Harris, Yeoman, Stonehouse, Clough, Taylor and Peacock floated across the turf and I was the small lad standing with his father on the terracing again. A Mackem supporter in the den of the enemy.

"The game started in a blur as I rediscovered the experience of live football. It took me some time to become accustomed to the fact that there were no action replays but the chants of the Holgate End were becoming infectious and I found myself shouting out 'Offside linesman', 'Never referee'.

"Suddenly I felt as though I had been 'Tangoed', because here I was gripped by the passion for the game again. Television did not compare to live football – this was the real thing.

"To the total surprise of Jamie and Daniel, my shouts were not for Sunderland but for the 'Boro. I'd fallen head over heels in love with the 'Boro and a 2-1 win was the perfect end to a perfect afternoon. It had started with apprehension and ended with requests for the details of the next game to ensure my place on the terrace to watch my new passion, Middlesbrough FC.

"A promotion season, quickly followed by relegation, but still I remained loyal to the 'Boro. Until one sub-zero afternoon came the biggest test of all, a return to Roker Park. As I stood on the Roker End of my childhood, with the 'Boro away supporters I wondered if 'Shack' and Charlie Hurley would ever forgive me. It certainly tugged at the heart strings.

"But then came the confirmation to blow away my remaining doubts. With the 'Boro losing 2-1 and well beaten a 'Boro fan shouted out 'I'm glad I'm not at home, sat in front of a nice warm fire watching this load of rubbish on the television.' A priceless comment which sums up a real 'Boro fan's black humour and the ability to laugh at themselves.

'Boro dropped the Milburns Band in 1938 because not all of the band members wore uniforms. They were replaced by the 'Boro Prize Band.

"I'm a 'Boro fan, through promotion and relegation, 'til death us do part, I'm totally committed. 'We're 'Boro, we're 'Boro, we're off..."

Richard Yale
Thornaby

The Gateway to Heaven

"My father was a turnstile operator at Ayresome Park and I was privileged to start watching the 'Boro at the end of the 1973-74 promotion season when I was five years old.

"I remember getting a ride to the ground on the crossbar of his pushbike along Acklam Road and sailing through those welcoming iron gates after a good shaking on the cobblestone leading up to them.

"At every match the chief steward would call out the names of the turnstile men in a different order to the previous game, so the operators were rotated round the ground. This meant that every fortnight my dad would be at a different turnstile which enabled me to view the matches from a variety of vantage points.

"The first match that I attended on my own was on 5 February 1983, against Newcastle United, who boasted Keegan and Waddle in their ranks. The game ended in 1-1 draw with Mick Baxter scoring the 'Boro goal.

"The particular game I remember vividly was the thrilling FA Cup replay at Ayresome Park on 3 February 1988 against Everton.

"A group of us from work used to meet on match days inside the ground at Holgate End and as usual the arrangements were the same this night. But as we were walking up St Barnabas Road at about ten to seven I was surprised at the number of fans streaming towards the ground. As I turned left into Addison Road I was amazed to see the queue for the Holgate End turnstiles nearly at the junction with St Barnabas Road. I had never seen so many people queuing to get into Ayresome Park before.

"As 7:30 approached some policemen on horses shouted that the Holgate End was full and the gates closed. By this time I was about 20 yards from the turnstiles. As the doors closed I squeezed my way towards the Clive Road turnstiles for the South Stand Terrace. Unfortunately there was only one open and there were about 1,500 fans trying to get in. With the turnstile operator working flat out I managed to get into the ground at about twenty to eight.

"The game was a classic Cup-tie. The floodlights blazed away through the frosty air and the crowd noise was tremendous. The game went into extra-time thanks to a last-minute goal by Tony Mowbray. Then Alan Kernaghan put 'Boro 2-1 up with only minutes to go and an old man beside me offered me a cigar as the ball went into the net. But when I turned round he'd been swept about 12 feet forward during the celebrations, waving his Hamlets at anyone who wanted one.

"Unfortunately Everton equalised right at the death to put a dampener on the occasion. Although the 'Boro were to go out in a second replay at Goodison Park, I'll never forget that marvellous night of FA Cup football at Ayresome Park."

Peg Newton
Middlesbrough

Damned with 'faint' praise

"The incident I recall happened around 1945-46 and concerned my father Albert Farrow, who was and continued to be a very keen 'Boro supporter until his death in 1983.

"I was curious to find out what caused this passion he had for his beloved 'Boro, so I asked him to take me along to a match one Saturday afternoon.

"The crowds I remember were enormous. It was the era of Mannion, Hardwick and Spuhler. When the first 'Boro goal went in there was a huge roar around Ayresome Park and I promptly fainted! I was later informed that I was passed over the supporters' heads and laid on the pitch. I came round to a good view of the players legs.

"Needless to say my dad never took me again."

D.T.Taylor
Middlesbrough

My pre-match routines and superstitions

"My pre-match preparations have often focussed on the way to get to Ayresome Park. One Saturday afternoon back in 1987 my car refused to start – too many away trips to grounds like Plymouth and Portsmouth had taken their toll – so I resigned myself to walk.

"From our house I took a short cut and trekked across Albert Park, going the wrong way around the boating lake and then cutting through the tennis courts to save time.

"The 'Boro won the match comfortably so needless to say I continued to persevere with my route march for the weeks to come, even though my ageing Cortina was back on the road.

"Staggering through the park to the ground I have never been so fit in my life. I even wrote an open letter to the *Sports Gazette* to suggest that Bruce Rioch and the lads enrolled in my fitness regime.

"They must have taken some notice of my suggestion because they went on an unbeaten run of 14 matches and climbed to the top of the table.

"Their luck finally ran out at Leeds – unusual that – and when two more defeats followed in quick succession I called it a day. To be truthful I was almost glad because I was wearing out my feet.

"Needless to say, now I drive to the match."

Paul Peacock
Coulby Newham

In appreciation of Bobby Thomson

When I think of the illustrious Scottish players who have pulled on the famous 'Boro red shirt, my mouth waters as I recall Baxter, Murdoch and Souness, players of class and distinction... And then there was Bobby Thomson who breezed into Ayresome Park as a replacement for David Armstrong declaring 'Believe me I'm no comedian', (a reference to the famous North-Eastern comic of the same name).

Why do I remember this player so well? Was it his silky ball skills or his deceptive turn of pace? No it was for his penalty taking prowess. On 30 January 1982, Bobby gave us a glittering display of his natural talent.

"The 'Boro were trailing to Southampton when they were awarded a penalty in front of the Holgate End. Confidently our hero strode up. The stands hushed with expectation as we waited for Thomson the executioner to deliver the final blow. As he sped towards the ball like a nimble gazelle, I thought to myself 'He'll bury this.'

"And sure enough he did, straight over the roof of the Holgate and into the bowels of Middlesbrough General Hospital next door.

"No this was not the first penalty miss I had witnessed, but it is permanently etched on my brain because of Bobby Thomson's hilarious after match comments when said, 'I knew I should have left it to someone else, I was suffering from double vision.'

"Well Bobby, you might have been suffering but not half as much as we suffered that day. Middlesbrough were duly beaten and relegated that season with Mr Thomson trekking back north from whence he came. He had claimed that he wasn't a comedian but he gave the travelling hordes from Southampton – all six of them – a good laugh that day in January 1982."

Jason Scott
Acklam

Wembley fever hits Teesside

"My enduring memory is quite unique in that there was no match in progress, not a player within a mile of Ayresome Park. Indeed it was midnight not midday.

"It was a chill February night back in 1990 and history had been made. At long last the Reds were to grace Wembley Stadium after disposing of the mighty Aston Villa in the Zenith Data Systems Cup semi-final. Now the hard work for the supporters was to begin, obtaining a ticket knowing that around 40,000 fans were suddenly crawling out of the woodwork to claim a lifetime of loyalty to the lads.

"I left nothing to chance, I approached Ayresome Park a good nine hours before the tickets were due to go on sale, confident that I would be one of the first in the queue.

"Then Bang! Reality hit me. A long, long line of sleeping bags, deckchairs and makeshift stools stretched out before me. Bonfires were already lit, the first of endless cups of coffee were being supped and yours truly was realising the hard way, what true commitment was all about. This was Cup fever. Just try telling those diehards that the ZDS was a Mickey Mouse affair. As the hours wore on it seemed that half of Teesside had descended on Ayresome Park. The late arrivals just stared in disbelief at the ever lengthening snakes of expectant fans.

"At last the word filtered back that the ticket office had opened early. Then suddenly the first fans began to dance down the street holding aloft their prized acquisitions. Joyous strangers hugged each other, kissed their tickets, then hugged some more.

"Then it was my turn… After 30 years of loyal support I held in my hands the passport to those Twin Towers of Wembley. Delirium overtook me and I went through all the backslapping, dancing and general euphoria of my predecessors.

"I would have loved photographs of it all, a camcorder heaven sent. But who cares, I'll remember that wonderful night for as long as I live."

Dick Mannion
Norton

Mini Memories

"One of the most humorous incidents to happen at Ayresome Park took place in the 1994 season. The 'Boro substitutes Craig Hignett and Nicky Mohan were warming up during the match by running up and down the touch-line in front of the North Stand. As they made their final sprint at speed, a wag near me on the terrace shouted out, 'Why don't you run that fast when you're playing.' You can guess the players' reaction."

Helen Jane Small
Hartburn

"The best performance I ever saw at Ayresome Park was in the first leg of the League Cup match against Brighton, 1993-94 when Craig Hignett scored four goals."

Craig Hignett, pictured scoring against Sunderland in 1993, grabbed four goals in one night against Brighton.

Simon McIntyre
Middlesbrough

"My favourite moment at Ayresome Park came when Paul Wilkinson scored against Bolton Wanderers to give the 'Boro a 1-0 victory. I was really chuffed because I could torment my grandad who came from Bolton and was a Bolton Wanderers supporter."

B.Stalker
Acklam

"Before World War Two there was no *Evening Gazette* scoreboard at the Bob End of the ground. I used to attend the reserve matches and the only way that the young lads could find out the first-team half-time score was to ask the reserve goalkeeper, who was usually Paddy Nash, when he came back on to the pitch for the second half."

John Brodie
Middlesbrough

"My favourite 'Boro player was John Hendrie. He had skill, speed and read the game so well. He always gave 100 per cent when he put a red shirt on. I wished they'd put him on the coaching staff when he retired."

Maynard V.Wilson
Thornaby

"The best team I ever saw the 'Boro put on to the field was in 1938-39 when they finished fourth in the League. The 12 stars were: Cumming, Laking, Stuart, Brown, Baxter, Forrest, McKenzie, Milne, Mannion, Fenton, Yorston and Chadwick."

Alan Robinson
Hartlepool

"My greatest memory of Ayresome Park was the night that the 'Boro knocked First Division Blackburn Rovers out of the FA Cup in 1963. Blackburn in those days had a team of stars with Ronnie Clayton, Bryan Douglas and Roy Vernon but they came a cropper against 'The Peach' and Arthur Kaye that night.

Some of my favourite players from that period were Bill Harris, Gordon Jones, Ian Gibson, Mick McNeil, Cyril Knowles, Alan Peacock, Eddie Holliday, Ray 'Yogi' Yeoman and Mel Nurse. They were the nucleus of a good side and it was quite surprising they didn't do anything."

Arthur Kaye, the 'Boro winger who scored in the outstanding FA Cup win against high flying Blackburn Rovers in March, 1963.

David Hodgson, the 'Boro striker who was highly rated by Alan Hansen.

Alan Knox
Acklam

"One of my favourite games was against Liverpool in February 1950. Middlesbrough won that particular encounter 4-1 with Dickie Robinson and Bill Whittaker literally marking those great Liverpool players Billy Liddell and Albert Stubbins out of the game. The Anfield attack was blunted and we went on to win in style. The match is special to me not only for its competitiveness and the fine victory secured by the 'Boro but also as I was accompanied to the game by my future wife Margaret."

Celebrity Memories

Alan Hansen, former Liverpool captain, Scottish international and BBC football pundit.

"In the Liverpool dressing-room we always thought that it was very difficult to get a result at Ayresome Park. I remember in particular the final match of the season in 1982 when Liverpool had won the First Division championship and Middlesbrough were bottom of the League and about to relegated. We came expecting an easy match and in the end although it was a draw 0-0, 'Boro could have easily won, so determined were they to finish off their disappointing season in style. David Hodgson played particularly well that night and in the summer he was transferred to Anfield.

"Just as a matter of interest, why does it always rain in Middlesbrough?"

John Motson, BBC Television football commentator.

"My most vivid memory of Ayresome Park was the FA Cup sixth-round tie between Middlesbrough and Wolverhampton Wanderers in March 1981. I was the *Match of the Day* commentator on that afternoon. The 'Boro could have made history and reached the FA Cup semi-final for the first time ever!

BBC football commentator John Motson has vivid memories of his early visits to Ayresome Park.

"I well remember interviewing 'Boro manager John Neal on *Football Focus* at lunchtime, on what an historic day it could be for all those concerned at Ayresome Park, and noticing the players had a lucky Teddy Bear in their dressing-room. Sadly, once again it was not to be. Before a crowd of 36,382 Terry Cochrane equalised Andy Gray's early header for Wolves and the tie went to a replay at Molineux which 'Boro lost 3-1 after extra-time.

"My first Ayresome Park commentary was in November 1975, when I covered the Final of the Anglo-Scottish Cup when Middlesbrough played Fulham, who boasted Bobby Moore and Alan Mullery in their ranks. 'Boro won the game 1-0 thanks to an own-goal by Strong and it proved good enough to win the trophy as the second leg was goalless."

Gordon Cox, 'Boro Website

Hickton Could Walk on Water

"For 28 years Ayresome Park was my spiritual home. I wouldn't pretend for one minute I enjoyed every minute there, far from it, but, in common with many football supporters, I could quite happily sit and watch the grass grow during the summer. To write dispassionately is impossible.

"How can you do that when something, or someone, has put you through a range of emotions you didn't know existed. My first taste of the Ayresome atmosphere was against

Ron Atkinson, making a spectacle of himself. In 1967 he skippered the Oxford United side which was crushed 4-1 at Ayresome Park.

Oxford United when Middlesbrough won 4-1 to clinch promotion from the then Third Division. I'm told John O'Rourke scored a hat-trick that day. I was seven at the time and not really sure what was going on! Many would say that's the same today.

"It was my father who was responsible for changing the course of my life. Not an over statement, a fact. Had he not taken me that day, who knows, I may never have gone. But he had been following the 'Boro since before World War One and as soon as it was seen fit to allow me to continue the family tradition that was it, I was in. The ground meant so much to my father that I spread his ashes across the playing surface when he sadly died in 1993.

"There was something about that first night against Oxford which must have whetted the appetite. That was the last game of the season. August couldn't come quickly enough as season 1967-68 edged nearer.

"My father and I used to watch from the East End. Success was limited, but I learned that John Hickton was the closest thing to a biblical experience Teesside was likely to have. Hickton could walk on water.

"In season 1973-74 I was fortunate enough to be chosen, through my school, to be a ball-boy for the season. That was the Jack Charlton era and to be in the same part of the changing area as the players and management taught me a lot.

"I still flick through the dictionary from time to time to see if some of the words used during the half-time interval against Luton one November do really have a meaning. That was a promotion year of course and the atmosphere was special, but the players had little to do with us ball-boys. We didn't mind, just to walk out through the tunnel before the game was enough for us.

"My mother kept father company during that season and for a few more as I moved on to a different responsibility, on the turnstiles. I worked on the gate for over four years. Waited for the dreaded announcement by the man who used to read the allocated turnstiles to the staff. 'Gordon Cox-34, or 49 or 9' meant a half-time gate.

"I'd had enough on the gates. Too much hassle from supporters as the game went through a more violent stage, and that quite frankly just wasn't my scene.

"I returned to the terraces, but quickly into the world of radio. Alastair Brownlee and I used to go to the same college, but he's older (had to get that in) and we rarely shared time. But we met up a few years later on an away trip to Chelsea. Ally had set up the Junior Reds a few seasons before and I joined forces with him. As a direct consequence I became associated with Radio Cleveland and later the *Hartlepool Mail.*

"Reporting from Ayresome gave me a sense of pride. It was hectic sometimes, especially when you were doing a written report for the *Hartlepool Mail* at the time and even more so when serving the old Clubcall service which we did for a year.

"But I was at Ayresome. It didn't matter what had to be done, how busy I was. I was at home."

Alan Green, Radio Five Live football commentator

"I know the weather is not always cold in the North-East… it just appears to be like that when I'm there!
Ironically my outstanding personal memory of Ayresome Park took place on a very warm spring evening in May 1988, when Middlesbrough played Bradford City in the second leg of the then Division Two Play-offs.

"On the same evening Chelsea were up against Blackburn Rovers and the BBC, not wanting to offend the unpredictable Chelsea chairman Ken Bates, had committed itself to a commentary of the Stamford Bridge game, even though Chelsea had won the first leg convincingly 4-1. So, Peter Jones, Bryon Butler and Trevor Brooking were duly dispatched to 'The Bridge' knowing that it was most unlikely that they would need to do any commentary. I went to Ayresome Park on my lonesome, knowing I'd probably end up commentating, but no one had arranged a summariser for me.

"My worst fears were confirmed as soon as I reached the ground. The powers that be had decided to take the Middlesbrough game as their main match and could I please find a

Gary Hamilton, remembered by BBC radio commentator Alan Green during the play-off semi-final against Bradford City.

summariser. Easier said than done on a match day, but I tracked down the then Sunderland manager Dennis Smith, who had just returned from a club tour in Majorca and had decided to spend his first night home by taking his wife out to see Middlesbrough play Bradford of all things.

"Being the lovely soul he is, Dennis left his wife alone in the directors' box and joined me in the commentary position from which we proceeded to do 120 minutes commentary (the match went into extra-time) on one of the most exciting games imaginable.

"After a pulsating match which Middlesbrough won of course 2-0, with goals from Slaven and Hamilton, they went on to secure a place in the First Division by beating Chelsea in the Play-off Final. But I will certainly remember that evening at Ayresome Park."

Tom Finney of Preston North End and England

Sheepdog trials were held at Ayresome Park on 8 September 1943, to raise money for Middlesbrough prisoners of war.

"The Ayresome Park pitch was always a good surface on which to play football and it suited my style of running with the ball. The Preston team enjoyed going to Middlesbrough because of the atmosphere inside the ground and the fact that the home supporters were very fair and appreciated good football, even

Preston and England legend Tom Finney always enjoyed playing at Ayresome Park, and was a big fan of Wilf Mannion.

if it was being played by the opposition.

"I remember two games in particular at Ayresome Park. The first was a match which Preston won 5-2 in 1951 and I scored a couple of goals. Middlesbrough had given a debut to a new full-back (Robert Corbett signed from Newcastle) who was marking me and he didn't have the best of games.

"The second was when Wilf Mannion returned to Ayresome Park after a spell out of the game in 1949 (Mannion had wanted to open a business in Oldham but a fee could not be negotiated) and received a hero's welcome.

"Wilf Mannion would be in my all-time greats team. He was an artist, the most complete inside-forward of his generation. He was tenacious, good in the air for his height and a shrewd passer of the ball. We formed a very productive partnership on the left wing for England and it was a real shame when he was seriously injured against Scotland in 1951 because I don't really feel he was the same player again.

"Yes I certainly have some favourable memories of Ayresome Park."

Liam Brady former Arsenal and Republic of Ireland midfield player

"Unfortunately for me I would have to say Ayresome Park is not one of my favourite grounds. I can remember as a youth team player losing an FA Youth Cup-tie against 'Boro when a certain Tony McAndrew was in the opposition.

"As my career progressed my luck did not seem to improve at Ayresome Park. I recall losing heavily 4-1 in the FA Cup in 1977 and David Mills scoring a hat-trick.

"However, my special memory is that Ayresome Park is the ground where I played my last game for Arsenal, before I left for Italy to sign for Juventus in May 1980. During the previous ten days we had lost in two Cup Finals, one against West Ham at Wembley and then on penalties to Valencia in the European Cup-winners' Cup. Going to Middlesbrough we needed to win to qualify for a UEFA Cup place. Once again we were on the receiving end of a very handsome victory for the home team by 5-0 and I recall Craig Johnston had a splendid match.

"So as you can see throughout my Arsenal career Ayresome Park was a rather unhappy ground for me."

Mark Page Riverside announcer

Goal Flash: D.J. Scores stunning hat-trick at Ayresome Park.

"It was my grandad, a one time Blyth Spartans goalkeeper who moved to Teesside in the 1930s, that I have to thank for my allegiance to the 'Boro. He used to take me to all the matches and I remember sitting in the same seats, D.95 and D.96, in the South Stand for years.

"One of the most exciting seasons at Ayresome Park was 1966-67 and the promotion from Division Three. I was attending Linthorpe Juniors and saw John Hickton make his debut at centre-half against Workington. John O'Rourke was the hero of the day and I used to sing 'Give us a goal John O'Rourke' morning, noon and night.

"The climax to the season was the

Mark Page, the Ayresome Park announcer during the 1990s and well-known local radio personality.

incredible 32,000 who came to watch us beat Peterborough with two goals from Big John and the man in the white coat from Wembley trying to conduct some community singing, followed a few days later by nearly 40,000 for the Oxford game to see us win 4-1 and go up. The ground just filled and filled that night, from out of the stands and on to the cinder track. It was the greatest spectacle I have ever witnessed.

"Next season I saw Eusébio play in a friendly against the 'Boro and my best mate Andy Gunn became the first club mascot. I remember being green with envy as he ran out on to the pitch and I never even got to be a ball-boy. In the 1960s, the half-time scores were put next to letters on pitch-side boards, so you needed a programme to work out the code. There was never quite the same effect as I can get now by announcing that either Sunderland or Newcastle, or preferably both, are losing.

"Suddenly, there were major technological advances at Ayresome Park with state of the art electronic score-board, sponsored by the *Gazette*, placed at opposite ends of the North Stand. Unfortunately a season or so later the bulbs started to go and eventually all the scores looked like L-L whatever the numbers were supposed to be.

"One of my greatest thrills has to be scoring a hat-trick on the hallowed turf of Ayresome Park. When attendances had reached an incredible low in the year before liquidation, I brought a Radio One team up to play a match. Three thousand people turned up to see us and despite spuds like Gary Davies being in the team I still managed to score three. Mind you it was against a Radio Cleveland side! Such happy memories."

The late Don Revie, manager of Leeds United and England 1961-77

Middlesbrough-born Don Revie was not only an outstanding manager with Leeds United but also had a successful playing career particularly with Sunderland and Manchester City. At the height of his managerial powers he was discussing the attributes of his team, players like Johnny Giles, Allan Clarke, Billy Bremner and Eddie Gray when he was asked about players from his own era that he admired. Without hesitation he named Middlesbrough's Wilf Mannion as his all-time favourite player.

"I only wish Wilf Mannion was playing today. He would walk into any team of mine. When he approached people with the ball to take them on, he used to remind me of a ballet dancer because he was so balanced in everything he did. He would go at defenders full pace and without even touching the ball he would sell so many dummies that the opposition would go in all directions and he'd run straight on with the ball.

"He could score goals, beat people, lay the ball off accurately, he had the lot. Whenever Wilf got the ball there was an expectant roar and he hardly ever let the crowd down. One match in particular at Ayresome Park when Middlesbrough beat Blackpool 4-0 said it all. Everyone in the ground gave him a standing ovation, even the entire opposition team lined up and clapped him off. You don't see that kind of individualism these days.

"I must have had 60 pictures of Wilf Mannion on my bedroom walls and I would have gladly swapped five or six of any other player to get one of him. Wilf would still be out on his own today, there was nothing he wasn't capable of doing."

Ron Atkinson, football manager and former Oxford United player

"My lasting memory of Ayresome Park occurred on 16 May 1967. I was captain of Oxford United and our last game of the season was against Middlesbrough, who needed to beat us to gain promotion to the Second Division.

"The one thing that sticks in my mind was the intensity of the crowd that evening. there must have been nearly 40,000 people in the ground that might with some of them sitting on the track around the pitch.

"I distinctly remember John O'Rourke scoring a hat-trick and what a very emotional evening it was for the Boro supporters.

"We also had a particularly marvellous time in the Fiesta Club in Stockton on the way home . . .!"

Steve Roberts Hemlington

Pylons in the sky

"My first memory of Ayresome Park was one of fascination. That big building with pylons reaching high into the sky that lit up my bedroom on winter afternoons. What was it all about?

"Brought up in Costa Street, close to the ground, I guess I had Middlesbrough FC in my blood right from the start, living with the hustle, bustle and noise on alternative Saturdays. The roar generated from the Holgate used to rattle the windows. I don't exactly recall my first game although it was watching the reserves and we were in a deserted Holgate End. My dad took me most Saturdays when the 'big' team played away. He perched me on the metal crash barriers right behind the goal for my first visits and as I got older, allowing me to retrieve the ball from the empty terracing. He also always bought me those freshly printed single-sheet programmes for one penny that had a distinctive smell. And I remember being puzzled by those letters on the terracing walls and the man putting numbers after them at half-time. An explanation didn't really enlighten me.

"My first floodlit game was a Youth Cup tie against local rivals Redcar Albion. At that match I was introduced to the smell of Oxo and the appearance of away supporters who made plenty of noise. My first league game at Ayresome Park was against Oxford in May 1967 and I'm sure everybody who attended that night has their own personal memories of a famous promotion-clinching match. I asked my dad if it was like this every time the 'big' team played. He didn't answer… He just stood there, transfixed, taking it all in. Now I know why."

Harry Green Former Middlesbrough Secretary

The signing of John Hickton

"In 1966/67 Middlesbrough were playing in Division Three for the first time in their history. The season didn't start too well with the team winning only one of their opening six games. It was obvious that some new blood was needed so when I received a phone call from 'Boro manager Stan Anderson one morning at 7.30am I wasn't surprised. Twenty minutes later we were on our way to Sheffield to try and sign John Hickton.

"When we arrived at Hillsborough we were met by the Wednesday manager Alan Brown who took us into his office to discuss a possible transfer. While we were talking, a knock at the door informed Mr Brown that Frank O'Farrell, the manager of Norwich City, was also there to see John Hickton. Brown left his office and it was obvious to us that the player was in demand.

"Ten minutes later Alan Brown returned to say that he had denied O'Farrell access to the player and that we would be the only ones allowed to speak to Hickton.

"The meeting with John Hickton was very amiable indeed and after discussing terms he agreed in principle to join Middlesbrough but informed us that the final decision would rest with his fiancée Rosemarie.

"As John left to drive to his home in Chesterfield we were taken to Alan Brown's home for lunch. When we arrived at the house Stan and I were escorted into the lounge from where we could see the dining table set out for two. Alan then took his wife into the kitchen for a chat and the table was reset for

For winning the Division Two title in 1973/74 Boro players shared a bonus fund of £25,000.

Former 'Boro secretary, Harry Green, first right, presents another trophy to fans' favourite John Hickton, a player he helped to sign.

three. Within five minutes Stan and I were called in for lunch, which was served by Mrs Brown. However, she did not join us so I can only assume that she was not forewarned of our arrival and we were eating her meal, which was all rather embarrassing.

"The following day John arrived in Middlesbrough with his fiancée, who was a beautiful young lady, to complete his transfer and the rest, as they say, is history. Not only did his performances help to revive the 1966/67 season and drive the 'Boro on towards promotion, but also he became one of the most popular 'Boro players of all time. I can honestly say that was one of the best pieces of business we did while I was secretary of the club."

Charles Hough
Wakefield

Enter Big John

"It was 1966 and Middlesbrough had been relegated to Division Three for the first time in their history. However, England had just won the World Cup so football was front-page news.

"At that time I was 14 and attended Bede Hall School in Billingham. I'd been going regularly to Ayresome Park with my friends on either the number 11 or 64 bus, which dropped us off at the Newport Bridge. The season started very badly and after six games it looked as though the 'Boro were heading straight for Division Four, never mind challenging for promotion. Then in late September manager Stan Anderson made an inspired signing prior to the home game with Workington Town.

"The match against the Cumbrians followed a similar pattern to the previous fixtures with the 'Boro going two goals behind in the first half. But just before half time they were awarded a penalty at the East End. As the players were low on confidence there didn't appear to be many volunteers willing to take the kick until a tall blond-haired lad calmly placed the ball on the spot, walked back for what seemed like miles, turned and smashed the ball past the keeper. John Hickton had announced his arrival at Ayresome Park.

"The rest of that season proved to be dramatic and being part of the Holgate End singing, 'Give us a goal John O'Rourke,' and 'David Chadwick, Alleluia, Alleluia' was amazing. It was a typical 'Boro rollercoaster ride with promotion only secured in the last game with a 4–1 victory over Oxford.

"Like many supporters of my generation that was the definitive season when my bond with the 'Boro was cemented and it will live long in the memory."

Alan Keen MP
House of Commons

Started badly and fell away

"I am sure we are all delighted with the statistics showing that in 2004 Middlesbrough's regular crowd contains a higher percentage of women than any other Premier League club. My first experience of tactics and teamwork on a match day took place a couple of hours before the Saturday afternoon kick-off – and it was at home in Grangetown. It was the two women of the house who were responsible. If only the football team in those days had been subject to the same preparation and planning! If Micky Fenton was half as quick as Grandad when he came home from the early morning shift at Dorman Long, changed out of his working boots, ate his dinner and dashed off to catch the 'trackless' to Doggy Market for the walk through Albert Park to the match, we would not have had to wait until 2004 to win something. It must have been the first season after the end of the war and I knew it must be something serious because we never moved anywhere near as fast on our way to the air-raid shelter in the back street when the siren went off! But it was a few years before I found out just how serious it really was.

"The suffering really started as soon as I was allowed to go to the games with pals rather than relatives. It was the 1950/51 season when we had been up with the league leaders until after Christmas before we faltered and Spurs ended as champions. I believe in the first game I saw we were three up against Burnley in the first half and could only get a draw. So my Ayresome experience followed the old football saying, "started badly and fell away". But there were so many moving memories. I was leaning against the wall immediately behind the goal to the Sunderland keeper's right when Lindy Delapenha's penalty slipped under the net and Kevin Howley gave a goal-kick. I stood regularly with that great character Astor and his friends half way up the embankment behind the goal at the 'Bob End' before he moved to the terrace in front of the North Stand. He always organised a 'forward sweep' for the first goal and I was still close enough to my Methodist roots to wonder if this counted as serious gambling.

"Late in the 1954 season I recall very clearly having to lean against a concrete support suffering from Asian flu and stupidly thinking I could not feel worse. But I was wrong again. We lost to Liverpool and slid into the second division. But I was there again at the first game the following season for the Plymouth match. A draw seemed disappointing but it turned out to be an excellent result when compared to losing the next eight games on the trot. At least there was the subsequent pleasure of watching Charlie Wayman getting the better of the great John Charles.

"I watched Cloughie score his five goals in the record 9–0 defeat of Brighton. It would not have been so bad had it not been the first game of the season, but I was there at the second home game when our hopes of promotion were dimmed by a nil–nil draw. And we complain nowadays when we fall away after Christmas! The hopes we had and the excitement of Eddie Holliday and Billy Day running at – and past – the opposing fullbacks. And the subsequent introduction of the twin centre-forward plan when Alan Peacock joined Cloughie and the goals flowed.

"There were many more disappointments to come, but all were extinguished at Ayresome Park that Tuesday night in May 1967. That exhilarating game when we won promotion by beating Oxford United 4–1. A win that brought promotion and success to Stan Anderson and the building of a great squad of players that eventually took us back to the top division under Big Jack. It was my first season working for the club and I recall talking to Stan outside the dressing room at Peterborough with six games left and discussing how, if only we had won that game and this game earlier in the season we could have been in with a chance of promotion. I remember, very well, someone passing and shouting a greeting as we were chatting. He sympathised with Stan on the disappointing season. Stan replied, "Aye, we started badly - and fell away!" But this time we were not finished, were we? That's why, "We love you 'Boro" – and we always will."

Sheila Middleton
Norton

Shoulder high

"The first match I saw at Ayresome Park was 'Boro v Blackpool in 1947. My sister had just been born and I think my father, a lifelong 'Boro supporter, had begun to realise that there was a distinct possibility he might never have a son to take to the game.

"I'd watched him many times getting ready to go to the match and had constantly pestered him to take me, until he finally relented.

"Walking down Ayresome Street to the ground I was so excited and could hardly wait to see my hero 'Golden Boy' Wilf Mannion. To make my special day complete 'Boro won 4–0 and from that day I never let my father go to the match without me.

"In those days it was like being part of one big happy family at Ayresome Park and being a girl I was spoilt rotten. I was often lifted shoulder high down to the front of the crowd for a better view and at half-time I enjoyed a hot drink and a pie with my dad and his friends.

"As I grew older the anticipation before a match never diminished and the thought of watching Wilf Mannion play, even now, makes me feel quite emotional.

"As the years went by, I graduated to watching from the stand and never missed a home game until I was married and went to live in America. Even then I still kept in touch with the 'Boro because my dad rang me every week with the result. When I returned to England I began saving 'Boro memorabilia and built up an extensive collection.

"Later, I was fortunate to meet my childhood hero, Wilf Mannion, many times and even presented him with a programme montage of some of the games in which he played.

"Like most supporters of my generation who grew up with Ayresome Park, I was disappointed when Middlesbrough left the old ground but I understood the reasons. In fact I think the Riverside Stadium is great, particularly for families. But I can still remember proudly walking to the match with my dad to see my team and being passed shoulder high down to the front of the terracing to watch Wilf Mannion. It's a feeling that was an important part of my life and can never be replaced."

Julie Wood
Guisborough

Don't you touch my Willie!

"Some of my favourite memories of Ayresome Park are the quips from the crowd directed towards the players.

"In the early 1990s, during a particularly uninspiring match, the shout went up, "Get stuck in Slaven, your shorts are cleaner than when you came on!"

"Another example occurred when blond winger Stuart Ripley was about to take a throw in near us. As he walked towards the touchline he appeared to be limping slightly, but that cut no ice with somebody behind me who yelled out, "It can't be cramp Rippers, you've done nowt." Whoever passed the comment was rewarded with a discreet single finger gestured response from the 'Boro forward.

"And during Falconer's stay at the 'Boro an unintentional comment from a female fan set all the supporters laughing when following a heavy tackle on the Scot a high voice piped up, "Don't you touch my Willie!""

'Boro were relegated from Division One in 1927/28 with the highest number of points (37) ever recorded by any relegated club under the old two points for a win system.

Harry Greenmon
Normanby

No penalties for Cloughie

"At the start of the 1958/59 season I went to my first 'Boro match against Brighton and Hove Albion. My father took me to the Boys' End turnstile and told me to meet him at the left-hand corner of the enclosure once I was inside. This I duly did and he lifted me over the wall. I will always remember as I entered the ground my first sight of the famous Ayresome Park pitch, I couldn't believe how green and immaculate it was.

"The match, which I watched from behind the Bob End goal, resulted in a memorable 9–0 record victory for the 'Boro with five goals from Brian Clough and two apiece from Alan Peacock and one of my all time favourites, Bill Harris. What an introduction to supporting the

Willie Falconer, back row third right, Stuart Ripley, middle row third right, and Bernie Slaven, front row second right, with the 'Boro squad of 1991/92, were all recipients of good-natured banter from the terraces.

In 1973 senior 'Boro players were earning £150 per week.

'Boro. I thought it was going to be like that every week! Harris's two goals came from the penalties and at the time I wondered why such a prolific goalscorer as Brian Clough didn't take spot kicks. It didn't take me long to realise that while Cloughie was brilliant at striking a moving ball he was hopeless at kicking a stationary one. Makes you wonder how many goals he would have scored if he'd taken the penalties.

"Welsh international Bill Harris was, in my opinion, one of the 'Boro's most underrated players, who did not gain the recognition he deserved. Many of the goals scored by Clough and Peacock during their Ayresome Park careers were created by the slide rule passing ability of Bill Harris.

"At a 'Boro Legends dinner a few years ago one of Harris's contemporaries was asked if the current 'Boro midfield players were as good as the Welshman. Taking his time before giving a considered response, he replied, "They probably are, but then Bill did pass away 10 years ago!"

Former 'Boro manager Jack Charlton's first club car was a basic Austin 1300 Countryman. Following promotion to Division One in 1974 it was upgraded to a Range Rover.

Alison Sigsworth
Coulby Newham

A smacker from Gazza

"My brother took me to my first 'Boro game at Ayresome Park, which was against Newcastle reserves in the late 1980s. I stood by the big red gates with my new autograph book collecting the players' signatures and even succeeded in getting a kiss from a Geordie!

"For the next few weeks I'd often ask my brother, "Which one kissed me again?" "Paul Gascoigne" he'd reply, but I had no idea who he was at the time. (To this day I still think it was that kiss which made him famous!)

"From then on I became a regular. "Half past two at the Yellow Rose" my brother would say. I was always on time, but he never was. Sometimes his mates would turn up and say, "Your brother's asked me to take you to the match he's running late." Other times he would collect me, get us both a "squeeze" at the Holgate End and then keep my £3.50!

"The atmosphere was always buzzing in the Holgate. I stood in the walkway behind the goal. Whenever we scored the players and the fans would jump up on either side of the metal fence to celebrate together. In fact I was once caught on TV hugging Bernie Slaven after he'd scored.

"The team from the 1980s was mainly home-grown talent. It was a daily occurrence to see the players either driving round town, in church or at the local Spar shopping. When I think of "my" 'Boro I think of players like Pears, Parky, Coops, Mogga, Hamilton, Pally, Slaven, Ripley and Kerr.

"One of the games I remember most was in 1990 when we beat Leicester 6–0. The Holgate fans were ringing out the chants of, "We want four," "We want five," "We want six," every time we scored another goal.

"In 1990 'Boro made history and reached their first Wembley final in the Zenith Data Systems Cup and I queued for hours to get tickets. The queue zig-zagged around Middlesbrough General Hospital car park about 10 times and my knuckles were white from holding on tightly to my vouchers. After what seemed like an eternity, we eventually reached the ticket office. As we approached the kiosk the stewards counted about 15 people behind me and said, "Sorry, that's the lot, they've all gone." Phew!!"

John Sowerby
Coulby Newham

Graduating from the reserves

"My grandfather first took me to Ayresome Park in the early 1950s to watch 'Boro Reserves in the old North Eastern League. The league provided a tough senior baptism for future 'Boro stars such as Brian Clough and Alan Peacock, who knew they'd been in a hard game after playing against some of the physical local colliery welfare sides.

"In those days even the reserve games attracted a few thousand Holgate spectators, most of whom had one eye on the game and the other on the large Bob End score box, which kept us informed about the first team's progress in their away match.

"By the end of the 1954/55 season I'd served my apprenticeship and was allowed to attend my first senior game against Port Vale. This time we stood in the Kensington Road corner of the East End. I remember vividly sitting on top of one of the large concrete barriers watching the 'Boro win 2–0 with goals from Lindy Delapenha and Charlie Wayman. Those two players, along with Ugolini, Robinson, Dicks, Harris and Fitzsimons, became my instant heroes and from that moment on I became totally enthralled by the 'Boro."

Gary Bolton
Guisborough

Sights, sounds and smells

"While 'Boro players, matches and seasons came and went the one constant in football life was Ayresome Park. The ground had one of the best pitches in the country and the lush green grass under floodlights produced an awe-inspiring sight for a youngster like myself.

"Various sights, sounds and smells all contributed to the match day experience. Passing the dressing rooms tucked underneath the North Stand the strong aroma of liniment wafted through the open windows. The North Stand, where according to the clock, time literally stood still, also had electronic score-boards. However, the bulbs never seemed to work properly which led to some bizarre half-time scores such as 8–6! A tiny box in the South Terrace housed the match announcer, Bernard Gent, whose tannoy would crackle into life at 2.30 with the amiable greeting, "Welcome to Radio Ayresome" accompanied by the signature tune *The Hustle*.

"The appearance of a stray dog on the hallowed turf was seemingly the norm

'Boro's England international winger, Eddie Holliday, right, in action in 1959. Clearly visible in the background is the giant East End scoreboard, fondly remembered by many Ayresome Park fans.

Harry Bell, front row first right, was not only a reliable wing-half from 1946 to 1955 but also a highly talented professional cricketer.

and energetic attempts by the players and officials to capture the intruder were often the highlights of the afternoon.

"At the Holgate End we all had our own square foot of terrace to stand on. However, by the mid-1980s only the diehards remained and there was so much space we all had our own barrier to lean on.

"Although it was old fashioned, the ground had great character and atmosphere. It's a decade since we left but it seems light years away. Thank goodness for our Ayresome Park memories."

Tony Elliott
Marton

Who's the referee?

"My earliest memory of Ayresome Park was straight after World War Two when a crowd of 40,000 plus for a big game was the norm. I remember the supporters, particularly those shoe-horned into the East End, would sway alarmingly from side to side in order to see the action.

"Another one of my initial recollections was when 'Boro keeper Dave Cumming knocked out Leslie Compton of Arsenal in a goalmouth mêlée. Then, before the inevitable sending off decision was even made, he removed his woollen jersey and walked to the touchline.

"The players I grew up with were Wilf Mannion, certainly the best forward I ever saw, closely followed by England captain George Hardwick, the reliable Harry Bell, who was also a fine cricketer scoring five centuries in a season for Middlesbrough and Lindy Delapenha, who possessed one of the hardest shots in football.

"Later in the 1950s I also remember watching Huddersfield's Denis Law and thinking what a fine player he was.

"The humour on the terraces was often worth the entrance money alone, particularly if it was a poor game. One of my favourite lines was when a fan asked, "Who's the referee?" The reply came straight back, "The fella in the black." And local comedian, Astor, could always be relied upon for a wisecrack especially when encouraging 'Boro's Jamaican-born forward Delapenha by calling out, "Come on our kid.""

Ron Redshaw
Teesville

Step on board the roller coaster

"Like most people of my generation I was hooked on the 'Boro when they were relegated to Division Three for the first time in their history in 1966. As a 15-year-old who had just started work, my rollercoaster ride as a 'Boro fan had begun. Gone were the days of being in the Boys' End and climbing over the wall when nobody was watching. I became an Ayresome Angel in the Holgate End. My first hero moved from defence to attack and there was no finer sight than Big John Hickton charging down the wing and then burying the ball in the back of the opposition's net. Or watching him take his 110-yard run up before dispatching a penalty past a shell-shocked keeper.

"For me personally there were so many great memories of Ayresome Park, starting with the promotion party against Oxford in May 1967. Then beating QPR 6–2 after being two down, demolishing Sheffield Wednesday 8–0 under the guidance of Jack Charlton and watching the best uncapped player in England, Willie Maddren. Also wondering how on earth the club nearly ceased to exist in the 1980s before it rose from the ashes of liquidation, thanks mainly to Steve Gibson, to regain its Premier League status in the last season at Ayresome Park under Bryan Robson. A fitting epitaph.

"The old ground may be gone but it's certainly not forgotten."

Bill Smith
Acklam

In praise of Bill Harris

"One of my favourite players of the 1950s–60s was Bill Harris. He was signed from Hull City in March 1954 to replace another fine servant, Jimmy Gordon. However, he couldn't prevent us from being relegated from Division One. Harris was not renowned as a midfield battler but he possessed wonderful skill and was an elegant passer of the ball from right-half. At the 'Boro his consistent performances were rewarded with six international caps for Wales. Eventually he was moved up to inside-forward, forming a good partnership with another player I admired, Arthur Fitzsimons. Bill Harris played over 375 games for Middlesbrough but I feel his attributes were never fully appreciated by the club's supporters."

Ian Clennitt
Ingleby Barwick

Mogga's TV Special

"It was St Valentine's Day 1988 and 'Boro's first live TV appearance against high-flying Aston Villa. Due to cup replays against Sutton and Everton, 'Boro had fallen behind in the Division Two promotion race and a home win from this difficult fixture was vital if they were to stay in contention.

"The game started badly when Gary Thompson put Villa ahead in the first half and at that point you couldn't really see the 'Boro getting back into the game. Then 10 minutes from the end substitute Alan Kernaghan grabbed an equaliser and the subdued atmosphere in the Holgate was suddenly transformed as 'Boro began to pile forward in search of the winner. It wasn't long in coming and

Former 'Boro director, Jack Hatfield, front row fourth left, pictured with the 'Boro squad of 1973, can trace his family's connection to the club right back to 1912.

that superb goal remains my abiding memory of Ayresome Park. With about five minutes to go a cross came into the box and Tony Mowbray athletically launched himself full length to powerfully head the ball past the stranded keeper. The Holgate End, including me, went wild. What a fantastic way to win a match in front of a live TV audience."

In 'Boro's Division Two championship-winning season of 1973/74 the most expensive season ticket was £14!

Jack Hatfield
Ingleby Greenhow

Family connections

"The Hatfield family association with Middlesbrough FC began when my father opened his first sportswear shop in 1912. From then on we supplied kit and equipment to the 'Boro for nearly 75 years. Over the years every 'Boro legend including Camsell, Mannion, Hardwick, Clough and Hickton must have visited our shops in Newton Street and Borough Road armed with their official club chits for new boots and shin pads. In 1966 we even had representatives of the North Korean World Cup party buying up 50 footballs because they were in short supply back home.

"Eventually, following a long association with the club, my father was invited to join the board in 1952 and he served as a diligent director until the mid-1960s.

"My own first memory of Ayresome Park was prior to World War Two when, as an impressionable youngster, I used to stand in the living room of my grandparents' house in Ayresome Street and watch the sea of people walking to the match, and hope that one day I might join them.

"I finally joined the masses in 1946 when I stood in the south-west corner of the ground and watched 'Boro legends Wilf Mannion, George Hardwick, Mick Fenton, Bobby Stuart, Dave Cumming and Jimmy Gordon beat Leeds 3–0.

"Unfortunately, as more of my time was devoted to the family business, attending matches became more difficult, but I remained an avid supporter and was devastated in 1966 when we were relegated to Division Three for the first time in our history.

"By 1972/73 changes were being made in the Ayresome Park boardroom and I was invited to follow in my father's footsteps and become a director. Initially, although I was very flattered by the invitation, I had serious reservations because of my business commitments. However, after positive encouragement from my brothers I accepted the kind offer.

"My early years spent on the board of Middlesbrough FC were some of the happiest of my life. Granted it coincided with the relatively successful Jack Charlton and John Neal eras but as a representative of the club I was privileged to meet so many interesting people. I visited all the leading grounds in the country and toured Australia and Asia where we made many friends and enhanced the reputation of the club by winning a prestigious international tournament in Japan.

"Also during that period I got a great deal of satisfaction from seeing local lads like Willie Maddren and David Mills do well. It was a shame that neither of them made full international appearances.

"Much has been written in other publications about the club in the 1970s and its sad demise when I left the board in the mid-1980s. The only comments I will make about individuals are to say that I thought Harold Shepherdson's overall contribution to Middlesbrough FC was immense, both as an ambassador and officer of the club. And that former chairman Charles Amer never really got the credit he deserved for ensuring the World Cup came to Ayresome Park in 1966 and that Middlesbrough were a competitive club throughout the 1970s.

"All in all I have some wonderful memories of Ayresome Park both as a supporter and director and I can honestly say that the Hatfield family were proud to have such a long association with Middlesbrough FC."

John Culley
Coulby Newham

Running the line

"How do you fall in love with concrete, steel (most of it rusty) and grass? I don't know. But like thousands of Teessiders before me, I just did. It seemed that Ayresome Park had always been there, the spiritual home of the 'Boro fan. It just felt right to be there. Even in the bad times you were drawn to the ground by some magnetic force every other week.

"In the summer, when there was no football, I have to confess that every now and again, I'd go down to the ground, walk in, look at the grass, and walk out again, just to check it was still there.

"Then when it closed it was like part of the family had passed away.

"In 1995 I was a local referee when I received a call from the Premier League official and staunch 'Boro fan, Jeff Winter, asking me if I'd run the line for him at Stephen Pears's testimonial match. My prayers had been answered. To be asked to officiate at the ground's last game when the Division One Championship trophy was being presented, well I'd have run through Albert Park on broken glass for the privilege.

"Official confirmation of my appointment arrived in the post from the club – still treasured – plus tickets for the 100 Club and an underground car park pass.

"When I saw the words 'underground car park pass' it set me thinking. Surely deep in the bowels of Ayresome Park there must be some discarded item I could keep as a memento of the old ground.

"On the night of the game I arrived three hours early with my son Chris, who was a ball boy that season. Once in the

Memorabilia from Ayresome Park was much sought after by supporters. The sign from the North Stand eventually resided in a local pub of the same name.

ground I saw what I was looking for. Against a wall, in among a haphazard pile of old goalposts and a groundsman's line marking machine, I could see the corner of a wooden board. Chris, who felt like disowning me as I ferreted away, helped to lever up a crossbar so I could pull it out. As I rubbed away the years of accumulated dirt and grime a three foot square red and white sign was revealed stating, 'North Stand Seats.'

"When I eventually walked in to the referee's room, covered from head to toe in dust and lime, Jeff Winter remarked, "You look more like a ragman than a linesman." But I didn't care, I had my little piece of Ayresome Park history."

Neil Robinson
Ingleby Barwick

Trapped with the opposition

"Before moving to Teesside my family were originally from Halifax. However, in 1989 I experienced the ultimate nightmare when 'Boro were drawn against my home town club in the league cup.

"The minute the draw was made I knew I was in trouble. The pressure, particularly from my father, to support Halifax Town and disown the 'Boro began to build. My dad really took the game seriously, going so far as sending the Halifax manager, Billy Ayre, a scouting report of what he perceived to be the 'Boro's strengths and weaknesses. Whether the Town boss ever read the letter I don't know, but it was certainly never acknowledged.

"Anyway, after much gentle persuasion, but ultimately for the sake of a quiet life, I decided to join my father in the Ayresome Park away end and what a strange experience it was. I felt like an intruder who'd gate-crashed a party as I was penned inside my own ground with about 600 Halifax supporters. I didn't want to be there, and to be the butt of the home chanting, "What's it like to see a crowd," etc was not a pleasant feeling.

"The game itself was a stroll for the 'Boro, who won 4–0 with two goals from Bernie Slaven and one apiece for Alan Comfort and Alan Kernaghan. But one of the worst things about standing with the away support was that I had no emotional release. As each goal hit the net I had to stand there impassively and show no emotion, while inwardly cheering and chanting to myself, "We want five." What a feat of self-control!

"After the final whistle it was also strange to find myself being kept in the away enclosure while the home support left and then being escorted from the ground surrounded by a police cordon.

"Since that game Halifax have unfortunately lost their league status and now play in the Conference. However, that doesn't stop me following their FA Cup progress hoping they don't reach round three and I have to go through the same charade again."

John Watts
Thorntree

Where's Stuart Boam?

"For eight years, from 1968–76, I was Middlesbrough FC's coach driver. From a personal point of view it was a great privilege to work for the team I'd always supported.

"At that time the well-known local coach firm, Bee Line, employed me and in 1974 when Middlesbrough won the Division Two title I drove the players' bus through the centre of town during the promotion celebrations. What a day that was, with people crowding the streets and hanging out of every vantage point on Linthorpe and Corporation Roads to cheer the achievements of Jack Charlton's champions.

In April 1969 a 'Boro scouting report noted, "Stuart Boam of Mansfield is not up to Division Two standard." Oops. Good job they took a second opinion.

Popular former 'Boro captain, Stuart Boam, was unintentionally left stranded on the M1.

A generation of supporters vividly remember this 1966/67 promotion winning team. Back row: Don Masson, Ray Lugg, John Hickton, Des McPartland, Willie Whigham, Arthur Horsfield, Jim Irvine, Dickie Rooks, Bill Gates. Front row: David Chadwick, Billy Horner, Geoff Butler, Gordon Jones (capt), Jimmy Lawson, Derrick Downing, John O'Rourke.

"But of all the memories I have from that period, and there were many, the one that sticks in my mind the most involved 'Boro skipper Stuart Boam.

"Stuart was signed from Mansfield and periodically he would return home to visit his relatives. On one particular occasion we were playing away at Leicester and it was decided that in order to save time we would pick him up on the M1 at the main Mansfield junction. It should have been no problem, up the slip lane and down the other side.

"On the day of the match everything was going well until we pulled into Filbert Street and the 'Boro trainer Jimmy Headridge (a smashing fella) said, "Where's Stuart Boam?" "Oh dear," (or colourful words to that effect) I replied, "We've forgotten to pick him up." There was great hilarity from all the other players on the bus when they realised what had happened and I certainly came in for a bit of stick.

"With no mobile phones in those days we had no way of contacting Boamy so we just had to hope that he'd somehow make his own way to Leicester.

"Eventually he arrived by car, not, you understand, in the best of humour. Apparently he'd seen us drive by from the flyover and thought we were just having a laugh.

"In fact I had visions of him frantically waving his arms at us as he ran down the slip road in a vain attempt to attract our attention.

"How embarrassing, leaving the skipper high and dry. All I could do was apologise. But in my defence I wasn't the only one who forgot about him, everybody on the bus did. Anyway he got his own back during the championship dinner held at the Ladle because he reminded everybody about my forgetfulness in his captain's speech.

"Needless to say we never made those arrangements again."

Harry Green
Former Middlesbrough Secretary

The Brian Clough transfer

"Over the years a great deal has been written and spoken regarding Brian Clough's transfer from Middlesbrough in the summer of 1961. Much of it, I have to say, was without foundation. The facts about his departure from Ayresome Park are really quite straightforward.

"In accordance with Football League and Football Association rules at the time, Clough was offered a new contract at Ayresome Park in May 1961. Without discussing the terms, the player informed the club that he would not be playing for the 'Boro again.

"The board took him at his word and instructed me to circulate Clough's availability to all clubs in the top two divisions and say that they were open to

Brian Clough, whose "confident personality caused dressing room unrest".

offers. Despite scoring over 200 goals in his 'Boro career, three weeks passed by without a solitary enquiry being received!

"At the next board meeting the chairman, Mr W.S. Gibson, informed the directors that a tentative enquiry had been received from Sunderland, and that he proposed to invite members of the Roker Park board to lunch at the Corporation Hotel to discuss their interest further. Prior to the meeting no other enquiries had been received so a deal was struck to transfer Clough for £45,000, with £25,000 down and the balance payable in December.

"A couple of days later Brian Clough came to see me in my office to tie up the loose ends of his transfer and I asked him straight why he wanted to move, particularly as the maximum wage had been abolished. He replied that he'd said many times in the press that he would go and he could not go back on his words now.

"At the time there were reports in the press that a famous Italian club wanted to sign him but when I phoned the club in question they replied, "Who is Brian Clough?"

"During his 'Boro career there is no doubt that Cloughie was an outstanding goalscorer but his confident personality caused dressing room unrest. It's very interesting to note that despite his playing attributes, the *only* offer received for his services was from Sunderland. I wonder why?"

Robert Nichols
Ayresome Park Estate

Big John an Ayresome Hero

"When we were all kids everyone wanted to be John Hickton. You had to be someone as you strode purposefully about the makeshift pitch in the park, before lamping the ball imperiously between the two jumper goalposts and Big John was first on every kid's wish list. You could forget Geoff Hurst, our hero was no TV zero he was up there with the big screen idols, he was Middlesbrough's John Wayne.

"My first memory of Ayresome is hazy but I do recall the shock of seeing John Hickton's name omitted from the teamsheet. Surely some mistake? It was a cold day, peering out through the pipe tobacco smoke across the biggest subbuteo green pitch I'd ever seen. It was all exciting apart from the score line, we were soon 1–0 down. Time to call on a substitute. "Come on Big John," cried a woman in front and like the gun-slinging superstar he was he duly obliged, driving straight through the opposition defence before despatching a finish like a missile into the corner. Deadly.

"What seemed like a football generation later, Big John became a playground hero all over again when his two cannonball penalties blasted Sunderland out of the FA Cup. The blue and black kit (why did we wear our away shirts at home?), the run up that started in the General Hospital car park, and the rocket shots were re-enacted time and time again around Teesside.

"Years later, memories such as these and a hundred images of the bravest of brave centre-forwards brushing off defenders like flies before charging for goal, caused me to queue up for a signed testimonial programme. It was a long queue, to one of those windows in the Ayresome Park Road ticket office, but at the end of it was our hero. I was more than a bit nervous as I drew closer and closer. I still remember the handshake, the two rings J and H and the beaming smile. John Hickton, a real Ayresome hero. And of course he scored a hat-trick in his testimonial, but we knew he would anyway."

Leaving for good? 'Boro's players collect their personal belongings from Ayresome Park before the gates are locked. Pictured foreground, left to right, are Gary Hamilton, Stuart Ripley, Gary Gill, Gary Parkinson and Gary Pallister.

'Boro in the Melting Pot

THE 92-year history of Ayresome Park was only minutes away from becoming an 83-year history. If the events of the summer of 1986 had taken a different turn, then professional football on Teesside would have come to a full stop. It would have been all over for Middlesbrough Football Club.

When the liquidator moved in, at the end of May, 'Boro were in a very sorry state. In fact things were much worse than could have been imagined. And 'Boro seemed to have few influential friends just when they needed them most.

The club had reached the brink as the result of four or five years of financial decline, allied to dwindling support and a struggling team. The financial problems had been greatly exacerbated by the building of the adjoining sports hall.

On the face of it, the sports hall should have been a club asset. But building started at the wrong time, especially as the major problems which developed in the sports hall proved a great strain on the club's finances and created a great white elephant which was a millstone around 'Boro's neck.

However, the sports hall was only the final nail in the coffin. When work first started on the building, 'Boro were a respected First Division outfit with valuable players and decent crowds.

It all started to go wrong at the birth of the 1980s, when the team began to break up. Quality players were allowed to leave and the money was virtually thrown away on a series of dreadful buys. As a result, 'Boro were relegated to the Second Division, and the fans deserted in droves, disillusioned by the poor standard of football and the club's apparent lack of ambition.

By the time that experienced boss Malcolm Allison took over the hot seat at the end of 1982, the club was already operating within severe financial restraints. Allison faced a long and odious task trying to turn things around without a massive cash injection. But time was not on his side.

Willie Maddren, one of 'Boro's great stalwarts from the 1970s, followed Allison into the manager's chair and went on to make several sensible buys within the tight restrictions of the club's budget. But it only seemed to be papering over the cracks, and 'Boro were struggling to stay in the Second Division as the crowds dipped dramatically to under 5,000.

In February 1986, when Bruce Rioch took over the helm, the club was approaching its lowest ebb. Relegation was a probability, and the low income from

The pressure in on. Provisional liquidator, Tony Richmond (left) meets Save The 'Boro Fund co-ordinator, Councillor Edmund Pearson, as the battle starts in earnest to try to save the club from oblivion.

meagre crowds was threatening to send 'Boro into oblivion. Rioch pitched in a few kids, and the team showed some fight in the closing weeks of the season as they battled to halt the slide.

However, a 2-1 defeat at Shrewsbury on the final day of the season sent 'Boro into the Third Division. It must have seemed to the fans that things couldn't get any worse. But they did.

The club was in crisis. The directors, well aware that they were dealing with a potential disaster, knew that drastic action was needed. There were several options, none of them guaranteed to bring any success. One was

The Dagenham Girl Pipers played at the Theatre Royal in Middlesbrough on 28 November 1949, and invited all the 'Boro players to attend the performance.

Peter Beagrie shows his aerial power when getting in a header in this home game against Barnsley. He is pictured alongside defender Don O'Riordan. Both players were to leave the club during the upheaval of 1986.

to go into voluntary liquidation and then build a new club from the ashes. This had already been achieved elsewhere in the Football League, notably by Bristol City.

Alf Duffield, the outspoken but committed chairman, had put a lot of his own money into the club to keep 'Boro afloat in the previous 12 months. However, for business reasons, Duffield handed in his resignation in the April. Duffield was having problems with his business interests in the oil industry.

His place at the helm was taken by 26-year-old Steve Gibson, a self-made businessman from the Park End area of Middlesbrough whose Bulkhaul company transported container vessels. Gibson had earlier been brought on to the board by Duffield.

Gibson consulted his solicitors for the best course of action. His first move was to ask the remaining 'Boro directors to grant him full executive powers to run the club. This was granted. Gibson said: "My next move was to dismiss the rest of the board."

Former chairman Duffield still promised to be a knight in shining armour. He petitioned in the High Court to wind up the club, and a date for the hearing was set for 30 June. It was still possible that the club might be allowed to die, and then resurrect itself.

However, the Football League had already decided to stamp down on this method of survival, after having attracted a lot of bad publicity from angry creditors elsewhere. They felt that this method of survival gave football a bad name, especially as the creditors of liquidated clubs received only a small percentage of the money they were owed, and then had to suffer the frustration of seeing the football club rise again and carry on trading as if nothing had happened. So the League slapped a ban on clubs being run by reformed companies.

In May 1950, 'Boro offered a certain Bobby Robson from Langley Park Juniors £4 a week to join the club as a part-time professional. Robson, 17, was already on amateur forms with the club. But the future England manager turned them down.

Even so, there were few alternatives at Ayresome Park. At the end of May, a provisional liquidator was appointed. He was Tony Richmond, from Peat Marwick McLintock, a firm of chartered accountants. Richmond's first and immediate task was to put the club up for sale. An advertisement was placed in the *Financial Times* on 3 June.

Estimates of 'Boro's debts varied, although at the time they were reckoned to be around £1.8 million. The debts included £605,000 owed to the Midland Bank, £120,000 to former chairman Charles Amer, £170,000 for ground improvements and the sports centre, £90,000 to Camerons Brewery, £595,000 to Alf Duffield, £200,000 for a Securities Pacific loan backed by Duffield's company ITM's shares, and £94,000 to Cleveland County Council for policing Ayresome Park rising to £102,500 with interest.

Richmond was looking to bring in whatever cash he could. He said: "I haven't got an asking price. I will be open to offers. I am inviting offers for the ground and all the staff at the moment because it's possible that the sports centre and Hutton Road training ground can be sold separately."

Unfortunately there was a very poor response to the advertisement in the *Financial Times*. There were ten enquiries, of which only three were prepared to follow up their initial enquiry. Within a matter of days this was down to one. It was not a very promising situation, to put it mildly.

The media began to look for saviours from elsewhere. Rock star Rod Stewart, who had indicated that he might be interested in taking over a football club, was linked with 'Boro. But the rumour was denied by Annie Challis, his publicity agent.

The main source of hope seemed to lie at home in Teesside. Edmund Pearson, a local businessman and councillor, and a keen 'Boro fan, launched the Save The 'Boro Fund. He opened a bank account at the Yorkshire Bank, and asked fans to commit themselves to whatever they could afford to help prevent the club from dying.

Pearson's plan was that the cash should be exchanged for shares when, and if, 'Boro were saved. Hundreds of fans pledged their support, and a balance of £20,000 was quickly reached.

But it was a long way short of what 'Boro needed, and the best chance of survival seemed to lie with Gibson. He had already financed a viability study to show that 'Boro could be run at a profit in the Third Division with crowds of 6,000.

However, at this stage, 'Boro's battle for survival looked hopeless. Even Gibson's legal advisors had recommended that his best possible move was one of non-involvement. Steve said: "They had told me to get out at the very start. But I couldn't do that. I felt that I needed to give it my best shot."

Top shareholder... Henry Moszkowicz invested £300,000 into Ayresome Park to save the club from going to the wall.

Gibson's plan was to put together a consortium to save the club, and his first move was to approach Middlesbrough Council through chief executive John Foster and council leader Mike Carr, who was Gibson's former schoolteacher.

Steve said: "The council said that they would come in, and fortunately they had contacts at ICI, so we were able to approach them, and they were interested because they didn't want the club to die. Then disc jockey Mark Page introduced me to Graham Fordy from Scottish and Newcastle Breweries and they were keen as well.

The next step was to place an advert in *The Times* looking for more support. We got Henry Moszkowicz out of that. All we knew at first was that he was a businessman in London who was a 'Boro fan. I went to meet him at Heathrow and he wrote out a cheque for

£200,000 as soon as we started talking. That gave us five members for the consortium."

At this stage the consortium had not made themselves public, although they had begun talks with Tony Richmond and were planning to have discussions with the major creditors.

At the end of June, 'Boro were given more breathing space when Alf Duffield asked for a two-week adjournment of his High Court winding-up order. Hopefully it would give the consortium time to come up with a survival package which was satisfactory to the provisional liquidator.

Even so, Richmond held a press conference to announce that the consortium was still 'miles short' of putting together a package which might be acceptable to the creditors. He said that if a solution was not found by 14 July, which was the High Court deadline, then the staff and players at Ayresome Park faced redundancy.

Richmond stressed that 'Boro's plight stemmed from the club's lack of playing success. He said: "Whether that means the wrong players were sold and the right players not bought is too intricate for me. However, very large amounts were spent voluntarily which the club could not afford, and in that I am also thinking of the sports centre."

Later, Richmond revealed that five members of the consortium had given him letters of intent, though he was still not in a position to give individual names. In addition, Scarborough millionaire Don Robinson, who was chairman of Hull City, had also inquired about the details of 'Boro's financial situation.

From the fans' point of view, they were being given little indication that anything positive was happening. It seemed a lost cause. The players, too, had good reason to be worried. They were behind with their wages and did not know if the club had a future.

Winger Peter Beagrie, whose contract was up, started to talk to other clubs. Physiotherapist Steve Smelt officially handed in his resignation and joined up with Lawrie McMenemy at Sunderland. Smelt said: "It was a difficult decision to make because of the time I had enjoyed at Middlesbrough. But with all the uncertainty hanging over the club and with a wife and four children at home, I couldn't afford to wait."

At this time, the make up of the consortium was starting to become public. Middlesbrough Council announced that they were prepared to pump £200,000 into the club, and Scottish and Newcastle Breweries pledged the same amount.

On 14 July, in the High Court, the club was handed another two weeks' reprieve. Soon afterwards ICI revealed that they had also met the £200,000 asking price and would be joining the consortium. Their representative was to be Colin Henderson, who was a former head of ICI's petrol producing works at Wilton and who now concentrated specifically on special projects.

Within 48 hours the consortium held a press conference, when Henry Moszkowicz was revealed as the fifth mystery member. It was a time for hope, though the consortium still faced a very rocky road ahead to deal with the creditors, the Football League and the provisional liquidator.

At the time the consortium had around £900,000 on the table, with four members providing £200,000 and Gibson £100,000 through his Bulkhaul company.

Richmond said that he thought the consortium could be in business if Duffield would agree to accept an offer of just £120,000 in full settlement of the monies owed to him. Duffield had already rejected the offer. The consortium were continuing negotiations with the other major creditors and remained confident, provided they could deal with the Football League, who were still adamant that all creditors must be paid in full.

The provisional liquidator informed the Press that the consortium was willing to make the £900,000 available only if: "The club carried no old debt; none of the past directors other than Steve Gibson should take part in the club's future management and that the club should be run on a proper business basis providing a community facility."

Meanwhile 'Boro's bemused players reported back for official training on 17 July. They were led by manager Bruce Rioch and first-team coach Colin Todd, both of whom had continued to maintain a positive stance throughout the troubles.

The returning squad included three players – Peter Beagrie, Archie Stephens and Brian Laws – who had taken the club to a Football League tribunal for alleged breach of contact. The trio had argued that they were entitled to free transfers.

The tribunal had agreed that 'Boro were indeed in breach of the players' contracts, but delayed announcing their final decision. The delay was to prove crucial because, although Beagrie eventually moved on, 'Boro were able to hang on to the other two players.

By this time the consortium had rubber stamped their determination to save the club by paying the players' wages. But it was still a very difficult time for the playing staff, especially as they were being fed so much gloom and doom by sections of the media about the club's alleged slim chance of survival.

On the other side of the fence, the Save the 'Boro Fund, created by Edmund Pearson, had now reached £23,000. Other fans were doing their bit as well. David Johnson of Ayresome Street applied to the council for a licence to hold street collections on behalf of the club, although he was turned down.

The consortium continued with their plans to come to agreements with the creditors and had fruitful talks with the bank. There was a distinct possibility that the £900,000 could be enough to settle the old debts through part payment, and also give a new club a fresh start.

However, all the time the Football League were digging their feet in and insisting that 'Boro must pay all creditors in full if they were to be re-admitted to the League. John Foster, Middlesbrough Council's chief executive, said: "We realise that the Football League would have to re-register the new club, despite them altering their rules to prevent this happening."

Steve Gibson said: "All we got from the Football League was pound for pound, pound for pound. They insisted that we should pay all claims. All that did was create an opening for all sorts of people to make claims against the club. We had cleaners from ten years ago making claims for a week's wages, and things like that. When all these extra claims flooded in, the debts topped the £2 million mark.

"There were four or five clubs on the brink at the time, and the Football League needed a scapegoat. So they picked on us. They wouldn't budge an inch. Yet we were funding the club, keeping everybody in a job, and desperately trying to keep football alive in Middlesbrough."

Duffield, despite his need to recoup his investment in the 'Boro, remained sympathetic to the club and announced that he no longer intended to proceed with his winding up order. It seemed that the Inland Revenue, who took Alf's place as the main petitioner, could not now produce a new winding-up order at the High Court until 6 October. This was because the High Court was about to adjourn for its annual holiday, known as the 'long vacation'. A further boost had come from former 'Boro chairman Charles Amer, who scrapped his claims for £120,000 from the club.

Unfortunately, a body-blow for the consortium was just around the corner. On 25 July, Middlesbrough Council withdrew from the consortium and took their £200,000 with them. The council blamed rate-capping for their decision. Steve Gibson said: "I had just stepped off the plane after a business trip, and the taxi driver told me. It was shattering news."

Colin Henderson immediately called the remaining members to a crisis meeting and appealed to them to stay together. He said: "I am sure that the council's decision will have surprised everybody. But we are getting used to new factors emerging everyday and creating different situations. The consortium will consider the new situation carefully and I am hopeful that it will not change anybody's resolve to try to save the football club."

The consortium did agree to stay together, with Henry Moszkowicz eventually pledging a further £100,000. The council was also welcomed back in, as a non-paying member.

However, this was only the start, because the body-blows continued. In a shock move, the Inland Revenue took control of Alf Duffield's winding-up order after being given special dispensation by the High Court over their £115,000 claim. Suddenly the consortium had to change tack completely. In fact they could do nothing but throw themselves at the mercy of the High Court and then react to whatever decision was afforded.

A consortium statement read: "Having taken specialist legal advice, we have concluded that to meet the requirement of the Inland Revenue would leave the members of the consortium at severe financial risk. The provisional liquidator, despite his strenuous efforts, does not have the power to deliver a package which will enable the consortium to proceed.

"We will remain together and will be ready to discuss a deal with whoever has control of the company affairs following tomorrow's court hearing. We very much regret that the uncertainty must continue but we remain hopeful that a deal can be concluded quickly."

The consortium's reluctance to settle with the Inland Revenue left the High Court judge with just one course of action. On 30 July, at a 30-second hearing, Middlesbrough Football Club (1892) Ltd was ordered to be wound up.

It had been the only option open to the High Court, but also the only option open to the consortium. It was clear that the old club now had to die, and a new battle had to begin immediately to bring a new club into being.

It was a difficult and potentially impossible task which lay before the consortium. First of all they had to come to an agreement with the Official Receiver and buy the assets of the former club.

Secondly they had to appease the Football League, who immediately laid down a set of conditions if a new club was to be admitted in the place of the old one.

The first condition was ongoing, that the consortium had to settle with the old 'Boro creditors in full. With this in mind, the consortium members had to sign a performance bond for £2.5 million, which would be called in to settle the debts if the consortium failed to meet their obligations.

The League also demanded that 'Boro must start the season with £350,000 of working capital, in addition to satisfying the Professional Footballers' Association that they had paid off all their commitments to the players. Lastly, the opening game of the season, at home to Port Vale, had to take place and finish before midnight on Saturday, 23 August.

The consortium had just over three weeks to save the club.

On 1 August, David Storry, the agent of the Official Receiver, padlocked the gates of Ayresome Park. Inside were the players' kit and training gear. Outside were the players, the coaching staff and the office staff. They were no longer employed by the football club because the football club ceased to exist.

The Football League must have felt there was hope, because they moved in quickly to secure the contracts of the players. Bruce Rioch and Colin Todd also played their part by convincing the players that they should continue to train and work together, and try to build up to the start of the new season as normal.

Rioch said: "My philosophy is to keep working unless I hear that the club definitely does not have a future. I will work with the players, training and coaching them, even though the circumstances are somewhat difficult.

"We don't want the players sitting at home twiddling their thumbs while these delicate negotiations are going on in the background. It's much better for them to go out on to the training ground each day, working physically to burn off their energy and frustration.

"Once they are out there they forget about what is going on elsewhere. I know a lot of work is being put in by the consortium to make sure the club survives, and that is the fundamental factor."

Local sports organisations were willing to help. 'Boro were offered the use of Stockton FC's facilities and also those of Longlands College. And they travelled to Maiden Castle at Durham City to play Huddersfield Town in a friendly.

While 'Boro battled on, others weren't convinced. The pools companies unceremoniously wiped 'Boro off their football coupons for the new season in the belief that football on Teesside was dead.

Meanwhile the consortium had gone underground. They had been willing to speak to the fans via the Press in July, but suddenly put up an iron curtain. However, the hard work was still going on. Negotiations were held with the Midland Bank and a basic compromise was reached over the purchase of Ayresome Park.

The major sticking point continued to be the Football League. The League's spokesman Andy Williamson said: "Any hopes the consortium have that we will bend the rules is nonsense. Its members have known for weeks what our conditions are in any rescue package.

"Their tactics were to put us under pressure, get us to lower our sights and make us out to be the bad boys. But I am afraid there is no prospect of the League being browbeaten into changing the conditions we have set on repaying creditors."

On 11 August, 'Boro suffered the anticipated loss of Peter Beagrie when he signed for Sheffield United under freedom of contract. The blow was doubled within 24 hours when skipper Don O'Riordan successfully negotiated a free transfer with the Football League. He later signed for Grimsby Town.

Rioch now faced an ever increasing struggle to keep his squad together, especially as the League were threatening to call in all the players' contracts and make them available to other clubs.

Rioch remained defiant, saying: "I don't think it will have a snowball effect because there are so many players who want to stay and play for Middlesbrough Football Club."

The manager was correct, but several players were still worried, particularly those with mortgages to pay. Gordon Taylor, chairman of the PFA, admitted that several 'Boro players had approached him inquiring about the possibilities of following O'Riordan's lead.

The closer 'Boro got to the start of the season, the worse it seemed to get. Ten days before the opening game, the consortium put forward salvage proposals which were turned down by the Football League. Then the League fanned the flames by officially giving 'Boro's players permission to talk to other clubs.

It was a dire situation, and because the players could not afford to leave too much to chance, several had discussions with other clubs and some received offers. But every one of them decided to leave their decisions until 24 August. It was a crucial moment in the eventual re-emergence of the club as a playing force.

'Boro's frustrated fans desperately needed some good news. It came three days later when the consortium made a public announcement that they believed they were well on the way to saving the club. Colin Henderson read a statement which said: "Following further communications with the Football League, the consortium is satisfied the League's conditions can be met in full and are proceeding to conclude arrangements."

It was a brave announcement, especially as it quickly became clear that nothing was yet cut and dried. The battle continued day and night to try to reach agreement on all the relevant parts of the intricate survival package.

One thing was obvious. There was no way that 'Boro were going to be able to play their first match against Port Vale at Ayresome Park. For a start, all of the ground's gates were locked and promised to remain that way for some time. In any case, the consortium did not own the stadium.

The League had already insisted that a postponement was out of the question, so the only answer was to switch the match to another ground. But where? Sunderland and Darlington quickly ruled themselves out of the running. The Darlington police had already requested that no game should be played at Feethams because of the Teesside Air Show on the same afternoon.

The Victoria Ground at Hartlepool seemed to be out of the running because they were scheduled to play a Fourth Division match at home to Cardiff City. Billingham Synthonia's Central Avenue ground was another worthy of consideration, though there were segregation and access problems, and police opposition.

However, there was a desperate need to find a quick solution, and the consortium came up with the answer thanks to the generosity of the Hartlepool directors. It was announced that – if 'Boro could solve all the other problems and were saved – they would play Port Vale at the Victoria Ground at 6.30pm on the Saturday. This meant the match would start less than two hours after the end of Hartlepool's own game.

It was good news, though 'Boro's worried fans were still no nearer to knowing if the club would be saved. Time was running short. Behind the scenes, the consortium's legal representatives were still in hectic protracted negotiations with the Official Receiver, the Football League, the Midland Bank and everybody else who had a vested interest in the survival battle.

At the same time, Bruce Rioch and his players were carrying on with their build-up just as they had done for the past four weeks, despite not knowing if they would have the chance to kick a ball on the Saturday evening.

It hadn't been easy for Rioch to orchestrate the kind of build-up he would have wanted, especially as the team had been training without proper facilities, showers and sometimes without goal-posts. Rioch said: "Things haven't gone well for us but we are not going to make any excuses despite the hiccups.

"We are representing Middlesbrough Football Club and I demand discipline, commitment and the desire to win. Without any of those, we will not have a good team and we will not have good players."

On the Friday afternoon, the local media were called to Middlesbrough Town Hall's Stainsby Room to hear the final outcome of the safety battle at a 3pm press conference. But it quickly became clear that there was no news to announce. Desperate last gasp negotiations were still going on in London. The club was not safe yet.

The minutes ticked by. The 5pm deadline which had been set by the Football League came and went. Still there was no news. It was starting to look black for the club.

'Boro had two camps set up, one in London and the other at the Town Hall, so both parties were able to keep in regular contact by telephone. The Press were becoming impatient, but were urged to stay put.

Finally, at exactly 6.30pm – 90 minutes after the death blow should have been struck – the consortium members emerged to announce triumphantly that the 'Boro had been saved. A relieved Colin Henderson said: "Nothing can go wrong now. This has been the final chapter and I'm delighted with the results."

Henderson also apologised for the way in which the fans had been kept in the dark over the developments of the past month. He said: "We are sorry that the fans have been kept in the dark but because of the great importance of the negotiations, the consortium has never felt in a position to make them public. At the end of the day we were trying to save the club for the fans and for the people of Middlesbrough."

Colin also made it abundantly clear that 'Boro must never end up in the same mess again. He said: "We can't risk creating another situation where the club is insolvent. We must endeavour to build a sound base and make sure that the club is run on proper lines."

'Boro still had to meet one of the Football League demands. They had to complete their opening match against Port Vale. This went ahead on a warm sunny evening at Hartlepool. The police had set a crowd limit of 5,600, but in the event a miserable crowd of 3,690 fans travelled across Cleveland to watch the game. The crowd included around 300 fans from the Potteries. It was not a clear indication that the people of Teesside actually wanted a League football team, though attendances were to increase dramatically over the next three years.

Hartlepool officials opened the gates at 5.45pm, which was 35 minutes after the last few fans had been cleared from the stadium following Pool's clash with Cardiff. Admission prices were £3.50 for seats, with £2 concessions, and £2.70 standing, with £1.50 for concessions. The match was keenly contested, Archie Stephens hitting a brace to put 'Boro well in control. But 'Boro's lack of proper fitness began to take its toll and as they tired, Vale took advantage to score twice and earn a share of the spoils.

'Boro were back at the Victoria Ground three days later, this time as the away side. They took on Hartlepool in the first round first leg of the Littlewoods Cup and drew 1-1, thanks to a goal from Bernie Slaven.

Hartlepool were also the first visitors to Ayresome Park under the new regime. The keys to the stadium had proved elusive, and it was not until 1 September that they were finally handed over by the Official Receiver. The crowd limit was set at 17,500 with the East End closed temporarily because it did not have a safety certificate. Pool arrived the following night, and 7,735 fans watched 'Boro win 2-0 with goals from Stuart Ripley and Gary Hamilton.

'Boro's Tom Woodward won the Professional Footballers' Golf championship at Liverpool in October 1950.

So, 'Boro were now fully up and running. The new directors were officially named as Colin Henderson, who was eventually to become chairman, Henry Moszkowicz, Graham Fordy and Steve Gibson, who was the only director to survive the pre-liquidation days. Reg Corbridge, a second representative from Scottish and Newcastle Breweries, later joined the board as a fifth director.

Moszkowicz was the leading shareholder, along with his wife Rosemary. The couple had pumped in £300,000, with ICI and the Breweries both investing £200,000, and Gibson's Bulkhaul company putting in £125,000. As a result, 825,000 £1 shares were issued. It was a very low capital base from which to start off a new company, and did cause occasional problems in later years.

The board appointed an acting chief executive in 30-year-old Ian Stokoe, a chartered accountant from Price Waterhouse. Stokoe's brief was to get the club on a sound financial footing as quickly as possible. He was given total control over the running of the club's affairs, and personally monitored all income and expenditure.

One potential injection of cash was not taken up by the directors. They declined to accept the £23,000 which had been raised by the Save The 'Boro Fund, led by Edmund Pearson.

The condition on which the cash would be handed over was that it would be exchanged for shares, to give the fans an opportunity to be involved in the club. But the board was unmoved. So Edmund eventually returned the cash to all the subscribers.

On the field, 'Boro were getting better all the time. In fact it was October before 'Boro were beaten for the first time. It was just as well, because Rioch was operating under a buying ban.

David Dent, the Football League's assistant secretary, said the ban had been imposed because "Middlesbrough were in

We've done it! 'Boro directors Steve Gibson and Graham Fordy celebrate the ceremonial unlocking of the gates to Ayresome Park after the key was handed over by David H.Storry, (seen here in the background), the Official Receiver's agent.

Keith Lamb, 'Boro's chief executive during the difficult years following liquidation.

default of payment to members of the Professional Footballers Association". No further details were released, though former 'Boro skipper Don O'Riordan, now with Grimsby, admitted that he was one of the players owed money by the old company.

On 1 December, 'Boro appointed a permanent chief executive in Keith Lamb, a chartered accountant who had been working for the Stephenson Group contractors in Hartlepool. Lamb, who was born in Port Clarence, was a keen 'Boro supporter who had played local football on Teesside for many years. For the previous three years he had been managing the Cassel Works team in the Teesside League.

He said: "I'm looking forward to the challenge. My role as chief executive will be to pull the strings together and control the administration of the football club. I can sense a wave of optimism running through the club and my aim is to make Ayresome Park a focus of the town for leisure and entertainment."

The ban on buying players was finally lifted shortly before Lamb's arrival, and 'Boro were able to move forward. But the road was never a straight one. Shareholders' feuding, relegations following promotions and occasional discontent among the supporters meant that the last few years at Ayresome Park were never mundane.

The four remaining members of 'Boro's boardroom team after the resignation of Henry Moszkowicz. Pictured left to right, at a match at Ayresome Park, are Steve Gibson, Reg Corbidge, Graham Fordy and chairman Colin Henderson. Gibson later won a battle for control, when acquiring Moszkowicz's shareholding, which led to the departure of Henderson.

Welcome to Ayresome! 'Boro skipper Tony Mowbray, right, greets new boy Dean Glover, watched by the rest of the first-team squad.

Ayresome's Final Years

MIDDLESBROUGH'S most wayward period in the whole history of Ayresome Park came in the few years following liquidation. One minute they were up, the next minute they were down.

The fluctuating fortunes were reflected in the gates, which changed rapidly from anywhere in the low 20,000s, to well below 10,000. One day the fans were on a high – the next they were deflated in the depths of despair.

However, there were a lot of good times, including two seasons in the top flight and a first-ever appearance at Wembley.

That game in front of the Twin Towers may have been in the Zenith Data Systems Cup Final, or Mickey Mouse Cup Final as it was more affectionately known, but nevertheless it was an appearance at Wembley. Even though 'Boro lost it by 1-0 to Chelsea, the result was of secondary nature to the tear-jerking huge sea of red and white who packed the national stadium.

In comparison to the good times, there were the dark days. 'Boro lost an awful lot of games at Ayresome Park in the Second and later the First Division, and in 1990 were saved by the skins of their teeth from falling back into the old Third Division.

At times there was a total lack of consistency in 'Boro's performances. They would blow hot for a while, whet the fans' appetites, and then let them down with an unexpectedly dismal display against seemingly lesser opposition.

In many respects, the fact that 'Boro had gone out of existence for a few weeks in 1986 was largely forgotten. The mere matter that the 'Boro was surviving as a going concern, was never at any time uppermost in the minds of the fans. They demanded success all the way along the line – and at first they got it.

The Ayresome Park that welcomed the fans back in 1986 was different in several ways to that of 1985. The North Stand was unchanged, though in 1986 the Holgate End was split laterally into three sections to prevent the fans moving sideways. There were also a couple of central gangways down the middle.

There was no seating in the lower terrace of the South Stand, while the East End was without its first ten rows of seats. The north-east corner still contained a high, elevated area. As a result the capacities of the different areas of the stadium were greater. If the club had possessed full safety certificates in 1986, the stadium would probably have accommodated in the region of 30,000.

Not that 'Boro were capable of attracting that kind of crowd immediately following relegation. The club lost the bulk of its support in the first half of the 1980s, and needed to attract a whole new generation of fans.

They managed to do just that, thanks mainly to Bruce Rioch's wafer-thin squad of largely inexperienced home-grown kids who marched straight from the Third Division to the First in successive seasons.

Rioch and his right-hand man, Colin Todd, engineered one of the greatest achievements in the 92-year history of Ayresome Park. They turned a bunch of wet-eared youngsters into a skilful and never-say-die fighting unit, which just would not accept defeat, no matter how much the chips seemed to be stacked against them.

Even so, it's still difficult to believe that Rioch started the 1986-87 season with only 13 senior professionals, almost half of whom had virtually no Football League experience.

Not that 'Boro deliberately planned it that way. The fact was that Rioch was operating under a ban from the

League, which prevented the club from signing players from other League clubs until they had got their financial accounts in order. In any case, any cash which the new directors had available was needed to pay overheads and wages and settle with pressing creditors.

So, what did Rioch have to build a team around? He did have 25-year-old Bernie Slaven, who was about to emerge as one of the most lethal finishers in Britain, and he did have 22-year-old local boy Tony Mowbray, who proved to be an inspirational and thoroughly committed leader throughout the Rioch years.

One of Rioch's first jobs was to make Mowbray club captain, and the player's bravery went on to win him many accolades, including from Rioch, who said that if he was on a rocket trip bound for the Moon, the man he would want alongside him was Tony Mowbray. Hence the title of the popular 'Boro fanzine, *Fly Me To The Moon*.

There was also goalkeeper Steve Pears, a quality player who was ideal to have around at a time when 'Boro's fledgling back four was trying to find its feet. Pears was born in the North-East at Brandon, but he learned his trade at Manchester United and, at the age of 24 with 'Boro, was just starting to develop into a top-class 'keeper.

Mowbray's central defensive partner was another local lad, Gary Pallister. The 20-year-old had come into League football only two years earlier and was still learning his trade. But he was a quick learner, and was destined to play for England within two years.

Manager Walter Rowley travelled to Ashington, to talk to a young inside-right called Bobby Charlton at his home, in May 1953. Charlton, a schoolboy international, told Rowley he was joining Manchester United.

In midfield, Rioch had Brian Laws, 24, who was a converted full-back, and Gary Gill, 21, who was a converted centre-back. Wide out on the left was former Scottish youth international Gary Hamilton, 20, who was right-footed but could play anywhere.

Up front, alongside Slaven, was the oldest member of the squad, 29-year-old Archie Stephens. A Merseysider by birth, Stephens had come into League football at a relatively late age with Bristol Rovers, but he was a useful attack leader who was particularly strong in the air. Stephens quickly formed a formidable striking partnership with Slaven, and the duo became the most feared front two in the Third Division.

The rest of Rioch's squad were teenagers. There was Colin Cooper at left-back. He was a right-footed player who had made his debut the previous season.

There was Gary Parkinson at right-back. The Thornaby lad was pitched in for his debut in the opening game against Port Vale and, like Cooper, went on to play all 46 League games in that first season after liquidation.

Stuart Ripley was 'Boro's right winger. Like Cooper he had broken through in the final few games of the previous season. And, like the other kids, he had a lot to learn. But Ripley's pace down the right flank and his ability to send over the crosses for the head of Stephens was a vital factor in 'Boro's successful promotion campaign.

The other members of the 13-man squad were Alan Kernaghan and Lee Turnbull. Kernaghan had arrived at Ayresome Park as a centre-forward, but was capable of turning his hand to anything. In fact Rioch played him just about everywhere except in goal, using him mainly as a replacement in that first season when other players were injured. Turnbull was a striker, and a close friend of Parkinson, the pair having come through the Stockton Schools ranks together.

So brittle looking was this squad, that the bookmakers gave them little chance of making much impact in the Third Division. In fact neither did anybody else. The general feeling on the streets was that success would be merely staying in the Third Division.

As it turned out, relegation had never entered Rioch's head, nor that of his players. 'Boro were unbeaten in their first nine games, and all the talk afterwards was of promotion.

People were impressed by the all-out efforts of the largely home-grown team, and attendances rapidly swelled to more than 9,000, which was quite good considering that less than 5,000 had regularly watched games in the Second Division the previous season.

The team continued to hold sway near the top of the Division and the stingy defence, admirably led by Mowbray, recorded nine clean sheets in a run of ten games in November and December. It was remarkable how the side had blended together so tightly.

Ayresome Park was buzzing when more than 14,000 turned up on Boxing Day to witness the 1-0 win against Carlisle United, thanks to Gary Gill's first League goal. Then 15,458 watched the FA Cup third-round tie against Preston North End, on a cold day, with a dodgy frozen pitch. Unfortunately both sides struggled to keep their feet with Fourth Division Preston winning as the result of a goal from diminutive midfielder Ronnie Hildersley.

Rioch had made his first signing in the November by bringing in Hartlepool-born striker Paul Proudlock from South Bank. Soon afterwards he signed midfielder defender Ronnie Coyle from Celtic, initially on loan, when the League ban was lifted.

In the January, Rioch spent money on a new player for the first time when signing 21-year-old Paul Kerr from Aston Villa. The Portsmouth-born player was a striker at Villa, but was converted to a midfielder almost immediately by Rioch and quickly settled into his new role and into the team.

The kids were starting to look a little jaded in February and early March, but a 1-0 defeat at Walsall on 14 March proved to be the last time the 'Boro flag was lowered that season.

Rioch managed to cajole his young team back into top gear and they finished their Third Division programme like an express train. 'Boro were unbeaten in their final 13 games, which was good enough to guarantee promotion behind champions Bournemouth.

Promotion was secured on a balmy May evening at Ayresome Park, when the best crowd of the season of 18,523 turned up to witness the marvellous occasion. 'Boro needed only one point for promotion, and that was what they got from a goalless draw against Wigan Athletic, who were one of the Division's better sides.

The 'Boro team on that historic occasion was: Pears, Hamilton, Cooper, Mowbray, Parkinson, Pallister, Slaven, Stephens, Turnbull, Kerr, Ripley.

During the season, Ayresome had become a fortress again. 'Boro had lost just twice at home in the League, to Blackpool and Chester. They were unbeaten in their last 14 games at the stadium.

Slaven, who had emerged as the new hero of the fans, top-scored with 21 League and Cup goals. He also scored the team's only hat-trick in the 3-0 home win against Blackpool in the first round of the FA Cup, which effectively erased the memory of the home League defeat by the same side.

Stephens was not far behind on 17 goals, while Laws did well to finish next best on ten. The converted midfielder grabbed all his goals in the first half of the season, having suffered a cruciate knee ligament injury in February which was to put him out of the game for eight months.

So, 'Boro had achieved the virtually impossible, but still had not fully found their feet as a club. Cash remained at a premium, and there was no huge sum available for Rioch to go out and strengthen his squad for the following season.

However, he did go back to Aston Villa for what proved to be another astute signing when paying £30,000 for 23-year-old Dean Glover. The Birmingham born player was a central defender, but previous positions didn't mean much to Rioch, who converted Glover to midfield, where his tough tackling made him a big crowd favourite.

There was a change in the boardroom at this stage. Leading shareholder Henry Moszkowicz, who had played a major part in saving the club from extinction 12 months earlier, resigned his directorship over disagreements in policy.

However, Moszkowicz continued to monitor the club's affairs and used his authority as holder of 36 per cent of 'Boro's shares to put pressure on the board on occasions over the next few years, often as an outspoken critic.

The stadium needed attention, and a spruce up cost the club in the region of £200,000 over the next 12 months. The main change was the addition of seats in the front, standing area of the East End, thus reviving the situation which was introduced in 1966.

On the playing side, everybody was looking forward to the new season. However, 'Boro at first found life tough in the Second Division and won just two of their first seven League and Cup games. Even so, four goals from Slaven in this spell indicated that he was going to be equally as effective in the higher sphere.

'Boro were now regularly attracting five-figure crowds to Ayresome Park again. Swindon Town were early 3-2 winners on Teesside, but otherwise 'Boro were not beaten again in the League on their own ground before the turn of the year. In fact an unbeaten run of 14 games launched them right into the middle of the promotion battle. And another two signings from Aston Villa, goalkeeper Kevin Poole and forward Mark Burke, increased the strength of the squad.

The good old days were well and truly back at Ayresome Park on Boxing Day, 1987, when a massive 23,536 crowd crammed into the stadium for the game against promotion rivals Blackburn Rovers. Ayresome had not seen a crowd like it since a derby clash with Newcastle United in early 1983. The battle against Blackburn was a thrilling and tense affair, with 'Boro having to settle for a single point thanks to a goal from Slaven.

'Boro then lost their way for a while, and their hopes of automatic promotion looked faint when rivals Bradford City completed a double with a 2-1 win at Ayresome in the February. But, once again, the young team gathered themselves for a late rally.

Trevor Senior, a prolific scorer in the lower divisions with Reading, was signed to add spice to the attack, and he scored twice in a 6-0 drubbing of Sheffield United at Ayresome. Stuart Ripley went one better that day, grabbing his first hat-trick for the club.

Wins against Plymouth and Barnsley in late April and early May left 'Boro the verge of the First Division. They needed only to beat middle of the table Leicester City at Ayresome Park in the final game to be certain of promotion.

Fans who hadn't attended Ayresome Park for years turned up in their droves to see the anticipated march back to the top flight. The crowd of 27,645 bettered the amazing Boxing Day gate against Blackburn by more than 4,000. It was the highest League attendance at the stadium since more than 35,000 watched 'Boro beat Sunderland 1-0 thanks to a Graeme Hedley goal in February 1981.

The air was one of great expectation. The new craze of painted faces was popular everywhere, so red and white visages abounded. There was a profusion of newly-bought scarves and hats, while red and white balloons were occasionally breezing across the pitch in the hot sunshine.

Unfortunately, the expectations of the fans were not to be realised. The occasion proved too much for 'Boro's young side. They were frozen, as if transfixed by the atmosphere. They were unable to provide the goods on the day.

The huge crowd was submitted into long spells of eerie quietness as Leicester came out to play with a determination which belied their meagre League position, and displayed uncanny passing skills which was normally 'Boro's trademark.

'Boro did find the net through Bernie Slaven, but Leicester scored twice through Peter Weir and Gary McAllister and the game was always out of 'Boro's reach. It was a stunning experience for players and fans alike. Nobody could understand why Leicester had played so well. Yet, in truth, they had played only as well as they had been allowed by nervous 'Boro.

The outcome was that 'Boro missed out on automatic promotion on goal-difference. Aston Villa pipped them for second spot behind champions Millwall, by virtue of a goalless draw at Swindon while 'Boro were losing to Leicester.

However, all was not lost. 'Boro still had a chance of reaching the First Division through the Play-offs, which had been introduced into English football for the first time. In the semi-finals of the Play-offs, 'Boro were paired with Bradford City, who also missed out on a place in the First Division on the last Saturday. If Bradford had beaten Ipswich at Valley Parade they would have taken advantage of 'Boro's slip-up against Leicester and been promoted instead of Villa. But they lost 3-2.

Naturally Bradford were favourites to reach the Play-off Finals at 'Boro's expense because they had already beaten Rioch's boys on two occasions in the Second Division.

'Boro lost a third time to Bradford in the first leg of the semi-finals, going down 2-1 at Bradford. However, 'Boro's goal, from Trevor Senior, proved to be crucial.

It also gave them a fighting chance in the second leg at Ayresome Park, and 25,868 fans crowded into the stadium on a Wednesday evening in May to witness the decider. They were not to be disappointed because the two sides gave everything in a hotly-contested battle which was in doubt until the final whistle. Nobody who was there will ever forget the intensity and remarkable level of commitment from both sets of players.

'Boro pulled themselves on to level terms on aggregate through Bernie Slaven, but it was the only goal in the opening 90 minutes. Extra-time was signalled, and Gary Hamilton quickly put 'Boro in charge with a goal shortly after the restart. It was nip and tuck all the way to the final whistle, but 'Boro kept their noses in front.

Their reward was a place in the Play-off Final against First Division Chelsea, who had crushed Blackburn in the other semi-final. This time the first leg was at Ayresome Park. Just over 300 fewer fans turned up for the clash against Chelsea than had watched the remarkable game against Bradford.

In all respects it was far less of a spectacle. 'Boro won more comfortably than they had done against Bradford. However, the scoreline was the same, goals from Trevor Senior and Bernie

This is one of the crucial goals which sent 'Boro on their way to the First Division. Trevor Senior heads home 'Boro's first goal against Chelsea in the Play-off Final, first leg.

Slaven giving 'Boro a 2-0 victory over 90 minutes. Chelsea were disappointing for a First Division side, but then proceeded to make several astonishing comments in the national Press, saying that 'Boro were unworthy opponents and would be stuffed out of sight in the second leg at Stamford Bridge.

In the event 'Boro did lose, in a match which was played throughout in a sickening pervading feeling of hatred. However, the 1-0 scoreline in Chelsea's favour was enough to put 'Boro in the First Division on aggregate.

Even the ugly crowd scenes which started before the kick-off and continued after the final whistle with a mammoth pitch invasion, failed to dampen 'Boro's glee. They were back in the First Division, and Rioch and his young side had pulled off another remarkable promotion feat.

Rioch said: "Nothing ceases to amaze me about the character of the guys. It's a privilege for me to be working with them. Deep down, they all love the club and they are all dedicated to working hard for themselves and for each other. They're a great bunch.

"Just when you feel that they have given all they can, they roll up their sleeves and give a bit more. It really hurts them deep inside when something goes wrong, and they are determined to put it right and learn from the experience."

At the same time, Rioch was privately a bit worried that the club had been promoted too quickly. There had been no opportunity to put together a large squad, and the two rapid promotions had left one or two players behind because they were not capable of coping with the higher standard of football. In addition, 'Boro were still not financially equipped to provide enough cash for the club to make a big impact in the First Division.

A major structural survey of Ayresome Park showed that a lot of work was necessary in the future to make the stadium a safe ground for the thousands of fans it was expecting to attract. The whole of the East End needed to be reinforced with steel columns because a lot of the concrete had decayed. Salt which had been thrown down in the 1940s and 1950s to make the terracing safe in the winter had mixed with water and created an acidic solution which had burned through the concrete.

It meant that another £200,000 of work was necessary over a period of time to strengthen that area of the stadium. Corrugated fencing had to be erected to stop supporters using the elevated sections of the two eastern corners, which led eventually to the elevated section of the north-east corner being knocked down and rebuilt in 1990.

During the summer of 1988, Rioch managed to make one big signing when he snapped up midfielder Mark Brennan from Ipswich Town for £350,000. Ironically he was the first out and out midfield player to be brought into the club by the manager.

Rioch's fears that his inexperienced side might find life in the First Division hard proved fully justified, though he battled to keep the players organised and determined, and in the event they came within a whisker of retaining their place among the country's élite.

'Boro lost their first three games, but made a good recovery and by the middle of November were comfortably placed in the top eight. Rioch then took an almighty gamble by paying £750,000 for Manchester United's England international striker Peter Davenport. It was a huge fee at the time and a club record, but the move was doomed to failure.

Rioch had rightly been aware that he needed a quality man up front alongside Slaven, and Davenport arrived at Ayresome Park with a great goalscoring record. However, the Merseysider was unable to reproduce this form for 'Boro, and managed just four goals in his first season. It was not enough.

If Davenport had been able to double his tally, then 'Boro would undoubtedly have stayed up because they ended up being relegated on goals scored, having an identical goal-difference to Aston Villa, who survived instead.

Promotion salute from Bruce Rioch as the manager acknowledges the packed crowd outside Middlesbrough Town Hall after the team had received a civic reception for winning promotion to Division One.

However, while Davenport was the wrong man for the job, he wasn't the major reason for 'Boro failing to beat the drop. 'Boro's young squad was just not experienced enough to cope with rigours of life among the best teams in the country. 'Boro were still well clear of the relegation positions at Christmas, but in the second half of the season they fell away badly and a slow slide gradually took them towards the bottom three. Rioch paid £300,000 to Sheffield Wednesday to bring back experienced midfielder Mark Proctor, but the youngsters around him were struggling.

Bernie Slaven continued to find the net and his eventual haul of 15 First Division goals was remarkable considering the lack of chances 'Boro created. From mid-January, 'Boro won just one game. It was a 2-1 victory at West Ham and, even then, 'Boro needed two last-gasp goals from Slaven to turn defeat into victory.

Somehow, 'Boro managed to keep out of the bottom three until the final day of the season. The last match was at Sheffield Wednesday and 'Boro knew they would be relegated if they lost and other teams won.

Unfortunately the team which Rioch was forced to field at Hillsborough hardly reflected his first-choice line-up. Six injured regulars were sitting in the stands of the stadium. As hard as Rioch's makeshift line-up tried, the outcome was predictable. 'Boro lost 1-0 and were relegated. In the event a draw would have saved them.

Later years were to prove that the 'Boro squad at that time contained so many quality players that it's fair to assume that 'Boro could have gone on to become an established top-flight side if they had survived that first season. But it was not to be.

At that time football was heading for change, with the Hillsborough disaster in April 1989, eventually spawning the Taylor Report, which was to lead to major alterations at Ayresome Park.

There were alterations to the squad at Ayresome. Rioch was naturally keen to bounce straight back. Trevor Putney was signed from Norwich City and Alan Comfort from Orient, and 21,727 turned up to see 'Boro trounce Wolves by 4-2 on the first day of the season.

However, it soon became evident that the spark had gone from the side. To make matters worse, Rioch was forced to concede that he was losing his England international defender Gary Pallister to Manchester United in the opening weeks of the season. Pallister was determined to get away to Old Trafford,

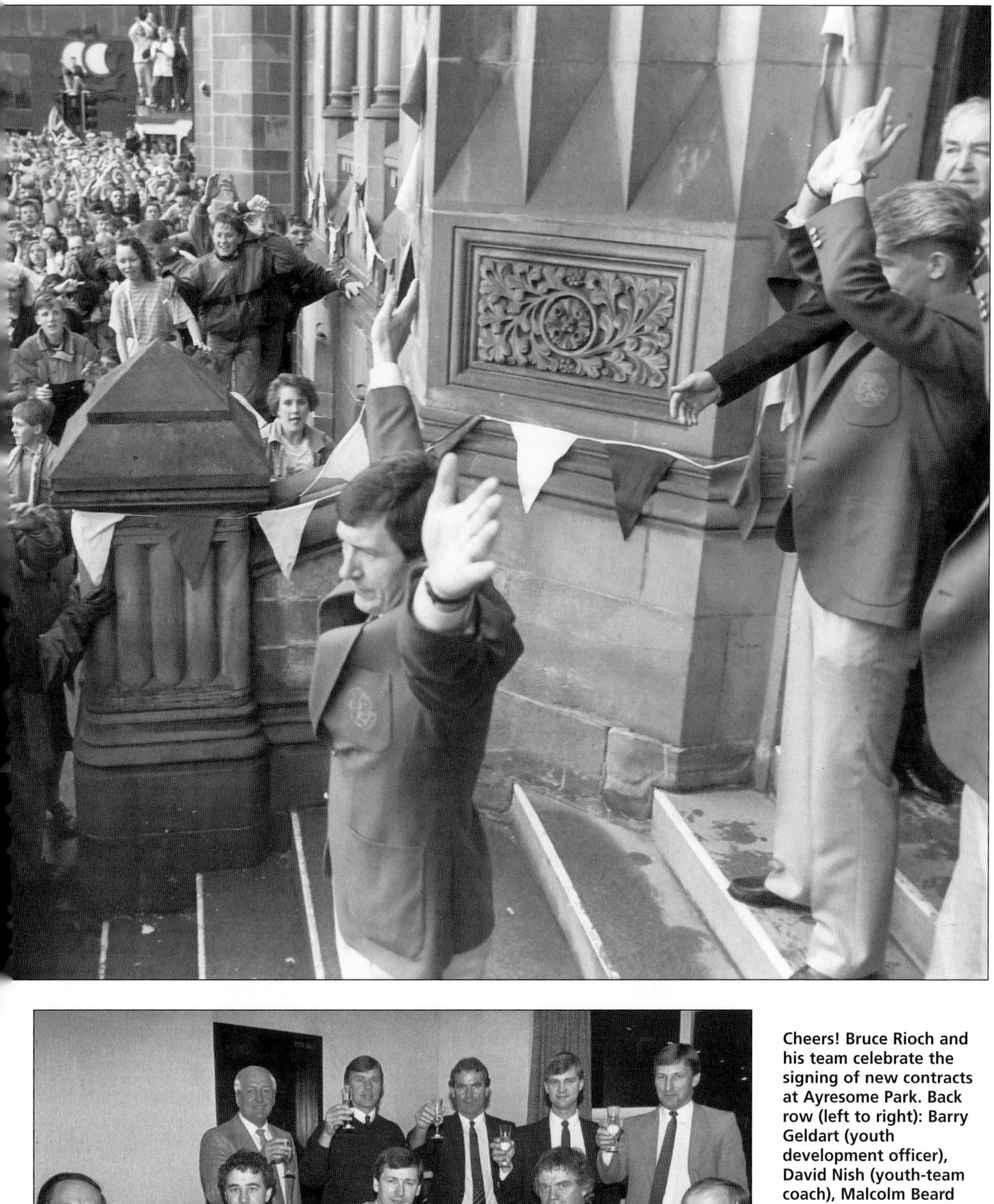

Cheers! Bruce Rioch and his team celebrate the signing of new contracts at Ayresome Park. Back row (left to right): Barry Geldart (youth development officer), David Nish (youth-team coach), Malcolm Beard (chief scout), Brian Little (reserve-team coach), Colin Todd (first-team coach). Front row: Reg Corbidge (director), Steve Gibson (director), Bruce Rioch, Colin Henderson (chairman), Graham Fordy (director).

and was no longer mentally committed to the 'Boro cause.

Rioch did not give up without a fight, and the result of his efforts was a remarkable British record transfer fee of £2.3 million. It was a huge fee at the time, and even 'Boro's most devout fans must have felt that the club had pulled off a good deal.

The money should have been just what 'Boro needed to bring in the players who could equip the team for quick return to the

Speedy winger Stuart Ripley takes on West Ham United's Paul Ince following 'Boro's return to the top flight.

So, on the League front, it turned out to be a miserable season. 'Boro lost no less than ten times at Ayresome Park, as crowds fell from just under 20,000 in the First Division to less than 17,000. Throughout the season Rioch retained the undying support of the fans, but he was losing the dressing-room. The players were no longer responding to him. There were several bust-ups, and the overall mood throughout the club was one of uncertainty and lack of confidence.

If Rioch had stayed in charge until the final match, then 'Boro would almost certainly have finished up back in the Third Division. The directors were left with a tough decision to make, though it was a necessary one. In early March, Rioch was sacked. The man who had done so much to build the new 'Boro with his hard work and dedication in all areas of the club, had outlived his usefulness. The marvellous team he had built out of nothing finally proved his undoing.

If Rioch was to have survived in the early months of 1990, he would have needed to institute a total clear-out and bring in a wealth of new faces, in order to build a new team. He might have done it, but for the fact that most of the players were on long-term contracts and could not be easily moved. The outcome was an ever-tightening noose which led to Bruce's dismissal on a Friday morning in early March.

When Oldham Athletic signed George Hardwick for £15,000 in November 1950. It was the largest transfer fee ever paid for a full-back.

First Division. But it wasn't. In the event all of the cash was frittered away on players who were not good enough to do the job which was needed for the club.

Familiar faces for 'Boro fans as John Hendrie, then with Newcastle United, takes on 'Boro's Gary Parkinson.

Within seconds of announcing that Rioch had left the club, the directors announced his replacement. Their choice was an unusual one. They opted for Colin Todd, Rioch's first-team coach, believing that they could appoint successfully from within. It was a system used consistently at Liverpool. But Ayresome Park was not Anfield. In the event Todd did a remarkable job. Not only did he avoid relegation in his 13 matches in charge at the end of the 1989-90 season, but he guided the 'Boro to a place in the Play-offs the following year. It was a complete turn-around.

This achievement came without the support of the fans, who turned against Todd virtually from the start. And in many respects it was also achieved with only basic support from the players, who were never able to totally clear the dressing-room cloud which had been generated in Rioch's last season. In the passage of time, Todd will be seen to be a much better manager than was appreciated at the time. More than anything, it was the fact that he was the successor to such a popular and initially successful manager as Rioch which counted against him at the end of the day.

The memories of Bruce Rioch lingered for a long time. One

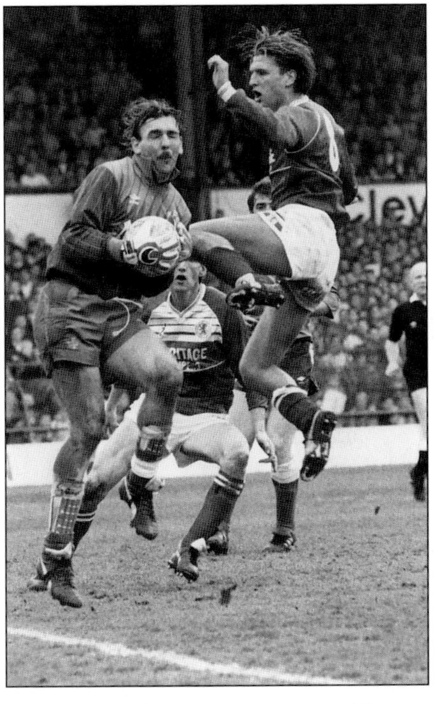

No way through for Gary Gill as Everton goalkeeper Neville Southall gathers during a 3-3 draw at Ayresome Park.

of his last achievements was to see 'Boro to Wembley for the first time in their history.

The team proved that they could still turn on the style for the big occasion by reaching the Final of the Zenith Data Systems Cup. It was a competition which offered a killing to any team which was committed to doing well.

The ZDS Cup was limited to First and Second Division clubs only and, judging by results, it was more of a nuisance to the big clubs than anything else – particularly in the early rounds. In 1989-90, 'Boro were also blessed with a series of home draws, which enabled them to reach the Northern Finals of the competition without having to travel.

Attendances crept up match by match. 'Boro opened their programme by beating Port Vale 3-1 in front of 6,691 fans, and then brought in another 2,000 for a crushing 4-1 win against First Division Sheffield Wednesday, with Bernie Slaven grabbing a hat-trick.

A derby crowd of just under 17,000 turned up for the Northern semi-final at home to Newcastle United. It was a cut and thrust clash, with both sides missing clear-cut chances. In the event a goal from 'Boro full-back Colin Cooper was enough to settle it.

'Boro's reward was a two legged Northern Final against First Division Aston Villa. The Midlands side had gone from strength to strength since just avoiding relegation at 'Boro's expense the previous year, and were now rightly regarded as one of the top club sides in the country.

It was a tough tie for 'Boro, and few outsiders would have given much for their chances. However, this was just the kind of match to bring the best out of 'Boro.

They went to Villa Park for the first leg and pulled out all the stops on a night of torrential rain to win 2-1. The winning goal was a stunning shot late in the game by Mark Brennan. 'Boro suddenly found themselves just 90 minutes from Wembley, and, bearing in mind they were in the lead with the home leg to come, they were nearer than they had ever been before.

With Wembley so close, Ayresome Park might have expected a better crowd than the 20,806 who turned up to see the return leg with Villa. More than 21,700 had watched the opening

That sports hall! Chairman Colin Henderson is pictured in the gymnasium of the notorious building which was reopened for public use.

The 'Boro Club Shop, where thousands of fans bought their strips and their memorabilia.

League game against Wolves, while Ayresome's capacity was around 26,000.

Perhaps it was the fact that some fans believed that 'Boro were already as good as at Wembley as a result of their first leg win. Perhaps it was that the ZDS Cup could hardly be regarded as a major cup competition.

As it was, 'Boro soon discovered that they were by no means on their way to Wembley. They had to battle hard all the way and could not fully settle into a rhythm. Villa looked a totally different side from the first meeting, and more like a First Division unit. 'Boro just could not hold on, the tie going into extra-time when Villa substitute Stuart Gray scored from a corner to leave the scores tied 2-2 on aggregate.

Ironically, 'Boro looked more settled in extra-time and began to put the pressure on their visitors. Even so, it needed a bit of magic from goal ace Bernie Slaven to turn the tie 'Boro's way again when he turned on a sixpence to score an incredible goal in the first extra period. Bruce Rioch later described it as a world-class goal.

Take your partners for a hoe-down! But there's a serious side to this picture as Bernie Slaven heads the equaliser in a 3-3 draw against Sheffield United.

Suddenly 'Boro looked all over winners, and the celebrations started on the terraces. They turned into a full scale party when Paul Kerr's low drive sailed through a sea of legs to put 'Boro 4-2 ahead on aggregate. Now there was no way back for Villa.

The final whistle was sweet music. 'Boro had finally made it to Wembley after more than 70 years of trying. It was a night to remember, with the town centre alive and throbbing into the early hours.

'Boro went on to take 35,000 fans to Wembley, and might have taken more if extra tickets had been available. Just where those extra 15,000 fans came from, or where they disappeared to after Wembley, will long remain a mystery.

One man who didn't make it to Wembley with 'Boro was Bruce Rioch. He was sacked after a midweek home defeat by Watford less than three weeks before the big game. New boss Colin Todd, fully aware that it was Rioch's team which had reached Wembley, asked skipper Tony Mowbray to lead the side out on to the hallowed turf. It was a fine gesture, especially as Mowbray was out injured with a pelvic problem.

The Wembley atmosphere was marvellous, but the match was a huge anticlimax. 'Boro suffered from stage fright on their big day, and lost 1-0 to First Division Chelsea.

Back in the real world, Todd was trying to get to grips with the task of keeping the team in the Second Division. Rioch had bought Simon Coleman from Mansfield as replacement for Gary Pallister, and Ian Baird was signed for £500,000 from Leeds United in February to try to pep up the attack. But 'Boro were still struggling, and Todd strengthened his defence by paying Oxford United £250,000 for left-back Jimmy Phillips.

There were signs of improvement in the closing weeks, but no consistency, and 'Boro needed to win their final League game to stay up. Unfortunately the last match was at home to

The most famous man at Ayresome Park in season 1989-90 was the 'Boro Bugler. Drummer Lee Matthews from the Green Howards, was a regular bugler at the stadium to sound the charge at corners and free-kicks, and after goals. Lee, who hails from Middlesbrough, is seen blowing his bugle for Gary Gill and Tony Mowbray, with the Green Howards Cup, before 'Boro travelled to Catterick Camp for their annual friendly match.

It's Bernie Slaven on the rampage as he holds off Sunderland's John Kay before testing goalkeeper Tony Norman. 'Boro won the match 3-0 in January, 1990.

arch rivals Newcastle United, who were pushing for promotion.

It was an agonising thought that the Magpies might send 'Boro back into Division Three. The daunting prospect also had an inspirational effect on the 'Boro players, who produced something special out of the bag to crush Newcastle 4-1.

Twin strikers Bernie Slaven and Ian Baird had a field day. Both players scored twice, with Slaven taking his tally of League and Cup goals for the season to a remarkable 32.

That summer, 'Boro had to make changes to comply with some of the demands of the Taylor Report. The seating in the

Peter Davenport, who was 'Boro's record signing when snapped up for £750,000 from Manchester United, leaps high to head home against Sunderland.

Weighing in at 9st 4lb, 'Boro midfielder Eric McMordie became one of the lightest footballers to play against England when he was capped by Northern Ireland.

South Terrace was reinstalled and all the lateral gangways were removed from the Holgate End, so that fans could move freely. The side fences were also removed around the pitch, including the notorious spikes which had been placed along the top of them in 1987.

The full cost of the work was £150,000 but 'Boro's board of directors still came up with plenty of cash for Todd to strengthen his struggling side during the summer. Todd was given more than £1 million to spend and used the bulk of the cash wisely.

He brought in four players, the best of which was unquestionably John Hendrie. The lively Scot had been a big thorn in the side of 'Boro three years earlier when he almost helped Bradford City to spike 'Boro's promotion aspirations.

Hendrie was known in the game as a tricky and speedy winger, and a good crosser of the ball, who could also play up front. He had moved from Bradford to Newcastle, and had 12 months with Leeds at Elland Road before Todd stepped in. The fee was £500,000, but it turned out to be money well spent.

Todd also splashed out £375,000 on Oxford United midfielder Robbie Mustoe, who was largely unknown in the North-East at the time. However, it was another case of money invested wisely. Mustoe went on to prove himself a tenacious fighter with self-charging batteries, who improved every season to become 'Boro's Player of the Year in 1994 and was third in the prestigious Hennessy Player of the Year awards.

The biggest name to join 'Boro that summer was Scottish international John Wark. At the age of 33, 'Boro's fans might have believed that Wark's best days were behind him, but the former Ipswich and Liverpool player had other ideas and Todd saw him as a valuable experienced head at the back. In the event the move was not to work out as well as both sides might have hoped. Todd's fourth incoming player was midfielder Martin Russell, who was signed from Scarborough for £175,000. This was one move which paid no dividends and Russell was eventually given a free transfer.

'Boro went on to show marked improvement that season, though there was a distinct lack of consistency. The team enjoyed a good run in the League Cup, beating First Division Norwich City by 2-0 at Ayresome Park, on the way to a fourth-round defeat at Aston Villa by 3-2. However, they did not fare so well in the FA Cup, losing 2-0 away to Third Division Cambridge United.

Despite some wayward League results, 19 goals from Bernie Slaven and 16 from Ian Baird kept 'Boro in the Play-off battle throughout most of the season. They virtually assured their Play-off place with consecutive 2-0 home wins against Wolves and Brighton.

After losing a terrific end-to-end night match at Oldham by 2-0, 'Boro went to Barnsley for their final game of the season knowing that only a 4-0 defeat would prevent them from reaching the Play-offs. They did lose, but only by 1-0.

Qualification for the Play-offs brought with it a genuine chance of promotion, but they were paired with in-form team Notts County in the semi-finals and went into the tie as underdogs. Confidence was not as good as it could have been at Ayresome Park, though 'Boro had beaten County by 1-0 in the previous League clash on Teesside and, on their best form, were well capable of winning through.

In the event 'Boro did not play well, and needed a scrambled goal from Jimmy Phillips to force a 1-1 draw in front of 22,343 fans in the home leg. The game lacked atmosphere, and 'Boro spent most of the time chasing the game after conceding an early goal.

The changing face of Ayresome Park... as demolition men get to grips with the North-East corner of the ground in the summer of 1990. The foundations of the Boys' End were unearthed and strengthened.

'Boro goalkeeper Tim Williamson is the only England player to score an own-goal on his international debut. It came in February 1905, at Ayresome Park.

Colin Todd adopted a sweeper system for the very first time in the second leg, with Tony Mowbray, Simon Coleman and Alan Kernaghan carrying out the central defensive duties. 'Boro were defensively strong, but they lacked impact at the other end and lost 1-0 to a late goal.

Todd's determination to change things around led to him placing 11 players on the list that summer. The board of directors did not stand in the way of this move, but at the same time wanted to vet Todd's list of transfer targets as replacements. Not surprisingly the overall situation created

This is the renovated East End for the start of the 1990-91 season, which included visitors' covered seating at the right-hand side of the picture.

turmoil within the club, and Todd resigned, citing boardroom interference.

'Boro advertised the position, but had a definite target in mind. They needed to restore stability within the club and their choice was Lennie Lawrence, an experienced and well-respected manager from his eight years in charge at Charlton Athletic. Lawrence was nicknamed Houdini for the way in which he had successfully avoided relegation from the First Division over several seasons at Charlton while operating with minimal resources.

His first task at Ayresome Park was to investigate the 11-strong transfer list, which led to a rapid clear-out. Eight players left Ayresome Park within a matter of weeks.

One man who didn't leave was defender Alan Kernaghan, who had been released on loan to Charlton at the end of the previous season. Lawrence had been on the verge of signing Kernaghan for £300,000 but now he had to change tack and convince the 24-year-old defender that his future lay at Ayresome Park after all. Not only did Kernaghan agree to stay but he became the mainstay of the defence.

Lawrence said: "I went through the players on the list and asked them if they wanted to stay or go. Some wanted to go because of things that had been said at the end of the last season. So I shifted them quickly because I didn't want any unhappy players standing in the way of us making a good start to the season.

"Kernaghan got a shock when he saw me arrive, but I knew I needed him at Middlesbrough and I got him to stay. The only blow was losing Colin Cooper. He was determined to leave and that was that."

Lawrence was also given money to spend, and spent it wisely. His major deal was to bring in centre-forward Paul Wilkinson for £500,000 and Willie Falconer for £300,000, both from Watford. Trevor Putney went in the opposite direction. Wilkinson, who had spells with Everton and Nottingham Forest in the First Division as a youngster, had matured into a strong attack leader and regular goalscorer. Falconer was a stylish midfielder who was being watched by Scotland boss Andy Roxburgh.

Ian Ironside also came in as reserve 'keeper from Scarborough for £80,000, while Lawrence signed promising full-back Curtis Fleming from St Patrick's Athletic for £50,000.

Lawrence said: "I was pleased to get those players in. We had a smaller squad, but we had a good one. Wilko fitted in well from the start and we had class in the side, with Stuart Ripley and John Hendrie on the wings, and a good defence."

The defence was given a huge boost by Steve Pears and Tony Mowbray both recovering from long injuries, and Kernaghan agreeing to stay at Ayresome. The overall look of the team was one of strength, and they were capable of beating anybody on their day.

'Boro were given a kick start by a run of six consecutive victories early in the season and afterwards they were always in the thick of the promotion shake-up. The team also did extremely well in both Cup competitions, and only the star-studded Manchester United eventually prevented them from going all the way to Wembley in the Rumbelows Cup.

A magnificent solo goal from Stuart Ripley gave 'Boro a 1-0 fifth-round replay win against Third Division Peterborough United in front of almost 22,000 fans at Ayresome Park in the Rumbelows Cup.

A near-capacity crowd of 25,572 then turned up to witness a

A magic moment for Robbie Mustoe as he guides home the winning goal against Millwall in Lennie Lawrence's first match.

This is how we are going to do it! Lennie Lawrence calls the full squad together to outline his plans following his arrival at Ayresome Park in the summer of 1991.

goalless draw against United in the first leg of the semi-finals at Ayresome. On a terrific night at Old Trafford in the second leg, full of atmosphere, 'Boro were beaten but far from disgraced when going down by 2-1 after extra-time.

Oh no you don't. Andy Peake challenges Peter Reid of Manchester City during 'Boro's FA Cup win in January 1992. Robbie Mustoe watches the action.

In the FA Cup, 'Boro beat First Division sides Manchester City and Sheffield Wednesday, before succumbing meekly to Portsmouth when 'Boro's weakened side was crushed 4-2 at home by the south coast club in a fifth-round replay.

In the November, Lawrence had sold enigmatic skipper Tony Mowbray to Celtic for £1 million to bring to an end the Redcar lad's illustrious career at Ayresome Park. In his ten years as a first-team regular on Teesside, Mowbray had epitomised everything that the fans were looking for from 'Boro's players. Mowbray, who never gave less than 100 per cent, was regarded as a captain courageous and a fine example to the players around him.

However, in the last couple of seasons, Mowbray had seen many of his contemporaries leave the club and needed a move himself to prevent staleness creeping in and provide a new challenge.

Nicky Mohan, a 21-year-old Middlesbrough lad who had just turned down a £200,000 move to Plymouth, came in as Mowbray's replacement and did well, while Lawrence used the Mowbray cash to sign the free-scoring striker Andy Payton from Hull City for £750,000.

Payton made a terrific initial impact by scoring after only four minutes of his debut against Bristol City. But he picked up a troublesome injury in the same match, and then had problems settling into the 'Boro dressing-room. His eventual departure became inevitable.

Debut delight from Andy Payton as he scores after only four minutes of his debut against Bristol City.

How about that! Steve Pears receives the Hennessy Player of the Year award from former 'Boro boss Jack Charlton. Pears was outstanding in 'Boro's promotion year of 1991-92 and earned a place in the England squad.

Teenager Jamie Pollock was another home-grown player to break through that season, and he was to go on and quickly establish himself in the side. Lawrence also brought in another key midfielder when paying his former club Charlton just £150,000 for Andy Peake.

The manager said: "I had to balance the books on transfers and Peaky turned out to be a real bargain. There was nobody like him at the club and he did exactly the job we needed.

Most League goals scored by Middlesbrough at Ayresome Park in a season was 78 in 1926-27. George Camsell scored 37 of them.

"Our away form had been poor in the first half of the season but it started to pick up in February. February-March was a key time for us, especially when you think how well the players did when some of them were carrying injuries. We only had 15 or 16 players at the best of times, but we were down to 13 or 14 at this time and still pulling out the stops in the Cups. It was phenomenal what we achieved."

'Boro overcame a run of injuries at this stage, and were delighted to welcome back Willie Falconer after five and a half months out of action with a knee injury.

Consecutive home wins against Oxford and Plymouth, both by 2-1, kept 'Boro in promotion contention, but a 1-0 derby defeat at Sunderland on 20 April was a body blow. So 'Boro approached their final three games knowing that Ipswich Town and Leicester City were hot favourites to take the two automatic promotion places.

The first two of these final three were at Ayresome Park. Two goals from Paul Wilkinson ensured that 'Boro scraped through by 2-1 in front of only 14,000 fans against Bristol Rovers.

A further 4,500 supporters turned up for the final home game the following Tuesday night against Grimsby Town. A penalty from Jimmy Phillips and another goal from Wilkinson produced a 2-0 victory.

It left 'Boro needing to win their final match at Wolverhampton to guarantee promotion. Once again, 'Boro's injury jinx struck, and Steve Pears had to drop out, so Ian Ironside was called up for his 'Boro debut after spending the previous 45 games watching from the touch-line.

Any fears that Ironside might be hit by nerves were quickly dispelled, but it looked like the Play-offs for 'Boro midway through the second half when they went down to ten men when Nicky Mohan was sent off, and then fell 1-0 behind.

Somehow these two events combined to bring the very best out of 'Boro. They lifted themselves for an all-out assault, and grabbed the equaliser when Jon Gittens, who was on loan from Portsmouth, scored from close range.

With time running out, 'Boro pushed more men forward, and there were goalscoring chances for both sides. However, it was 'Boro who finally broke the deadlock.

Jamie Pollock showed terrific resilience into a tackle and turned quickly to cross into the box, where Paul Wilkinson spectacularly headed in. Five minutes later came the final whistle, and 'Boro were members of the inaugural Premier League.

Lawrence said: "We delivered, against all the odds. It was a tribute to the great character of the side."

Money was made available for the manager to strengthen his side, and the Jon Gittens loan deal was quickly turned into a £250,000 permanent move. However, Stuart Ripley was keen for a change of scenery so he was sold to Blackburn Rovers for £1.3 million, with Lawrence using half the cash to bring in winger Tommy Wright from Leicester City. The Scot had scored 22 goals the previous season.

At the same time, Ayresome Park had undergone its last major ground repair. Toilet renovations under the North Stand revealed massive corrosion of the columns supporting the stand. It was a shock to the directors, and needed a £250,000 outlay to put it right. If nothing else, the discovery made the directors realise that the club's future lay away from Ayresome Park, being fearful that more and potentially very expensive problems could develop in the foundations in future years.

Lawrence was still given more cash to spend, and initially it looked as though he would hold on to the money until the season was under way. However, 'Boro were defensively dismal in pre-season, and Lawrence decided to act immediately by making two last-gasp signings.

He went to Celtic to sign two internationals – Derek Whyte of Scotland and the Republic of Ireland's Chris Morris. Whyte cost a club record £900,000 and was brought in to play alongside Alan Kernaghan at centre-half, and Morris, costing £600,000, came in as right-back. Striker Andy Payton went in the opposite direction as part of the deal.

The double deal left both players very little time to settle in. They signed on the dotted line only two days before the start of the season and met their new colleagues for the first time 24 hours before the opening Premier League match at Coventry City.

'Boro played poorly at Coventry and lost 2-1, but they quickly moved into gear in two remarkable matches at Ayresome Park. First of all a brace of goals from Bernie Slaven produced 2-0 win over Manchester City, then 'Boro produced one of their best Ayresome Park performances when humbling reigning champions Leeds United by 4-1. Leeds were outfought and outplayed as two goals from Paul Wilkinson and others from Tommy Wright and John Hendrie, against his former club, secured the victory.

By the middle of September, 'Boro were among the Premier League pacesetters and looking capable of giving anybody a good game. That was despite the fact that both goalkeepers, Steve Pears and Ian Ironside, had been injured at the same time. Lawrence brought in Barry Horne on loan from Millwall and

Jimmy Phillips, an often under-rated defender and great value for money buy at £250,000, takes on Manchester United's Mike Phelan.

Chris Morris, an experienced Republic of Ireland defender, battles to escape the attentions of Chris Bart-Williams of Sheffield Wednesday.

the 'keeper did well, if at times a little rusty as a result of lack of match practice.

However, by the beginning of October, the bubble had burst. A succession of bad results and a crippling run of injuries sent the team hurtling down the table.

Lawrence used his remaining cash to sign goalscoring midfielder Craig Hignett from Third Division Crewe Alexandra

Derek Whyte, who as 'Boro's record buy when signed from Celtic for £900,000, gets in a tackle on Aston Villa's Dean Saunders.

for £450,000. The Merseysider showed plenty of promise, but it was big step-up to the Premier League and the most valuable commodity which 'Boro were lacking was experience.

With the coffers now empty, there was little that Lawrence could do to halt the slide. 'Boro won just two games in the first three months of 1993 and the writing was on the wall.

The injury crisis abated in the closing weeks of the season to give the fans renewed hope, though deep down they expected the inevitable relegation. Despite winning 3-2 at Sheffield Wednesday on the penultimate weekend of the season, 'Boro were relegated to the First Division after a brief flirtation with top flight football.

Ironically the final home game brought back memories of the start of the season, as 'Boro drew 3-3 with Norwich City in a thrilling game. 'Boro had scored three times in each of their last three games, including a victory over Spurs in which Tommy Wright scored twice, so if nothing else it helped to generate the belief that 'Boro might start off the next season well.

Lawrence looks back on several events from that season as the turning point in the history of Ayresome Park, and of his own career.

He said: "We surrendered four needless points in September which made a lot of difference to our confidence. Bernie Slaven missed a last-minute penalty against Ipswich at Ayresome Park and then we went to QPR and were three times in front, but failed to win it as a result of an unnecessary last-minute trip by Chris Morris.

"Those two things, allied to the fact that we failed to sign Robert Lee from Charlton, made it harder for us. I thought we were on the verge of signing Robert Lee, but then Newcastle nipped in, and the rest is history."

Lawrence added: "Alan Kernaghan's injury at Liverpool in the November was a huge blow but we got to Christmas with 27 points and it was touch and go which way we would go.

"Then the home games against Crystal Palace and QPR decided it. We had all the pressure against Palace but missed chances and good goalkeeping by Nigel Martyn cost us the points. After that we were outmanoeuvred by QPR and I knew we were up against it. January and February were terrible months, especially as we had a lack of experience due to injuries to key players.

"We ended up with 44 points, which in another season might have been good enough to keep us up. Then again, I didn't get the help I needed. There were no board meetings between November and March. With a bit of help, we might still have done it."

The fewest goals scored by the opposition in a season at Ayresome Park was eight in 1973-74 when Jack Charlton's team took the Second Division by storm.

Another goal from the golden boot of John Hendrie (right) this time against Birmingham City in a 2-2 draw at Ayresome Park.

'Boro never ever managed an unbeaten League season at Ayresome Park. The closest they came was one home defeat in seasons 1926-27, 1936-37, 1968-69, 1971-72 and 1973-74.

The lack of help that Lawrence was referring to was partly due to the increasing battle for control of the boardroom, which was linked to the desperate need to sort out the shareholding issue.

Life in the boardroom had never been dull since liquidation, especially when the Football League called in the bond which had been lodged with them because the directors had failed to pay off all the old company's creditors in full. All the shareholders had been 'surcharged', which was a considerable extra outlay for Henry Moszkowicz, ICI, Bulkhaul, and Scottish and Newcastle Breweries.

Shortly afterwards the Breweries decided to withdraw their involvement in the 'Boro, and their shares were offered for sale pro rata to the remaining shareholders. All of them took up their option, leaving Moszkowicz with 396,000 shares, which represented 48 per cent. ICI had 265,000 shares and Bulkhaul 164,000.

Clearly it was not desirable for the 'Boro board to have almost 50 per cent of the shares retained by a person who had no official involvement in the day-to-day running of the club, especially as it tended to create internal problems.

Henry Moszkowicz was always quick to make his opinion heard on major matters and was generally a thorn in the side of the directors, as he had every right to be when he disagreed with club policy.

It might not have been an unsurmountable problem for the directors, but for the fact that a new rift had developed in the boardroom. Chairman Colin Henderson and Steve Gibson, who had the support of Reg Corbridge and Graham Fordy, were no longer thinking and working together in harmony. There had been a gradual breakdown of their working relationship.

The situation became critical in April 1993, when Henderson resigned from the chair, but retained his directorship. He demanded a total restructure of the boardroom, and greater shareholder involvement on the board, including the reinstatement of Henry Moszkowicz.

At the time it seemed to be an impasse, and there was no obvious way forward for the club until the boardroom battle and the shareholding issue was sorted out.

It was with this veil of uncertainty and behind the scenes bickering hanging over the club that Lawrence and his players had to prepare for the new season.

To make matters worse, there was no money in the kitty to strengthen the side for a new campaign. 'Boro's year in the Premier League had brought a financial strain on the club, in addition to being a failure on the pitch.

In fact Lawrence said that he had to sell players to raise funds, before any new faces could be brought in.

The first to go was left-back Jimmy Phillips, who rejoined his home-town club Bolton Wanderers for £250,000. Phillips was still vitally important to 'Boro, especially as he was the only experienced left-back at the club, but he had become unpopular with the fans and was happy to get away. So 'Boro accepted Bolton's offer even though it created a major problem at Ayresome Park.

Phillips was followed out of the club by Willie Falconer, who had been in and out of the side the previous season. Falconer returned to Scotland, where he joined up with Celtic in a £450,000 deal.

So 'Boro started the new season two players down, and soon sold another when Alan Kernaghan joined Premier League Manchester City for a huge fee of £1.66 million. Kernaghan, who had recently broken through into the Republic of Ireland side, had been a slow developer in his career but had become 'Boro's biggest asset. The fee was a very good one as far as 'Boro were concerned.

Lawrence said: "I sold Phillips and Falconer because I thought nobody was coming in for Kernaghan. Eventually Kernaghan signed a new contract, but I lost him as well when Manchester City came in."

The manager was publicly offered the Kernaghan cash to spend by the 'Boro board, but he failed to spend it quickly and, the amount of money available seemed to diminish as the season progressed.

However, 'Boro made a marvellous start to the season, with the teenage trio of Richard Liburd, Jamie Pollock and Alan Moore all making terrific contributions, and there was real hope for a while that the team might bounce straight back.

Liburd, who was playing non-League football with Eastwood Town just a few months earlier, was a right-footed defender who was drafted in to Phillips' left-back spot because he was the only option. The youngster repaid this faith by having a superb season considering his complete lack of experience.

Pollock, who had represented England in the World Youth Cup in Australia the previous season, had now developed into a dominant force in midfield, while Moore was a richly-talented Irish lad who had been knocking on the door the previous season.

Moore's impact was dramatic. He scored two breathtaking goals as 'Boro won 3-2 at Notts County on the opening day. The media immediately called him the new George Best, which was an unfair tag to hang on to the lad's shoulders at such an important stage of his development.

'Boro's next game was at Ayresome Park, at home to promotion favourites Derby County. 'Boro promptly destroyed the Rams, winning easily by 3-0 thanks to a terrific team performance which was reminiscent of the display which had beaten Leeds United 4-1 at the same stage of the previous season.

A 4-1 victory at Barnsley followed, with Moore again netting twice and John Hendrie grabbing the other two. It was a breathtaking start to the campaign which left 'Boro sitting proudly at the top of the First Division.

Unfortunately the team could not maintain this devastating run. A 1-0 defeat at Southend United followed and then results adopted a haphazard nature. Then the injuries returned, and suddenly 'Boro were sliding down the table.

Lawrence, who had still not entered the transfer market, became the target of the fans' frustrations and the supporters began to desert Ayresome Park in their droves.

The manager had hoped to hang on to the cash until the New Year, and then bring in the right player or players who might prove the critical pieces in the promotion jigsaw. But circumstances forced Lawrence's hand. Attendances were dropping dramatically and the alarm bells were ringing when they dropped below the 7,000 mark. 'Boro were on the verge of the bad old days again.

An injury to top scorer John Hendrie left Paul Wilkinson as 'Boro's only orthodox striker and the fans were hoping that Lawrence would bring in a striker. In the event he strengthened the defence instead by signing £750,000 centre-back Steve Vickers from Tranmere Rovers.

Vickers, born and bred in the North-East at Bishop Auckland, had spent all of his professional career with Rovers in the North-West. He was a good defender and a committed player, and a most valuable addition to the squad. However, the fans still felt that a forward should be brought in and thousands continued to stay away from the club.

Lawrence said: "I was determined to spend the money wisely. I didn't want to waste it on two or three inferior players who would have done nothing for the club. I wanted to buy quality and Vickers was the only player who was good enough who I could find."

Even so, the problem of the weakened attack was not resolved until Hendrie returned from injury at the end of February, by which time 'Boro looked more in danger of relegation than having any chance of making a late surge for the Play-offs.

In the event, several injuries cleared up at the same time. Lawrence was able to field his first-choice line-up for the first time in months, and suddenly the team began to zoom up the table. A series of wins, culminating in a 1-0 victory against promotion favourites Crystal Palace at Selhurst Park, took 'Boro to the verge of the Play-offs and gave the team a live chance of going up.

'Boro's newest director. George Cooke took over the reins as ICI's boardroom representative shortly before the shareholding battle was sorted for once and all.

However, while Hendrie's return to action was the first of several events on the field which led to 'Boro's revival, a much more important occurrence happened off the field.

In February, 'Boro sorted out their boardroom battle and shareholding issue at one fell swoop. It came about after an extraordinary meeting of the shareholders, when George Cooke was nominated as ICI's replacement director for Colin Henderson. At the same time, ICI made it clear that they had officially withdrawn their support for Henderson.

Even so, the matter was not decided in its entirety until Steve Gibson took control of the club by purchasing Henry Moszkowicz's shares. It left Gibson's Bulkhaul company with 68 per cent of the shares, leaving ICI as the only other shareholder with 32 per cent.

In many respects, this event was as big a change at the club as had taken place immediately following liquidation in 1986. It was the end of one boardroom regime and the start of another, and the total switch-around of the shareholding. It was the start of a new era.

There were no baddies and goodies in the battle for control. Henderson and Gibson had been at loggerheads for some time, though Henderson's part in building a new 'Boro from the ashes of liquidation should never be forgotten. Neither should the financial contribution of Moszkowicz, without whose huge cash input the consortium would not have been able to function in 1986.

'Boro still had four directors, with Steve Gibson installed as new chairman and in a position to pursue his personal plans for the club's future. Those four directors soon became two, however, with former Scottish and Newcastle Breweries representatives – Corbidge and Graham Fordy leaving the boardroom to take up paid positions on the club's expanding commercial side. Corbidge became development manager for the new stadium and Fordy commercial manager.

However, as far as Lawrence was concerned, there were no immediate changes on the playing side. The manager and the team carried on as normal in their battle to keep the season alive, without any financial investment before the transfer deadline.

Yet the bubble was bursting on the pitch. The players had put a lot of effort into reaching the verge of the Play-offs and were finding it difficult to maintain the momentum.

They were always in with an outside chance of a Play-off place until the final fortnight of the season, but there was no gas left in the tank to spark a renewed assault. It was a disappointing end to a frustrating season, especially as 'Boro's first-choice 11 was arguably as good as that of any of the four sides which did make the Play-offs.

The major problem was that the squad was too small. 'Boro did not have the strength to cope with injuries in key positions, and they got plenty of them during the season.

During the campaign Lawrence had been forced to pitch in a full team of youngsters, many of whom were blooded well ahead of their time. In particular, 'Boro had used the kids in a disastrous Anglo-Italian Cup campaign in which they lost three times and drew once.

Lawrence said: "We finished eighth, and considering all the circumstances of the season I think it was a better achievement than anything I did at Charlton. But it was not good enough for the fans, and I fully understand their feelings."

The club as a whole ended 1993-94 on a downer and were facing a potentially difficult summer. Season ticket sales were certain to be a financial disaster. The fans believed both that the club lacked ambition and that the manager was not good enough.

The player with the shortest first-team playing career at Ayresome Park is Malcolm Poskett, who appeared as substitute against Hull City on 13 October 1973, and played for only 12 minutes.

The directors, who were desperate to turn the club around now that news of the new stadium had been announced, did what most directors do in these situations. They sacked the manager. In truth they were left with very little alternative, just as they had been left with none over Bruce Rioch four years earlier. There was no animosity involved, it was just a crucial business decision.

Steve Gibson said at the time that there would be money to spend the following season, and he was not sure whether Lennie was the right man to spend it.

Lawrence was gutted when he received the news, but not surprised. He told the *Evening Gazette* that nobody could have done better with the players available and the lack of spending money. He left with his head held high.

Lennie said: "I've no quarrel with anybody at Middlesbrough. I don't blame the board of telling me to cut costs when we were relegated. And, at the end of the next season, I can understand them electing for change and wanting to bring a big name in.

"I just hope that with the passage of time, some of the fans who were not happy will look back and think that I didn't do too bad a job after all with the resources available. That's all I ask."

Remarkably Lawrence's contribution to 'Boro's fortunes was not yet over. He was to play a leading part in bringing his replacement to Ayresome Park. Lennie informed the directors that they should go after Manchester United's former England skipper Bryan Robson as his successor. Ironically the board were already thinking along the same lines. Robson had just ended his illustrious playing career at Old Trafford and presented a great capture for any club who could convince him that their ambition matched that of his own.

It was Lawrence, acting on behalf of the 'Boro directors, who made the first approach to Robson with news of the Teesside club's interest. Lennie then drove to Wetherby to meet up with Robson, and ferried him to a secret meeting with the 'Boro directors.

Gibson and Cooke, by this time, had devised far reaching and wildly ambitious plans for the 'Boro. With the new stadium to back them up, they could court Robson from strong ground. Robbo liked what he heard and liked what he saw, and a deal was struck quickly.

In fact the 37-year-old was thrilled at the prospect of returning to his native North-East and reviving 'Boro's fortunes. Everything went through without a hitch, and Robson was officially unveiled as 'Boro's new player-manager before the end of May.

Robson wasted no time in naming his assistant. He contacted his former England teammate Viv Anderson, who had spent the previous 12 months learning the art of football managership in charge of First Division Barnsley. Anderson had already started planning to build on his first year at Oakwell, but the lure of joining up with Robson again was too great and he agreed to the link-up.

The new framework was in position at Ayresome Park and there was an immediate response from the 'Boro fans. Robbo mania set in, and Teesside was buzzing with anticipation throughout the rest of the summer.

As far as Lawrence was concerned, there was never any doubt that he would be installed in the hot seat of a new club in time for the start of the new season. In the event he had several offers and eventually plumped for Second Division Bradford City.

There was a lot of potential at Bradford, especially considering that they had almost reached the First Division instead of 'Boro in 1988. So it was a job which Lawrence could do well.

Lennie did come back to Ayresome Park to snap up his assistant. He offered the post to 'Boro youth-team coach George Shipley, who jumped at the chance to take a career step forward.

However, it was a blow for 'Boro because Shipley had led the 'Boro Juniors to the Northern Intermediate League championship and the semi-finals of the FA Youth Cup the previous season.

Welcome to Ayresome! 'Boro's new goalkeeper Alan Miller is greeted by Viv Anderson and Bryan Robson just five days before the opening match against Burnley.

The Last Season

BRYAN Robson breezed into Ayresome Park on an unprecedented wave of optimism and expectancy. The signing of one of England's most-capped players of all time as 'Boro's player-manager created an air of eager anticipation throughout Teesside.

Robson was one of the biggest names in the game, an internationally respected England World Cup captain who had been the driving force behind Manchester United for many years. And now he was at Middlesbrough!

Robbo Mania set in during the summer, and 'Boro doubled their season ticket sales to around 10,000. The fans believed that Robson would guide the club back to the Premier League, and it was a united dream that Ayresome Park's last season would end with a successful promotion campaign.

Clearly that was the aim of 'Boro chairman Steve Gibson and director George Cooke, who had pushed the boat out to bring Robson to Teesside. It was all part of a new feeling of positive thinking and ambition throughout the club, which had started with the announcement of the new stadium at Middlesbrough Dock.

The Riverside Stadium was the first step, and the securing of Robson's services was the second step. It was a new commitment and determination to make 'Boro great again.

Robson, who could have gone to virtually any club in the country as player, coach or manager, was back in his native North-East. But the 37-year-old admitted that he had chosen to come to Middlesbrough purely because of the club's ambition and potential.

He said: "When I first met the chairman I realised that his ambitions matched my own. He wanted the club to compete with the best in the country, and he was building a stadium with which to do it. The new stadium was crucial to me agreeing to come here. I could see that 'Boro had the capability to achieve things."

At the same time Robson was under a certain amount of pressure to win promotion at the first attempt. The 'Boro board had backed their judgement by putting cash on the table, and Robson needed to spend it wisely and bring immediate results. But there were no guarantees, especially as he was taking his first steps into management and had a learning period ahead.

The first step was to find an experienced assistant, and Robson went for his former England and Manchester United colleague Viv Anderson. The two were like-minded in their views on how the game should be played, and were great friends.

Anderson was already in management, having had a hard first season in the hot seat at Barnsley. It was a useful learning year for the 38-year-old, and he had acquired a good working knowledge of First Division teams and players.

The duo quickly sat down together to devise their plans for a promotion campaign. 'Boro already had a decent squad. Anderson knew that fact well, because 'Boro had beaten Barnsley three times the previous season. But the squad was small, and had scope for improvement, so Robson and Anderson set out to bring in several quality signings.

Clayton Blackmore was a valuable free transfer signing from Bryan Robson's old club Manchester United.

John Hendrie scored 'Boro's first two goals of the final season at Ayresome Park and the last two goals.

When James McClelland scored a club record all five goals for 'Boro in a 5-1 FA Cup third-round victory over Leeds United on 9 January 1926, it was a day of double celebration for the Scot. His wife gave birth to their son Charlie on the same afternoon.

Robson said: "One problem that 'Boro had encountered the previous season was that the squad was not big enough to cope when the injuries came along. It was important that it didn't happen again. We needed to bring in quality players, and improve the size of the squad, so that we could cope with a gruelling 46-match season."

The new manager also wanted to put together a squad which was not only good enough to win promotion, but also to stay up in the Premier League. He said: "I wanted to sign players who I felt were too good for the First Division. This could help us to win promotion, and would give us the experience we needed once we got up. There was no point signing players who would not be good enough in the Premier League."

Robson did not have to reach for the chequebook for his first signing. He moved quickly to snap up Welsh international utility player Clayton Blackmore, who had been awarded a free transfer by Manchester United. Blackmore, 29, had vast experience of football at the highest level. He had been a member of the United first-team squad for the previous ten years, and had played all over the world for Wales.

Having signed Blackmore for nothing, Robson then forked out a club record fee of £1 million for Aston Villa's Neil Cox. Like Blackmore, 22-year-old Cox was a utility player who could play at right-back, centre-back or in midfield. However, Robson saw the England Under-21 international essentially as a right-back.

The board continued to make cash available for team strengthening, so Robson moved for his third Premier League player. This time he signed Sheffield Wednesday's tough-tackling central defender Nigel Pearson. The 30-year-old had fully recovered from two broken legs which had interrupted his career at Hillsborough. Robson saw Pearson providing the mental toughness and inspiration which 'Boro badly needed at the back, and promptly made him captain.

With Robson himself intending to play on, the 'Boro squad had been bolstered by four Premier League players within a matter of weeks. The squad already had much more depth, though there was still a distinct lack of cover up front where Paul Wilkinson and John Hendrie were the only two recognised strikers with experience.

And the incoming signings were countered by outgoing players. Andy Peake who, at £150,000, had been arguably Lennie Lawrence's best value for money buy, negotiated a free transfer and joined the police force in his native Leicestershire.

Then Lennie came back to Ayresome Park to snap up full-back Richard Liburd, who had enjoyed a remarkable debut season with 'Boro over the previous 12 months. The 20-year-old, a right-footed player, had played at left-back throughout the

Alan Moore, the Irish Under-21 star gained in strength during the season and was often a match winner.

Paul Wilkinson was a key 'Boro player for three and a half seasons and scored almost 70 goals.

1993-94 season and done very well. However, the arrival of three Premier League defenders at Ayresome Park put Liburd's future place in the team in jeopardy, and he was happy to complete a £150,000 transfer and link up again with Lawrence at Bradford City.

Home-grown defender Nicky Mohan who was out of contract, also felt that his opportunities at Ayresome Park might diminish over the coming season. So he joined up with former 'Boro youth-team boss Brian Little at Leicester City. It was a good move for Mohan, because Leicester had just been promoted to the Premier League.

The two clubs were unable to agree on a fee, and so the matter was referred to a tribunal, who ordered Leicester to pay £330,000. There could be few complaints by 'Boro because the fee was only £20,000 less than their asking price.

Even so, it's always sad to see Middlesbrough-born lads leave the club. Mohan was joined on the way out by another home-town player, Michael Oliver, who joined Stockport County under freedom of contract. Oliver had skippered the 'Boro youth team to the semi-finals of the FA Youth Cup the previous season and helped them win the Northern Intermediate League title for the first time since 1982. Oliver's fee was also fixed by a tribunal. 'Boro received £15,000 down, plus £15,000 after 20 appearances and a further £20,000 after another 20. 'Boro were also awarded 5 per cent of any sell-on fee.

As the season approached, Robson moved to solve his shortage of strikers by agreeing to pay Bolivian side FC Blooming £250,000 for international forward Jaime Moreno.

From Bolivia to 'Boro. Jaime Moreno received a terrific ovation from the 'Boro faithful when he was introduced to the crowd before the start of the derby match against Sunderland.

The Bolivian, who was only 20, was reported to have played in 30 internationals. He had twice come on as substitute for Bolivia in the World Cup finals in the United States.

Moreno had first impressed Robson on a video, sent to the club by an agent. Robson brought the youngster, who could speak no English, over for a trial and he greatly impressed in a 3-0 friendly win at Darlington. Moreno put 'Boro ahead from the penalty-spot after he had been fouled and added another in the second half. Craig Hignett completed the scoring in the closing minutes.

'Boro had started pre-season well. They kicked off with a short tour of the West Country, where they beat Torquay and Exeter. They returned home to play Darlington, and then went off on their travels again to Scotland. They started off badly with a 1-0 defeat at Raith Rovers, which was watched by Robson from the stands. However, the player-manager then laced up his boots again and scored both goals as 'Boro bounced back with a 2-1 win at Ayr United.

The pre-season build-up was concluded with a 3-1 home win against Scottish Premier League side Hearts at Ayresome Park on the Saturday prior to the start of the League season. Goals from Paul Wilkinson, Neil Cox and John Hendrie gave 'Boro a surprisingly easy win.

Unfortunately regular goalkeeper Steve Pears missed the whole of the pre-season friendly programme with rib and calf injuries, and clearly was not going to be fit in time for 'Boro's opening First Division game at home to Burnley. Reserve goalkeeper Andy Collett was also injured, having picked up a knee injury in the warm-up before the start of the match at Raith.

It left 'Boro with only 19-year-old Ben Roberts as a fit, recognised goalkeeper, so Robson moved into the transfer market again in the week leading up to the team's opening First Division match. Robson acted quickly to snap up the England Under-21 international Alan Miller, who had been understudy to England 'keeper David Seaman at Arsenal.

Miller, a product of the FA's soccer school at Lilleshall, had very little previous League experience, but came highly recommended. He had turned down the offer of a new contract at Highbury to try to win a regular first-team place elsewhere.

Nigel Pearson had also missed most of 'Boro's pre-season games with a knee injury. However, the new skipper had a run-out in the second half against Hearts, and then played the full 90 minutes of a reserve game at Spennymoor on the Monday night.

It was enough to convince Robson that Pearson was fully fit, and the manager announced that his skipper would play against Burnley on the Saturday. It was another bonus in a big week for the club. Advance ticket sales had gone really well, and Teesside was heaving with anticipation.

In the event, 'Boro went very close to achieving a sell-out for the first match of their last season at Ayresome Park. The

In 1936, the London & Northern Eastern Railway introduced express locomotives named after Football League clubs. No 61655 with red panel colours, was called Middlesbrough. It was scrapped in 1959 after 765,000 miles and the solid brass nameplate was offered to the club for scrap price. They did not take up the offer. So what happened to the nameplate?

The man himself. Bryan Robson is pictured in action early in the season against Jason McAteer of Bolton Wanderers.

The least number of games won by 'Boro at Ayresome Park in one season was five, when they were relegated from Division One in 1981-82.

capacity had been reduced to 24,299, and the clash against Burnley attracted 23,343 supporters.

It was a lovely warm afternoon, and there was a huge wave of expectancy among the short-sleeved fans. This clearly had an effect on the team's performance, because the 'Boro players were very nervous and their passing was poor.

However, Burnley, newly promoted from the Second Division, were dreadful in defence. They virtually handed two goals on a plate to John Hendrie, both of which were gratefully accepted by the lively Scot before the half-time whistle. With the points in the bag, 'Boro cruised through the second half for a 2-0 victory. It wasn't a spectacular start, but it was a sound one.

Three days later, on Tuesday, 16 August, almost 20,000 fans were back at Ayresome to see Manchester United in action. Clayton Blackmore had been on the verge of completing his testimonial season at Old Trafford when he signed for 'Boro, and was given special permission by the 'Boro board to stage his testimonial match at Ayresome. It made sense that Manchester United should be the opponents.

Clayton could hardly have expected a better turn-out if the match had been played at Old Trafford and there was a good buzz before the kick-off. However, like many testimonials, the game lacked a bit of excitement, especially as neither side was at full strength. Even so, United were a class apart and won 3-0 with two goals from Mark Hughes and another from Lee Sharpe.

'Boro were back in action on the Saturday, playing their first away game at Southend United. Once again 'Boro were tentative, but they grafted hard and deservedly won 2-0 with another brace from the clinical feet of Hendrie.

Bryan Robson raised a few eyebrows throughout the football world the following Monday when he announced in the *Evening Gazette* that he had approached former England teammate Gary Lineker. Robson had offered Lineker the chance to play for 'Boro for six months, once his contract with Japanese club Grampus Eight ended in December.

Lineker would have had a lot to offer 'Boro, even at the age of 33, but he later informed the 'Boro boss that he was taking up a job with the BBC.

'Boro switched competitions on the Wednesday when Piacenza visited Ayresome Park in the Anglo-Italian Cup. More than 5,000 fans turned up, which was something of an achievement. However, the match was dismal to watch, and ended goalless.

It was also a frustrating night for Paul Wilkinson, who came on as a second half substitute and was on the pitch only 20 seconds before being shown the red card for kicking one of the Italian defenders. The good news for Wilko was that he was banned from playing in the next two Anglo-Italian games.

'Boro faced their toughest test yet on Saturday, 27 August, when entertaining Bruce Rioch's Bolton Wanderers. It was a closely contested scrap throughout, with Paul Wilkinson giving 'Boro all three points when he converted a cross from Jamie Pollock. Even though the League season was only three games old, this was a very important game to win.

Deep in concentration. 'Boro's inspirational skipper Nigel Pearson leads the team out before the start of the very last derby match at Ayresome Park against Sunderland.

'Boro won the John White Footwear Supporters Award in May 1969, for having the best behaved and most sportsmanlike supporters in the Second Division.

Four days later 'Boro travelled to Derby County and won again, this time Clayton Blackmore grabbing the winning goal. The win was easier than the scoreline suggested, and meant that 'Boro had gone through their August programme without conceding a goal. The Endsleigh League, in their wisdom, decided against selecting a Manager of the Month award, which clearly would have gone to Robson.

Steve Vickers picked up a calf strain at Derby, and failed a late fitness test before 'Boro's trip to Watford on the Saturday. Derek Whyte came in as replacement and did well.

Watford went down to ten men in 22 minutes when goalkeeper Kevin Miller was dismissed for bringing down Bryan Robson outside the box. Thirteen minutes later Blackmore fired 'Boro in front, but Watford equalised after the break when a shot from Richard Johnson took a wicked deflection off Nigel Pearson. It was the first goal that Robbo's men had conceded. The match ended 1-1.

On Tuesday, 6 September, 'Boro were officially informed by the Department of Employment that Bolivian striker Jaime Moreno was to be awarded his work permit. The 20-year-old had been kicking his heels for six weeks while all the paperwork was processed.

Moreno was paraded to the Ayresome Park faithful before the start of the televised derby clash against Sunderland eight days later. Moreno, who received a standing ovation, said: "I've never received a reception before like that in Bolivia."

However, the crowd was soon silenced as two goals from Craig Russell gave Sunderland a two-goal lead by the 56th minute. The Rokermen were well and truly on top, with the woodwork denying Phil Gray a third goal.

'Boro looked dead and buried going into the closing stages. But Alan Moore scored a remarkable solo goal on 79 minutes and skipper Nigel Pearson equalised two minutes later to earn a 2-2 draw. It was a get out of jail free card, but 'Boro had shown that they possessed plenty of battling qualities.

Steve Vickers, seen in action against Don Goodman of Sunderland, had a great season in defence for 'Boro.

'Boro bounced back to winning ways by beating West Bromwich Albion by 2-1 at Ayresome Park on Wednesday, 14 September. However, they left it late, Craig Hignett ramming

Craig Hignett proved a match winner on more than one occasion in 'Boro's promotion campaign.

home a last-minute penalty after Paul Wilkinson was tripped by Craig Herbert. Albion had taken a 35th minute lead through Lee Ashcroft, but Robbie Mustoe equalised seven minutes later. Mustoe had come on as a substitute after 13 minutes for Bryan Robson, who had suffered a nasty kick in the first minute.

Injuries left 'Boro without Nigel Pearson, Bryan Robson and goalkeeper Alan Miller for their trip to Port Vale the following Saturday. Their places went to Derek Whyte, Robbie Mustoe and Steve Pears, the latter playing his first competitive game since May.

'Boro led 1-0 at the interval through a Jamie Pollock goal and controlled 70 per cent of the play. But a defensive lapse by Derek Whyte early in the second half enabled Vale to equalise, and the home side went on to win 2-1. It was 'Boro's first defeat.

A 4-1 win at Scarborough in the second-round first leg of the Coca-Cola Cup put 'Boro back into gear. The game was played throughout in heavy rain, but 'Boro were undeterred and cruised home with goals from John Hendrie, Jamie Pollock, Alan Moore and Robbie Mustoe.

'Boro were back in League action at Bristol City on Saturday, 24 September when a goal from John Hendrie was sufficient to bring all three points in a comfortable victory.

Jaime Moreno then made his competitive 'Boro debut as the team returned to Ayresome Park to beat Scarborough by 4-1 for the second time, to bring an 8-2 aggregate win in the second round of the Coca Cola Cup.

Moreno failed to score, but Paul Wilkinson had a field day, ending his lean spell with a hat-trick. However, Moreno made his mark on the match, setting up Wilko's third goal and another for Craig Hignett. The win meant that 'Boro had suffered just one defeat in their opening 12 games up until the end of September.

Clayton Blackmore returned after injury for Saturday's match at home to Millwall, taking the place of Alan Moore, who failed a late test on a groin injury.

'Boro were always in control, but missed the chance of an interval lead when Craig Hignett had a 42nd-minute penalty brilliantly saved by Millwall goalkeeper Kasey Keller.

However, 'Boro had the points in the bag early in the second half. John Hendrie scored his seventh goal of the season within 65 seconds of the restart, and then Paul Wilkinson grabbed his fourth goal in five days. 'Boro completed a 3-0 victory with an own-goal from Millwall full-back Mark Beard.

The following week Bryan Robson revealed that Tommy Wright was available for transfer if the right offer came along. The experienced winger had not started a League game under

Neil Cox, pictured in action against Tranmere Rovers, was the first million pound player at Ayresome Park.

Robson, though he was in the line-up for the midweek Anglo-Italian Cup-tie at home to Cesena. Once again the Cup-tie was a disappointment, 'Boro being held 1-1.

At least 'Boro managed to score their first goal in the competition at Ayresome Park in two seasons of trying. Jaime Moreno was the man who ended the search after 'Boro had spent 326 goalless minutes.

However, Cesena equalised when a free-kick from Dario Hubner was deflected into the net off Graham Kavanagh.

The following Saturday, 8 October, 'Boro produced their best performance of the season so far and suffered their worst result. They battered Tranmere Rovers for virtually the whole 90 minutes at Ayresome but could not score, and lost 1-0. Craig Hignett came closest to scoring for 'Boro when he hit the post in the first half. Tranmere, who rarely left their own half in the second period, broke upfield to take all three points when Steve Vickers slipped in going to meet a cross from Johnny Morrissey, and John Aldridge headed home.

In the closing minutes, Robbie Mustoe picked up a thigh injury and was later ruled out for three weeks. Bryan Robson tried to fill the gap by taking Manchester City's experienced Steve McMahon on a month's loan, but City were interested only in a permanent deal.

'Boro could have done with McMahon the following Saturday, because they were totally overrun at Luton Town and lost 5-1. There was no fluke about the scoreline. 'Boro failed to compete and were taken to the cleaners by the lively Hatters. Derek Whyte scored a late consolation for 'Boro.

Looking back, Robson said: "It was my worst moment of the season. We didn't compete and we paid the penalty. But I told the players that they had to learn from this defeat and make sure that it never happened again. Nobody turned us over after that."

'Boro travelled for their first away game in the Anglo-Italian Cup on the Tuesday, when tackling Udinese in north-east Italy. They were without Paul Wilkinson, who was suspended, John Hendrie, who was playing in Gavin Oliver's testimonial at Bradford City, and Jamie Pollock, who was rested.

The trip threatened to turn into a nightmare when Derek Whyte, Clayton Blackmore and Craig Hignett were all injured on Udinese's training pitch on the morning of the match. The

Curtis Fleming successfully switched from right-back to left-back in Ayresome's last season.

injuries were extended to four when Neil Cox limped off at half-time with a hamstring injury.

However, 'Boro managed to put together a ramshackle side, with the injured players on the bench. They also did surprisingly well, forcing a goalless draw, and going close to winning it. Craig Liddle made his 'Boro debut in defence, and did well.

'Boro faced a trial by TV as they battled to wipe away the memories of their Luton hammering in a televised match at Portsmouth. There was never any danger of a Luton repeat. 'Boro were in control from the start and missed a handful of great chances before having to settle for a goalless draw. Jaime Moreno made his League debut, but it was not a memorable match for him because the Bolivian limped off with a thigh strain.

On Wednesday, 26 October, 'Boro were beaten 1-0 at Aston Villa in the Coca-Cola Cup third round. It was not a great game, the Premier League side winning it when a shot from Andy Townsend was deflected in off Derek Whyte.

Finally, 'Boro were back at Ayresome Park on 29 October to beat Swindon Town 3-1. Neil Cox's first goal for the club gave 'Boro a great start after only two minutes, though it was never plain sailing after that.

Jan Åage Fjørtoft, later to join 'Boro, equalised after the restart and then Swindon had what looked a good goal by Keith Scott ruled out for offside. Soon after, John Hendrie restored 'Boro's lead and then Paul Wilkinson settled it from the penalty-spot.

'Boro then made it six points in four days by beating Oldham Athletic by 2-1 at Ayresome. They had to come from a goal behind, the equaliser coming from Alan Moore after the restart.

Clayton Blackmore, who had twice hit the woodwork, was substituted by Craig Hignett, who hit the underside of the bar himself from a free-kick. However, it was Hignett who grabbed the crucial winner, finishing off a glorious through ball by Derek Whyte. The only bad news was the loss of Curtis Fleming with a knee injury and a booking, which also brought him a three-match ban.

The following Saturday 'Boro went to Grimsby Town and were two goals down after 12 minutes. Only brilliant goalkeeping by Alan Miller prevented a rout. However, 'Boro rallied in the second half and reduced the arrears from the penalty-spot through Craig Hignett. But the equaliser just would not come.

Bryan Robson sent his reserve side to Ancona for the final Anglo-Italian game and the lads did well. Chris Morris gave them an early lead, but the Italians went on to win 3-1. It was a frustrating night for Andy Todd, who was sent off in the closing minutes.

However, it was a momentous night for Jamie Pollock, who made his England Under-21 debut as a second-half substitute against the Republic of Ireland at St James' Park. It was a proud night for 'Boro, because Graham Kavanagh and Alan Moore were in the Irish side.

'Boro played their most important match so far on Sunday, 20 November, when entertaining First Division leaders Wolves in a televised game. Almost 20,000 fans packed into Ayresome Park to see 'Boro absolutely batter Graham Taylor's side. However, 'Boro's winning goal was delayed until the middle of the second half, when John Hendrie struck his ninth goal of the season thanks to a deflection off Wolves midfielder Geoff Thomas. The win put 'Boro back on top for the first time

Jamie Pollock broke into the England Under-21 international squad as a result of his committed displays.

since mid-September. The following week, Nigel Pearson returned at Charlton Athletic for his first game since September. Bryan Robson opted for a sweeper system and 'Boro won comfortably with goals from John Hendrie and Jamie Pollock, though the latter picked up a booking which brought him a three-match ban.

Pearson was left out for the home game against Portsmouth on 3 December, though they were never threatened at the back and romped to a 4-0 victory with two goals each from Paul Wilkinson and Craig Hignett. Pompey striker Gerry Creaney was sent off in the second half.

Robbie Mustoe suffered the first sending off of his career at Reading on the Tuesday. Nigel Pearson was back for the match, which ended 1-1. 'Boro had gone ahead from the penalty-spot through Paul Wilkinson and looked in no danger until substitute Scott Taylor grabbed a late equaliser. Reading's Keith McPherson was also given his marching orders.

'Boro then went into their home game against Southend United five points clear at the top and looking to extend their lead. The visitors had other ideas and won 2-1, with 'Boro's late goal coming from John Hendrie. 'Boro badly missed the suspended Jamie Pollock and also Craig Hignett, who had been injured at Reading.

Bryan Robson made his long-awaited return to action at Burnley on 18 December, having been side-lined for three months through injury. His return coincided with 'Boro's best display for some time and they won easily, thanks to John Hendrie's third hat-trick for the club. Curtis Fleming also played well on his return after injury as 'Boro went six points clear at the top.

'Boro could have been pioneers on all-weather pitches. In 1969 they received an estimate of £9,340 from En Tout Cas for providing an all-weather pitch at Hutton Road. The matter was debated, but eventually discarded.

'Boro faced a more testing match at Sheffield United on Boxing Day, when they had to roll up their sleeves to earn a 1-1 draw thanks to a goal from Craig Hignett. 'Boro were without suspended duo Jamie Pollock and Robbie Mustoe, but Graham Kavanagh did well in his first game of the season.

Back at Ayresome Park, 'Boro had to work hard to overcome struggling Notts County by 2-1, the goals coming from Craig Hignett and Nigel Pearson. However, 'Boro suffered a blow when Neil Cox had to leave the field with a broken collarbone.

On Saturday, 31 December, Robson discarded the previously successful sweeper system at Stoke City, and 'Boro struggled to earn a 1-1 draw after taking the lead through Steve Vickers' first goal of the season.

The New Year started on a cold note when the home game against Barnsley was abandoned at half-time. The pitch was clearly unplayable before the start because it was frozen solid. Oldham referee Paul Harrison decided to go ahead and the match was a farce.

When he finally called a halt, 'Boro were leading 2-1 thanks to goals from John Hendrie and Alan Moore.

Many fans were incensed by the abandonment and demanded their money back. A Tannoy announcement at the end of the game only served to increase the confusion. Eventually 'Boro made it clear that ticket and voucher holders would be admitted for half price when the match was rearranged, but this infuriated a lot of fans who felt that they should be admitted free of charge.

'Boro switched their attentions to the FA Cup on Saturday, 7 January, earning a 1-1 draw at Second Division Swansea City in the third round. The Swans led 1-0 at the interval, forcing 'Boro to scrap their sweeper system at the interval by bringing on Alan Moore for Derek Whyte, who had picked up a foot injury.

Moore went on to head 'Boro's equaliser and they should have settled the issue on the day, but the winner just would not come.

The following week Paul Wilkinson missed his first game of the season with a knee injury as 'Boro went down 2-1 at Swindon Town. A first-half sending off of Curtis Fleming for a second bookable offence proved crucial. Craig Hignett scored 'Boro's goal, while Jan Åage Fjørtoft netted the first of Swindon's replies. Two days later 'Boro were back in action in their FA Cup third-round replay at home to Swansea City. It turned out to be their worst home performance of the season.

'Boro had most of the play, but were ineffective in attack and made some dreadful errors. Swansea were far from overawed by the occasion and took full advantage to take a two-goal lead through Steve Torpey and David Penney.

John Hendrie finally broke through for 'Boro 12 minutes from time, but the Swans deservedly held on. The most galling point was that 'Boro missed out on what would have been a mouth watering fourth-round derby battle at Newcastle United.

Bryan Robson said: "We let ourselves down. It was the most disappointing performance of the season at Ayresome Park. We didn't function at all. It happens in football, but it's frustrating when it happens in a game that you would normally win nine times out of ten."

'Boro had problems breaking down the Swansea defence, and they encountered the same trouble the following Saturday when Grimsby Town came to Ayresome Park and forced a 1-1 draw. On a cold and rainswept afternoon, 'Boro fell behind for the fourth time in a row at home when Neil Woods scored from a breakaway for the Mariners.

Earlier Craig Hignett had missed from the penalty-spot when his effort was saved by goalkeeper Paul Crichton, but Robbie Mustoe finally broke through to salvage a late point. Sadly, it was the last game of the season for Curtis Fleming, who was side-lined with a hip injury.

After the match, Robson revealed that he had signed German striker Uwe Fuchs on loan from 1.FC Kaiserslautern until the end of the season. Fuchs had watched the Grimsby match from the North Stand.

'Boro had hoped to play their abandoned match against Barnsley on FA Cup fourth-round day of Saturday, 28 January, but the game once again fell victim to the weather. The pitch was iced up on the Friday, and waterlogged the following day when the frozen pools of water on the pitch thawed.

'Boro had failed to win any of their games in January, and suddenly they were under pressure to find a victory from somewhere. They were starting to struggle, and Reading – one of their promotion rivals – took full advantage at Ayresome Park on 4 February. 'Boro failed to perform on the day, and Paul Holsgrove's strike early in the second half was enough to give Reading all three points.

The defeat was enough to cost 'Boro the top spot in the First Division for the first time since mid-November. Suddenly there was an air of desperation over the need to halt the slide. The players were losing confidence and needed inspiration.

It came at home to Charlton on 18 February, from Bryan Robson and Uwe Fuchs. Robson returned after injury to add stability to the midfield, while he also blooded Fuchs in place of Paul Wilkinson, who was destined not to start another game for the club.

Wilko had been the main man in the 'Boro line-up for almost four years, but the switch paid immediate dividends when Fuchs grabbed a fine goal after only 15 minutes. The goal settled 'Boro's nerves, and they held on for the three points.

Three days later, 'Boro faced their biggest test of the year so far at Wolves. It was a six-pointer of magnitude proportions, but 'Boro were simply brilliant and won very easily by 2-0. It was a huge confidence boost for Robbo's boys, and a major blow for Wolves in front of a shocked crowd of 26,611.

Both goals came in the second half, Steve Vickers scoring with a looping header and Uwe Fuchs netting for the second game in a row. It might have been 3-0, but Chris Morris had a late penalty saved.

'Boro followed up with a trip to Millwall, and again gave a positive account of themselves. But they struggled to cope with the difficult playing surface, and had to settle for a goalless draw. In his desperation to score a late winner, Bryan Robson

The goal which turned the tide. Uwe Fuchs grabs the winner against Charlton Athletic which restored 'Boro's confidence at a crucial time of the season.

Willie Whigham was suspended indefinitely with pay for assaulting coach Jimmy Greenhalgh in the dressing room in December 1968. The 'Boro goalkeeper was dropped from the team to play at Blackpool and his place taken by Maurice Short. Whigham later apologised to Greenhalgh and sent a written apology to the board, and the suspension was lifted.

threw himself bravely at a corner and suffered a nasty gash above his left eye which needed a dozen stitches.

Despite this injury, Robson kept his place in the line-up for the home game against Bristol City the following week. However, the real hero was new fans' favourite Uwe Fuchs, who rammed home all three goals in a 3-0 victory. The match signalled the return of Neil Cox after injury, while Jaime Moreno also had his first start of 1995 in place of the injured Jamie Pollock.

'Boro then made it two home wins in four days by beating Watford 2-0 at Ayresome Park on 7 March. The feature of the game was a remarkable solo goal from Robbie Mustoe, who ran 40 yards and blasted the ball into the top corner from outside the box. Fuchs scored the other to give him six goals in five starts.

Robson, who had rested himself against Watford, returned to action on the Saturday for the big, big game at Bolton Wanderers. Robbo hit the post in the first half, but Bolton were in the driving seat from the 14th minute when Mixu Paatelainen scored, and Wanderers took the points.

The outstanding match against Barnsley finally took place at Ayresome Park on Tuesday, 14 March and was a disappointment because the visitors grabbed a deserved 1-1 draw. Jaime Moreno put 'Boro ahead when finishing off a good run by Alan Moore, but the home side slackened off in the second half and former 'Boro striker Andy Payton headed the equaliser.

The following Saturday, 'Boro called up teenager Keith O'Halloran to make his debut at home to Derby County. The Irish lad played at right-back with Neil Cox moving over to the left for the injured Derek Whyte.

In the event O'Halloran was given very little support and had a nightmare match. In fact he was replaced at half-time, when 'Boro were three goals down through Lee Mills (2), and Mark Pembridge.

'Boro staged a remarkable revival at the start of the second half. They scored through Uwe Fuchs and Jamie Pollock in quick succession and threatened to win the game. However, Marco Gabbiadini grabbed a great solo goal for the Rams, and 'Boro's gallant effort faded as the visitors won 4-2.

Three days later Jamie Pollock revived 'Boro's promotion hopes with a crucial winner at Sunderland. He picked up a through ball from Robbie Mustoe, raced clear and forced the ball home.

Mustoe had bravely played on after suffering a broken cheekbone in the opening minutes as a result of a challenge by Richard Ord. The midfielder was to play no further part in the promotion push.

'Boro were back in action at Ayresome Park in a televised game against Port Vale, on Sunday, 26 March. The match was notable both for 'Boro's 3-0 win, and Bryan Robson's first goal for the club.

Robbo produced a great early strike to score from the edge of the box and send 'Boro on their way to a comfortable victory. Steve Vickers and Uwe Fuchs also scored.

The player-manager revealed: "It must be the new boots. My old pair had split so I had to switch to a new pair to play in against Port Vale. It looks like I'll have to change my boots every match!"

Not content to rest on his laurels, Robson made a double transfer swoop on transfer deadline day. In came record signing

It's that man Uwe again. The popular German striker is in the thick of the action against Port Vale.

Jan Åage Fjørtoft, a £1.3 million snip from Swindon Town, and England Under-21 defender Phil Whelan for £300,000 from Ipswich Town.

Norwegian international Fjørtoft was top scorer in the First Division with 25 goals to his credit in all competitions and promised to be very good value at the price. Whelan also offered great value for money, especially as he had been playing regularly in the Premier League for Ipswich.

However, a mix-up with the registration forms meant that 'Boro were not allowed to play Whelan in First Division games. The Football Association claimed that the forms had arrived after the 5pm registration deadline.

It meant that Whelan could not make his debut in 'Boro's game at West Bromwich Albion on Saturday, 1 April – which was a blow, because skipper Nigel Pearson was suspended. In fact 'Boro were left with a dearth of centre-backs because Andy Todd was on loan at Swindon until the end of the season.

The answer was for 38-year-old assistant manager Viv Anderson to put his boots on again. Anderson had not played a League game all season, but in the event did so well that he was one of the best players on the pitch.

Even so, 'Boro struggled early on and trailed at the interval to a Tony Rees goal. They needed some inspiration, and got it from Alan Moore, who was told by Bryan Robson early in the second half that he was about to be substituted. Moore responded with ten minutes of magic in which he set up the equaliser for Jamie Pollock, crossed for West Brom defender Paul Raven to turn the ball into his own net, and then scored the third himself as 'Boro won 3-1.

'Boro followed up with another away game, at Oldham Athletic. In a dull match, they never looked in trouble, and went close to taking the lead when Fjørtoft lobbed the ball against the crossbar midway through the second half.

Unfortunately 'Boro then suffered a blow in the closing minutes when Nigel Pearson was concussed in a late challenge by Oldham substitute, Andy Ritchie. Pearson was still in a dazed state when Oldham staged a late attack and it was Ritchie who fired home to give the home side a last-minute winner.

At this point, all the promotion-chasing sides were starting to feel the pressure at the top, especially as there was only one automatic promotion spot to go for. Tranmere,

Norwegian international Jan Åage Fjørtoft who, at £1.3 million, was the most expensive player ever to wear 'Boro's famous red shirt at Ayresome Park.

A bird's-eye view of the gateway to Ayresome Park, taken on a match day near the end of the season.

Wolves and Bolton, who were 'Boro's main challengers, were all starting to drop unexpected points and continued to do so until the end of the season.

'Boro were back at Ayresome Park on 8 April to entertain Stoke City, with Graham Kavanagh coming into midfield for Bryan Robson and John Hendrie coming back for the injured Uwe Fuchs.

The home side were given a great start when skipper Nigel Pearson put them in front, but slack marking at the back then allowed Paul Peschisolido the equaliser.

It looked all over a draw until Moore conjured a bit of magic from his box of tricks 15 minutes from time. The Irish lad started and finished the move, cutting in strongly from the left before playing a 1-2 with Fjørtoft and going on to slam home the winner.

Moore was unfortunately injured for 'Boro's next match away to struggling Notts County, so his place was taken by Jaime Moreno. It was not a memorable match, and 'Boro looked like losing it when Devon White put County ahead in the second half.

However, Uwe Fuchs proved the goal hero again. The German came off the bench to convert a cross from Neil Cox six minutes from time for his ninth goal for the club.

'Boro were back at Ayresome on Easter Monday for what turned out to be a gruelling clash against Sheffield United. Jan Fjørtoft's first goal for the club gave 'Boro a seventh minute lead, but Nathan Blake equalised 11 minutes later and the match developed into a stalemate.

The game was notable for the controversial refereeing of Bill Burns from Scarborough, who regularly incensed the 'Boro players and the fans with his second-half decisions.

It started when Mr Burns merely cautioned United's Craig Veart for bringing down Jamie Pollock from behind as the 'Boro man hared in on goal, just outside the box. The game then got out of hand, and goalkeeper Alan Kelly escaped with only a caution when he handled outside the area.

Mr Burns did correctly produce the red card on just one occasion, to send off Uwe Fuchs for a reckless foul on Kevin Gage.

Afterwards Bryan Robson risked an FA fine when he said: "The referee did not want us to win the match."

'Boro played their last Saturday match of the season on 22 April in a torrential downpour at Barnsley. Viv Anderson made his second appearance, at his former Oakwell stamping ground, in place of skipper Nigel Pearson, while Chris Morris and John Hendrie came in for the suspended Derek Whyte and Uwe Fuchs.

The match was memorable mainly for a terrific solo goal from Jan Fjørtoft, which should have been good enough for all three points. But 'Boro allowed Andy Liddell a tame equaliser and had to settle for a 1-1 draw. Remarkably, after three consecutive draws, 'Boro were still three points clear at the top.

So, the scene was set for the very last League game at Ayresome Park at home to Luton Town on Sunday, 30 April. 'Boro made sure that it was a memorable day for the fans by organising a series of celebratory events, including a parade of dozens of former 'Boro stars before the kick-off.

It was a glorious, hot afternoon, and the capacity crowd of 23,903 were in position a good hour before the kick-off to enjoy the pre-match entertainment, which included several songs from 26-year-old Suzannah Clarke, the nationally recognised soprano who hailed from Normanby. The highlight of this was *You'll Never Walk Alone*, which had thousands of red and white scarves raised aloft and received full vocal backing from the stands and many a tear.

'Boro, who had Bryan Robson, Derek Whyte and Nigel

You'll Never Walk Alone. **The Holgate End join in a heart rending rendition of the famous soccer anthem shortly before the start of the last match against Luton Town.**

Back home. Bernie Slaven salutes the fans as he parades with the 'Boro greats before the Luton match. Also pictured is his fellow striker Archie Stephens.

The message tells the story. Another shot from the Luton match, which indicates the fans' feelings about the stadium.

Pearson all back in action, received terrific support. But it was a pressure situation for the team because of the high level of expectation and, despite creating a host of chances, they struggled to put them away.

John Hendrie finally broke the deadlock just before the interval when his shot was deflected in off Dwight Marshall, but 'Boro faltered after the restart and John Taylor silenced the crowd by heading Luton level in the 63rd minute.

It was a testing time for the home side, but 11 minutes later came the winning goal and the last to be scored in official competition at Ayresome, fittingly in the Holgate End goal. Jamie Pollock did the spadework on the left, and Derek Whyte cleverly took it on before setting up Hendrie for his second goal and the honour of scoring the last one at Ayresome.

Afterwards 'Boro might have finished with six or seven goals, but burnt-up adrenalin and the hot sun took their toll.

Hendrie said: "It was very, very hot out there, and the players were under a lot of pressure because of all the expectation. We ran ourselves into the ground to make sure that we won it."

'Boro now stood one point from the First Division

Action from the last game against Luton Town as Jan Åage Fjørtoft sends a header over the bar.

The crowds have gone, but 'Boro marvel Wilf Mannion stays on to say his own personal goodbye to the stadium which he graced for so many years.

A final farewell. 'Boro goalkeepers Steve Pears and Alan Miller salute the crowd following Pears' testimonial game, which was the very last match to be played at Ayresome Park on Tuesday, 16 May 1995.

championship, and would be crowned champions without playing if remaining rivals Bolton Wanderers failed to win their game in hand at Stoke City the following Wednesday night.

It was a tense night, with thousands of Teesside fans and players alike crowded around the radio to hear live broadcasts from both Radio Cleveland and TFM. In the event Stoke forced a draw, and the title belonged to Robbo's men.

Robson said: "I think we have deserved it because we have been the best team over the course of the season. We had a couple of hiccups, but so did everybody else. We were the most consistent team at the end of the season and it proved to be crucial."

'Boro were able to go to Tranmere for the last game of the season in party mood. They took 3,200 official fans with them, while many more were dotted around the Tranmere areas of Prenton Park. For most of the match they outshouted the home supporters.

Robson took the opportunity to make changes and gave Craig Liddle his League debut in midfield, and he did well. Chris Morris, Philip Stamp and Jaime Moreno were also given a taste of the action.

'Boro dominated the first half, but found themselves with it all to do when Kenny Irons fired Tranmere in front shortly before the interval. However, Jan Fjørtoft equalised six minutes after the restart and 'Boro were never in any danger of losing.

The 1-1 draw was 'Boro's fourth in their last six games, but it was still a level of consistency which their promotion rivals had been unable to match. In fact 'Boro lost just one of their last ten games – at Oldham – and even then would surely have avoided defeat but for concussion to skipper Nigel Pearson.

Once all the promotion celebrations had settled down, Bryan Robson announced his retained list. There were few surprises. Paul Wilkinson, who had failed to start a League game since February, was made available for a fee, and so, too, was Craig Hignett. Tommy Wright, who had seen little of the first-team action, was given a free transfer, along with Steve Pears, who was celebrating his testimonial season after giving 'Boro ten years tremendous service.

The biggest disappointment as far as the fans were concerned was that Uwe Fuchs was not signed on. The German was available for transfer from his club 1.FC Kaiserslautern for £500,000, and obviously represented good value at that price. His nine goals had been invaluable for 'Boro, and without him the club would not have won the title.

However, Robson made it clear that he would be scouting around for much bigger fish during the summer, and asked the fans to be patient and wait to see what he could come up with, before making a hasty judgement on the Fuchs decision.

All that remained now was the Ayresome Park finale, which was Steve Pears' testimonial match against a Select XI on Tuesday, 16 May. It was the culmination of the testimonial year for the former England squad goalkeeper, who had been

Lest we forget. This aerial shot of the magnificent old North Stand – 92 years old – was taken as the final curtain was pulled down on the much loved stadium.

outstanding throughout his time at the club. In fact many fans were surprised to see Pears awarded a free transfer because they felt he still had a lot to offer the club.

'Boro's first-team players had to hurry back from a short break in Portugal to play in the game, and in the end most of them played only the opening 45 minutes. Before the kick-off they were awarded their First Division championship medals, and the trophy was handed to 'Boro skipper Nigel Pearson by Mike Naylor, managing director of Endsleigh Insurance. Almost 20,000 fans turned up to afford 'Boro rousing adulation during their lap of honour.

Pears' Select XI included former 'Boro heroes like Bernie Slaven, who scored the first goal and celebrated in true fashion by leaping on the Holgate fence. Peter Beardsley also scored, just before Paul Wilkinson replied for 'Boro.

Ten minutes from time, the Select XI were awarded a penalty and Steve Pears came forward to slam the ball home for a 3-1 victory.

It was the final goal at Ayresome Park.

'Boro made a second lap of honour at the final whistle, with Pears carrying the championship trophy. It was the last time that professional football was to grace Ayresome Park, and it was fitting that it should be commemorated with a trophy – and the knowledge that 'Boro were back in the Premier League.

Ninety-two years of history had come and gone. The gypsies' curse held strong, but didn't prevent thousands of fans and players collecting the memories of a lifetime. Goodbye Ayresome, Hello Riverside!

Going, going, gone. Rubble lies on part of the Ayresome Park pitch as the demolition men with their digging machines prepare to do their worst in the late summer of 1996.

Ayresome Lives

IN THE autumn of 2002, the North Koreans were back on Teesside. The diminutive heroes of the 1966 World Cup made an emotional return to the site of their greatest sporting achievement. They had flown to these shores for a week-long trip, having accepted an invitation to attend an England international in Southampton and a film festival in Sheffield. But it was only natural that the centre of their pilgrimage halfway across the world should be Ayresome Park.

This was the stadium where North Korea had played their three historic World Cup group games, winning the hearts of all those supporters who saw them in action in the matches against Russia, Chile and that memorable victory against Italy. However, the Ayresome Park which the surviving seven players from that heroic team revisited was not the Ayresome Park which was etched into their memories.

On Wednesday 23 October, the North Korean party alighted from their coach to see Ayresome Park as it is now, a vibrant, colourful and proudly maintained small housing estate in the centre of Middlesbrough. They discovered that bulldozers had long since moved in to demolish the town's 92-year-old football icon, razing the ageing stands to the ground and ripping up the hallowed turf to create homes for Middlesbrough people and their families.

What once belonged to the people had been given back to the people.

In their hearts and minds, the North Koreans may again have heard the deafening roar of the crowd, smelt the cigarette smoke from the terraces and the football boot dubbing from the dressing room, and even seen Pak Do Ik run forward to repeat his unforgettable winning goal against the Italians.

But Ayresome Park had long ceased to be the base for football on Middlesbrough and the cultural home of thousands of local supporters.

Domestic football had moved a couple of miles from the Ayresome borough, to the heart of the former industrious Middlesbrough dockland. The Middlehaven site now housed the purpose-built, ultra-modern Riverside Stadium, where the 'Boro played their football in the Premiership, the greatest league in the world.

Three days after their eye-opener at Ayresome Park, the North Koreans would have the opportunity to gape at the sights of a packed Riverside. In fact Pak Do

An aerial view of the new Ayresome Park estate as it takes shape.

A fee of £10,000 was paid to European champions Ajax for playing a friendly at Ayresome in August 1978.

Ik would even repeat his memorable goalscoring achievement in front of the appreciative 'Boro faithful, who stood to cheer him in the stadium's North Stand.

Who knows what emotions the Asian players felt that day. Maybe, deep down, they would have preferred to have seen the wood and concrete of the original Ayresome Park, standing in all its majesty and glory.

But they were too late. The North Koreans returned to the site of the old stadium more than seven years after competitive football was last played there. John Hendrie's wonderful brace of goals in 'Boro's final match against Luton Town in Division One had ended Ayresome Park's chequered history on a high. A few days later, Steve Pears's testimonial match brought down the final curtain.

"Boro moved to the Riverside in August 1995, though only for matches. In fact Ayresome Park still remained intact and was used as a training base for the club's playing staff for another season. However, it was only ever intended that Ayresome Park should provide 'Boro with temporary training facilities. While 'Boro celebrated their return to the Premiership by playing in a new stadium down by the Riverside, the club were making progress with their plans to provide an off-the-field training base of the same high quality. Work was already underway to develop state-of-the-art training headquarters at a secluded site at Rockliffe Park, near Croft, which had recently been relinquished by the members of a religious order. The work at Rockliffe Park initially involved levelling a large area of land to provide several training pitches, and this would not be fully completed until the summer of 1996.

So 'Boro continued to use Ayresome Park as their training base and the coaches and players arrived there every morning. The old stadium held all the facilities which Bryan Robson and his squad needed, from changing rooms with baths and showers, to a perfect playing surface. Ayresome Park also offered a degree of security and privacy, allowing the team to train behind closed doors when necessary.

The 'Boro players returned for pre-season training to Ayresome Park on 13 July 1995. The only player missing on that day was striker Jan Aage Fjortoft, who had been allowed an extra few days holiday because he had been on duty with Norway during the summer.

Nine days later a programme fair was held at Ayresome Park and 2,000 fans turned up to rummage through the items for sale and also to pay homage to the old stadium. They were allowed to walk around the pitch and take photographs for the final time.

The 'Boro squad trained at Ayresome Park throughout the winter months, except for a brief break in February when the pitch became unplayable due to heavy rain and 'Boro were offered the use of the excellent sports facilities at the nearby Holme House Prison. The players would travel by bus to the prison, be guided through the thick prison walls, and then train on a near-perfect grass pitch while prisoners watched from cell windows in an often eerie atmosphere.

'Boro had taken steps to try to improve the state of the Ayresome Park pitch in December 1995, by forking out the cash to install extra drainage. But the work did not bring the desired results in what was a particularly wet winter.

In addition to offering training facilities for the players, Ayresome Park had provided a base for the club's commercial staff for a few extra months following the opening of the Riverside Stadium. Work on the infrastructure at the Riverside had not been fully completed, even though games were being played there, so office staff continued to work from Ayresome Park for several weeks. In fact the ticket office at Ayresome Park remained open until the end of September, even though tickets were being sold for games at the Riverside.

Eventually the move was fully completed, though not everybody made it away from Ayresome Park. On 26 September the *Evening Gazette* reported that Keegan, the club's black and white cat and official mouse catcher, had died. So he never had the chance to catch mice down by the Riverside.

The new stadium was quickly awarded its first international, when England Under-21s entertained Austria on 14 November. The cream of England's young talent trained at Ayresome Park in preparation for the match. A few days later the first snow of the winter arrived, and 'Boro's new superstar Juninho was famously pictured making snowballs at Ayresome Park. Juninho was later joined on Teesside by his Brazilian compatriot Branco, who was to play in a match which remains a genuine contender for the official title of 'Last Game Ever Played At Ayresome Park'.

On 2 April 1996, 'Boro played a full 90-minute match, with qualified referee, linesman, corner flags and everything else, against the Norwegian side Tromso. The Norwegians were touring Britain to play warm-up fixtures in preparation for their own domestic season, which was just about to start, and 'Boro agreed to play them.

For some reason, this friendly was not played at the Riverside, so Ayresome Park hosted the match. As the stadium no longer held a licence to accommodate spectators, the match was played behind closed doors. The only people present were the officials from both sides, plus one or two 'Boro reserve team players.

The game was played at a competitive pace, and Tromso won 3–1. All their goals were scored by the big striker Sigurd Rushveldt, who had been linked with a potential £600,000 move to 'Boro early in 1995. Rushveldt fired Tromso ahead after 23 minutes, but 'Boro's Bolivian striker Jaime Moreno equalised with a solo goal 10 minutes later.

Branco went close to scoring for 'Boro with a piledriver which came back off the crossbar, but Rushveldt earned victory for the Norwegians with two further goals in the 83rd and 85th minutes. The 'Boro team for that last-ever match was: Miller (Payne 46), Morris (Ward 46), Byrne, Vickers, Liddle, Branco, Hignett, Blackmore, Fjortoft, Moreno, Skingsley (Campbell 81).

Later that month, on Tuesday 23 April, the stadium was given its final send-off. That was the date of an official auction to sell off any remaining parts of the stadium which would attract buyers. The book *Robson and the 'Boro*, published by Juniper Publishing in 1996, reported: "Fittingly, it was a damp and depressing day for the auction, which was a particularly sad event for the fans.

"The auction lasted for much of the day and the goods which were sold off included the floodlights, stand seats and turnstiles.

"Non-league clubs bought most of the items for installation at their own grounds but many 'Boro fans also turned up to bid for some of the lots, concentrating on buying wooden signs and other small pieces of memorabilia.

"The North Stand clock was bought by Dave Stokes to hang in the Ayresome Park pub in Albert Road.

"Even former 'Boro goal ace Bernie Slaven got in on the act by buying a section of the Holgate End fencing, from where he used to salute the fans after scoring one of his many goals at the stadium."

Fans had little opportunity to pay a final pilgrimage to Ayresome Park. Work on demolishing the stadium began almost immediately after 'Boro vacated the premises to take up residence at Rockliffe Park. Builders Wimpey Homes had been contracted to erect 138 terraced and semi-detached homes on the site, effectively taking up every inch of land which had previously been occupied by the stadium.

However, before the hallowed turf was ripped up, employees from Wimpey decided to play one final game on the pitch. Two teams were selected from the company's employees, representing England and Scotland. It was a close international match, which the Scots won 1–0.

George Cowens, the Wimpey Homes site manager, puts the finishing touches to one of the new street signs on the Ayresome Park estate.

Then the contractors moved in. Work began immediately on digging up the pitch, while the stands were quickly reduced to rubble.

It was at this stage that the full impact of the loss of the old stadium, as it disappeared from the Middlesbrough skyline, became apparent. All fans must have found it particularly poignant to walk, or drive, past the site. The view down Warwick Street, which for many, many years had provided the comforting view of the prized metal gates, now revealed nothing but a scene of desolation. The gates, the North Stand and the pitch had gone. Huge mounds of rubble lay everywhere.

Not everybody was pleased to see that the old was being replaced by the new.

An Italian journalist rang the *Evening Gazette* to ask whether it was true that Ayresome Park had been demolished. He said: "Ayresome Park should be a lasting memorial to the greatest failure in Italian football. Pak Do Ik is a household name in Italy because he scored the winning goal for North Korea in Middlesbrough.

"So football supporters in Italy are very interested to see what will happen to Ayresome Park.

"We threw so many rotten tomatoes at our national team when they arrived home in 1966, that we were rather hoping, that if the stadium had to be knocked down, it would be turned into a supermarket for canned tomatoes."

However, it was quite clear that a housing development held priority over a supermarket, and Wimpey's construction staff worked diligently and quickly to redevelop the Ayresome Park site. Outlines of the first houses began to take shape in Ayresome Park Road. These were also the first homes to be occupied, having been erected on the area of land underneath the East Stand, or the Linthorpe Road End as it was originally known.

By the end of 1999, the estate was almost complete. At this time, the final four houses were put up for sale. These were the show homes, which ranged from £49,950 to £59,950 in price. The signing of contracts on these homes was the final act which ensured the complete disappearance of the old stadium.

But it was not the end of football. Familiar names like The Holgate, The Turnstile and The Midfield were still surviving at Ayresome Park. These were the street names which had been given to the array of pleasant cul-de-sacs which now occupied the land.

The demand for homes on the new estate had been strong from day one, and had never wavered. A lot of Middlesbrough people wanted to live on the attractive new development, and Wimpey claimed that the homes had helped breathe new life into the Ayresome region of the town. Kevin Thubron, the sales and marketing director at Wimpey Homes, said: "Ayresome Park has played a significant role in the regeneration of the area. The response from day one has been overwhelming."

In addition to giving the streets names with football themes, there was a push to ensure that some of the vital parts of Ayresome Park would be allowed to live on as visible signs to both residents and visitors. So Wimpey Homes agreed, in collaboration with Cleveland Arts, to intermingle the houses with art works.

The former penalty spot – part of a resident's front garden – was marked by a bronze football and painted to resemble a children's ball. The centre spot attracted a pair of football boots and pitch puddles in bronze. And garden walls were branded with enormous sandblasted text, highlighting areas of the ground.

The carefully sculpted memorabilia was the work of celebrated artist and sculptor Neville Gabie, who was specifically commissioned to carry out the work. Neville, formerly the artist in residence at the Tate Gallery in Liverpool, had worked closely with Liverpool Football Club in the past on other football orientated projects.

Neville's first task at Ayresome Park was to pinpoint the exact areas where the penalty spot and the centre spot had stood. He also used photographic evidence to mark the point from where Pak Do Ik hammered home his World Cup match-winning goal in 1966.

Neville, who was delighted by the response to the project from people in and out of the new estate, was inspired to carry out the project by his own love of football. He revealed: "When I started the project, what I did was to mark things in such a way that, if you were not looking at the estate as a former football ground, then you would see it only as a housing estate.

"But the signs of what was there before the houses are easy to find for those people who are looking for them.

"We have the centre spot, and the Holgate penalty spot, and the corner flags.

"We also have the words 'Enclosure' and 'Away' sandblasted into walls, and they have been done very subtly so that they aren't always obvious in different lights.

"I wanted to be as subtle as possible. A bronze football marks the penalty spot but I wanted to make it look like a kid had been playing and left it there so that it wouldn't look out of the ordinary."

The extra touches were much appreciated by the residents.

Robert Nichols, editor of the 'Boro fanzine *Fly Me To The Moon* and one of the first residents to move into a house

A poignant moment as Wilf Mannion's funeral cortege passes hundreds of fans paying their respects to the former 'Boro legend outside the site of Ayresome Park.

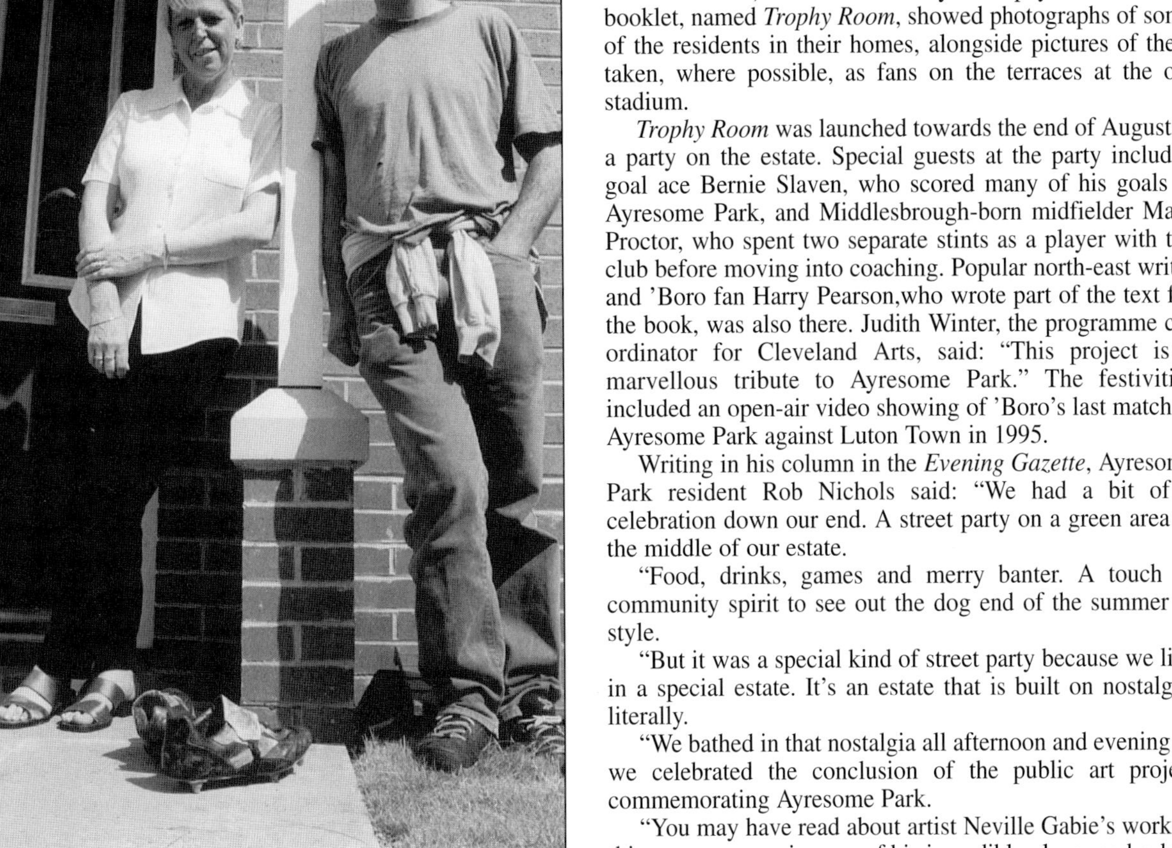

Artist Neville Gabie, who fashioned the unique pair of bronze football boots to mark the old Ayresome Park centre spot, which stand on Mary Griffith's front doorstep.

The bronze football boots that mark the old Ayresome Park centre spot.

on the new estate, said: "It's engendered a real feeling of pride with the people who live here."

Mary Griffith, who moved into the house which was sitting directly across the centre spot, as highlighted by a pair of bronze boots on her doorstep, said: "I think it's a brilliant idea."

The finished work was much appreciated by Philip Reilly of Cleveland Arts, who said: "We are really pleased with it. We like the idea of having different objects rather than just one piece and having them on different properties."

In August 2001, Ayresome Park old and new was commemorated by a booklet which was produced by Cleveland Arts. The publication featured lots of pictures of the old, much-loved stadium, and of the housing estate which now occupies the site. The booklet was compiled by Neville Gabie, and financed by Wimpey Homes. The booklet, named *Trophy Room*, showed photographs of some of the residents in their homes, alongside pictures of them taken, where possible, as fans on the terraces at the old stadium.

Trophy Room was launched towards the end of August at a party on the estate. Special guests at the party included goal ace Bernie Slaven, who scored many of his goals at Ayresome Park, and Middlesbrough-born midfielder Mark Proctor, who spent two separate stints as a player with the club before moving into coaching. Popular north-east writer and 'Boro fan Harry Pearson,who wrote part of the text for the book, was also there. Judith Winter, the programme co-ordinator for Cleveland Arts, said: "This project is a marvellous tribute to Ayresome Park." The festivities included an open-air video showing of 'Boro's last match at Ayresome Park against Luton Town in 1995.

Writing in his column in the *Evening Gazette*, Ayresome Park resident Rob Nichols said: "We had a bit of a celebration down our end. A street party on a green area in the middle of our estate.

Four 'Boro players were killed in action during World War Two: H. Cook, Andrew Jackson, Don McLeod and Archie Wilson.

"Food, drinks, games and merry banter. A touch of community spirit to see out the dog end of the summer in style.

"But it was a special kind of street party because we live in a special estate. It's an estate that is built on nostalgia, literally.

"We bathed in that nostalgia all afternoon and evening as we celebrated the conclusion of the public art project commemorating Ayresome Park.

"You may have read about artist Neville Gabie's work in this paper or seen images of his incredibly clever and subtle sculptures on TV. But unless you were there you won't have experienced the spine-tingling fanfare of Cyril Stapleton's Power Game, trumpeting in a re-run of the final Ayresome game, projected onto the back wall of the Holgate.

"It was so eerie hearing the incessant roar from the startlingly red terraces. We covered our faces when Neil Cox missed his penalty. Punched the air in delight when Hendrie's deflected shot beat Davis into the net and bit deeply into our nails as Taylor pulled Luton level. It was impossible not to get drawn into the drama all over again.

"A mere six years seems like a lifetime ago, such are the immense changes seen since.

"Bernie Slaven was up on the fence again, Proc returned to sign autographs and Marrie Wieczorek came down to coach the kids.

"Then it was time to take a wander around the trail of football artefacts that Neville Gabie has positioned marking key points in the old ground.

"With classic 'Boro songs pumping out of the PA system we spotted a jumper here, a discarded scarf, a pair of boots parked up by a doorstep, all cast in bronze but painted to look totally lifelike. They are all links and entry points to another world, the world of hopes, triumphs and disasters of generations past."

After the hangovers had subsided, the residents settled down to get on with their lives. That is, until they received some very, very special visitors in October 2002. That was when the seven surviving members of the 1966 North Korea World Cup side, plus coach Myong Rye Hyon, revisited the scene of their greatest triumph.

To mark the return of the Koreans, the *Evening Gazette* printed a special supplement which was handed to goal hero Pak Do Ik by *Gazette* Chief Sports Writer Eric Paylor when

Back home! Pak Do Ik, wearing the black jacket, and his North Korean teammates, make a tour of the Ayresome Park housing estate on their emotional return to Teesside.

he alighted from the coach and touched base with Ayresome Park for the first time in 36 years.

Pak Do Ik, whose goal in front of the Ayresome Park faithful gave them victory over the mighty Italians, and his teammates were given a guided tour of the estate and were shown the sculptures. Pak Do Ik was particularly amazed to be shown the bronze casting which marked the spot from where he struck his winning goal.

Pak Su Jin, who scored the equaliser in a 1–1 draw against Chile during the tournament, said: "We have great feelings for the people of Middlesbrough because they looked after us and took us in their hearts in 1966.

"I have very vivid memories of the game here against Italy and can recall the winning goal. It was a great moment for us.

"We were surprised to come back to the stadium and see that it has gone. It was such a wonderful place for us.

"But life must go on and we are now to see that Middlesbrough has a new stadium for the people of the town."

Pak Do Ik said: "The English people took us to their hearts and vice versa. I learned that football is not only about the winning.

"Wherever we go, playing football can improve diplomatic relations and promote peace."

Later the North Korean party moved on to Billingham Synthonia's Central Avenue ground, where they had trained when preparing for their World Cup campaign. Three days later they were the special guests of the 'Boro at their Premiership game against Leeds United at the Riverside Stadium.

The 'Boro fans gave all seven members a special reception when they took to the pitch, while Pak Do Ik received a deafening reception as he re-enacted his legendary Ayresome Park goal in front of the North Stand at the Riverside. Karen Shields, one of the trip's organisers, said: "We had a chat with them and they were all very, very emotional.

"When they went on to the pitch at the Riverside, the reaction from the fans was just gobsmacking. They were totally overwhelmed.

"Pak said that when he scored on Saturday, he could picture what went through his head in 1966 – that's why he picked the ball out of the net after he scored."

The North Koreans were accommodated at the Middleton St George Hotel at Teesside International Airport, which is where they had stayed during their epic World Cup campaign.

In addition to the trips to Ayresome Park and the Riverside, a series of civic visits were also organised, including a reception at the Town Hall following the Leeds match. Middlesbrough's speaker, Ken Hall, hosted a party for the visitors, and the team was greeted by councillors from the Tees Valley when they arrived. Councillor Hall said: "That they speak so highly of the town when they were here for only a week is brilliant.

"The occasion speaks for itself. It's brought a lot of smiles to people's faces. People are so happy about the whole thing – it's very special."

The guests burst into spontaneous applause as Councillor Hall raised Pak Do Ik's arm aloft as he entered the Town Hall suite. The North Korean team presented gifts, including a signed vase and football, to the town. Redcar and Cleveland Mayor Eric Jackson said: "I think a lot of people in the area took the Koreans to heart. People always like to see the underdog do well and it was a great occasion when they dumped out the Italians."

North Korean goalkeeper Li Chan-Myong – nicknamed 'The Cat' – said: "It's amazing that although a long time has passed, the people of Middlesbrough still remember us.

"We've been very busy because so many people want to meet us, but it is our pleasure. It feels like meeting some of my relatives, because people have been so welcoming."

The team were also special guests at a sportsman's dinner at the Riverside. Former 'Boro manager Jack Charlton, another hero of the 1966 World Cup, was guest speaker.

After five days, the party left for a film festival in Sheffield, wearing Billingham Synthonia ties given to them by the club. The Koreans had earlier been guests of honour at the England v Macedonia Euro 2004 qualifier at the St Mary's Stadium, Southampton, and were honoured with an official Football Association reception to which members of both the 1966 England and Italy squads were invited.

Retaining the legendary Holgate Wall, pictured in September 2003, became the subject of intense local debate.

The whole trip had been organised by documentary makers Daniel Gordon and Nicholas Bonner, who produced an 80-minute film charting North Korea's glorious World Cup campaign. Virgin Atlantic had agreed to fly the former players over free of charge.

The documentary, *The Game of Their Lives*, received a gala screening at the Sheffield International Documentary Film Festival and had further showings in Middlesbrough, London, Liverpool and Shanghai. Dan said: "The people of Middlesbrough get really animated and passionate about the film whenever we show it. They are rightly proud of the team their town adopted – and that warmth is reciprocated.

"When the North Korean team came over to England they were genuinely touched by the incredible welcome they got on Teesside.

"We had just come back from a photo opportunity at the old Ayresome Park and were driving towards the town hall when one of the players started shouting: 'Stop the bus!'

"He had spotted the North Korean flag flying above the town hall and was amazed and touched by such a gesture. They all trooped off to look. They were so proud.

"Then when we introduced them to the crowd before the Leeds game it was just overwhelming for them all.

"There was a full house and they got the most tremendous warm applause and cheering and they were enormously moved. Several were in tears of pride when they came off.

"Now they are all keen 'Boro fans. I was back in North Korea and met up again with some of the players and they were all very anxious to know how the team was getting on. They have a genuine love for Middlesbrough."

While the North Koreans flew home to tell their families and friends about their many new memories of Middlesbrough, not everything was hunky-dory on the former Ayresome Park site. In fact the new-found worries, fears and disagreements were all centred around a landmark of the old stadium. It was a fact that, eight years after the demolition men moved in, not all of Ayresome Park had completely disappeared.

In September 2003, a campaign was launched by a group of 'Boro fans to save the Holgate Wall, which still formed part of the perimeter boundary of Middlesbrough General Hospital. The 'Save The Holgate Wall' campaign was started after Newcastle-based builders Barratt were granted planning permission to develop the hospital site with 382 homes.

The planning permission included authority to knock down sections of the historic wall in order to connect the new project to the existing estate that grew up on the old Ayresome Park.

The frustration was felt most not by fans, for whom thoughts of the Holgate Wall would be forever etched in their memories, but by those residents who had bought houses on the Ayresome Park land in the belief that they would be living in cul-de-sacs.

Robert Nichols was one of the residents who had two reasons to be angry. Not only was he a fierce advocate of all things 'Boro, but he lived on Ayresome Park, and he felt the residents had been let down. He said: "The whole original plan was to develop the Ayresome Park site carefully and sympathetically.

"The 'Boro heritage has been preserved in a really interesting way with important parts like the penalty spots marked out in people's houses and gardens and residents are rightly very proud of that.

"And the wall plays a big part in that. Not only does it give security and privacy, but it marks the historic boundary of Ayresome. It was supposed to be the final piece of the jigsaw.

"Neville Gabie had planned for the wall, which is set against an open green space, to be the centre-piece of a spectacular bit of landscape gardening.

"The original plan was that beds of red and white flowers were to be planted to represent scarves waving against the Holgate Wall. If the wall goes that won't happen.

"The residents stand to lose a big part of their environment and 'Boro fans stand to lose a big part of their history."

The demolition plan led to a petition being launched. Soundings were even taken to get the wall made a listed building, citing its significant historical and cultural significance. The Department of Culture, Media and Sport said they were ready to listen to any application and that, as many diverse structures have been listed, there was no reason why a wall could not be judged to be significant.

The campaign was kick-started when passionate former Holgate Ender John Donovan read of the plan to demolish the wall in the *Evening Gazette*. He said: "This is outrageous. We cannot possibly allow what is left of our old home be demolished.

"Many, many thousands of people have stood looking at the wall during 'Boro's years at Ayresome and I bet it has heard many reasoned and ridiculous arguments in its time – not to mention some colourful language.

"I recently took my daughter to show her where Ayresome used to stand and I showed her the wall and enlightened her with many a tale of times gone by – she was thrilled!

"With the town celebrating its 150th year it would be a crying shame for the Holgate Wall to be bulldozed now. We cannot let this happen."

The organising cyber-power of the *Fly Me To The Moon* website was harnessed as petitions to council chiefs were distributed. Campaigners also hoped the club would add its weight. But, with the council having already given consent to the development, the campaigners faced a tough task.

Barratt Homes were planning 117 flats and 212 houses on the 20-acre site of the former hospital. Gerard Abbiss, a partner in Design Developments, the architects for the scheme, told Middlesbrough Council's planning committee that the 16 different home types would range from one bedroom flats to four-bedroom luxury town houses. He said the development would have a public open space at its heart. But he confirmed it was proposed to remove part of the boundary wall to link the open spaces of the new and the existing developments. He said: "Retaining all the wall will divide two communities."

Local councillors Jackie Elder and Martin Booth both backed residents who wanted the wall retaining, or the whole wall rebuilt. Councillor Booth said: "Residents fear it will become a throughway and that will bring problems, particularly at night."

Councillor Elder said: "To allow part of the wall to be taken down would be a bad day for local democracy."

George Melville, for Linthorpe Community Council, said the community council agreed in principle with homes being built on the site, but it had some concerns. He said: "Holgate area residents at the moment live in what is a cul-de-sac and they do not want the wall taken down and a through route created."

Planning committee member Councillor Steve Bloundele said: "This will be a prestige housing development but we cannot ignore what the residents say about the wall."

Councillor Francis McIntyre said: "It is a small part of the wall that would come down and it will help pull the communities on both sides together."

With planning permission already granted, it seemed inevitable that part of the wall would come down and a thoroughfare would be created. It's all part of the changing landscape which was once one of the greatest football stadia in England.

Maybe change is perpetual. Perhaps, one day, our great-great grandchildren will be witnessing another form of progress, as the 'old' houses on the Ayresome Park estate make way for a brand-new football stadium.

One thing is for certain. Ayresome Park will never be forgotten, as long as football is played in Middlesbrough.

Middlesbrough in the FA Cup 1904-1995

Middlesbrough's record in the FA Cup at Ayresome Park is P 108, W 52, D 34, L 22.

Home games are in capitals. * Denotes after extra-time

	Season	*Round*	*Opposition*	*Result*	*Scorers*	*Attendance*
	1903-04	a 1	Millwall A	W 2-0	A.Brown 2	
	1903-04	a 2	Preston NE	W 3-0	A.Brown 2, Atherton	
	1903-04	a 3	Manchester C	D 0-0		
1	1903-04	H 3r	MANCHESTER C	L 1-3	A.BROWN	34,000
2	1904-05	H 1	TOTTENHAM H	D 1-1	ASTLEY	20,340
	1904-05	a 1r	Tottenham H	L 0-1		
3	1905-06	H 1	BOLTON W	W 3-0	COMMON, HEWITT, THACKERAY	22,000
	1905-06	a 2	Brighton & HA	D 1-1	Hewitt	
4	1905-06	H 2r	BRIGHTON & HA	D 1-1*	COMMON	15,000
	1905-06	n 2 2r	Brighton & HA (at Bramall Lane, Sheffield)	W 3-1	Common 3	
	1905-06	a 3	Southampton	L 1-6	Walker	
5	1906-07	H 1	NORTHAMPTON T	W 4-2	BLOOMER 2, COMMON, BRAWN	15,000
	1906-07	a 2	Brentford	L 0-1		
	1907-08	a 1	Notts C	L 0-2		
	1908-09	a 1	Preston NE	L 0-1		
6	1909-10	H 1	EVERTON	D 1-1	THACKERAY	25,000
	1909-10	a 1r	Everton	L 3-5	Common, Cail, Thackeray	
7	1910-11	H 1	GLOSSOP	W 1-0	CAIL	15,000
8	1910-11	H 2	LEICESTER F	D 0-0		17,000
	1910-11	a 2r	Leicester F	W 2-1*	Cail, Dixon	
9	1910-11	H 3	BLACKBURN R	L 0-3		30,369
10	1911-12	H 1	SHEFFIELD W	D 0-0		24,719
	1911-12	a 1r	Sheffield W	W 2-1	James, Windridge	
11	1911-12	H 2	WEST HAM	D 1-1	ELLIOTT	12,327
	1911-12	a 2r	West Ham	L 1-2	Elliott	
	1912-13	a 1	Millwall A	D 0-0		
12	1912-13	H 1r	MILLWALL A	W 4-1	J.CARR 3 (1 pen), ELLIOTT	12,780
13	1912-13	H 2	QUEEN'S PARK R	W 3-2	ELLIOTT 2, EYRE	27,774
	1912-13	a 3	Burnley	L 1-3	Eyre	
	1913-14	a 1	Blackburn R	L 0-3		
14	1914-15	H 1	GOOLE T	W 9-3	J.CARR 3, ELLIOTT 3, TINSLEY 3	8,650
	1914-15	a 2	Bradford C	L 0-1		
15	1919-20	H 1	LINCOLN C	W 4-1	ELLIOTT 3, W.CARR	17,746
	1919-20	a 2	Notts Co	L 0-1		
	1920-21	a 1	Derby Co	L 0-2		
	1921-22	a 1	Hull C	L 0-5		
	1922-23	a 1	Oldham A	W 1-0	Birrell	
16	1922-23	H 2	SHEFFIELD U	D 1-1	WILSON (pen)	38,067
	1922-23	a 2r	Sheffield U	L 0-3		
17	1923-24	H 1	WATFORD	L 0-1		24,192
	1924-25	a 1	Bradford	L 0-1		
18	1925-26	H 3	LEEDS U	W 5-0	McCLELLAND 5	29,000

	Season	Round	Opposition	Result	Scorers	Attendance
	1925-26	a 4	Clapton O	L 2-4	McClelland, Birrell	
19	1926-27	H 3	LEICESTER C	W 5-3	CAMSELL, WILLIAMS, PEASE, BIRRELL 2	30,000
	1926-27	a 4	Preston NE	W 3-0	Camsell 3	
	1926-27	a 5	Millwall	L 2-3	Pease, Williams	
20	1927-28	H 3	SOUTH SHIELDS	W 3-0	PEACOCK 2, CAMSELL	25,000
	1927-28	a 4	Southport	W 3-0	Camsell 3	
	1927-28	a 5	Huddersfield	L 0-4		
	1928-29	a 3	Walsall	D 1-1	Camsell	
21	1928-29	H 3r	WALSALL	W 5-1	CAMSELL 2, PEASE 2, WILLIAMS	14,917
	1928-29	a 4	West Bromwich A	L 0-1		
	1929-30	a 3	Chesterfield	D 1-1	Bruce (pen)	
22	1929-30	H 3r	CHESTERFIELD	W 4-3	CAMSELL 2, BRUCE 2	18,793
23	1929-30	H 4	CHARLTON A	D 1-1	MUTTITT	35,707
	1929-30	a 4r	Charlton A	D 1-1	Bruce	
	1929-30	n 4 2r	Charlton A (at Maine Road, Manchester)	W 1-0*	McKay	
24	1929-30	H 5	ARSENAL	L 0-2		42,073
25	1930-31	H 3	BRADFORD C	D 1-1	WARREN	21,698
	1930-31	a 3r	Bradford C	L 1-2	Barkas (og)	
26	1931-32	H 3	PORTSMOUTH	D 1-1	BRUCE	22,949
	1931-32	a 3r	Portsmouth	L 0-3		
	1932-33	a 3	Manchester U	W 4-1	Bruce 2, Williams, Blackmore	
27	1932-33	H 4	STOKE C	W 4-1	BLACKMORE 2, CAMSELL, BAXTER	29,457
28	1932-33	H 5	BIRMINGHAM	D 0-0		27,705
	1932-33	a 5r	Birmingham	L 0-3		
	1933-34	a 3	Sunderland	D 1-1	Camsell	
29	1933-34	H 3r	SUNDERLAND	L 1-2	FERGUSON	40,882
30	1934-35	H 3	BLACKBURN R	D 1-1	WILLIAMS	34,637
	1934-35	a 3r	Blackburn R	L 0-1		
31	1935-36	H 3	SOUTHAMPTON	W 1-0	CUNLIFFE	29,550
32	1935-36	H 4	CLAPTON O	W 3-0	CAMSELL 2, CUNLIFFE	34,470
33	1935-36	H 5	LEICESTER C	W 2-1	CAMSELL, FORREST	42,214
	1935-36	a 6	Grimsby T	L 1-3	Camsell	
	1936-37	a 3	Wolverhampton W	L 1-6	Birkett	
34	1937-38	H 3	STOCKPORT CO	W 2-0	FENTON 2 (1 pen)	34,757
	1937-38	a 4	Nottingham F	W 3-1	Mannion, Camsell, Milne	
	1937-38	a 5	York C	L 0-1		
35	1938-39	H 3	BOLTON W	D 0-0		32,790
	1938-39	a 3r	Bolton W	D 0-0*		
	1938-39	n 3 2r	Bolton W (at Elland Road, Leeds)	W 1-0	Fenton	
36	1938-39	H 4	SUNDERLAND	L 0-2		51,080
	1945-46	a 3 1L	Leeds U	D 4-4	Dews 2, Fenton, Murphy	
37	1945-46	H 3 2L	LEEDS U	W 7-2	FENTON 3, GORDON, DOUGLAS, HARDWICK (pen), SPUHLER	24,000
	1945-46	a 4 1L	Blackpool	L 2-3	Suart (og), Spuhler	
38	1945-46	H 4 2L	BLACKPOOL	W 3-2	FENTON 2, SPUHLER	46,556
	1945-46	n 4r	Blackpool (at Elland Road, Leeds)	W 1-0	Hardwick (pen)	
	1945-46	a 5 1L	Bolton W	L 0-1		
39	1945-46	H 5 2L	BOLTON W	D 1-1	FENTON	51,612
	1946-47	a 3	Queen's Park R	D 1-1	FENTON	
40	1946-47	H 3r	QUEEN'S PARK R	W 3-1	FENTON 2, MANNION	31,270
41	1946-47	H 4	CHESTERFIELD	W 2-1	SPUHLER 2	42,250
	1946-47	a 5	Nottingham F	D 2-2	Mannion, Spuhler	
42	1946-47	H 5r	NOTTINGHAM F	W 6-2	MANNION 3 (1 pen), SPUHLER, FENTON 2	26,907
43	1946-47	H 6	BURNLEY	D 1-1	WALKER	53,025
	1946-47	a 6r	Burnley	L 0-1		
	1947-48	a 3	Hull C	W 3-1	Dobbie 2, Mannion	
	1947-48	a 4	Brentford	W 2-1	Spuhler, McCormack	

	Season	*Round*	*Opposition*	*Result*	*Scorers*	*Attendance*
44	1947-48	H 5	DERBY CO	L 1-2	SPUHLER	43,708
	1948-49	a 3	Brentford	L 2-3	Walker, Spuhler	
	1949-50	a 3	Aston Villa	D 2-2	Linacre, McKennan	
45	1949-50	H 3r	ASTON VILLA	D 0-0*		49,850
	1949-50	n 3 2r	Aston Villa	W 3-0	McCrae 2, Mannion	
			(at Elland Road, Leeds)			
	1949-50	a 4	Chesterfield	L 2-3	Walker, Spuhler	
	1950-51	a 3	Leeds U	L 0-1		
46	1951-52	H 3	DERBY CO	D 2-2	MANNION 2	35,850
	1951-52	a 3r	Derby Co	W 2-0	Delapenha 2	
47	1951-52	H 4	DONCASTER R	L 1-4	BELL	41,560
	1952-53	a 3	Aston Villa	L 1-3	Fitzsimons	
48	1953-54	H 3	LEICESTER C	D 0-0		38,701
	1953-54	a 3r	Leicester C	L 2-3	Spuhler, Mannion	
49	1954-55	H 3	NOTTS CO	L 1-4	WAYMAN	30,503
	1955-56	a 3	Bradford	W 4-1	Scott 2, Delapenha, Wayman	
	1955-56	a 4	Tottenham H	L 1-3	Scott	
50	1956-57	H 3	CHARLTON A	D 1-1	SCOTT	32,863
	1956-57	a 3r	Charlton A	W 3-2	Day, Clough, Fitzsimmons	
51	1956-57	H 4	ASTON VILLA	L 2-3	CLOUGH, HARRIS	42,396
52	1957-58	H 3	DERBY CO	W 5-0	PEACOCK 2, DAY, HOLLIDAY, CLOUGH	29,530
	1957-58	a 4	Stoke C	L 1-3	Clough	
53	1958-59	H 3	BIRMINGHAM C	L 0-1		36,587
	1959-60	A 3	Sheffield W	L 1-2	Clough	
	1960-61	a 3	Manchester U	L 0-3		
54	1961-62	H 3	CARDIFF C	W 1-0	PEACOCK	29,260
	1961-62	a 4	Shrewsbury T	D 2-2	Peacock 2	
55	1961-62	H 4r	SHREWSBURY T	W 5-1	KAYE, HARRIS, PEACOCK, HOLLIDAY 2	34,751
	1961-62	a 5	Blackburn R	L 1-2	Burbeck	
	1962-63	a 3	Blackburn R	D 1-1	Orritt	
56	1962-63	H 3r	BLACKBURN R	W 3-1	PEACOCK 2, KAYE (pen)	39,595
57	1962-63	H 4	LEEDS U	L 0-2		39,672
	1963-64	a 3	Brentford	L 1-2	Kaye	
58	1964-65	H 3	OLDHAM A	W 6-2	IRVINE 3, HORSFIELD 2, KAYE	17,178
	1964-65	a 4	Charlton A	D 1-1	Nurse	
59	1964-65	H 4r	CHARLTON A	W 2-1	GIBSON, NURSE	30,460
60	1964-65	H 5	LEICESTER C	L 0-3		31,099
	1965-66	a 3	Tottenham H	L 0-4		
	1966-67	a 1	Chester	W 5-2	O'Rourke 3, Downing, Hickton	
61	1966-67	H 2	YORK C	D 1-1	HICKTON	20,573
	1966-67	a 2r	York C	D 0-0		
	1966-67	n 2 2r	York C	W 4-1	Lawson, Lugg, Horsfield, Jackson (og)	
			(at St James' Park, Newcastle)			
	1966-67	a 3	Mansfield T	L 0-2		
62	1967-68	H 3	HULL C	D 1-1	CROSSAN	28,509
	1967-68	a 3r	Hull C	D 2-2	Horsfield 2	
	1967-68	n 3 2r	Hull C	W 1-0	Downing	
			(at Bootham Crescent, York)			
63	1967-68	H 4	BRISTOL C	D 1-1	PARR (og)	29,086
	1967-68	a 4r	Bristol C	L 1-2	Hickton	
64	1968-69	H 3	MILLWALL	D 1-1	ALLEN	29,960
	1968-69	a 3r	Millwall	L 0-1		
65	1969-70	H 3	WEST HAM U	W 2-1	McILMOYLE, DOWNING	32,585
66	1969-70	H 4	YORK C	W 4-1	McMORDIE, G.SMITH, LAIDLAW, HICKTON (pen)	32,283
	1969-70	a 5	Carlisle U	W 2-1	Hickton, Downing	
67	1969-70	H 6	MANCHESTER U	D 1-1	HICKTON	40,040
	1969-70	a 6r	Manchester U	L 1-2	Hickton	
	1970-71	a 3	Manchester U	D 0-0		

	Season	Round	Opposition	Result	Scorers	Attendance
68	1970-71	H 3r	MANCHESTER U	W 2-1	McILMOYLE, DOWNING	40,040
	1970-71	a 4	Everton	L 0-3		
	1971-72	a 3	Manchester C	D 1-1	Mills	
69	1971-72	H 3r	MANCHESTER C	W 1-0	HICKTON	39,971
	1971-72	a 4	Millwall	D 2-2	Hickton, Downing	
70	1971-72	H 4r	MILLWALL	W 2-1	HICKTON (pen), DOWNING	36,489
	1971-72	a 5	Manchester U	D 0-0		
71	1971-72	H 5r	MANCHESTER U	L 0-3		39,671
	1972-73	a 3	Plymouth Argyle	L 0-1		
	1973-74	a 3	Grantham	W 2-0	Mills, Armstrong	
	1973-74	a 4	Wrexham	L 0-1		
	1974-75	a 3	Wycombe W	D 0-0		
72	1974-75	H 3r	WYCOMBE W	W 1-0	ARMSTRONG (pen)	30,128
73	1974-75	H 4	SUNDERLAND	W 3-1	HICKTON (2 pens), MURDOCH	39,400
	1974-75	a 5	Peterborough U	D 1-1	Mills	
74	1974-75	H 5r	PETERBOROUGH U	W 2-0	FOGGON 2	34,303
	1974-75	a 6	Birmingham C	L 0-1		
75	1975-76	H 3	BURY	D 0-0		20,728
	1975-76	a 3r	Bury	L 2-3	Brine, Hickton (pen)	
	1976-77	a 3	Wimbledon	D 0-0		
76	1976-77	H 3r	WIMBLEDON	W 1-0	ARMSTRONG (pen)	22,485
77	1976-77	H 4	HEREFORD U	W 4-0	ARMSTRONG 2 (1 pen), SOUNESS, WILLEY	25,163
78	1976-77	H 5	ARSENAL	W 4-1	MILLS 3, ARMSTRONG	35,208
	1976-77	a 6	Liverpool	L 0-2		
79	1977-78	H 3	COVENTRY C	W 3-0	MILLS 2, McANDREW	18,015
80	1977-78	H 4	EVERTON	W 3-2	MILLS 2, MAHONEY	33,652
81	1977-78	H 5	BOLTON W	W 2-0	ASHCROFT, CUMMINS	36,662
82	1977-78	H 6	ORIENT	D 0-0		33,426
	1977-78	a 6r	Orient	L 1-2	Armstrong	
83	1978-79	H 3	CRYSTAL PALACE	D 1-1	ASHCROFT	21,447
	1978-79	a 3r	Crystal Palace	L 0-1		
	1979-80	a 3	Portsmouth	D 1-1	Cochrane	
84	1979-80	H 3r	PORTSMOUTH	W 3-0	COCHRANE, JOHNSON, ARMSTRONG	22,551
	1979-80	a 4	Birmingham C	L 1-2	Hodgson	
	1980-81	a 3	Swansea C	W 5-0	Hodgson 2, Ashcroft, Angus, Cochrane	
85	1980-81	H 4	WEST BROM A	W 1-0	BAILEY	28,285
86	1980-81	H 5	BARNSLEY	W 2-1	PROCTOR, JANKOVIC	37,557
87	1980-81	H 6	WOLVERHAMPTON W	D 1-1	COCHRANE	36,382
	1980-81	a 6r	Wolverhampton W	L 1-3*	Hodgson	
	1981-82	a 3	Queen's Park R	D 1-1	Thomson	
88	1981-82	H 3r	QUEEN'S PARK R	L 2-3*	OTTO, THOMSON (pen)	14,819
89	1982-83	H 3	BISHOP'S STORTFORD	D 2-2	BELL 2	13,207
	1982-83	a 3r	Bishop's Stortford	W 2-1	Shearer 2	
90	1982-83	H 4	NOTTS CO	W 2-0	HANKIN, BEATTIE (pen)	17,114
91	1982-83	H 5	ARSENAL	D 1-1	OTTO	20,790
	1982-83	a 5r	Arsenal	L 2-3	Shearer 2	
92	1983-84	H 3	ARSENAL	W 3-2	MacDONALD, SUGRUE, BAXTER	17,813
93	1983-84	H 4	BOURNEMOUTH	W 2-0	SUGRUE 2	20,175
	1983-84	a 5	Notts Co	L 0-1		
94	1984-85	H 3	DARLINGTON	D 0-0		19,084
	1984-85	a 3r	Darlington	L 1-2	McAndrew	
95	1985-86	H 3	SOUTHAMPTON	L 1-3	O'RIORDAN	12,703
96	1986-87	H 1	BLACKPOOL	W 3-0	SLAVEN 3	11,205
	1986-87	a 2	Notts Co	W 1-0	Hamilton	
97	1986-87	H 3	PRESTON NE	L 0-1		15,458
	1987-88	a 3	Sutton U	D 1-1	Pallister	
98	1987-88	H 3r	SUTTON U	W 1-0*	KERR	17,932
	1987-88	a 4	Everton	D 1-1	Kerr	
99	1987-88	H 4r	EVERTON	D 2-2	MOWBRAY, KERNAGHAN	25,235
	1987-88	a 4 2r	Everton	L 1-2	Ripley	

	Season	Round		Opposition	Result		Scorers	Attendance
100	1988-89	H	3	GRIMSBY T	L	1-2	SLAVEN	19,190
101	1989-90	H	3	EVERTON	D	0-0		20,075
	1989-90	a	3r	Everton	D	1-1*	Parkinson	
	1989-90	a	3 2r	Everton	L	0-1		
102	1990-91	H	3	PLYMOUTH ARGYLE	D	0-0		13,042
	1990-91	a	3r	Plymouth Argyle	W	2-1	Baird, Kerr	
	1990-91	a	4	Cambridge U	L	0-2		
103	1991-92	H	3	MANCHESTER C	W	2-1	KERNAGHAN, WILKINSON	21,174
	1991-92	a	4	Sheffield W	W	2-1	Hendrie, Wilkinson,	
	1991-92	a	5	Portsmouth	D	1-1	Kernaghan	
104	1991-92	H	5r	PORTSMOUTH	L	2-4	WILKINSON 2	19,479
105	1992-93	H	3	CHELSEA	W	2-1	WRIGHT, FALCONER	16,776
	1992-93	a	4	Nottingham F	D	1-1	Falconer	
106	1992-93	H	4r	NOTTINGHAM F	L	0-3		20,514
	1993-94	a	3	Cardiff C	D	2-2	Wilkinson, Moore	
107	1993-94	H	3r	CARDIFF C	L	1-2	KAVANAGH	10,769
	1994-95	a	3	Swansea C	D	1-1	Moore	
108	1994-95	H	3r	SWANSEA C	L	1-2	HENDRIE	13,940

In their last ten years at Ayresome Park Middlesbrough won only four of the FA Cup-ties played at the ground.
Highest FA Cup Attendance at Ayresome Park: 53,025 v Burnley, 1946-47 (round 6).
Lowest FA Cup Attendance at Ayresome Park: 8,650 v Goole T, 1914-15 (round 1).
Lowest FA Cup Attendance at Ayresome Park since World War Two: 10,769 v Cardiff C, 1993-94 (round 3r).
Biggest FA Cup win at Ayresome Park: 9-3 v Goole T, 1914-15 (round 1).
Worst FA Cup defeats at Ayresome Park: 1-4 v Doncaster R, 1952-53 (round 4),
1-4 v Notts C, 1954-55 (round 3).

Football League Cup 1960-1995

Middlesbrough's record in the Football League Cup at Ayresome Park is P 48, W 21, D 17, L 10

Home games are in capitals. * Denotes after extra-time

	Season	Round		Opposition	Result		Scorers	Attendance
1	1960-61	H	1	CARDIFF C	L	3-4	CLOUGH 2, PEACOCK	15,695
	1961-62	a	1	Tranmere R	W	6-3	Peacock 3, Burbeck 2, Day	
2	1961-62	H	2	CREWE ALEX	W	3-1	KAYE 2, PEACOCK	9,830
	1961-62	a	3	Norwich C	L	2-3	Holliday, Allcock (og)	
	1962-63	a	2	Hull C	D	2-2	Burbeck 2	
3	1962-63	H	2r	HULL C	D	1-1*	GIBSON	15,612
	1962-63	a	2 2r	Hull C	L	0-3		
	1963-64	a	2	Bradford	D	2-2	Peacock 2	
4	1963-64	H	2r	BRADFORD	L	2-3	PEACOCK, HARRIS	11,991
	1964-65	a	2	Charlton A	L	1-2	Irvine	
	1965-66	a	2	Colchester U	W	4-2	Irvine 2, McMordie, Horner	
5	1965-66	H	3	MILLWALL	D	0-0		12,927
	1965-66	a	3r	Millwall	L	1-3*	Gibson	
6	1966-67	H	1	YORK C	D	0-0		9,758
	1966-67	a	1r	York C	L	1-2	Chadwick	
7	1967-68	H	1	BARNSLEY	W	4-1	HICKTON 3, D.SMITH	15,968
8	1967-68	H	2	CHELSEA	W	2-1	McMORDIE, D.SMITH	30,417
	1967-68	a	3	Blackburn	L	2-3	Hickton (pen), O'Rourke	
	1968-69	a	2	Bristol C	L	0-1		
	1969-70	a	2	Manchester U	L	0-1		
	1970-71	a	2	Oldham A	W	4-2	Hickton, Laidlaw, McIlmoyle, Downing	
	1970-71	a	3	Chelsea	L	2-3	Hickton, Jones	
	1971-72	a	2	York C	D	2-2	Downing, Hickton	
9	1971-72	H	2r	YORK C	L	1-2	CRAGGS	21,021
10	1972-73	H	2	WREXHAM	W	2-0	MILLS 2	5,808
11	1972-73	H	3	TOTTENHAM H	D	1-1	HICKTON	23,822
	1972-73	a	3r	Tottenham H	D	0-0*		
	1972-73	a	3 2r	Tottenham H	L	1-2*	Hickton	
	1973-74	a	2	Manchester U	W	1-0	M.Smith	
	1973-74	a	3	Stoke C	D	1-1	Brine	
12	1973-74	H	3r	STOKE C	L	1-2	FOGGON	26,068
	1974-75	a	2	Tottenham H	W	4-0	M.Smith, Mills, Hickton (pen), Armstrong	
13	1974-75	H	3	LEICESTER C	W	1-0	MILLS	23,901
	1974-75	a	4	Liverpool	W	1-0	Maddren	
14	1974-75	H	5	MANCHESTER U	D	0-0		36,005
	1974-75	a	5r	Manchester U	L	0-3		
	1975-76	a	2	Bury	W	2-1	Hickton, Mills	
15	1975-76	H	3	DERBY CO	W	1-0	FOGGON	25,740
16	1975-76	H	4	PETERBOROUGH U	W	3-0	BOAM, HICKTON (pen), ARMSTRONG	17,749
	1975-76	a	5	Burnley	W	2-0	Mills, Maddren	
17	1975-76	H	SF	MANCHESTER C	W	1-0	HICKTON	34,579
	1975-76	a	SF	Manchester C	L	0-4		
18	1976-77	H	2	TOTTENHAM H	L	1-2	McANDREW	19,042
	1977-78	a	2	Sunderland	D	2-2	Armstrong 2 (1 pen)	
19	1977-78	H	2r	SUNDERLAND	W	1-0	BOAM	29,572
	1977-78	a	3	Everton	D	2-2	Woof, Mills	
20	1977-78	H	3r	EVERTON	L	1-2	MILLS	28,409
21	1978-79	H	2	PETERBOROUGH U	D	0-0		12,510

	Season	Round	Opposition	Result	Scorers	Attendance
	1978-79	a 2r	Peterborough U	L 0-1*		
	1979-80	a 2	Derby Co	W 1-0	Armstrong (pen)	
22	1979-80	H 2 2L	DERBY CO	D 1-1	JANKOVIC	19,466
23	1979-80	H 3	NOTTINGHAM F	L 1-3	ARMSTRONG	29,869
24	1980-81	H 2	IPSWICH T	W 3-1	SHEARER 2, PROCTOR	14,430
	1980-81	a 2 2L	Ipswich T	L 0-3		
25	1981-82	H 2	Plymouth Argyle	W 2-1	ASHCROFT, THOMSON	8,201
	1981-82	a 2 2L	Plymouth Argyle	D 0-0		
	1981-82	a 3	Liverpool	L 1-4	Shearer	
	1982-83	a 2	Burnley	L 2-3	Otto, Cochrane	
26	1982-83	H 2 2L	BURNLEY	D 1-1	HANKIN	10,389
27	1983-84	H 1	CHESTERFIELD	L 0-1		7,163
	1983-84	a 1 2L	Chesterfield (Lost 5-3 on penalties)	W 1-0*	Otto	
	1984-85	a 1	Bradford C	L 0-2		
28	1984-85	H 1 2L	BRADFORD C	D 2-2	BUCKLEY, SUGRUE	3,980
	1985-86	a 1	Mansfield T	L 0-2		
29	1985-86	H 1 2L	MANSFIELD T	D 4-4	ROWELL 2 (1 pen), CURRIE, POLLARD (og)	4,051
	1986-87	a 1	Hartlepool	D 1-1	Slaven	
30	1986-87	H 1 2L	HARTLEPOOL	W 2-0	RIPLEY, HAMILTON	7,735
31	1986-87	H 2	BIRMINGHAM C	D 2-2	STEPHENS, RIPLEY	9,412
	1986-87	a 2r	Birmingham C	L 2-3*	Laws 2 (1 pen)	
	1987-88	a 1	Sunderland	L 0-1		
32	1987-88	H 1 2L	SUNDERLAND	W 2-0	SLAVEN, MOWBRAY	15,570
33	1987-88	H 2	ASTON VILLA	L 0-1		11,424
	1987-88	a 2 2L	Aston Villa	L 0-1		
34	1988-89	H 2	TRANMERE R	D 0-0		12,084
	1988-89	a 2L	Tranmere R	L 0-1		
35	1989-90	H 2	HALIFAX T	W 4-0	SLAVEN 2, COMFORT, KERNAGHAN	10,613
	1989-90	a 2 2L	Halifax T	W 1-0	Slaven	
36	1989-90	H 3	WIMBLEDON	D 1-1	SLAVEN	12,933
	1989-90	a 3 2L	Wimbledon	L 0-1		
37	1990-91	H 1	TRANMERE R	D 1-1	MOWBRAY	10,612
	1990-91	a 1 2L	Tranmere R	W 2-1	Slaven, Mustoe	
38	1990-91	H 2	NEWCASTLE U	W 2-0	MUSTOE 2	15,042
	1990-91	a 2 2L	Newcastle U	L 0-1		
39	1990-91	H 3	NORWICH C	W 2-0	KERR, HENDRIE	17,024
	1990-91	a 4	Aston Villa	L 2-3	Slaven 2	
40	1991-92	H 2	BOURNEMOUTH	D 1-1	WILKINSON	10,577
	1991-92	a 2 2L	Bournemouth	W 2-1	Parkinson (pen), Hendrie	
41	1991-92	H 3	BARNSLEY	W 1-0	WILKINSON	9,381
42	1991-92	H 4	MANCHESTER C	W 2-1	MUSTOE, WILKINSON	17,286
	1991-92	a 5	Peterborough U	D 0-0		
43	1991-92	H 5r	PETERBOROUGH U	W 1-0	RIPLEY	21,973
44	1991-92	H SF	MANCHESTER U	D 0-0		25,576
	1991-92	a SF	Manchester U	L 1-2	Slaven	
	1992-93	a 2	Newcastle U	D 0-0		
45	1992-93	H 2 2L	NEWCASTLE U	L 1-3	WILKINSON	24,390
46	1993-94	H 2	BRIGHTON	W 5-0	HIGNETT 4, HENDRIE	5,651
	1993-94	a 2 2L	Brighton	W 3-1	Wilkinson, Hendrie, Hignett	
47	1993-94	H 3	SHEFFIELD W	D 1-1	HENDRIE	14,765
	1993-94	a 3r	Sheffield W	L 1-2	Mustoe	
	1994-95	a 2	Scarborough	W 4-1	Hendrie, Pollock, Mustoe, Moore	
48	1994-95	H 2 2L	SCARBOROUGH	W 4-1	WILKINSON 3, HIGNETT	7,739
	1994-95	a 3	Aston Villa	L 0-1		

Highest League Cup Attendance at Ayresome Park: 36,005 v Manchester U, 1974-75 (round 5).
Lowest League Cup Attendance at Ayresome Park: 3,980 v Bradford C, 1984-85 (round 1 2L).
Biggest League Cup win at Ayresome Park: 5-0 v Brighton 1993-94, (round 2 1L).
Worst League Cup defeats at Ayresome Park: 4-3 v Cardiff C, 1960-61 (round 1),
3-1 v Nottingham F, 1979-80 (round 3),
3-1 v Newcastle U, 1992-93 (round 2 2L).

Average League Attendances at Ayresome Park

From 1903 to 1925 the attendances recorded at Middlesbrough home games were approximate and were often rounded up or down to the nearest thousand by the local Press. The Ayresome Park attendances since 1925-26 are based on the official figures submitted to the Football League.

The post-World War Two football boom period of 1946-47 to 1950-51 provided the peak in attendances at Ayresome Park with all average crowds for those seasons in excess of 34,000. The highest average in the history of Ayresome Park was achieved in the championship challenging season of 1950-51 (36,123) when over three-quarters of a million people passed through the turnstiles. By Easter, Boro were still in with a realistic chance of their first Championship but they lost six and drew two of their last eight matches to finish in a disappointing sixth position, after a season of much promise. The most depressing season for attendances was 1984-85, when in the depths of 'Boro's financial crisis the average crowd was a paltry 5,135 with the lowest ever League crowd recorded on 9 February 1985, when only 3,364 supporters turned up for the game against Notts County. This was a sad indictment on the state of a club, who were now only one year away from liquidation.

SEASON	*AVERAGE ATTENDANCE*
Division 1	
1903-04	18,000
1904-05	12,500
1905-06	13,500
1906-07	17,000
1907-08	18,000
1908-09	13,300
1909-10	11,500
1910-11	14,500
1911-12	14,419
1912-13	11,601
1913-14	15,543
1914-15	10,500
1919-20	20,210
1920-21	23,800
1921-22	22,380
1922-23	17,760
1923-24	17,950
Division 2	
1924-25	14,390
1925-26	13,259
1926-27	21,836
Division 1	
1927-28	22,635
Division 2	
1928-29	18,724
Division 1	
1929-30	19,172
1930-31	16,858
1931-32	13,890
1932-33	12,157
1933-34	12,364
1934-35	14,376
1935-36	18,771
1936-37	22,390
1937-38	24,260
1938-39	21,188
1946-47	35,912
1947-48	35,901
1948-49	34,292
1949-50	35,407
1950-51	36,123
1951-52	28,775
1952-53	27,077
1953-54	27,002
Division 2	
1954-55	21,108
1955-56	17,866
1956-57	21,127
1957-58	24,398
1958-59	24,876
1959-60	25,550
1960-61	15,859
1961-62	15,810
1962-63	16,528
1963-64	18,786
1964-65	14,612
1965-66	13,450
Division 3	
1966-67	16,540
Division 2	
1967-68	18,906

SEASON	AVERAGE ATTENDANCE
1968-69	21,063
1969-70	19,856
1970-71	18,534
1971-72	17,943
1972-73	10,418
1973-74	22,498
Division 1	
1974-75	28,605
1975-76	23,223
1976-77	21,840
1977-78	19,874
1978-79	18,459
1979-80	18,739
1980-81	16,432
1981-82	13,413
Division 2	
1982-83	10,018
1983-84	8,473
1984-85	5,135
1985-86	6,257

SEASON	AVERAGE ATTENDANCE
Division 3	
1986-87	10,174
Division 2	
1987-88	14,528
Division 1	
1988-89	19,999
Division 2	
1989-90	15,307
1990-91	17,020
1991-92	14,695
FA Premier League	
1992-93	16,724
Football League Division 1	
1993-94	10,400
1994-95	18,641

Index